MOSCOW PRIME TIME

MOSCOW
PRIME TIME

HOW THE SOVIET UNION BUILT THE MEDIA EMPIRE THAT LOST THE CULTURAL COLD WAR

KRISTIN ROTH-EY

CORNELL UNIVERSITY PRESS   ITHACA AND LONDON

First published 2011 by Cornell University Press
Printed in the United States of America

Library of Congress Cataloging-in-Publication Data

Roth-Ey, Kristin Joy
    Moscow prime time : how the Soviet Union built the media empire that lost
the cultural Cold War / Kristin Roth-Ey.
        p. cm.
    Includes bibliographical references and index.
    ISBN 978-0-8014-4874-4 (cloth : alk. paper)
    1. Mass media policy—Soviet Union.   2. Motion picture industry—
Government policy—Soviet Union.   3. Radio broadcasting policy—Soviet
Union.   4. Television broadcasting policy—Soviet Union.   5. Soviet
Union—Cultural policy.   I. Title.
    P95.82.S65R654   2011
    302.23'09409045—dc20   2010047282

Cornell University Press strives to use environmentally responsible
suppliers and materials to the fullest extent possible in the publishing
of its books. Such materials include vegetable-based, low-VOC inks
and acid-free papers that are recycled, totally chlorine-free, or partly
composed of nonwood fibers. For further information, visit our
website at www.cornellpress.cornell.edu.

Cloth printing   10 9 8 7 6 5 4 3 2 1

For my father, John J. Roth (1940–2004),

who would have loved to see this book,

and for David Roth-Ey, whose love

means more than all books

CONTENTS

ABBREVIATIONS

Moscow, Russia

GARF	Gosudarstvennyi arkhiv Rossiiskoi Federatsii
RGALI	Rossiiskii gosudarstvennyi arkhiv literatury i iskusstva
RGANI	Rossiiskii gosudarstvennyi arkhiv noveishei istorii
RGASPI	Rossiiskii gosudarstvennyi arkhiv sotsial'no-politicheskoi istorii
RGASPI-m	Rossiiskii gosudarstvennyi arkhiv sotsial'no-politicheskoi istorii-m (formerly Tsentr khraneniia dokumentov molodezhnykh organizatsii)
TsAOPIM	Tsentral'nyi arkhiv obshchestvenno-politicheskoi istorii Moskvy (formerly Tsentral'nyi arkhiv obshchestvennykh dvizhenii Moskvy)
Gosteleradiofond	Gosudarstvennyi fond televizionnykh i radioprogramm

Kyiv, Ukraine

TsDAHOU	Tsentral'nyi derzhavnyi arkhiv hromads'kykh ob'ednam' Ukrainy
TsDAVO	Tsentral'nyi derzhavnyi arkhiv vishchikh organiv vladi ta upravlinnia Ukrainy

Budapest, Hungary

OSA	Open Society Archive

MOSCOW PRIME TIME

INTRODUCTION

SOVIET CULTURE IN THE MEDIA AGE

There is a famous photograph of Soviet premier Nikita Khrushchev surrounded by young women dressed as cancan dancers. Khrushchev was in Hollywood (the year was 1959), and although the photo shows him beaming, the scene it captured would soon give way to a minor scandal: Khrushchev found the performance that followed risqué, concluded his hosts had staged it to embarrass him, and let an eager international press corps know it. This was one of the Soviet leader's many foreign trips—part dog-and-pony show for socialism, part reconnaissance mission, and part personal journey—and he had chosen to visit Hollywood himself. Khrushchev was curious (perhaps even a little starstruck), and he was also well aware of Hollywood's power internationally. He did not, however, bow down to it, and this was the point of his cancan sermon. When Khrushchev came to Hollywood, he came representing the cultural formation destined, he said, to consign it to the dustbin of history: "Soviet culture." He had genuine grounds for boasting; already in 1959, the USSR had one of the most extensive infrastructures for culture the world had ever seen, and it was in the midst of explosive expansion. And yet there was the Soviet leader, smiling arm in arm with starlets one moment, and banging his proverbial shoe for "dignity" and "Art" the next, in images soon seen round the world. Khrushchev's fascination with capitalist mass culture and his prickliness when confronted with that fascination; his pride in Soviet culture, backed by real achievements, and his insecurity in the face of competition; his dead certainty about the importance of culture and fuzziness about how to define it, especially beyond the halls of the Bolshoi Theater; his love-hate relationship with modern media practices; the very fact of a Soviet leader caught up overseas in an international celebrity event—all these things were emblematic of the new cultural position in which the Soviet Union found itself and that it made *for* itself in the 1950s, '60s, and '70s. Soviet culture in the media age demonstrated both terrific strengths and crushing weaknesses.[1] It was, on its own terms, a very successful failure.

Across the world, the three decades after the close of the Second World War were a period of profound cultural change, grounded in the miracle working of

---

1. See Alena Ledeneva's discussion of the "self-subversive nature" of Soviet institutions in her *Russia's Economy of Favours: Blat, Networking, and Informal Exchange* (Cambridge, 1998), and, on the same theme, Stephen Kotkin's *Magnetic Mountain: Stalinism as a Civilization* (Berkeley, 1995).

postwar economies and technologies and in the lifestyle shifts they authorized. Never had mass culture in such volume been so accessible to so many and so regularly. In the industrialized West, and in many new postcolonial states as well, governments turned their attention to print, film, and broadcasting as matters of state policy, essential to both national integration and international prestige.[2] The Soviet Union was not only a participant in this new media age; it built a media empire. Soviet people were the most active moviegoers in the world in the 1960s and '70s. A romantic fantasy film called *Amphibian Man* (*Chelovek-amfibiia*) sold more than 65 million tickets or, in raw statistical terms, one ticket for every 3.4 inhabitants. The USSR's main movie magazine, *Soviet Screen* (*Sovetskii ekran*), brimming with photographs of foreign and Soviet stars, had a print run of roughly 4 million in the sixties and still sold out at newsstands in a heartbeat. The Soviet Union also boasted the world's most extensive broadcasting network. Radio ownership reached near-saturation levels by the early sixties, and television, a glimmer in the eye of a few technological enthusiasts before the war, burst onto the scene soon thereafter. In 1962, Soviet TV spawned its first national craze, a game show known as *KVN*.

Though blockbusters and game shows pointed to the galloping success of mass culture inside the Soviet Union, the authorities took great care to present a more dignified portrait: prima ballerina Maia Plisetskaiia, the great quantities of poetry sold in Soviet bookstores, a World War II–theme film like *Ballad of a Soldier* (*Ballada o soldate*, 1959, prizewinner at Cannes)—these were the sorts of things most often mustered as evidence of cultural power in the USSR. The term "mass culture" (*massovaia kul'tura*) itself served as a slur in the Soviet lexicon: "mass culture" was the soulless and exploitative culture of the capitalist West. (To convey this distinction, I will use the term "masscult.")[3] The USSR declared itself home to the world's first noncapitalist mode of cultural production and consumption: an anti-masscult culture for the masses.[4] This socialist, or Soviet, culture was as integral to the promise of communism as ample housing for all, men and women in space, and sausage on every table.

But what exactly *was* "Soviet culture"? As the Communist Party's historic 1961 program explained it, with the advent of full-fledged communism—projected, for the first time, as within reach for the "present-day generation"—culture would be truly global, "absorbing and developing all the best that has been

2. See Asa Briggs, *Serious Pursuits: Communications and Education*, vol. 3 (Urbana, IL, 1991), 77–81.

3. I've adopted (and adapted) the term "masscult" from Dwight MacDonald's "Masscult and Midcult," originally published in *Partisan Review* in 1961, reprinted in *Against the American Grain* (New York, 1962).

4. Cf. Katerina Clark, *Petersburg: Crucible of Cultural Revolution* (Cambridge, MA, 1995), 20. The ideological framework ("socialism as the antidote to capitalism") was of course comprehensive. Kotkin, *Magnetic Mountain*, 152.

created by world culture"; it would also be accessible and universal, "common to the whole people and to all of humanity."[5] In a communist society, the program promised, all distinctions between mental and manual labor would be eliminated: manual laborers would be "elevated in their cultural-technical level to the level of people who perform mental labor."[6] The intelligentsia as such would cease to exist because, in effect, every Soviet person would have joined its ranks as an active consumer and producer of authentic art. Communism would endow all Soviets with both the opportunity *and* the capacity for cultural fulfillment on an everyday basis. Ten years later, in 1971, Leonid Brezhnev told the party's Twenty-fourth Congress how much had already been achieved: "Socialism has not only given the working masses wide access to spiritual values," the Soviet leader said, "it has made them creators of culture."[7]

If all of this sounds rather more along the lines of ballerinas, poetry readings, and serious World War II films than amphibian men and game shows, so it was. Soviet propaganda made much of the idea that there was no distinction between low and high or mass and elite cultures in the USSR.[8] But as Aleksandr Iakovlev observed in 1965, Soviet culture operated according to an implicit "table of ranks" that placed the fine arts, and especially literature, above those cultural products that won mass audiences but were not defined as art.[9] Iakovlev, a future architect of perestroika, was then a point man for broadcasting within the Central Committee (CC) of the Communist Party, and he made his comments in the context of promoting TV development; he had a far keener sense than many of his Kremlin colleagues for media's mounting significance, and we will meet

5. *Programma Kommunisticheskoi partii Sovetskogo Soiuza priniata XXII s"ezdom KPSS* (Moscow, 1962), 278–279.

6. Ibid., 137.

7. Quoted in B. R. Shcherbina et al., *Ideologicheskaia bor'ba i sovremmenaia kul'tura* (Moscow, 1972), 58–59.

8. For this reason I refer to "Soviet culture" rather than "Soviet popular culture." Authenticity claims—which cultural forms enjoyed genuine mass acclaim (popularity as audience approval) and which were genuine mass products (popularity as audience participation)—are not my main concern. All Soviet culture was popular in both senses by definition and design, and the fate of the design is the locus of my interest. The Soviet authorities did promote something labeled "popular" or "folk" (*narodnaia*) culture. But though this had roots in the varied peasant cultures of the USSR, it was rapidly professionalized and canonized. What Soviet culture prided itself on was the elevation of folk cultures to high-culture status. See Richard Stites, *Russian Popular Culture* (New York, 1992), 71–79; Karen Petrone, *Life Has Become More Joyful, Comrades!* (Bloomington, 2000), 35–39.

9. A. Iakovlev, "Televidenie: Problemy, perspektivy," *Kommunist*, no. 13 (1965): 71. See also Svetlana Boym, *Common Places: Mythologies of Everyday Life in Russia* (Cambridge, 1994), 168–214; P. Vail' and A. Genis, *60-e: Mir sovetskogo cheloveka* (Moscow, 1996), 324–329.

him several times in this book. But even Iakovlev advocated not so much a reca-libration of the Soviet cultural model as expansion to build new channels for its diffusion. Soviet culture and art were indivisible, he agreed. "Masters" and "mas-terworks" were the keystone of Soviet culture's identity. Because culture aimed to elevate everyone to connoisseurship and artistry, it was inherently, unapolo-getically elitist and pedagogical: Soviet culture was full of lessons to teach, typi-cally via heroic role models, and of authorities to teach them; it had an inbred inclination for the collective, the public, and the declamatory. The audience it-self was a perpetual work in progress, subordinate and needy; mass taste was un-trustworthy by definition, and when the authorities tipped their hats to it, it was by way of concession: Soviet workers had the right to use culture for relaxation, and it was acknowledged that many unfortunately still preferred show tunes to opera. Yet recreation was less a value in and of itself than a functional category: one relaxed primarily to restore one's energies for work, that is, for the build-ing of the communist future.[10] Soviet culture, then, was characteristically both future-oriented and nostalgic; past and prospective glories were its polestars.[11] The present, the ordinary, and the personal, when not connected to the grand march of history, tended to slide off the cultural map into meaninglessness.

This Soviet cultural model had a number of critical implications. First, it gave the creative intelligentsia exceptional clout in ideological terms (a clout that might also be parsed as culpability, and often was). In many ways, artists were Soviet society's true heroes, because though the proletariat was the demiurge of history, artists were today's representatives of the radiant future; only artists were living as everyone ought to live, in a contemporary state of grace. Sec-ond, since Soviet culture was global by definition, a kind of safe house for the world's best, there was a constant counterargument within the system to the idea of rigid borders, an innate disposition to cosmopolitanism—meaning not only Marxist-Leninist internationalism, but a sophisticated, confident cultural diversity—that could not be ignored.[12] At the same time, though, the Soviet cul-tural model was grounded in a bedrock exceptionalism whose vagueness only contributed to its power. Soviet culture was Soviet by dint of origin (it had the "good genes" of a socialist mode of production), but it still had to prove itself both sovereign and superior. This made negotiating similarities with the capi-talist antimodel a tricky, and sometimes treacherous, affair. What is more, in an

10. David Crowley and Susan Reid, eds., *Pleasures in Socialism: Leisure and Luxury in the Socialist Eastern Bloc* (Evanston, IL, 2010); Diane Koenker, "Whose Right to Rest? Contest-ing the Family Vacation in the Postwar Soviet Union," *Comparative Studies in History and Society* 51, no. 2 (2009): 401–425.

11. Katerina Clark, *The Soviet Novel: History as Ritual,* 3rd ed. (Bloomington, IN, 2000), 145–146, 172–176.

12. On Soviet culture as guardian of the European tradition, see Eleonory Gilburd, "Picasso in Thaw Culture," *Cahiers du monde russe* 47, nos. 1–2 (2006): 74–83.

age of mounting mass-media power, with culture's borders growing more porous by the moment and with the moment itself—the here and now—growing ever more central to cultural experience, setting boundaries and rallying people around them grew increasingly difficult. Finally, the Soviet cultural model set the stakes for its success exceedingly high: not only was culture at the heart of the socialist project at home, but it was integral to the Soviet Union's mission in world history. Culture—education, inspiration, mobilization—was the royal road to the radiant future not only for Soviets, but for people everywhere.

The ideal type for Soviet culture was forged in the 1930s and transmitted largely intact to the postwar world. So too were the major mechanisms for administering and controlling Soviet culture: the professional organizations such as the Writers' Union that authorized people to work as cultural producers and doled out perquisites; the censorship organs, including the KGB, that screened all work for political errors and the betrayal of state secrets; and the state and party structures (the various ministries, Central Committee departments, and party cells) that organized cultural production and meted out rewards and sanctions. Yet while this ideological and bureaucratic framework remained basically stable, the context for achieving a Soviet culture shifted—and shifted radically.

One of the most vital changes was, of course, mass media's quickening pulse and power in the postwar era, and Soviet media—radio and television broadcasting, film, and (to a lesser extent) print media—are the heart of this book. Other historians might well choose to focus on different cultural spheres, and many have. Literature and book publishing, the visual arts, theater and dance, classical music, circus, sports—cultural production in the USSR was capacious, and in choosing to focus primarily on broadcasting and film, I do not wish to imply that they were either the sum of Soviet culture or its essence. They were, however, tremendously important, and I believe their story is essential to understanding the fortunes of the Soviet bid to create an anti-masscult for the masses in the post–World War II context. First, all mass media are synthetic; they comprise other cultural forms, and so the issues associated with any single form—popular music, say, and the challenge to Soviet music of rock 'n' roll—are embedded in their histories as well. Second, the kind of consumption associated with mass media as they developed after the war challenged Soviet culture's traditional modes and mores in fundamental fashion. Third, mass media were the Soviet Union's largest cultural industries, and in studying them, we gain an incomparable view of the tangle of social and political networks, and economic interests, that was Soviet cultural production. Finally, and crucially, Soviet media had profound symbolic importance; they spoke—and failed to speak—for the Soviet Union's success as a modern, globally competitive cultural power. Never was this truer than in the 1950s, '60s, and '70s: this was, for better and for worse, Moscow's "prime time."

This book, we should note, regularly refers to decades, whereas the more common approach among Soviet scholars is to mark time by political regimes or using the terms "thaw" and "stagnation." (The "thaw"—*ottepel'*—is typically defined as an era of relative cultural liberalism beginning around 1956, with Khrushchev's partial repudiation of Stalin, and running until either his ouster in 1964 or the Soviet-led invasion of Czechoslovakia in 1968. "Stagnation"—*zastoi*—is the thaw's converse—an era of comparative cultural conservatism and partial re-Stalinization under Leonid Brezhnev, 1964–82.) Who sat in the Kremlin was of course crucial to culture's producers and consumers, and insofar as concepts like the thaw were themselves Soviet artifacts—generated, circulated, and disputed by Soviet people—they are relevant to cultural history.[13] But using labels in a diagnostic fashion can stunt historical analysis; by foregrounding certain values and figures associated with them, we risk distorting others and obscuring important continuities.[14] Many of the phenomena we want to understand in the cultural life of the Soviet Union—film fandom, for example, or the role of social networking in production—were long-term trends that span the familiar chronological and conceptual borderlines. This is a history of Soviet culture across the postwar decades because across the decades is how Soviet culture developed.

What is more, although the familiar dates remain significant, they can be misleading markers for the purposes of cultural history. Nineteen fifty-three, the year of Stalin's death, is often presented as the end of Soviet cultural autarky as well, and it was celebrated as such at the time, inside and outside the country. But in thinking about autarky, we must consider not only aspirations, but also everyday realities. In truth, even Stalin's USSR was never walled off altogether from masscult, and a good deal of contemporary high culture from the West continuously flowed into Soviet space as well. During World War II, millions of Soviet people, service personnel and civilians alike, came face-to-face with capitalist culture when they crossed Soviet borders. And with the USSR's annexation of vast new territories along those western borders, millions of bourgeois consumers were transformed into new Soviet subjects. Elements of capitalist culture circulated widely in the late Stalinist USSR—in material form (leather jackets, Spam, jazz recordings) and in the imaginative associations of millions (a Red Army soldier's tales of well-stocked Polish shops, civilian memories of wartime radio shows about the Allies.)[15] In a fascinating historical twist, the Soviet regime was itself

---

13. See Stephen Bittner, *The Many Lives of Khrushchev's Thaw: Experience and Memory in Moscow's Arbat* (Ithaca, NY, 2008).

14. The right wing of the political-cultural spectrum, in particular, remains understudied and inadequately integrated into our overall view of post-Stalinism. See Yitzhak M. Brudny, *Reinventing Russia: Russian Nationalism and the Soviet State, 1953–1991* (Cambridge, MA, 1998); Nikolai Mitrokhin, *Russkaia partiia: Dvizhenie russkikh natsionalistov v SSSR 1953–1985 gody* (Moscow, 2003); Alexander Yanov, *The New Russian Right: Right-Wing Ideologies in the Contemporary USSR,* trans. Stephen P. Dunn (Berkeley, 1978).

15. Elena Zubkova, *Russia after the War* (Armonk, NY, 1998); Juliane Fuerst, ed., *Late Stalinist Russia: Society between Reconstruction and Reinvention* (London, 2007); Amir

responsible for delivering the most potent dose of masscult to postwar Soviet audiences with so-called trophy cinema—films seized from the vanquished Germans in the last days of the war and then marketed countrywide.

But if autarky was never quite an everyday reality in the USSR, the vision of a sovereign, superior Soviet culture was elemental, and in a Cold War context it took on a new and dangerous urgency. As early as November 1945, Stalin was castigating members of his inner circle for failing to recognize the ideological threat posed by the Allies and the danger of Soviet people's falling prey to Western influence.[16] In 1946, the regime launched a ferocious ideological campaign to secure, it said, Soviet culture's purity and preeminence. Artists and intellectuals of all stripes stood accused of admiring capitalist culture to excess—"groveling before the West" was the current phrase, along with "rootless cosmopolitanism" (a sin delineated after the 1948 declaration of the state of Israel and attributed almost entirely to people of Jewish origin). "Soviet patriotism" was the correct and compulsory line: everything from the light bulb to radio to romantic poetry traced its origins to Soviet territory and, in nearly all cases, to the genius of its vanguard people, the Russians.[17] Secretary of Ideology Andrei Zhdanov hammered the point in a speech to Soviet writers in 1946:

> It goes without saying that our literature, which reflects an order that stands higher than any bourgeois democratic order, a culture that is many times superior to bourgeois culture, has the right to teach others the new universal morals.... We know the strength and advantages of our culture very well.... It is not for us to bow to all things foreign or to take a passive position of defense![18]

The world of the Soviets and of Soviet culture was complete unto itself, in other words, and all the more so given its glittering new satellites, the people's democracies of Central and Eastern Europe. To intimate otherwise was to signal treachery. As the Cold War heated up, the Soviet regime's tack was to bellow so loudly as to drown out any hint of doubt. Soviet cultural autarky was always about more than self-sufficiency; it was both an assertion of imperial power and a life-and-death exercise in self-defense.

Weiner, *Making Sense of the War* (Princeton, 2001); Vassily Aksyonov, *In Search of Melancholy Baby,* trans. Michael Henry Heim and Antonia W. Bouis (New York, 1985); Joseph Brodsky, *On Grief and Reason* (New York, 1997).

16. R. Pikhoia, *Moskva. Kreml'. Vlast'. 40 let posle voiny* (Moscow, 2007), 169–172.

17. For the Russian chauvinism at the core of Soviet patriotism, see David Brandenberger, *National Bolshevism: Stalinist Mass Culture and the Formation of Modern Russian National Identity, 1931–1956* (Cambridge, 2002).

18. Andrei Zhdanov, "The Duty of a Soviet Writer," *Literaturnaia gazeta,* 21 September 1946, translated in *U.S. House of Representatives, 80th Congress: The Strategy and Tactics of World Communism* (Washington: Government Printing Office, 1948).

Bravado and paranoia, universality and insularity—all familiar modes for Soviet culture in general, but the very essence of late Stalinist culture as it stiffened its back against the gusts of a changing world. Stalin died too soon to witness the West's spectacular postwar transformation. Great Britain would not end wartime rationing for another full year, and standards of living remained low in many parts of Western Europe well into the 1950s.[19] But signs of the postwar "economic miracle" and the mass consumer society, with mass culture at its core, were already on the horizon. Broadcasting was plainly a major force to be reckoned with in the new era. Radio, which had first shown the extent of its powers during the war, expanded its reach rapidly after 1945, blurring familiar boundaries (geographical, for instance) in some places and reinforcing them (generational, linguistic) in others. Television was not a major force in most countries until the 1960s, but wherever it was introduced, audiences embraced it with alacrity and intensity. It affected everything from the way political campaigns were run to the way families ate dinner and states promoted languages and cultures. Commercial jet travel, too, although, like television, in its infancy in the early fifties, was clearly on the rise and set to transform the way people moved across and thought about borders. Decolonization was already bringing the first large populations of former colonial subjects to European cities. And although it would be several years before Dwight MacDonald reported on the power of the American "teenager" for the *New Yorker* magazine, and a few years more until the new breed flexed its muscles on the other side of the Atlantic, the baby boom was in full swing, and one could hear rumblings in the mass cultural scene of the "youthquake" to come.[20]

What would Stalin have said about TV dinners (and about political leaders presenting important issues on screen as viewers blithely slurped their stew), about English workers plotting not only strikes, but package holidays in Spain, about rock 'n' roll radio shows, pushy reporters heady with the speed and sway of electronic media, shaggy-haired activists, Brigitte Bardot? It is not difficult to imagine some possible reactions, given what we know about the dictator's personal tastes and also about how many of his contemporaries reacted. Stalin was famously prudish about on-screen kisses; Francisco Franco's censors made film distributors paint over Jane's bare midriff in the *Tarzan* films.[21] And anxiety and revulsion were in no way limited to the dictators; many adults in the democratic West recommended a similar approach to broadcasting Elvis Presley's lower half and shook their heads at the spectacle of 1960s youth activism. Surely it was an

19. For a brilliant discussion of Europe's long "postwar," see Tony Judt, *Postwar: A History of Europe Since 1945* (New York, 2005).

20. Dwight MacDonald, "A Caste, A Culture, A Market," *New Yorker,* 22 November 1958, 57–94, and 29 November 1958, 57–107.

21. Helen Graham and Jo Labanyi, eds. *Spanish Cultural Studies, An Introduction* (Oxford, 1996), 210. See also Aurora Bosch and M. Fernanda del Rincón, "Franco and Hollywood, 1939–1956," *New Left Review* 1, no. 232 (November–December 1998): 112–127.

unusual person who, having been raised in the nineteenth or early twentieth century, did not find much of the new culture bewildering, if not alarming.

Stalin's successors were themselves very much men of the ancien régime when it came to culture—a fundamental fact. But they did shift the Soviet Union's stance in other ways that proved essential to cultural development. The most significant change across the board was the renunciation of mass terror. Although the Soviet Union remained a dictatorship, the scale of its repressive actions diminished dramatically after Stalin's death, and the impact on Soviet culture's producers was profound. Internationally, the post-Stalinist regime, with Khrushchev at the helm, signaled its desire for "peaceful coexistence" with the West. The new line established that the Soviets did in fact have a great deal to learn from the world beyond their borders; increasing cultural interactions would also help decrease Cold War tensions, it was said, reducing the risk of nuclear cataclysm and leading to greater understanding of the Soviet system abroad.[22] "Cultural exchange" thus became a watchword of the Khrushchev era. Soviet culture's cosmopolitan strain was decriminalized and then actively promoted in the name of peace and progress. The USSR opened its doors to new foreign theatrical productions and art exhibitions, tourist groups, students, and scientific delegations. Meanwhile, foreign broadcasters stepped up their efforts to reach Soviet listeners at their radio sets, and foreign businesspeople came calling to sell their wares. And so, for the first time in a generation, Soviet culture after Stalin found itself in *open* competition on its own terrain. In 1962, rivaling Soviet cinema's amphibian man, Vladimir Korenev, for the affection of Soviet audiences were Yul Brynner, Steve McQueen, and the other stars of an American Western, *The Magnificent Seven* (1960).

This story of cultural infiltration—let us call it the "parting the iron curtain" story, after an influential 1997 study—has proved enormously engaging over the years.[23] Contemporary Western journalists like Harrison Salisbury of the *New York Times* reported with undisguised glee on the Soviet crowds for Western films and art exhibitions; seasoned newspapermen who would never accept an assignment to cover a sock hop at home appeared to relish writing about teenagers dancing to rock 'n' roll in the USSR and their efforts to dress in the latest foreign fashions. For Salisbury and his colleagues, these were all welcome signs of health and sanity behind the iron curtain.[24] The theme continued through the

---

22. See Vladislav Zubok, *A Failed Empire: The Soviet Union in the Cold War from Stalin to Gorbachev* (Chapel Hill, NC, 2007), 103–104.

23. Walter J. Hixson, *Parting the Curtain: Propaganda, Culture, and the Cold War, 1945–1961* (New York, 1997). See also Yale Richmond, *Cultural Exchange and the Cold War: Raising the Iron Curtain* (University Park, PA, 2003), xiv.

24. Two examples: "Bobby Soxers—Moscow Style," *New York Times,* 17 February 1952; Harrison Salisbury, "'Lost Generation' Baffles Soviet; Nihilistic Youths Shun Ideology," *New York Times,* 9 February 1962.

seventies and eighties, when every well-read tourist to the USSR knew to bring gifts of blue jeans and Beatles albums. With the collapse of the USSR and the masscult deluge that followed, the notion of cultural infiltration was enshrined on the level of popular wisdom. "Their" love for what was "ours" clearly equaled a rejection of what they had, or rather, what had been imposed upon them by the old men in the Kremlin—a culture hostile to artistic innovation and fearful of youthful energy and spontaneity, frumpy, joyless, and hidebound.[25] Once the curtain was parted and Soviets got a good glimpse of the alternative, it was only a matter of time before it all came tumbling down.

Popular wisdom is not called wisdom for no reason, and Western observers did not fabricate stories about Soviet passions for masscult: they did not need to. Equating such behavior with political disaffection was actually as much a Soviet media trope as a Western one.[26] Yet we need not peg the saxophone as an agent of either liberation *or* sedition to see how important masscult could be in introducing new imagery, ideas, and modes of self-expression into Soviet space. The parting-the-iron-curtain story is not altogether wrong, but it is inadequate, and in allowing it to dominate our horizons, we lose sight of what may well be the bigger story for postwar history: the success of *KVN, Soviet Screen,* and *Amphibian Man,* that is, the phenomenal growth of homegrown Soviet culture in the everyday life of Soviet people and the new images, ideas, and modes of expression it offered. The fact is that it was not until the late fifties that the regime was materially capable of making any culture a part of everyday life on a mass scale. What made this possible was a vast postwar expansion in the cultural infrastructure—a veritable revolution in the world of Soviet media. And this revolution, in turn, was authorized by the regime's continued ideological commitment to cultural exceptionalism—to a *Soviet culture.*

Khrushchev spelled out the Soviet regime's position in no uncertain terms: though peaceful coexistence was the correct line in foreign diplomacy, it did not contravene the laws of history, whose engine remained the struggle between labor and capital: there could be no peaceful coexistence in the realm of ideology. Under Brezhnev, the regime attempted to broker what it defined as a more stable

25. A good example of this attitude is Reinhold Wagnleitner, "The Empire of the Fun, or Talkin' Soviet Union Blues: The Sound of Freedom and US Cultural Hegemony in Europe," *Diplomatic History* 23, no. 3 (Summer 1999): 499–524. Cf. David Caute, who mostly ignores the popular culture Wagnleitner champions, but draws an equally devastating portrait of Soviet inadequacy: "[T]hey were losing the wide *Kulturkampf* from the outset because they were afraid of freedom and were seen to be afraid." Caute, *The Dancer Defects: The Struggle for Cultural Supremacy during the Cold War* (Oxford, 2003), 2.

26. Though the popularity of the theme in Western media needs little explanation, a more intriguing question is what these stories were doing in Soviet media. See Kristin Roth-Ey, "Mass Media and the Remaking of Soviet Culture, 1950s–1960s" (PhD diss., Princeton University, 2003), chap. 1.

relationship with the ideological opponent; and culturally speaking, Brezhnev's USSR showed more willingness to co-opt enemy trends and more financial savvy in exploiting actual masscult products in certain, delimited spheres. But dé-tente in the seventies did not spell accommodation or convergence any more than peaceful coexistence in the fifties and sixties had. The Soviet ideological commitment—what Vladislav Zubok and Konstantin Pleshakov have called the "revolutionary-imperial paradigm" and, more colorfully, "the delirium tremens of Soviet statesmen, the core of the regime's self-legitimacy"—endured.[27]

The USSR was at base a "propaganda state"; culture in the Soviet context was always in the business of educating, training, motivating, and mobilizing.[28] But it was also, fatefully, in the business of proving to audiences worldwide Soviet culture's superiority to masscult. Easy access to high-quality cultural experience on an everyday basis was a bedrock promise of socialism. Or, to put it in media-age terms, Soviet culture itself was essential to the Soviet brand. And the regime's continuing commitment to the brand throughout the Cold War guaranteed that there would be intensive, ongoing, and much-ballyhooed investment. How much investment? According to one Soviet publication, the overall expenses for "culture" (including, in this case, education and scientific research) in 1980 accounted for around 27 percent of the national income, for a total of 98.8 billion rubles, more than twenty-four times the level in 1940.[29] These figures should be taken as illustrative rather than definitive, and with the unreliability of Soviet record keeping, we may never have verifiable economic data. In a global sense, though, we do not need them. The growth of the Soviets' infrastructure for mass-media culture was nothing short of explosive. Television went from a novelty item—one set for every twelve thousand people on average in 1950—to a staple of Soviet life—one set for every fifteen people in 1970 and one for four in 1980.[30] Radio reached saturation levels far earlier, with the number of radio sets topping 70 million by the early sixties and reaching 95 million by 1970, a sevenfold increase over 1950 levels. In cinema, the media boom meant dramatic expansion in both production and distribution and translated into a stunning annual box office of over 4 billion tickets for much of the sixties and seventies. Finally, there was the mass Soviet press, with print runs to make any Western managing editor's head spin. Magazine circulation inside the Soviet

27. Vladislav Zubok and Constantine Pleshakov, *Inside the Kremlin's Cold War: From Stalin to Khrushchev* (Cambridge, MA, 1996), 276. See also Nigel Gould-Davies, "Rethinking the Role of Ideology in the Cold War," *Journal of Cold War Studies* 1, no. 1 (Winter 1999): 90–109.

28. For "propaganda state," see Peter Kenez's pioneering *The Birth of the Propaganda State: Soviet Methods of Mass Mobilization, 1917–1929* (Cambridge, 1985).

29. B. A. Miasoedov, *Strana chitaet, slushaet, smotrit* (Moscow, 1982), 11.

30. Ibid., 66.

Union reached 2.6 billion by 1970—an overall increase of over fourteen times from the 1950 level.[31]

The postwar media boom gave Soviet culture unprecedented, imperial scope and reach. Yet it also entailed historic changes to the Soviets' mass culture formation—to the ways culture was produced, marketed, consumed, and spoken about within the USSR.[32] Historians have long emphasized the role of the creative intelligentsia in cultural change after Stalin, following and confirming in large measure the intelligentsia's own accounts. This book looks beyond the fabled intelligentsia gatherings around the kitchen table to consider cultural terrains of a different type: bureaucracies, technologies, social networks, and everyday life practices. From this new vantage point, it becomes clear how many of the most significant changes in media-age Soviet culture relate to the fundamental facts of expansion itself—not in a deterministic sense, but rather in a dynamic and interactive one.

On the production side, it is undeniably easier to administer and control a film industry that produces a dozen or so movies a year, as did the Soviet in the late forties, than one that churns out a hundred or more, as was the case by the sixties. Similarly, it is one thing to be on top of a broadcasting system with a few hundred employees, mostly in Russia, and responsible for twenty or thirty hours of programming daily; it is something else again to run a high-tech, multichannel, multiregional network employing tens of thousands of people and striving to fill airtime around the clock, as did the Soviets in the 1970s. The point is not that most Soviet culture makers were waging subterranean warfare against the system by pushing the boundaries of the permissible—far from it. Nor should we imagine that Soviet media managers grew lax over the decades; they did not. But there were many more of them, and more people involved in production and

---

31. *Narodnoe khoziaistvo SSSR v 1970 g.* (Moscow, 1971), 678, 466.

32. I have adopted the term "mass culture formation" from Marilyn Ivy in an effort to move beyond the idea of mass culture as something produced by one group of people, controlled and administered by another, and consumed by a third in a tidy system. (In Soviet history, this was an "official culture" generated by the intelligentsia, censored and delivered by apparatchiki, ingested by the people). In practice, all groups have a tendency to overlap, and all cultural packages shape-shift in the hands of new technologies and in different social and political contexts. Soviet culture's context was dictatorship: shapes never shifted in any way they pleased. But its modes of production and consumption had commonalities with other modern mass cultures, and for this reason, Soviet culture is better understood as a "formation": a set of cultural products, industries, bureaucratic institutions, social networks, and, not least, a discourse—the ongoing and often conflicted conversation that mass cultures have about themselves as experience and ideal. Marilyn Ivy, "Formations of Mass Culture," in *Postwar Japan as History,* ed. Andrew Gordon (Berkeley, 1993), 239–258. Ivy's definition does not include the discursive element I describe. See also Leszek Kolakowski's "Communism as a Cultural Formation," *Survey* 29, no. 2 (Summer 1985): 139–148.

distribution, too; careers, egos, personal pleasures were on the line all over the Soviet Union. As the industries and institutions for culture grew, people found more spaces within to pursue their own interests, as they defined them. And sometimes, in a media-age environment, they were able to pursue them even as they appeared to contradict big-picture ideological and economic goals.

Imagine a party secretary in a provincial town who decided to set up a local TV station because it was prestigious and because he liked the idea of watching movies at home with his family. Moscow said the project made no sense—the town would soon be connected to central TV by cable—but our party secretary went ahead and built his station nevertheless. Local technological buffs were eager to give it a try, and the secretary was able to work out an understanding with republic-level party bosses for protection. Picture a film director who yearned to create a serious biopic about a little-known artist. Everyone knew it would never sell enough tickets to cover the cost of production; and everyone knew that cinema, like all Soviet art, was supposed to reach out to a universal audience. Yet our director secured funding for his niche project all the same because he had powerful friends and the studio hoped it would compete well at international festivals.

Soviet culture had many taboos still, and people could be harshly punished for violating them. But with the renunciation of mass terror after Stalin's death, these were penalties of an altogether different order. Now there were roomier pockets within the Soviet culture formation for individuals and institutions to pursue various interests—not freedom of action, but a broader scope for leveraging relationships, ignoring instructions, and playing one principle against another in the name of a third. The people who made mass culture in the USSR and administered it spent years of their lives in meetings, telling each other just how things should work according to economic plans and ideological campaigns and scolding each other (and sometimes worse) for their failings. Some shared a personal commitment to those plans and campaigns and to the vision of Soviet culture they embodied: this was particularly true in the Khrushchev era, the peak of postwar optimism about the Soviet system's prospects and an era of enthusiasts, or self-defined socialist cultural activists later known as "people of the sixties" (shestidestiatniki); we will meet several of them in this book. And yet, even then, all sorts of things happened in Soviet culture that should not have by any conventional playbook (do-it-yourself TV stations, movies targeted to elite audiences). They happened because they could and because they met other needs.

We can spot the Soviet mass culture formation's new flexibility and dynamism on the consumption side of the equation, too, as it intersected with and, in many ways, reinforced the great sociological shifts of the postwar era. Taken alone, the production boom need not have translated into higher levels of consumption. But the Soviet regime also made a major push to widen access to culture in the early postwar era and, more important still, Soviet villagers voted with their feet for an urban lifestyle. As of 1962, for the first time in Soviet history, the majority of the population lived in urban areas, and urbanization brought unprecedented numbers of people squarely into the orbit of mass media culture.[33] So too did the mass construction of individual family apartments in the fifties, sixties, and seventies and the promotion of home-based cultural technologies; the expansion of the educational system and extension of adolescence in the Soviet life cycle; and the substantial increases, across the social spectrum, in both leisure time and disposable income. The sociological context for cultural experience in the Soviet Union was profoundly, irrevocably altered.

All these factors encouraged engagement with mass culture, but they could not, of course, command it. Enter the Soviet audience. Whereas the parting-the-iron-curtain story tends to summon up images of masscult-mad consumers, or vaguely dissident high-culture ones, most of what the media boom brought to Soviet audiences was in fact Soviet-made and ideologically orthodox. It is this culture that consumers in the postwar USSR chose to make part of their every-day life in ever-increasing volume. Average annual visits to the cinema shot up from only six in 1950 to nearly twenty a decade later. Sociological research also indicated that people were devoting more time than ever before to media cul-ture, particularly broadcasting. One mid-sixties study in several cities found that men in families with TV sets (roughly two-thirds of the total) were watching eleven hours per week and women six.[34] By the mid to late sixties, over three-quarters of Soviet people reported listening to radio programming on a daily basis, and even more said they read newspapers and magazines.[35] Young people appeared to be the most avid consumers of all: researchers estimated that the average Soviet child was devoting sixteen hours a week to broadcasting and cinema in the mid-sixties, a steep rise from their estimate of six hours for the 1930s.[36] Media consumption continued to rise in the seventies and beyond.

This was, once again, a remarkable achievement on paper for the propaganda state, but one that altered the terms of Soviet cultural engagement in a funda-mental fashion.[37] For what the boom meant on the ground was that, more than

33. A. Vishnevskii, *Serp i rubl': Konservativnaia modernizatsiia v SSSR* (Moscow, 2000), 91.

34. Research from L. A. Gordon and E. V. Klopov, *Chelovek posle raboty* (Moscow, 1972), cited in B. M. Firsov, *Puti razvitiia sredstv massovoi kommunikatsii* (Moscow, 1977), 118. Gordon and Klopov conducted their research in 1965–67 in Dnepropetrovsk, Zaporozh'e, Odessa, and Kostroma.

35. Firsov, *Puti razvitiia,* 120.

36. L. Pressman and D. Poltorak, "Net, oni ne passivny," *Sem'ia i shkola,* no. 1 (1971), cited in I. Levshina, *Liubite li vy kino?* (Moscow, 1978), 31.

37. Compare with Lewis Siegelbaum's discussion of the Soviets' burgeoning car culture: "The more time one spent in and with one's own car the less there was for performing other functions, whether social, professional, or otherwise." *Cars for Comrades: The Life of the Soviet Automobile* (Ithaca, NY, 2008), 7.

at any point in the Soviet Union's history, Soviet people were able to interact with mass culture on their *own* terms. One person could, for example, use her radio solely for light music programs, while another might choose to go to the movies only when they were showing comedies. Soviet audiences had always made choices. But with the postwar media boom people saw their options expand exponentially, and this could not help but change both their expectations and their experiences of mass culture. What is more, with the rise of home-based cultural technologies, people across the USSR were increasingly making their choices in private rather than public settings and on their own time rather than in a collectively organized fashion. Broadcasting—radio and television—epitomized the new dynamic, and along with broadcasting, we must bear in mind the important role of small-scale, domestic recording technologies. Soviet consumers of the 1950s played "X-ray" records (recordings from radio and other sources printed on disused X-ray plates), whereas in the sixties and seventies people used reel-to-reel tape recorders.[38] In the early 1980s the spread of video technology in the USSR set about transforming the consumer experience of cinema and television, too.

As home-based technologies combined with the relative abundance of cultural production to empower consumers in ways both unprecedented and unpredictable, the nature of what was on offer was changing as well. Soviet culture in the media age remained steadfast in its pedagogical mission, but it also grew more entertainment-oriented and more eclectic, faster, more immediate, and increasingly oriented toward daily life—culture in a personal key and the here and now. *Swan Lake* came to the Soviet television viewer in a jumble with game shows, soccer matches, and lectures on agricultural policy, all to be consumed at the viewer's pleasure in a domestic setting.[39] Individual TV programs also ran the risk of blurring crucial cultural distinctions by mixing high and low (e.g., having an opera diva and a satirist share one stage). Eclecticism, a sense of immediacy and intimacy, and the empowerment of personal choice were all particularly vital in television broadcasting, making the TV boom exceptionally important to Soviet culture. But these trends were also characteristic of radio, film, and even print media in the fifties, sixties, and seventies.

38. Tape recorders were both Soviet-made and foreign: for the Soviet recorders alone, estimates run to 50 million sold between 1960 and 1985. Adele Marie Barker, ed., *Consuming Russia: Popular Culture, Sex and Society since Gorbachev* (Durham, NC, 1999), 83. On political power and cultural technologies in Russian-Soviet history, see S. Frederick Starr, "New Communications Technologies and Civil Society," in *Science and the Soviet Social Order,* ed. Loren Graham (Cambridge, 1990), 19–50.

39. Here I am building upon Raymond Williams's concept of "flow" as the "central experience" of television. Flow as a mode of cultural consumption was, I argue, an awkward fit with Soviet cultural ideals that prized clear, hierarchical boundaries, canons, and control (see chapter 4). Raymond Williams, *Television: Technology and Cultural Form* (Hanover, NH, 1974), 72–112.

Moreover, thanks to the improvements in infrastructure and to shifting everyday life patterns, especially the boost in leisure time, the very function of Soviet culture was changing in many people's lives. Gathering around an outdoor loudspeaker to hear the radio orchestra play or marching off with your factory brigade to see this season's movie at the local club embodied old-style Soviet culture—collective, public, event-driven, with clear genres and goals—and there was still plenty of it around straight through the seventies. But with expansion and technological change, with the world outside the USSR pressing in and many people inside reaching out, with producer and consumer demands in play in all sorts of ways, Soviet culture changed. Paradoxically, for all its gigantism, it grew smaller; for all its straining toward Art, History, and other Big Ideas, it became more everyday and ordinary.

Soviet cultural conservatives railed against the mutations of the postwar era, defending the brand "Soviet culture"—and with it a Soviet way of life—from enemy assault. "[W]estern propaganda...is using all possible measures to penetrate socialist countries and, first and foremost, the USSR, with elements of so-called 'mass culture,' which carry a powerful charge of bourgeois psychology and the petty bourgeois way of life," warned one leader of the Soviet youth organization, the Komsomol, in 1967.[40] The official Soviet version of a vast, tightly organized, and massively funded intergovernmental campaign to assault the USSR with masscult was a dark fantasy (albeit one that resonated with the dreams of many a Cold Warrior in the West).[41] Nevertheless, when Soviet cultural conservatives spied suspicious changes at home—a growing similarity to the dreaded masscult in Soviet culture's own look, feel, and function—this was not mere paranoia; they were right. Workers relaxing before their TV sets hardly looked the part of builders of communism; young film fans mooning over Vladimir Korenev or Bollywood star Rishi Kapoor did not bring to mind the heroic youth construction brigades of the 1930s or the enlightened connoisseur of tomorrow's communist society. But it was Soviet culture that provided these opportunities. By self-definition, Soviet culture always had work to do, but in the media age it was in many ways a culture increasingly oriented away from work and toward cultural consumption as a value in and of itself. The bonds that tied culture to mobilization and the Soviet grand narrative—the march from heroic past to radiant future—were steadily coming undone. And so Soviet culture was in the paradoxical position of getting worse as it got better, of undermining its

40. RGASPI-m, f. 1, op. 34, d. 127, ll. 13–14.

41. Compare this view with contemporary Western arguments about U.S. "cultural imperialism," especially Herbert Schiller, *Mass Communications and American Empire* (New York, 1969, 1992). For a more recent, exceptionally sophisticated argument in this vein, see Victoria de Grazia, *Irresistible Empire: America's Advance through Twentieth-Century Europe* (Cambridge, MA, 2005).

own stated values and cherished goals while also achieving its greatest reach, penetration, and power.

The postwar mutations in the Soviet mass culture formation brought it closer in line with the rest of the industrialized world, and although this shocked cultural conservatives in the USSR, it should not shock us. The media boom was of course a common phenomenon across postwar Europe and the United States and Japan as well; it was an integral component of what Eric Hobsbawm has called "the greatest and most dramatic, rapid and universal social transformation in human history."[42] On both sides of the iron curtain, mass media were instrumental in spreading images of the good life that helped fuel mass consumption. They were also prominent and very powerful symbols of the good life in their own right: to be able to go to the movies once a week or even more, to bring a transistor radio along on a picnic, to have a TV set in your own home—all these were flagpoles for a modern lifestyle, and people rallied around them enthusiastically, often choosing to spend their money on mass culture before they invested in practical appliances like washing machines. Mass culture was more than just a symbolic good, in other words, more than just a sign of a modern lifestyle; it was a lived good, a modern lifestyle enacted and enjoyed. In the USSR, most people did not much concern themselves with which model TV to buy (acquiring a set, any set, was trouble enough for most), and they saw no advertising campaigns to whet their appetites for one program or another. But they knew they wanted a TV because it was defined early on by Soviet media as a must-have of modern life, and this resonated with their own experience; they found they enjoyed watching. And in this, as in their appreciation for light music with a danceable beat, big-budget genre cinema, and news stories with flashes of scandal, people in the Soviet Union were like people all over the developed world.

Western European political and cultural elites tended to have a far more ambivalent reaction to the brave new world of postwar mass culture than did the everyday consumer.[43] Some aspects of the media boom they did embrace. The sheen of technological modernity radiating off mass media was universally prized. A modern media system was a must for any modern state. This was a point of pride on the international stage, much like a national airline company, and a perceived competitive advantage in a globalizing economy as well. Postwar mass culture, then, was conceptualized as a public good tightly linked to the idea of national prosperity. This meant that most European film industries and

42. Eric Hobsbawm, *The Age of Extremes: A History of the World, 1914–1991* (New York, 1996), 288. Cf. Arthur Marwick, *The Sixties: Cultural Transformation in Britain, France, Italy and the United States c. 1958–c. 1974* (New York, 2000), 13–20.

43. Andrew Ross, *No Respect: Intellectuals and Popular Culture* (New York, 1989); D. Hebdige, "Towards a Cartography of Taste, 1935–1962," *Block*, no. 4 (1981): 39–65, reprinted in *Hiding in the Light: On Images and Things* (London, 1988), 45–76.

many publishers won substantial state subsidies. But it was broadcasting above all that registered as an engine of progress, and although some countries did open their doors to commercial ventures over the years, the bulk of broadcasting in Western Europe remained very much in state hands and operated according to a public service model.[44] Public broadcasting systems varied in the mix of programming they offered, but they all made a goal of improving educational levels and raising cultural standards. The BBC's postwar concept of a "cultural pyramid"—programming on three distinct levels, low, middle, and highbrow, and training the population to advance from one to the next—was perhaps more elaborated than most, but the approach was typical.[45] By the end of the fifties, even a highly skeptical Franco had been convinced that television broadcasting was necessary to improve the educational levels of Spaniards and spur economic growth.[46]

Yet for all that, many leading figures in Europe's political and cultural life remained anxious about the potential hazards of a booming mass culture. The problem was usually framed in terms of "Americanization," a term that cut a very wide swath, from flooding a country with American products to the political and economic manipulation of markets to the influence of supposedly American ideas on cultural and social life. The postwar debate over Americanization already had a long history in Europe, and it touched on genuine phenomena. The issues, however, were always more complex than the label implied.[47] What had many people concerned were the changes in cultural experience—the speed and immediacy of the new culture and the way it seemed to destabilize traditional hierarchies and privilege the personal realm, for example—as well as the transformation of social experience that came with urbanization and rising living standards. All these factors were intimately related, but it is impossible to isolate

44. Asa Briggs and Peter Burke, *A Social History of the Media from Gutenberg to the Internet* (Malden, MA, 2005); Richard Collins, *From Satellite to Single Market: New Communication Technology and European Public Service Television* (New York, 1998).

45. Andrew Criswell, *An Introductory History of British Broadcasting* (London, 2002), 83.

46. Manuel Patricio, "Early Spanish Television and the Paradoxes of a Dictator General," *Historical Journal of Film, Radio and Television* 25, no. 7 (October 2005): 599–617.

47. Highlights of the extensive literature on Americanization include de Grazia, *Irresistible Empire;* Robert Kuisel, *Seducing the French: The Dilemma of Americanization* (Berkeley, 1993); Richard Pells, *Not Like Us: How Europeans Have Loved, Hated, and Transformed American Culture since World War II* (New York, 1998); Ute Poiger, *Jazz, Rock, and Rebels: Cold War Politics and American Culture in a Divided Germany* (Berkeley, 2000); Reinhold Wagnleitner and Elaine Tyler May, eds., *"Here, There, and Everywhere": The Foreign Politics of American Popular Culture* (Hanover, NH, 2000); R. Kroes et al., eds. *Cultural Transmissions and Receptions: American Mass Culture in Europe* (Amsterdam, 1993); Alexander Stephen, ed., *The Americanization of Europe: Culture, Diplomacy, and Anti-Americanism after 1945* (New York, 2006).

causal links among them. The denim-clad teenagers on the corner probably did take fashion cues from Hollywood, and if they had a transistor, they were likely to be listening to American-style music, too. But their presence was made possible by many other new facts of life, including the fundamental fact that they, unlike earlier generations, did not *have* to be working and had cash in their pockets for things like jeans and radios. Much the same might be said of their parents sitting alone at home watching TV. The problem of postwar mass culture and Americanization was also the problem of postwar economic success.

Faced with the new realities, Soviet political and cultural elites reacted much like their Western counterparts. Soviet leaders would not have appreciated the comparison, but when they railed against "bourgeois cultural infiltration" and touted Soviet culture's superior "spiritual" qualities, they sounded very much like Spain's Franco—and Franco could sound like anti-Americanization speakers throughout Europe. To defend culture's traditional hierarchies, to worry about changing modes of cultural consumption and social mores (and draw a bright line connecting them analytically) were common stances on both sides of the iron curtain.[48]

But the Soviet Union's encounter with the postwar media age was also very different from the West's, and its progress and outcome had different implications for the rest of the world. The Soviet regime had branded itself with cultural power in a distinctive manner from the very beginning. When a foreign dignitary was visiting Moscow, he or she would be escorted to the Bolshoi without fail and often presented to the artists after the performance. Khrushchev, in his day, enjoyed telling foreign guests how he, a mere country bumpkin, had learned to appreciate art thanks to Soviet power. The folksy bluster was vintage Khrushchev, but the attitude was all Soviet apparatchik, and every subsequent leader kept up the tradition. This was Soviet culture. Read almost any political memoirist from the Soviet era, and you will find the "some of my best friends were artists" cliché, brandished as proof of personal *kul'turnost'* (cultured-ness) and an enduring commitment to the Soviet cultural brand.

Thirty years ago, literary historian Vera Dunham put *kul'turnost'* at the center of what she called a "Big Deal" struck between the late Stalinist regime and an aspiring middle class: acceptance of the status quo in exchange for social stability and a chance at personal enrichment and status. The role of mass culture (her focus was mass-produced fiction) was to promote the deal, which in her eyes held a lurid gleam because it trampled *kul'tura* in the name of *kul'turnost'*. *Kul'tura* was "higher culture, a synthesis of ideas, knowledge, and memories," she said, while *kul'turnost'* merely "encode[d] the proper relationship between

---

48. Even some Americans expressed concerns about what Europeans were calling Americanization of their culture. See Michael Kammen, *American Culture, American Tastes: Social Change and the Twentieth Century* (New York, 2000).

people through their possessions and labels"; it was "a refurbished, victorious, conservative force in Soviet postwar life, embodying a slick decorum and a new kind of self-righteousness—stable, prudent, heavy."[49]

Dunham's Big Deal argument was a scholarly tour de force, and it has been widely accepted as an explanation for Soviet stability and the seeming incongruity of a revolutionary political regime in bed with a conservative artistic and social one—a regime that could hail bearded third world rebels one moment while promoting quiet nights by the TV and blacklisting bearded Soviet TV performers the next. However, to sense an incongruity, one has to hold a standard, and the question is, whose? Lurking behind Dunham's argument was the shadow of an authentic Soviet culture, untainted by any deals and true to socialist values; she could scarcely temper her scorn for orange lampshades in Soviet living rooms radiating their owners' respectability; for "Soviet citizens in a Rumanian coastal resort, carrying their cameras and their suntan oil, and flashing their eager roubles"; and for all the other trappings of false cultural consciousness.[50] In this regard, Dunham channeled the traditional disdain of the Russian-Soviet intelligentsia for the market and reflected the discomfort many foreigners felt when faced with the Soviet Union's "tacky" goods and the "embarrassingly pathetic aspect" of people pursing them.[51] But what if there was no contradiction between revolutionary politics and conservative cultural and social values in the eyes of history's actors?

The hypothetical Soviet vacationer in Romania may well have packed a volume of Pushkin in his luggage. It mattered little whether he spent more time sunbathing than reading Pushkin; nor did it make much difference if he also read *Playboy* when he could get it. The Soviet tourist was not necessarily embarrassed; he still had Pushkin in his pocket and a sense of confidence that this was proper and Soviet. Inconsistency is not necessarily the same thing as cynicism. It was possible to remain committed to the brand in the abstract—Soviet culture as distinctive and spiritually superior, the clear victor in the historic battle (in the long run, but still)—while also taking other personal pleasures in the here and now. It was tenable, as Alexei Yurchak has argued, for a Komsomol activist to extol the genius of Deep Purple one moment and condemn the soulnessness of masscult the next without being a hypocrite.[52]

49. Vera Dunham, *In Stalin's Time: Middleclass Values and Soviet Fiction,* 2nd ed. (Durham, NC, 1990), 22.

50. Ibid., 240.

51. On the intelligentsia's disdain for the market, see especially Clark, *Petersburg,* and Boym, *Common Places.* The comments on "tacky" goods and "embarrassingly pathetic" pursuits are from sociologist Allen Kassof's (positive) review of Dunham in the *American Journal of Sociology* 84, no.1 (1978): 194.

52. Alexei Yurchak, *Everything Was Forever Until It Was No More: The Last Soviet Generation* (Princeton, 2005).

Yet even if, as Yurchak claims, a brokered relationship with Soviet culture and masscult was second nature for what he calls (generalizing from the activist to the general youth population) the "last Soviet generation," brokering was always brokering: it did not mean recalibrating values on a *systemic* level; it was not the same as rebranding the product, Soviet culture. Pushkin worship never ended, the pilgrimages to the ballet went on, and with them, a very powerful sense of cultural identity endured. The prima ballerina Maia Plisetskaia recalled being chastised by the minister of culture, Ekaterina Furtseva (1962–74): "Put on a skirt, Maia, you have to cover up your bare thighs. This is the Bolshoi Theater, comrades."[53] It was Furtseva's and Khrushchev's generations (born, respectively, in 1910 and 1894) who set the standards for the success and failure of Soviet culture.[54] And its success, as they defined it, was always a matter of global, historic significance.

It is this sense of mission that sets the Soviet media age story apart. In Europe, the best analogy to the USSR would be De Gaulle's France, whose minister of culture, André Malraux, had the temerity to escort the Mona Lisa on tour to the United States in the name of *French* cultural leadership in the world.[55] But even Malraux and De Gaulle did not promise a global "Frenchified" culture along the lines of the Soviet brand, and, more to the point, France's cultural identity was never linked to a political program of self-defined world-historic proportions. France would go on even if the rest of the world was perverse enough to ignore French culture. Franco's Spain emerged from official cultural autarky about the same time as the USSR and pushed a very strong idea of Spanish culture, though not a universal one.[56] The only real comparison—and the only one the Soviets themselves bothered making—was to the Americans. American culture was indeed, like Soviet culture, a universal model, grounded in (if not entirely delimited by) a crusading economic and ideological system, capitalism. If the United States had no mass, government-sponsored program of Americanization, that was only, one could argue, because it would have been superfluous. American culture did not need a minister of culture. It was everyone's idée fixe, and the Soviets' most of all.

The flip side of postwar cultural Americanization was the failure of Sovietization, and failure, too, was a Soviet idée fixe.[57] It is true that Soviet-made culture

53. Maya Plisetskaya, *I, Maya Plisetskaya* (New Haven, CT, 2001), 276. "Plisetskaia" conforms to the Library of Congress transliteration system used throughout this book. "Plisetskaya" is an alternative spelling.

54. On the graying of the Soviet leadership, see Amir Weiner, "Robust Revolution to Retiring Revolution: The Life Cycle of the Soviet Revolution," *Slavonic and East European Review* 86, no. 2 (April 2008): 208–231. On the importance of communism's success and failure to communist elites, see Stephen Kotkin, *Uncivil Society: 1989 and the Implosion of the Communist Establishment* (New York, 2009).

55. Olivier Todd, *Malraux: A Life,* trans. Joseph West (New York, 2005), 361–370.

56. Graham and Labanyi, *Spanish Cultural Studies,* esp. 196–228.

57. I am not speaking of the Sovietization of cultural institutions (the creation of Soviet-style cultural bureaucracies) in Eastern and Central Europe after World War II. This *was*

reached greater numbers of foreign consumers in the postwar era than ever before. There were Soviet cinema buffs in cities from Cairo to New York to Tokyo to Buenos Aires. But the Soviet film industry never came close to Hollywood for international mass reach, and the situation for the dominant media-age format, television, was even more calamitous from the point of view of the Soviet brand. Radio Moscow was more successful in foreign markets, particularly in the developing world, where television was not a factor. But this was a relative success, and the negative assessment is the Soviets' own, not mine. Although there is an important story to be told of Soviet high culture capturing the imaginations of educated elites, notably in the developing world, no one claimed the impact was comparable to American cultural influence.

Within the postwar USSR, various cultural streams circulated beyond the American (and it is debatable whether we can identify something like rock music as exclusively American in any event).[58] Yet there was no denying Soviet culture's fixation with and growing similarity to its self-defined antithesis, mass-cult. Some of this came from Soviet media adapting to Western models in the face of competition. But many of the similarities can be traced to the changes in technology and consumption patterns I sketched out earlier. Everyday culture in a mass-media age did not look, feel, or function like culture in the prewar or wartime eras. Marching in a parade or attending a ballet was not the same as watching these things at home on TV; going to watch the one movie in town with your workmates and discussing it afterwards with an agitator was not the same as arguing with your friend between the war drama and the Indian musical and agreeing to see one today and the other next week. These are simply different experiences of a culture, independent of the content involved. The first fit in far more readily with Soviet culture's role as a mobilizational and educational tool, but it was also the experience of a society with very limited resources. A culture that offered options, that enabled people to domesticate and to some extent personalize their experiences, and that tended to present itself in an everyday, here-and-now key was part of the postwar standard for the good life in the East as much as the West.

The Soviets could have stuck to their earlier operating manual. They could have put a radio loudspeaker on every corner instead of mass-producing home sets and transistors; they might have released a limited number of films every

---

successful, yet also more structural than ideational and clearly less powerful than Americanization in the long run.

58. On expanding our vision of cultural influence in the Soviet Union beyond the West, see Sudha Rajagopalan, *Leave Disco Dancer Alone! Indian Cinema and Soviet Movie-Going after Stalin* (New Delhi, 2008); Roman Szporluk, ed., *The Influence of East Europe and the Soviet West on the USSR* (New York, 1975); Amir Weiner, "Déjà Vu All Over Again: Prague Spring, Romanian Summer and Soviet Autumn on the Soviet Western Frontier," *Contemporary European History* 15, no. 2 (2006): 159–194.

year, ensuring everyone's cinema diet was identical, and organized mass campaigns around them. Soviet audiences could have come to know TV via giant public projections rather than tiny screens in their homes. The South African regime went so far as to ban television broadcasting altogether, so concerned was it about possible destabilizing effects. Soviet leaders might have taken any one of these approaches, but there were always many compelling reasons not to, and they were promoted best by people who produced and consumed culture in the USSR.

In the context of Cold War competition, the failure to Sovietize world culture *was* a failure. At home in the USSR, the enduring enthusiasm of audiences for masscult and almost any Soviet approximation of it was a kind of failure as well. If we take seriously the terms of Soviet culture's identity—educational, mobilizational, inspirational—the cultural landscape of the Soviet Union's final decades is strewn with signs of its ebbing vitality.

The fifties, sixties, and seventies had altered the Soviet mass culture formation. It was the same house with the same roof and nameplate on the door as in Stalin's day. But now it was a house of many more rooms, corridors, closets; for various reasons, people got to work on the wiring, bringing in new things from outside and routing cultural flows in new ways within. The mistakes and failures—all those elements in the culture that seemed to violate house rules—were also signs of strength: what they showed was that people and groups were now able to promote their own interests. They could do this in the name of a bigger and more imposing house (always a compelling argument in the Soviet context) or with the idea of creating a more comfortable place for one group or another. The expansion of the mass culture formation had allowed for greater adaptation and co-optation than had ever been possible. It is true that this wore away at Soviet claims to distinctiveness and superiority—and these were bedrock claims of Soviet culture and, by extension, of socialism. But one could always skirt the issue as needed. If we examine production figures alone (not what people watched but what films were made), the French and Italians had far more worries about the Americanization of their film industries than the Soviets did. Besides, it was the very wearing down of boundaries and eliding of rules that rendered Soviet culture a more workable experience for the people who made it, a more livable one for those who used it. The Soviet culture formation was a most successful failure. It was very good at being bad.

In the end, however, there are only so many alterations you can make to any house without undermining its structural integrity. Soviet culture did not collapse of its own weight, nor did it implode and carry off the whole system with it. Yet by the time the Soviet political system began to disintegrate in the late 1980s, its mass culture formation was plainly incapable of mobilizing builders, fighters, or defenders. As the bonds that tied culture to mass mobilization and the Soviet grand narrative came undone, Soviet culture failed to function as it was supposed to. And it failed, in large measure, because it had found many *other* meaningful functions: it had long provided people with experiences and ways of being in the world unconnected to broader political projects of any kind. In this story of the Soviet media empire in the Cold War, we find a window on both the remarkable resiliency of the Soviet system and its ultimate vulnerability, fragility, and collapse.

THE SOVIET FILM INDUSTRY

DEFINING CINEMATIC SUCCESS AFTER STALIN

"Cinema for us is the most important of the arts" (Lenin) was the essential slogan of the Soviet cinematographic world, cited in every publication, recited at every meeting. Unlike radio and television, or magazines and newspapers—all typically described as mass media (*sredstva*)—film was mass art, "Soviet cinema-art" (*sovetskoe kinoiskusstvo*). The distinction was critical, and cineastes defended it to the bitter end.[1] Cinema's status as an art form[2] determined the way it was funded and administered; it set the parameters for how film professionals saw themselves and their work, for their relationships with the political regime they lived under, and for the production process as well. Film as art, and its troubled fate in the USSR, is also the dominant mode in historical writing. For the post-Stalinist 1950s and the 1960s, the main narrative is that of the thaw, when, in the words of film scholar Valerii Fomin, "Soviet cinema reemerged from nothingness; it grew and developed almost as if in a fairy tale."[3] "Thaw cinema" meant the search for historical and emotional truths

1. I use "cineaste," "filmmaker," and "film professional" interchangeably.

2. This chapter discusses full-length fiction or feature films, but the Soviet film industry produced many other kinds. Children's and documentary cinema were particularly well developed.

3. Valerii Fomin quoted in Bernard Eisenschitz, *Lignes d'ombre: Une autre histoire du cinéma soviétique: 1926–1968* (Milan, 2000), 151. By and large, the history of Soviet cinema in this period (like that of Soviet broadcasting) has been written by participants—scholars, critics, and cineastes who were then studying or beginning their careers—and it tends toward the nostalgic. See the volumes edited by V. Troianovskii, ed., *Kinematograf ottepeli: Kniga pervaia* (Moscow, 1996) and *Kinematograf ottepeli: Kniga vtoraia* (Moscow, 2002); V. Fomin's commentary in his documentary collections *Kino i vlast': Sovetskoe kino, 1965–1985 gody: Dokumenty, svidetel'stva, razmyshleniia* (Moscow, 1996), and *Kinematograf ottepeli: Dokumenty i svidetel'stva* (Moscow, 1998); M. P. Vlasov, *Sovetskoe kinoiskusstvo 50–60-x godov* (Moscow, 1992); Neya Zorkaya, *The Illustrated History of Soviet Cinema* (New York, 1989); I. Shilova, . . . *I moe kino: Piatidesiatye, shestidesiatye, semidesiatye* (Moscow, 1993); Jeanne Vronskaya, *Young Soviet Film Makers* (London, 1972). Josephine Woll's *Real Images: Soviet Cinema and the Thaw* (New York, 2000), now the authoritative history in English, takes an approach similar to that of the participants, with a central focus on the

and the revival of Soviet artistic experimentation. In the Brezhnev era of stagnation, it is said, the fairy tale turned dark, as ideological repression and cynicism stalked the thaw; Soviet cinema-art struggled valiantly to survive.

This chapter grows from an obvious yet little-discussed dimension of this history. Soviet cinema-art was an *industry:* in fact, it was in many respects the powerhouse industry of Soviet culture, and never more than in the post-Stalinist era, when its every sector underwent terrific expansion. By the sixties the Soviet Union had one of the most impressive film industries in the world. Only a handful of countries produced a larger number of feature films annually, and of these, few had industries to rival the Soviets' in sheer size; none approached the Soviets' in geographical and linguistic scope.[4] Each of the fifteen Soviet republics had film studios (the Union had a total of forty-two in the sixties), and together they employed roughly twenty-five thousand people. Several hundred thousand Soviets connected their livelihood to cinema in some fashion.[5] Annual box office figures grew dramatically to reach 4 billion tickets in 1968 and stayed at that level until around 1980.[6] This, at least, was no dark fairy tale. Against a backdrop of faltering film industries in much of Western Europe and shrinking audiences across the industrialized world, Soviet cinema was, by many lights, a shining success.[7]

In the next chapter, I look more closely at the mass postwar audience in the USSR and at the emergence of new ways of engaging with cinema in everyday life—a new Soviet movie culture for the media age. Here I track the Soviet film industry in its boom years—moviemaking as a vital nexus of social, political, and economic interests—and explore the many paradoxes of cinematic success in the postwar USSR. Like all Soviet culture, Soviet cinema-art's identity was grounded in its competition with masscult: it was anticommercial by definition; it claimed to unite and inspire audiences, rather than divide and conquer them in the name of profits. Soviet cinema-art was also international by definition, leading the way to a future worldwide socialist culture. The message of cinema-art as a cultural system and the messages of the films themselves were always addressed, in principle, to audiences the world over. Last, but far from least, Soviet

cinematic intelligentsia and its artistic and political struggles. See also Alexander Prokhorov's recent work in a film studies vein, *Springtime for Soviet Cinema: Re/Viewing the Soviet 1960s* (Pittsburgh, 2001).

4. Though the United States, India, Italy, and Japan beat the USSR in sheer volume, they were, India aside, all monolingual cinemas. "US Fifth in Movies," *Washington Post,* 1 June 1966.

5. Fomin, *Kinematograf ottepeli,* 75.

6. I. E. Kokarev, *Rossisskii kinematograf: Mezhdu proshlym i budushchim* (Moscow, 2001), 30–31.

7. The U.S. box office reached its historic high of just over 4 billion tickets in 1946, dropping to 1.5 billion by 1959 (and continuing to fall). Paul McDonald, *The Star System: Hollywood's Production of Popular Identities* (London, 2000), 72.

cinema-art, in insisting on its mass nature, defined itself as beloved, esteemed, *successful* with audiences.

The history of Soviet moviemaking is far more complex than cinema's textbook definition—not because people proved defiant per se but because the ideology itself came embedded with many fruitful contradictions. While Soviet culture was inherently cosmopolitan, it was also inherently chauvinistic and defensive: a superior Soviet culture was understood to be in a pitched battle with a predatory capitalist foe, putting audiences in the USSR under constant threat. For cinema, this made the terms of the ideology useful in both promoting foreign imports and anathematizing them, in building up international connections in the film world and restricting or even punishing them. Similarly, while Soviet cinema was mass art by definition and rejected the notion of an elite-mass split in audiences as a capitalist perversion, it was also grounded in a bedrock hierarchy: people with educated aesthetic and political sensibilities outranked people without them. The goal was to elevate everyone; the consumption of art was supposed to further the goal. But in the meantime—and the meantime might be a long time, indeed—people at the top of the hierarchy could claim exceptional rights and privileges. And everyone else, ordinary consumers, could also stake claims to culture that met their as yet inferior taste for entertainment. In this way, the terms of the ideology justified making a self-defined mass art that the masses did not care to watch, browbeating them for their poor taste, *and* circulating inferior—and even ideologically harmful—cinematic product.

The most important contradiction in Soviet cinema-art as an ideological category, however, was its definition of success and its relationship to markets. Soviet cinema identified itself as anticommercial but also as drawing huge audiences and generating revenues for the state. Unlike other mass-cultural experiences—radio listening, for instance—cinematic experience was something bought and sold in the Soviet Union:[8] the impact of market-related values and relationships reverberated throughout this entire antimarket cinematic system. Success was framed in ways that encouraged people across the spectrum to blur the lines between art and commerce, self-expression and self-interest, and public service and budgetary windfall.

Cinema's fruitful contradictions did not originate in the post-Stalinist era; on the contrary, the cinematic system as a whole showed great continuities across the 1953 divide. The Soviet film industry was ever a hierarchical, centrally controlled state monopoly where power was unequally distributed by design. It was also a web of patron-client relationships: Soviet cinema-art always depended on the art of the Soviet deal.

---

8. This was not exclusively the case: the USSR also had many nonpaying venues for cinema, such as clubs and workplace theaters. See chapter 2.

With Stalin's death and the great boom that followed came not some new cinematic system but rather many more opportunities, and far less risky ones, for people at different levels to play their hands in the old one. It is not that the Soviet regime ever lost control over cinema. The big-picture story for the post-Stalinist fifties through the Brezhnev era is in fact one of increasing bureaucratization and regulation. Yet in a close-up shot, this picture grows variegated and far more interesting because control was now exercised in many more locations and in manifold ways. It was these post-Stalinist openings inside the Soviet cinematic system that allowed for its many in-built contradictions to come to the fore and bear fruit in an unprecedented fashion. Notably, success did not extend to the international sphere, where Soviet cinema botched its campaign for world leadership. Though the regime could control and exploit the internationalization of screens at home, it was mostly ineffectual abroad. The dream of Sovietizing world cinema was just that. Still, back in the USSR, the film industry's blockbuster hits and the population's level of engagement with cinema overall—the oft-cited 4 billion-strong audience—were enough to turn even a Hollywood mogul green with envy. In the media age, Soviet cinema was very big business, authorized, structured, and promoted by an ideology whose raison d'être was the end of business. It was a paradox that allowed for great successes and crushing failures alike.

CINEMA'S NEW OPENINGS, INSIDE AND OUT

In Stalin's final years, few observers would have predicted the cinematic boom on the horizon. The Soviet film industry was in crisis—a near-death experience later known as "the era of few pictures" (*malokartin'e*). Stalin had kept a keen eye on cinema throughout the thirties, acting as screenplay editor, casting expert, cinematography critic, and ultimate censor on every film shown in the country. The pressure on filmmakers was extreme. With the end of the New Economic Policy (NEP) and the consolidation of party control in the arts in the early thirties, production levels dropped precipitously, from 128 films in 1930 to fewer than 30 three years later.[9] After the war, the situation grew worse as Stalin ratcheted up his personal supervision even further and commanded perfection: "We must shoot fewer pictures, but every one should be a masterpiece," he reportedly told the Politburo, and in 1948, the USSR Council of Ministers passed a resolution in the same spirit.[10] As the regime pursued its witch hunt against "rootless cosmopolitans," the number of new productions plummeted. In 1951, at the depths of the era of few pictures, the Soviets released only 9 new feature

9. Julian Graffy, "Cinema," in *Russian Cultural Studies,* ed. C. Kelly and D. Shepherd (New York, 1998), 174.

10. G. Mar'iamov, *Kremlevskii tsenzor: Stalin smotrit kino* (Moscow, 1992), 41; L. Arkus, ed., *Noveishaia istoriia otechestvennogo kinematografa, 1986–2000: Kino i kontekst,* vol. 5 (St. Petersburg, 2004), 65.

films. Even at the height of the war, from 1942 to 1945, when every major studio in the country had evacuated to central Asia, they had managed nearly 70.[11]

Although the Soviet authorities acknowledged the crisis, it took the dictator-mogul dead in his coffin and out of the screening room for the world of cinema to open up.[12] Cineastes responded rapidly to the end of terror as a mode of cultural administration, and they found a post-Stalinist regime eager to develop the industry. Production exploded. By 1956 the Soviet film industry could boast over 100 new features per year; from 1960 through 1985 annual production ranged between 116 and 151.[13] The country's main film studio, Mosfil'm in Moscow, underwent a mass expansion and modernization in the 1950s. In the republics, the post-Stalinist boom amounted to nothing short of a resurrection. Armenian, Uzbek, Kazakh, and Georgian cinema, and even the Ukrainian industry, historically the strongest of the lot, had all ground to a halt after World War II. But by the sixties every Soviet republic was producing at least a handful of new features a year, and there were also brand-new national cinemas in Kyrgyzstan, Moldavia, and Lithuania.[14] In a few short years, the Soviet film industry had risen from humiliating prostration to become one of the world's top producers. And it was also connected to the world in new and dynamic ways. With the post-Stalinist regime's decision to promote "cultural exchange" and the growing sophistication of global media circuitry, Soviet cinema—film, filmmakers, and audiences—was internationalized as never before.

The sheer expansion of the cinematic system in the USSR had wide-ranging implications that went largely unrecognized at the time. It was years before the regime had bureaucratic structures in place that it considered adequate. The central state administration for film had a staff of fewer than one hundred in the 1950s, but it ballooned to four times that size by 1963 and to seven hundred in 1972.[15] It also underwent a series of reorganizations as the regime searched for

---

11. Many films listed as new releases after the war were not even real features but rather filmed theatrical performances. Peter Kenez, *Cinema and Soviet Society, 1917–1953* (London, 2001), 188; Peter Kenez, "Black and White: The War on Film," in *Culture and Entertainment in Wartime Russia,* ed. Richard Stites (Bloomington, IN, 1995), 166. On wartime cinema, see N. Zorkaia, *Istoriia sovetskogo kino* (St. Petersburg, 2005), 256–272; V. Fomin, *Kino na voine: Dokumenty i svidetel'stva* (Moscow, 2005).

12. See Louis Harris Cohen, *The Cultural-Political Traditions and Developments of the Soviet Cinema, 1917–1972* (New York, 1974), 230–231.

13. "Segida-Info," *Iskusstvo kino* [hereafter *IK*], no. 4 (1996): 76.

14. Of the republic-level studios, the largest were the Dovzhenko in Kiev (twelve to fifteen features annually in the sixties) and the Georgian in Tbilisi (six to ten features). The studios of central Asia, the Caucasus, and the Baltics produced a handful of features per year. Cohen, *Cultural-Political Traditions,* 515–528; Anna Lawton, ed., *The Red Screen: Politics, Society, Art in Soviet Cinema* (New York, 1992), 296.

15. Figures from an interview with V. Baskakov, Goskino deputy chairman in the sixties. Troianovskii, *Kinematograf ottepeli: Kniga vtoraia,* 325.

more effective measures of control and development. Soon after Stalin's death in 1953, the Ministry of Cinematography was liquidated, and film was placed under the direction of the USSR Ministry of Culture, with different divisions in the ministry responsible for different aspects of cinematic affairs. Critics inside the industry complained that the setup gave cinema short shrift and lobbied for a freestanding film administration—an idea that came of age in 1963 as part of a broader regime initiative to shore up ideological control over culture. The new administration, Goskino, the State Committee for Cinematography (Gosudarstvennyi komitet Soveta Ministrov SSSR po kinematografii), then remained in place until the collapse of the USSR but not without further bureaucratic shuffles. The most consequential of these, in 1972, was again part of a wider ideological clampdown and involved a large-scale purge of the film bureaucracy and a changing of the guard at the top. Filipp Yermash, Goskino's forceful new chairman, came directly from the Central Committee apparat, cinema division—in effect, he went from monitoring the store to running it—and he remained at the top until the Gorbachev era, ensuring stability (or, in critics' eyes, stagnation) in the regime's handling of cinematic affairs.[16] But at least until 1972, the problem of how best to administer and exploit cinema was very much on the table.

What under Stalin had been a tightly controlled, comparatively small-scale production unit—in effect, the dictator's personal *artel* (workshop) for cinematic dreamweaving—had morphed into something sprawling, complicated, and diverse: the post-Stalinist Soviet film industry. To be sure, ideological control remained constant and pervasive in these years. Although cinema saw periods of greater and lesser openness, they were relative, and it would be wrongheaded to imagine that Soviet filmmakers were ever autonomous actors—or, indeed, that most held autonomy as a goal. But if control was a central, perennial feature of the Soviet cultural system, the difference was that now it was enacted in a decentralized fashion, in manifold sites and, crucially, through manifold relationships.

Bringing a movie to the screen in the USSR always entailed an intricate choreography of institutional and social relationships. It was as much a bureaucratic-political process as an artistic one. The term "censorship" does not begin to capture the intricacy of the dance. As a first step, all would-be directors had to secure approvals for their screenplays at the studio level, including approvals from the working group within the studio that would have responsibility for the film—the *tvorcheskoe ob"edinenie*—and the studio as a whole. (Here, as in broadcasting, the figure of the *redaktor,* editor, was critical: it was the studio's chief *redaktor* who carried ultimate responsibility for the ideological viability of

---

16. The first Goskino(1963–65) was succeeded by the State Committee for Cinematography under the USSR Council of Ministers (1965–72), the State Committee of the USSR Council of Ministers for Cinematography (1972–1978), and the State Committee of the USSR for Cinematography (1978–1991). For more on the 1972 shakeup, see below.

its output.)[17] Next, the project would be brought before the republic-level insti-tutions for cinema: the state film administration and the republic's Central Committee apparat.[18] These approvals in hand, a director would then set out to win over the central state authorities at Goskino, specifically, its redoubtable Main Screenplay-Editorial College (Glavnaia stsenarno-redaktsionnaia kollegiia). And, of course, no project could ever get off the ground should the central party apparat harbor any objections. The Central Committee's Department of Culture, cinema division, had ultimate control over all aspects of the film industry and acted as judge and jury for all other institutional claims.

To be clear, we have been speaking thus far only of the very first stages in the moviemaking process. Even assuming a project had met green lights along the way, it still had many more approvals to secure: for the production plans, for casting, for revisions to the screenplay, for the rushes—the list went on. What is more, any number of institutions beyond the basic studio-Goskino-party axis might throw up roadblocks to production at any moment. Most important was the KGB, which had a healthy share of in-house film critics, in addition to spies on the lookout for subversive elements within the movie industry. And depending on the subject matter, the Komsomol, the navy, or the Ministry of Health or Mining might weigh in as well. A Soviet institution was duty-bound to protect its image in the public eye, and in this context, concerns about a film "defaming sailors" or "denigrating miners" were actionable: something would have to be altered, excised, improved.

The final stage for productions from all over the USSR was the submission of a print to Goskino in Moscow, which screened films in-house and often also sent them out to top-ranking leaders, whose opinions could also prove critical to a film's fate. Bringing a film to the screen, then, meant jumping through multiple hoops—some visible, some veiled—multiple times, and with no guarantee of success. It was entirely possible to secure approvals all along the line only to be told at the final moment that your work was unacceptable.

Consider the troubles director El'dar Riazanov faced with *Hussar Ballad* (*Gusarskaia ballada,* 1962), a film about the war against Napoleon in 1812, all be-cause he had cast Igor Il'inksii, a famous comedic actor, as Field-Marshal Kutuzov. Although any number of people would have signed off on the cast list and pos-sibly even watched the screen tests, then minister of culture, Ekaterina Furtseva, called Riazanov on the carpet after the film was finished to say he had "misrep-resented, one might say, slandered a great Russian commander. I love Il'inskii

17. On the role of the *redaktor,* see Fomin, *Kino i vlast',* 61.

18. The RSFSR (Russian Soviet Federated Socialist Republic) was a partial exception to this rule. All the largest feature film studios were located in the RSFSR and reported directly to central Goskino (not Goskino RSFSR, which did control other issues, including nonfiction film). Val S. Golovskoy, *Behind the Soviet Screen: The Motion-Picture Industry in the USSR, 1972–1982* (Ann Arbor, MI, 1986), 43.

very much," she said, "he's an outstanding comic—but Kutuzov!...The viewer is going to laugh at the sight of him." Riazanov would have to replace Il'inski and reshoot his scenes.[19]

Many—perhaps most—filmmakers suffered the hoop jumping as a form of harassment, both degrading and unnecessary. It is easy to understand why. The amount of time and energy involved could be astounding. One Lithuanian director made six separate trips to Moscow to have a screenplay approved in 1968, despite the fact that it had full support from the authorities in Vilnius. The completed picture barely made it to the screen anyway and was granted only a limited release.[20] Filmmakers often did not know who was behind the demands placed on them. "There is an opinion" (Est' mnenie) was the standard phrase.[21] The demands themselves were often mutually contradictory and unworkable. Andrei Tarkovskii listed in his diary thirty-five of the changes required of his poetic science-fiction drama *Solaris,* noting that if he "took them all into account (which would be impossible), there would be nothing left of the film." He described them as "ridiculous." Here is a sample: "1. Show more clearly what the world of the future looks like....3. Which camp does [the character] Kelvin belong to—socialist, communist, or capitalist?...5. Get rid of the God concept....10. We should not be left with the impression that Kris is a loafer."[22]

For some people in the cinematic world, fear also remained a fact of life, even without the terrifying perfectionist in the Kremlin. Nonna Mordiukova, one of the most famous actors of the postwar era, recalled how nervous she was at her first "picnic" for Soviet notables at Khrushchev's dacha. Like all the guests, Mordiukova said, she hung on the premier's every word and laughed demonstrably at his every quip. But she also worried that fellow actor Nikolai Rybnikov was a little too demonstrative and found herself wondering about all the black cars she had seen around the dacha and the men waiting with them; surely not all of them could be drivers, she thought. And then Rybnikov had the temerity to interrupt Khrushchev during a speech: "Nikita Sergeevich! Tell us about Cuba instead!" Mordiukova's thoughts turned instantly to arrest and imprisonment. Recounting the incident years later, she described herself as typical of her generation. "Fear had struck deep roots" in everyone, she explained, even those, like her, who had no personal experience of Stalinist terror.[23] Censorship,

19. E. Riazanov, *Ne podvedennye itogi* (Moscow, 2000), 89.

20. The director was Raimondas Vabalas. Troianovskii, *Kinematograf ottepeli: Kniga vtoraia,* 363.

21. See the interview with screenwriter Anatolii Grebnev in Troianovskii, *Kinematograf ottepeli: Kniga vtoraia,* 354–355.

22. Quoted in Feodor Razzakov, *Zhizn' zamechatel'nykh vremen, 1970–1974* (Moscow, 2004), 480–481.

23. Nonna Mordiukova, *Kazachka* (Moscow, 1995), 149.

institutional harassment, intimidation—these were real and important factors in people's personal lives and in the way cinema functioned as a system in the USSR. None of them, though, could compare with the psychological and physical costs of making movies under Stalin, and cinema blossomed in the new environment.

It was in these post-Stalinist years that cineastes campaigned successfully for a creative union, the kind of organization that writers, composers, and other arts professionals had long enjoyed and that Stalin had personally opposed. Khrushchev granted his approval in 1957, and the Filmmakers' Union took shape under the leadership of the renowned director Ivan Pyr'ev and was formally established in 1965.[24] Pyr'ev was also the man in charge of the expansion at Mosfil'm and one of the leading lobbyists for a freestanding cinema administration in the early sixties.[25] He has been described in post-Soviet times as Soviet cinema's leading "producer" (a term usually reserved in Soviet times for the grasping, wheeler-dealer types in Hollywood). In post-Soviet memoirs, many cineastes recounted how Pyr'ev intervened in their careers at crucial moments: to have them reassigned from a republican studio to Moscow, to set them up to shoot their first feature, to save a film from a ban, or, on the contrary, to put up roadblocks to its release. Pyr'ev had special clout given his position at the union and Mosfil'm, and he was also, by all accounts, an extraordinary personality.[26] But Pyr'ev's powers, however formidable, were far from exclusive.

Soviet cinema was a system of power brokers. The "cult of the director" in Soviet cinema and the organization of the film education system around directors was one critical factor.[27] At the country's premier institution, VGIK (Vsesoiuznyi gosudarstvennyi institut kinoiskusstva /All-Union State Institute for Cinematography) in Moscow, leading directors, or "masters," selected their students individually, trained them in groups, and very often hired them for their first jobs

24. Richard Taylor and Derek Spring, eds., *Stalinism and Soviet Cinema* (London, 1993), 167. V. Fomin published a series of documents and commentary on the history of the Filmmakers' Union, 1957–165, http://www.film.ru/sk-news. The union had 3,923 members at its founding congress, 5,210 in 1976, and 6,902 in 1981. *Chetvertyi s"ezd kinematografistov SSSR, 19–21 maia 1981 goda: Stenograficheskii otchet* (Moscow, 1982), 107.

25. Excerpts of Pyr'ev's letter to the party's Central Committee in Arkus, *Noveishaia istoriia*, vol. 6.

26. "Imena: v plenu u Gaidaia," *Rossiiskie vesti*, 31 January 1998; "Pyr'ev segodnia: Sergei Solov'ev, Vladimir Dashkevich, Aleksandr Mitta, Gleb Panfilov," *Kinovedcheskie zapiski*, no. 53 (2001), 4–14; M. I. Kosinova, *Istoriia kinoprodiuserstva v Rossii* (Moscow, 2004), 207–225.

27. Ian Christie traces the origins of the Soviet director cult to the 1920s and the canonization of the "Five" (Sergei Eisenstein, Lev Kuleshov, Aleksandr Dovzhenko, Dziga Vertov, and Vsevolod Pudovkin). Christie, "Canons and Careers: The Director in Soviet Cinema," in Taylor and Spring, *Stalinism and Soviet Cinema*, 142–170.

or became their most important patrons.[28] A student who studied with Mikhail Romm was considered his student for life—and, more than likely, she was pleased to be one out of respect for Romm as an artist and practical considerations as well. It was natural to want to "belong" to someone, to be a "Romm person" (*chelovek Romma*), or a "Bondarchuk person" (*chelovek Bondarchuka*). He might intervene on your behalf with other important people, who often "belonged" to someone, too. Networks overlapped. Filipp Yermash, for instance, was a "Kirilenko person," and Kirilenko sat on the Central Committee. If you had a good relationship with Bondarchuk, and Bondarchuk had a good relationship with Yermash (or, say, his wife was friends with Yermash's sister), doors just might open.

The contours of these patron-client relationships and behind-the-scenes deals are familiar enough from the Stalinist period.[29] This is how cultural production was brokered in the USSR. But the removal of Stalin at the center of all networks, the end of the terror, and the system's ramification—its opening *out* and not just opening up to the non-Soviet world—produced an essential and enduring difference. There was more space in the system. If Lenfil'm rejected your screenplay about the Battle of Kursk, you could try your luck somewhere else. After the Hungarian crackdown in 1956, many young directors who would later rise to prominence left Moscow for republic-level studios in an effort to evade tighter ideological controls in the center.[30] In the sixties several filmmakers stonewalled by republican officials appealed successfully to Moscow for support or moved to the capital for work. And in the seventies the pendulum swung back again, and many republics had a "softer" hand in cinematic censorship than the center.[31] The point is that more people in the cinematic process introduced not only more obstacles but also more relationships; sometimes, relationships could be leveraged.

Riazanov's *Hussar Ballad* made it to the screen unaltered because Aleksei Adzhubei, Khrushchev's son-in-law and editor of *Izvestiia* at the time, saw it at a special screening and liked it. Furtseva's ministry then picked up his signal from a positive review in the newspaper and organized a grand premiere. This, at least, was Riazanov's interpretation of events. Other forces may well have

28. The working of patron-client networks began with VGIK admissions. See the comments of Brezhnev's niece, Luba Brezhneva, in *The World I Left Behind: Pieces of a Past,* trans. Geoffrey Polk (New York, 1994), 134.

29. On patron-client networks in Soviet culture more broadly, see Juri Jelagin, *Taming of the Arts,* trans. Juri Jelagin (New York, 1951); Kiril Tomoff, "'Most Respected Comrade...': Patrons, Clients, Brokers and Unofficial Networks in the Stalinist Music World," *Contemporary European History* 11, no. 1 (2002): 33–65; Vera Tolz, "Cultural Bosses as Patrons and Clients: The Functioning of Soviet Creative Unions in the Postwar Period," *Contemporary European History* 11, no. 1 (2002): 87–106.

30. Eisenschitz, *Lignes d'ombre,* 143, 152

31. Troianovskii, *Kinematograf ottepeli: Kniga vtoraia,* 332. On the seventies shift, see N. M. Zorkaia, *Istoriia sovetskogo kino* (St. Petersburg, 2005).

been at work. Perhaps Il'inskii had friends of his own in high places. Riazanov himself claimed he had no hand in arranging to show the film to Adzhubei, but special screenings for the elite were an essential gear in the moviemaking machine. Top-level officials regularly watched films outside mainstream venues—the most common site was the dacha—and their opinions and those of their families could play a decisive role in a film's fate. Senior Goskino officials spent their Monday mornings fielding telephone calls from the dacha set with critiques. Opinions often varied. One official from the Filmmakers' Union recalled Yermash's predecessor at Goskino, Aleksei Romanov, telling him that every Monday he went to work "in an awful mood" anticipating the telephonic onslaught.[32] Positive dacha reviews could work miracles for filmmakers, though. Vladimir Motyl''s film *The White Sun of the Desert* (*Beloe sol'ntse pustyni*, 1969) was in bureaucratic purgatory: Mosfil'm refused to approve it, Motyl' resisted further changes, and it seemed destined for a ban. By chance, Goskino's "special department," the section that serviced the top-level political elite, misplaced a masscult picture destined for the Brezhnev dacha and sent *White Sun* instead. The Brezhnevs liked it, and soon it was released—albeit only after several changes insisted upon by Romanov. "What kind of minister would he be if he didn't put his two cents in," was Motyl''s comment in 2000.[33]

It was often a grueling ordeal for filmmakers to satisfy the Aunt Tanyas and the ministers of mining, the top brass in the CC apparat and the Moscow party committee and their families, along with the bureaucrats at Goskino, the film critics at the KGB, and all the rest. Sometimes it was impossible, and in many ways the process of bringing a film to the screen had been more straightforward when Stalin was the only producer to please. Georgii Daneliia quipped to a colleague in West Berlin who boasted that one hundred thousand people had watched a film there in a single month, "In our country, we have that many people in just the approval process."[34] The number of dacha screenings and demands for changes mounted over time, becoming especially onerous after the Prague Spring, 1968, when ideological control was ratcheted up. The number of films banned outright (put "on the shelf" was the phrase) also swelled in the Brezhnev era.[35] Careers sputtered; nerves faltered. Film scholars like Fomin emphasize that cinema-art was deformed by the process. Nonetheless, we must

---

32. Fomin, *Kino i vlast'*, 146. See also the comments of Goskino chairman Armen Medvedev, "Sed'moi ministr posle semi let v stroiu," *Novye izvestiia*, 13 February 1999.

33. V. Motyl', "Za derzhavu po-prezhnemu obidno," *Novaia gazeta*, 18 September 2000.

34. G. Daneliia, *Bezbiletnyi pasazhir* (Moscow, 2003), 210.

35. "The shelf" (*polka*) was also a real place: the film storage facilities of Gosfil'mofond in Belye Stolby. We have no comprehensive figures on the number of banned films, but according to Fomin (who once worked there), a special Filmmakers' Union commission considered more than two hundred features, documentaries, and cartoons for "rehabilitation" in the eighties. One union official estimated that about one hundred features were

recognize the fundamental difference between these scenarios and those that had played out when Stalin sat in the Kremlin theater with the fate of that year's ten or twenty films in his hands. Although an expanded cinematic sphere did not translate into expanded freedoms across the board, it did open up more opportunities for maneuver than had ever existed before. This was a difference relevant to the experience of individual filmmakers and to the functioning of the system as a whole.

The other vitally important opening for Soviet cinema after Stalin's death was, of course, its opening out to the world, or internationalization. Beginning in 1954, the USSR concluded a series of cultural exchange agreements that brought increasing numbers of new foreign films to Soviet theaters.[36] The Ministry of Culture also began to purchase large numbers of films abroad—from 63 in 1955 to 113 in 1958, with plans for over 150 in 1960, according to one Central Committee decree.[37] In fact, the number appears to have leveled off in the sixties at roughly 100 new purchases per year. These included productions from the socialist bloc, including, for a brief period in the late fifties, a large number of Chinese productions; films from Western Europe (with French and Italian cinema especially well represented), and, increasingly in the 1960s and '70s, from India, the Middle East, and Latin America.

Film professionals, like film lovers across the USSR, could celebrate the new diversity in the movie house. They were also now encouraged to develop and flaunt their foreign ties—a signal change after the dark days of late Stalinism. And other developments—jet travel, improved telephone connections, and a rapidly globalizing mass media environment—proved vital to the film industry as well. The Soviet film world was drawn into cinema's transnational circuitry, both mediated and material, in a whole new way in the post-Stalinist era. The emphasis on cultural exchange brought a wave of international film weeks and festivals; there were now more foreign cineastes in the USSR than at any time since the 1920s. Some Soviet film professionals also joined the privileged minority permitted to travel outside the socialist bloc, and they found their participation at foreign events the subject of media coverage abroad and at home. "Naturally," *Soviet Screen* told its readers, "the question every participant and the press asked from the very first day [of the festival] was: What are the Russians

---

banned over his twenty-three-year tenure (1965–88). See V. Fomin, *Polka: Dokumenty, svidetel'stva, kommentarii* (Moscow, 1992); Fomin, *Kino i vlast'*, 147.

36. Many films, though new to the Soviet market, were not new productions: the Soviets often bought older films because they were cheaper.

37. E. S. Afanas'eva and V. Iu. Afiani, eds., *Ideologicheskie komissii TsK KPSS 1958–1964: Dokumenty* (Moscow, 1998), 186.

going to show? There is enormous interest in Soviet art in Italy.... The Soviet delegation's press conference was the most crowded and lively."[38]

Soviet media laid it on thick, as a matter of course, because Soviet cinema's international clout was essential to its identity. Film scholar Naum Kleiman remarked in a 2000 interview that the "great discovery" of the perestroika period was that "Soviet cinema was not at the center of everything."[39] Contemporary readers can hear echoes of this in interviews with former Soviet actors, who often claim that the only thing that prevented them from starring in Hollywood and European pictures—so persistent were the offers—were jealous bureaucrats at Goskino. The invitations and the interest never matched the mythology.[40] Even Stanley Kramer, one of the most visible Western cineastes, mentioned Soviet cinema only once in his memoirs, and that was to recount how he had lectured an audience at the Moscow Film Festival about freedom of expression.[41]

Still, Soviet cinema did have moments of international chic, especially in the Khrushchev era. This was *succès d'estime*—Soviet pictures, directors, and actors all won important international awards—and it was also a reflection of a widespread fascination with things Soviet in the age of Sputnik, Gagarin, and the Bomb. (In the seventies the glamour of presumed dissidence would shine a different kind of light on filmmakers like Tarkovskii.) "Some people looked upon us with delight, others with terror, but no one was indifferent," recalled director Grigorii Chukhrai of his experiences at the Cannes Film Festival in 1956.[42] Chukhrai's younger colleague, Andrei Konchalovskii, also reflected on the international attention to Soviet filmmakers in his memoirs, but he took a more critical (some might say jaundiced) view. Sartre called a film Konchalovskii had worked on a "masterpiece" in the French press, and when he and Simone De Beauvoir visited Moscow, the young Soviet was summoned to meet them. "[T]his kind of thing could not help but affect us and go to our heads [*takoe ne moglo ne podeistvovat', ne sbit' s nog*]," Konchalovskii wrote.[43]

The film Sartre praised so highly, *Ivan's Childhood* (*Ivanovo detstvo*, 1962), a darkly poetic exploration of war through the eyes of a child, was not one initially favored by the bureaucrats at Goskino. (It did not receive wide publicity or distribution.) Nor was it a major hit with the Soviet moviegoing public, selling about 17 million tickets in the year of its release. By contrast, *Amphibian*

38. D. Pisarevskii, "Krylatye l'vy pobedy," *Sovetskii ekran [hereafter SE]*, no. 21 (1962): 14–16. The magazine published photos of Italian newspapers to prove its point.

39. Eisenschitz, *Lignes d'ombre*, 19.

40. For example, Iu. Slavich and E. Lyndina, *Rossiiskie kinozvezdy rasskazivaiut* (Moscow, 1998).

41. Stanley Kramer, *A Mad, Mad, Mad World: A Life in Hollywood* (New York, 1997).

42. G. Chukhrai, *Moe kino* (Moscow, 2002), 117.

43. Andrei Konchalovskii, *Nizkie istiny: Sem' let spustia* (Moscow, 2006), 143.

Figure 1.1. The Amphibian in love. Anastasiia Vertinskaia and Vladimir Korenev in the USSR's first blockbuster, *Amphibian Man*, 1962. RIA Novosti. Used with permission.

Man (*Chelovek-amfibiia,* 1962), a fantastical romance featuring beautiful young stars and state-of-the-art underwater photography, sold 65.5 million. But Soviet cinema-art had both Ivan *and* the Amphibian, international esteem *and* a gigantic domestic audience. It was the kind of thing that went to people's heads, and not only Soviet filmmakers'. Goskino officials traveled internationally in the post-Stalinist era, too, and they could share a sense of pride in Soviet cinema: the prestige of high art and the clout and dynamism of a mass audience (all the sweeter to savor as audiences were seen shriveling on the vine across Western Europe). It was easy to gloss the details: that Soviet viewers adored the Amphibian even if Sartre and the cinematic community loved Ivan—audience dynamism rarely correlated with artistic prestige—and that they also showed great affection for the heroes of foreign commercial cinema, say, the American Western *The Magnificent Seven* (1960). These were "shortcomings" in Soviet parlance, sometimes probed in meetings and in the media but easily evaded in favor of a generalized notion of Soviet cinema-art: outsized, upstanding, unique.

FOREIGN FILMS ON SOVIET SCREENS: SWINGING WITH
TARZAN, INVITING BRIGITTE BARDOT

While the thaw has often been celebrated as the moment when the USSR emerged from Stalinist cultural autarky, the history of cinema presents a more complicated picture. Foreign-made films were a powerful presence in the Russian-Soviet cultural marketplace for nearly all of the twentieth century. The 1930s were an anomaly: the only decade when domestic productions had a conclusive lock on audience affections and the only decade when foreign imports were almost entirely suppressed. In the pre-1917 period, French, American, and German productions ruled the screen, with a nearly 80 percent share of the market in the Russian Empire's cities, and for most of the twenties foreign domination was equally pronounced.[44] Once again in the post–World War II era, foreign cinema had a leading position, beginning almost immediately at the war's end. If we consider the volume of foreign-made movies proportionate to the overall market, the high point was late Stalinism. In 1951, only one in four films in distribution in the Soviet Union was Soviet-made.[45] In 1952, the top of the box-office ratings in the USSR—all four slots—were occupied by four *Tarzan* pictures from Hollywood. Although actual attendance figures are not available, we know that each sold more than 31.6 million tickets (as that was the figure for the fifth-place film, a Soviet civil war drama "starring" Stalin).[46] And 1952 was in no way exceptional for foreign cinema's triumph. The most widely seen picture in the USSR for the 1940s was neither a thirties classic nor a postwar masterpiece but a German musical production, *The Girl of My Dreams* (*Die Frau meiner Traüme*, 1944).[47]

Tarzan, Marika Rokk (the girl of their dreams), and other foreign exotica came to the USSR by way of Nazi Germany; they were war booty and so exceptional by definition. This at least is how the authorities presented them to Soviet audiences. Yet the story of these films' careers in the USSR reveals fundamental, long-term trends in the Soviet approach to masscult—trends in popular and bureaucratic tastes, mechanisms for control, and the centrality to the system of "commercial considerations," to use the Soviet bureaucratic trope. In most respects, it turns out, the trophies were not exceptional at all.

It took the Soviets less than a week after the Nazi surrender to have someone from the Ministry of Cinematography on the ground in Germany and hunting for movies. The official, I. Manevich, picked up new boots from Mosfil'm's wardrobe

44. Denise Youngblood, *Movies for the Masses: Popular Cinema and Soviet Society in the 1920s* (New York, 1992), 20; Neia Zorkaia, "O 'massovom segodnia'—Neskol'ko elementarnykh istin," *Kinovedcheskie zapiski*, no. 45 (2000): 27–37.

45. Fomin, *Kinematograf ottepel: Kniga pervaia*, 3.

46. The film was *Nezabyvaemyi 1919* (*The Unforgettable Year 1919*). Box-office figures at http://www.nashekino.ru/.

47. D. B. Dondurei, ed., *Otechestvennyi kinematograf: Strategiia vyzhivaniia: Nauchnyi doklad* (Moscow, 1991), 71.

department and went directly to the "German Hollywood" at Babelsberg, where he found a specially designed, bunkerlike movie archive surrounded by Red Army men. The soldiers were as eager as Manevich, "shouting, demanding the pictures, and proposing to break down the doors to the bunker with grenades," he later wrote. Manevich seized over 17,000 films and selected around 3,700 features and about 2,500 shorts for immediate shipment to Moscow.[48] Among them were a large number of genre productions—adventures, comedies, musicals, and love stories. Most dated to the prewar period and were American and Western European (especially German) in origin.[49]

At the very highest levels, Soviet authorities treated their cinematic war booty with loving care. Stalin scheduled regular late-night screenings for members of the Politburo and watched a good number, if not all, of the films himself, with simultaneous translation provided by the minister of cinematography.[50] The films were also vetted by the CC, which gave precise instructions about what to release, where, and in what form.[51] All trophy pictures were to be accompanied by "a specially prepared text that correctly orients the viewer as to the content of the film" and "carefully edited explanatory subtitles," the CC advised.[52] *Stagecoach* (renamed *The Journey Will Be Dangerous*), recalled one Muscovite, began with an on-screen announcement: "This film displays the morals of bourgeois society, and the hypocrisy and bigotry that are its distinctive characteristics. It will not be difficult for the Soviet viewer to discern that the film does not accurately show America's colonialist policies vis-à-vis the Indian tribes."[53] All the

48. The official numbers cited by Manevich were 17,300 total: 6,400 feature films, 3,500 shorts, 4,800 advertising spots, and 2,600 newsreels. I. Manevich, "Chuzhie trofei," *SE*, no. 18 (1991): 5.

49. The German trophies were combined with pictures seized during previous military operations (from western Ukraine and Belorussia in 1939 and the Baltics and Bessarabia in 1940) to form a special fund housed in Belye Stolby. About 40 percent of the films were American in origin, and roughly 50 percent were Western European. RGASPI, f. 17, op. 132, d. 88, ll. 3–4. The Soviets had also acquired (by purchase or as gifts) a number of American and British films prior to and during World War II, including *Sun Valley Serenade* (1941), *The Thief of Baghdad* (1924), and *Bambi* (1942). Though often lumped together with the trophies, these films were on Soviet screens much earlier, and they were legal. Yale Richmond, *Cultural Exchange and the Cold War: Raising the Iron Curtain* (University Park, PA, 2003), 129; M. Semenov, "'Trofeinoe kino'? Net, vorovannoe," *Novoe russkoe slovo*, 19 February 2002, and 12 March 2002.

50. Archival documents make occasional mention of a film's release "according to Comrade Stalin's instructions." RGASPI, f. 17, op. 125, d. 576, l. 60.

51. A 1948 report on a batch of seventy films rejected nineteen "as politically alien or base from an artistic point of view"; twenty-six were approved for "limited" use in trade unions and clubs; and twenty-four were authorized for general distribution. RGASPI, f. 17, op. 132, d. 92, l. 11.

52. Ibid.

53. Semenov, "'Trofeinoe kino'?"

films also had their opening credit sequences cut and replaced by a title page that identified them as the spoils of war.[54] In some cases the films were edited so clumsily as to be nonsensical in parts or to alter their original meanings altogether. In the Soviet version of *Mr. Deeds Goes to Town* (renamed *The Dollar Rules*), Deeds, a millionaire accused of insanity because he had decided to give his money away, was *not* vindicated in court in the end. Soviet audiences saw only the judge threatening to expel the millionaire's vociferous supporters, followed by shots of an empty courtroom and the millionaire's beloved in tears.[55]

Mr. Deeds joined Tarzan, Ali-Baba and the Forty Thieves, and the King of California in winning Soviet viewers' hearts all the same. In Tula, all four of the city's movie theaters were showing the foreign films in the fall of 1947, while in Barnaul, the Oktiabr' theater offered forty-five days of trophy cinema that season and only two days of the Stalin cult film *The Oath* (*Kliatva*, 1946). One Riga house was showing *Girl of My Dreams* practically around the clock, from the first screening before noon to the last at one in the morning.[56] In Baku, movie theaters held screenings even later, at two and four in the morning, and some ardent viewers went from one to the next.[57] A whole series of political and workplace organizations in Moscow petitioned for special screenings of *Girl of My Dreams*, from the Academy of Sciences to large factories such as Krasnyi Oktiabr'. Even the CC apparat chimed in with its request.[58] Many contemporaries, particularly people who were then youngsters, recall going to see trophy pictures over and over again. Moscow's courtyards sprouted rope swings for adventuresome young Tarzan imitators, and boys sported the *tarzanets* haircut after their hero.[59] Grown-up Russian men "practically drooled" at the mention of the American Deanna Durbin,[60] while women swooned over Robert Taylor, star of the British love story *Waterloo Bridge* (1940).

The stunning success of the trophy films elicited some murmurs of concern and even protest at the time. After the release of *Girl of My Dreams* in 1947, officials from a variety of regional party organizations contacted the CC questioning

54. This was also an attempt to avoid copyright disputes: the Soviet authorities were well aware of the potential for lawsuits and concerned that film sales abroad would be jeopardized and Soviet film distributors held liable. See RGASPI, f. 17, op. 132, d. 92, l. 5.

55. V. Demin, "Nostalgiia—greshnoe protivoiadie," *SE*, no. 18 (1991): 3.

56. RGASPI, f. 17, op. 125, d. 576, l. 57.

57. Elena Kurbanova, "Eiramdzhan, ulozhivshii Kuravleva v ginekologicheskoe otdelenie," *Moskovskaia pravda*, 11 May 1999.

58. RGASPI, f. 17, op. 125, d. 576, l. 4.

59. Aleksei Kozlov, *Kozel na sakse* (Moscow, 1998).

60. Oriana Atkinson, *Over at Uncle Joe's: Moscow and Me* (New York, 1947), 136. Deanna Durbin's popularity appears to have been extraordinary and enduring. See Irving R. Levine's comments in *Main Street, USSR: Selections from the Original Edition* (New York, 1960), 141; Serge Fliegers, "Liz Taylor Mistaken for Deanna Durbin," *Chicago Daily Defender*, 28 January 1958.

the wisdom of showing the films, as did the head of the Komsomol.[61] In 1948, L. Il'ichev (of the CC Department of Agitation and Propaganda) reported that the department had received "a large quantity of letters from workers" about the trophy films with "harsh criticism and, in many cases, demands for their removal from the screen."[62] One man in 1952 wrote of his frustration that Soviet theaters were, as he put it, "engaged in real bourgeois propaganda."

> The harmful effects of showing these films can be seen in every courtyard— including ours, where dozens of children play "Tarzan and Cheetah," in particular—and also in relations between adults. It seems to me that the state of affairs is reminiscent of the situation in the well-known fairy tale by Andersen, when everyone had to admit that "the emperor had no clothes."[63]

But with the emperor out naked on parade, Soviet media carefully avoided drawing attention to the spectacle. Few indignant missives like this one appeared in the central press; movie critics kept their distance, too.[64] Trophy films were at once official—the mainstay of everyday cinema culture in the late Stalinist USSR—and unofficial, everywhere on view, yet rarely reflected in orthodox visions of Soviet life.

The story of the trophy films captivates people now in its very strangeness. Tarzan and Stalin in one sentence—on one screen, in fact, as any *Tarzan* showing would have been preceded by newsreels featuring Stalin—is difficult to fathom. Factor in the world beyond the theater, and your head spins. This was a time when the Soviet regime forbade marriage to foreigners, when scores of artists and scientists suffered public persecution, and often worse, for their alleged lack of "Soviet patriotism." If drooling over Deanna Durbin did not qualify as groveling before the West, what did?

Historian Peter Kenez has suggested that Soviet leaders were willing to tolerate the trophies because they considered them light and frivolous and also because officials were banking on them to distract people from pressing economic and social problems.[65] Yet other light cultural forms from the capitalist world— jazz in particular—were under heavy ideological assault in the same period.

61. RGASPI, f. 17, op. 125, d. 576, l. 2; ibid., l. 58.

62. RGASPI, f. 17, op. 132, d. 92, l. 63.

63. RGASPI, f. 17, op. 133, d. 383, l. 208.

64. When *Komsomol'skaia pravda* ran an editorial critiquing the trophy film phenomenon in 1947, the Ministry of Cinematography sent a formal objection the CC. RGASPI, f. 17, op. 125, d. 576, l. 59. Seven years later, another Komsomol critique appeared in *IK* and won the journal an official rebuke and the Komsomol a warning from the CC. The offending article criticized Soviet filmmakers for failing youth and effectively throwing them into the arms of Tarzan. It was apparently quoted by an Associated Press reporter. See E. S. Afanas'eva and V. Iu. Afiani, eds., *Apparat TsK KPSS i kul'tura 1953–1975: Dokumenty* (Moscow, 2001), 285.

65. Kenez, *Cinema and Soviet Society,* 192.

What was the difference between jazz bands and Tarzan? Imagine, for a start, the sound of millions of kopeck coins jingling in cash drawers across the USSR. As Manevich, the official in charge of seizing the Nazi film fund, explained in 1991, trophy films were a cash cow, helping the film distribution bureaucracy overfulfill its plan, and its officials win tidy bonuses, for many years. In the sixties a new Soviet picture that sold 40 million tickets (at 25 kopecks per ticket, for a gross take of 10 million rubles) was considered a smash success.[66] In 1948, when the potential audience was far smaller, the Soviets anticipated an income of 35–40 million rubles for a *limited* release of the American *Viva Villa!* (1934).[67] And the film came free of charge. There were dozens of *Viva Villas!*

The story of the trophies, then, while captivating, is not so strange after all. With the new wave of imports after Stalin's death, many things changed, but the Soviet audience's taste for foreign, commercial cinema held fast. The children of Tarzan's fans in the USSR crowded theaters for *The Magnificent Seven* and *Bobby* (a 1975 Bollywood teen romance); yesterday's droolers for Durbin and Taylor now lusted after Sophia Loren and Rishi Kapoor. Moreover, the fondness of the USSR's cultural bureaucracy for masscult endured over the decades.

In the early postwar period, the framework for authorizing this taste was war booty—a just reward to the victors, like wristwatches seized from POWs. In later years, the official basis for imports was mutual cultural understanding. The USSR also used cultural exchange agreements as a mechanism for promoting Soviet cinema abroad: Soveksportfil'm, the organization in charge of import-export deals, chose a packet of films from, say, India, and India, in exchange, accepted a selection of Soviet pictures.[68] The Soviets also bought films outright. In the Brezhnev era, they were spending US$50,000–150,000 for a picture made in a capitalist country. Films from the developing world came far cheaper and were often bartered for goods, a fact that made them even more attractive. With socialist countries, the typical method was exchange.[69] (The division of cinematic production into "capitalist," "socialist," and "developing world" is an artifact of Soveksportfil'm's own classification system.) The Soviets never paid percentages or royalties—a sale was a sale—and they were also known to circulate film prints until they shredded.[70] The most popular film of all time in the USSR, Soviet or foreign, was a Mexican-made melodrama with a gypsy theme, *Yesenia* (1971),

66. Zorkaia, "O 'massovom segodnia,'" 28.

67. RGASPI, f. 17, op. 132, d. 92, l. 5. See also the three CC decrees on projected profits in Oleg V. Naumov and Andrei Artizov, eds., *Vlast' i khudozhestvennia intelligentsia: Dokumenty 1917–1953* (Moscow, 1999).

68. See Sudha Rajagopalan, *Leave Disco Dancer Alone! Indian Cinema and Soviet Movie-Going after Stalin* (New Dehli, 2008), 76–83.

69. Arkus, *Noveishaia istoriia*, 5:98–103

70. Films from capitalist countries were typically licensed for a limited period—a legal arrangement not always respected on the Soviet side.

which the Soviets bought for only U$20,000 in 1974. *Yesenia* sold 91 million tickets.[71] Even with the costs of copying, distribution, theater management, and so on, the clatter of kopeck coins was thunderous. Soveksportfil'm had a reputation as the most profitable foreign trade sector in the economy, and it was not thanks to exports. For every ruble in its budget, Soveksportfil'm estimated income from foreign film purchases at 5 rubles; in the case of some masscult pictures, it could reach 250.[72]

Comprehensive statistics on the foreign-film market in the USSR are not available at this time, but all indications suggest that films from capitalist countries attracted more viewers as a rule than either Soviet productions or films from the socialist bloc. A CC investigation in 1960 found that in the first nine months of that year, each film from the capitalist world drew an average audience of more than 500,000 in Moscow, while Soviet productions averaged 357,000 and socialist bloc pictures, 133,000.[73] Using other indicators, historian Sudha Rajagopalan concluded that Indian-made films were even more successful than capitalist productions on the Soviet market. The USSR imported 206 films from India in the period 1954 to 1991, nearly all of them (175) Hindi-language melodramas made in Bombay (so-called Bollywood cinema). Rajagopalan counted the number of films surpassing the 20-million mark for ticket sales in their first year of release and found that fifty productions were from India, more than from any other country. (The United States was second with forty-one, France third with thirty-eight.)[74] Until 1962's blockbuster, *Amphibian Man,* the record holder for any film was one of the first Indian productions to come to the USSR: Raj Kapoor's *The Vagabond,* released in 1954. At nearly 64 million tickets, *The Vagabond* still ranks in the top twenty films at the box office for the entire Soviet era.[75]

In 1960, Central Committee investigators concluded that the country's cinematic network had "received an excessively large diffusion of films from capitalist countries" and that "as a result, the attentions of a wide sphere of Soviet people are riveted on themes and ideas far from our tasks in ideological work and not infrequently contradicting those tasks."[76] This was one of several attacks on cinema repertoire, by the Central Committee and others, between 1958 and 1961, and some modifications did follow. Never again (in the Soviet era) would the

71. Dondurei, *Otechestvennyi kinematograf,* 73. See also Neia Zorkaia, "Sovetskii kinoteatr, ili chto tam bylo na samom dele v proshlye gody," *IK,* no. 11 (1995): 121.

72. Arkus, *Noveishaia istoriia,* 5:98–103.

73. Afanas'eva and Afiani, *Ideologicheskie komissii,* 258.

74. Sudha Rajagopalan, "A Taste for Indian Films: Negotiating Cultural Boundaries in Post-Stalinist Soviet Society" (PhD diss., Indiana University, 2005), app. A.

75. Sergei Kudriavtsev, *Svoe kino* (Moscow, 1998), 391. Rajagopalan, "Taste for Indian Films," 149.

76. Afanas'eva and Afiani, *Ideologicheskie komissii,* 258.

U.S. Information Agency be able to boast that nearly half of Moscow's theaters were showing Hollywood films, as it did in the summer of 1960.[77] After a high of ten U.S. releases in 1960 and seven in 1961, the years 1962–70 saw numbers ranging from two to six annually. (The 1960 level was then surpassed only once, in 1977, with eleven U.S. releases.)[78] As a rule, according to one official in 1966, two to three times fewer copies of capitalist pictures than Soviet releases were also being printed.[79]

Yet it is important to recognize that the new approach—restricting the number of new titles and copies, especially for U.S. films—did not always limit audience size. Twenty-four million viewers managed to watch the mere 360 copies of the French *Les Misérables* (1958).[80] *Some Like It Hot* (1959) with Marilyn Monroe reached even more spectacular heights: 211,000 viewers per copy.[81] Visitors to the Soviet Union continued to remark on the prevalence and popularity of masscult. One young Yugoslav scholar was surprised to count more than eighty Moscow theaters showing capitalist films in the summer of 1964. Well over a third of them were playing the same picture, the Italian comedy *Divorce Italian Style* (1961).[82] In the 1970s, the policy of restricting the number of new titles continued, and with it came a general shift away from films made in the capitalist West and toward Middle Eastern, Latin American, and especially Indian products.[83] One expert estimated that only 65 percent of ticket sales in the seventies were for Soviet-made productions, with the rest attributable to foreign films.[84] The head of the Filmmakers' Union gave an even lower figure for 1975 at the union's congress: 50 percent. He may have been pleased to report that the number had risen to 70 percent by 1981, but that still left nearly one-third of ticket sales outside the Soviet camp.[85]

---

77. "USIA Report Notes Huge Increase in U.S. Films Shown in Soviet Union," *Washington Post,* 19 September 1960.

78. Golovskoy, *Behind the Soviet Screen,* 133.

79. The Moscow party organization complained in 1961 that the city's largest theaters and stadiums were still showing capitalist films (though trade union clubs and TV were not). TsAOPIM, f. 4, op. 139, d. 52, l. 6.

80. RGALI, f. 2936, op. 4, d. 1307, l. 106.

81. Average viewership per copy was twenty-five to thirty thousand. Dondurei, *Otechestvennyi kinematograf,* 71; Kudriavtsev, *Svoe kino,* 392. The Soviets bought *Some Like It Hot* for 54,000 convertible rubles. Evgenii Zhirnov, "Arkhiv: Kremlevskie piraty," *Kommersant-vlast',* 14 October 2002.

82. Mihajlo Mihajlov, *Moscow Summer* (New York, 1965), 51. See also William Taubman, *The View from Lenin Hills: Soviet Youth in Ferment* (New York, 1967), 136.

83. Peter Kenez estimated there were only twenty Western films on Moscow screens in 1969–70. Kenez, "Notes on a Moscow Movie Season" (August 1975), OSA, box 300-80-1-316.

84. Golovskoy, *Behind the Soviet Screen,* 137.

85. *Chetvertyi s"ezd kinematografistov SSSR.*

Here we can draw a straight line back to the trophy film era: the Soviet cultural bureaucracy was consistently canny when it came to imports. For all the complaints about greedy officials pushing lowbrow movies and talk of their corrupting influence, these films never left the screen. They were essential to the smooth functioning of the Soviet cinematic system. Boris Pavlenok, Goskino's deputy chairman in the seventies, described the rationale in 2003:

> In order to make ends meet, we "invited Brigitte Bardot," as we used to say. This is a normal approach for producers. It is not important where I get the money—the main thing is to pay off my debts and obtain credits for the following year. Sometimes, the head of Gosbank would call Yermash and say: "Listen, buy some *Yesenia* or another, my accounts are empty." So we bought Indian melodramas, tossed them in the theaters in many copies, and filled up the budget.[86]

Soviet officials naturally did not speak in public about the Bardot technique, nor did they share the details of another important continuity with the past: acquisition practices. Soveksportfil'm representatives made a preliminary selection of films abroad and sent copies to Moscow to a special commission for review. The commission comprised people from Goskino, the CC apparat, the Ministry of the Interior and sometimes other ministries, the KGB, the Filmmakers' Union, and also representatives of "the public," such as writers and teachers, and it generated reports with recommendations. Until 1965, every acquisition of a capitalist production required an official go-ahead from the CC sekretariat.[87] But even after 1965, "the final word in any case rested with the CC," said one former participant, and in practice, the tastes of the top-level authorities carried enormous weight. *Divorce Italian Style,* for example, reportedly made the cut because Adzhubei was a fan.[88]

Soveksportfil'm for this reason played it very safe in its proposals. The selection it sent for review was always narrow, and this was especially true as much of cinema outside the USSR grew more sexually explicit, violent, and morally ambiguous. It was not enough for a film to contain stringent social criticism, to be anti-American, anticapitalist, or even Marxist. If it might be considered "formalist" (read: a nonlinear plot or abstract or experimental cinematography), "naturalist" (naked bodies), or "brutal" (graphic violence), Soveksportfil'm had good grounds to assume it would be rejected. This is one reason why Bollywood productions—typically free of these defects—were perennial favorites for acquisition. Politics could come into play in other ways as well. Soveksportfil'm's former deputy head recalled that the buying commission's favorable recommendation of Milos Forman's *Amadeus* (1984) was blocked by the Czechoslovak

86. Evgenii Zhirnov, "Arkhiv: Rentabel'nost' sovetskogo kinematografa sostavliala 900% v god," *Kommersant-vlast',* 10 March 2003.

87. RGALI, f. 2918, op. 5, ll. 40–42.

88. Zhirnov, "Arkhiv: Kremlevskye piraty."

communist leadership, who made it known how offended they would be should their Soviet comrades purchase a film made by a "traitor" to their homeland.[89]

If, as was sometimes the case, the Soviets decided to acquire a picture with objectionable scenes, they altered it, and this too was a link with the past. Audiences in the USSR saw a *Divorce Italian Style* almost entirely stripped of its storyline about a local communist, deemed too controversial. Censors were known to cut as much as thirty minutes of a standard two-hour feature. They also edited—changing the sequencing of scenes, for example—and purposefully mistranslated dialogue in dubbing. These practices reached historic heights in the seventies and eighties, but by then they were a Soviet tradition stretching back to the twenties.[90] Titles were changed wholesale; color films were printed in black–and–white; Soviet artists copied and recorded songs from foreign film soundtracks as their own. In the hands of the Soviet cultural system, embattled by definition, masscult films were always a kind of war booty. The attitude was at once cavalier with respect to the rights of creators and mindful, even fearful, of the potential power of the creation.[91] These movies were there to generate revenues and demonstrate the Soviet state's commitment to providing art and leisure (even if of dubious quality). They were also objects of intense attraction from the very top of the system down. The Soviet love affair with masscult cinema was no fling; it was an enduring, fruitful passion at the very heart of the cultural system.

DEFINING CINEMATIC SUCCESS

Cinema's superprofitability in the USSR is a historical chestnut that deserves to be cracked open and examined. In Soviet times, officials often bragged about their multibillion-strong audience, and although they mostly refrained from grubby talk of rubles and kopecks, the message was clear enough. Internal reports from Goskino and the Filmmakers' Union did include financial data, and in the mid-sixties they put gross ticket sales at roughly 1 billion rubles annually, of which the state was said to have collected 440 million in "pure profit."[92] Boris Pavlenok claimed in his post-Soviet memoirs that cinema had a 900 percent profit margin during his tenure. He also cited the figure of 1 billion rubles for an annual box office and estimated 440 million rubles or so as the annual take.[93]

All these figures should be taken as notional rather than actual because they were notional in their original historical context. The 1 billion-ruble gross sales

89. Arkus, *Noveishaia istoriia*, 5:102.

90. Ibid., vol. 4 (Moscow, 2002), 109–111.

91. Foreign literature fared no better. See Maurice Friedberg, *A Decade of Euphoria: Western Literature in Post-Stalin Russia, 1954–1964* (Bloomington, IN, 1977), esp. 16–57.

92. Fomin, *Kinomatograf ottepeli*, 6.

93. Zhirnov, "Arkhiv: Rentabl'nost' sovetskogo kinematografa." See also Boris Pavlenok, *Kino: Legendy i byl': Vospominaniia, razmyshleniia* (Moscow, 2004), 91.

number, for example, was not an actual box-office figure but rather an estimate derived from the number of tickets sold. The USSR, unlike most countries at the time, evaluated cinema in tickets, not cash (and tickets were also often sloppily equated with viewers, which had the effect of inflating audience size, since individuals frequently saw a film more than once). Taking an average price (itself an estimate) of 25 kopecks per ticket and an audience of 4 billion (also estimated), one arrives at a box-office take of 1 billion rubles. Similarly, the 440 million derived from the organization of the film financing system: by plan, 55 percent of all receipts from movie ticket sales went to local budgets. That would leave roughly 440 million of the 1 billion in "pure profit."[94]

Overall, we can say that cinema *was* a moneymaking venture for the Soviet state through the seventies.[95] The boon to city and regional coffers, in particular, was substantial: movie money helped pay the salaries of teachers, doctors, and many others on municipal payrolls across the USSR. My point here is not to mock the Soviets for either their pride or their bookkeeping but rather to draw our attention to how they framed cinematic success. Two important themes emerge. The first is the centrality of profit to cinema's very identity in the Soviet context. Though the term "profit" itself was shunned, the conventional wisdom—false but durable—was that film ranked second only to vodka in generating revenues for the state. The most important of the arts was always marked by its Midas touch, and filmmakers did not hesitate to point this out. Cinema, the Filmmakers' Union and Goskino reminded the CC in 1966, "is the only art in our country that brings in stable, constant, and ever-increasing revenues."[96]

The second important theme to note is the opacity of Soviet film finances as a matter of policy and not mere incompetence. Along with audience research, economics was the least well-tended and most secretive field in the entire cinematic sphere. It is not only that the Soviets did not collect accurate, comprehensive data.[97] They also rarely publicized and discussed what they did know. Box-office figures were almost never published, and even filmmakers rarely knew how their work had fared in theaters—nor were they particularly interested. The perpetual, systemic cloudiness about the facts on the ground and demands for "performance," however vaguely defined, opened filmmakers up to periodic assaults for squandering resources and undermining a winning sector of the socialist economy. Yet this kind of systemic cloud cover also worked to

94. Kosinova, *Istoriia kinoprodiuserstva v Rossii,* 20.

95. Birgit Beumers contended that returns on ticket sales exceeded expenses until 1983. Beumers, "Cinemarket, or The Russian Film Industry in 'Mission Impossible,'" *Europe-Asia Studies* 51, no. 5 (July 1999): 871; Arkus, *Noveishaia istoriia otechestvennogo kino,* 5:125.

96. Fomin, *Kinomatograf ottepeli,* 85.

97. Aleksandr Fedorov, "Gorkaia pravda luchshe vsiakoi lzhi?" *SK-Novosti,* no. 43, http://www.film.ru/sk-news.

their advantage.[98] It was, in this way, one of the most fruitful contradictions of the Soviet film industry. Movie theaters were packed, film was profitable overall, and digging into the details could well be considered beneath the dignity of the socialist artist or even a socialist cultural bureaucrat.[99] The image of Soviet cinema's profitability was essential to the smooth functioning of a system that had many bumpy patches.

Art or no, cinema was also an industrial process, and it suffered production problems typical of Soviet industry. The plan was the organizing principle. In the case of film, production plans were set by the film administration and the appropriate Central Committee departments, and they were organized by theme: a thematic plan (*tematicheskii plan*) specified the number of films a studio would produce in a given year—seven films in the historical-revolutionary thematic slot, three social dramas, and so on.[100] There were also plans for shorter periods—quarterly plans, for example. Studios routinely failed to meet them all. Sally Belfrage, an American who worked briefly on a Mosfil'm production in the late fifties, noticed very little happening on the set until the very end of the month, when there was a flurry of activity.[101] This was storming to meet the plan, much as Belfrage would have found in a refrigerator plant. And since half or more of all film productions in the early sixties were not completed until the final quarter of the fiscal year, storming must have been very common.[102] Other productions—again, an estimated 50 percent—simply ran over schedule.[103]

Why was this so? A 1963 evaluation of the industry gave a typical litany of problems, from overshooting and unnecessary travel to rewriting screenplays and recasting actors midway through productions.[104] If Soviet filmmakers were

98. Sloppiness in data collection could also make it easier to cook the books. Vladimir Motyl' claimed that the figures for *The White Sun of the Desert* (*Beloe sol'ntse pustyni,* 1970) were lowered so that those for another film would appear higher. "Vladimir Motyl': V kino nuzhno gospolitika," *Kommersant-Daily,* 6 November 1998.

99. My argument is not that the Soviet film industry was the only one to cook the books (Hollywood was, and is, famous for it) but that recipes differ by system. See Edward Jay Epstein, *The Big Picture: Money and Power in Hollywood* (New York, 2006).

100. Thematic plans varied yearly and were subject to interest-group lobbying. Plans for 1965, for example, set an increase in the military-patriotic category to commemorate victory in World War II. The late 1950s saw a spate of movies featuring honest police officers—part of a mediawide campaign to burnish the reputation of the police force. Denis Gorelov, "Chelovek-amfibiia," *Izvestiia,* 24 March 2000. The KGB in the seventies rallied for films on Soviet counterintelligence as a retort to a wave of anti-Soviet films in the West. Fomin, *Kino i vlast',* 143.

101. Sally Belfrage, *A Room in Moscow* (London, 1958), 147. The film was *Pamiat' serdtsa* (1958).

102. Afanas'eva and Afiani, *Ideologicheskie komissii,* 475.

103. RGALI, f. 2936, op. 4, d. 1307, l. 25.

104. RGALI, f. 2944, op. 1, d. 20, l. 185.

here to defend themselves, they would protest—with good reason—that the problems were not their fault. Given the execrable quality of Soviet film stock—an estimated 10 to 15 percent of the costs of production were related to problems with defective film—the amount of wasted footage was massive and reshooting inevitable.[105] "Rewritten" was often another word for censored. What choice did a director have if, say, military top brass decided the character of the soldier in his film was not sufficiently heroic? He reworked the script. He found an actor with a stronger chin, broader shoulders, and better connections, and he reshot the soldier's scenes. Many filmmakers did whatever they could to beat the system, and sometimes this meant shooting material they knew would likely raise objections, but they were willing to sacrifice to satisfy the bureaucrats.

All these changes drove up the costs of filmmaking substantially: in 1970, the average Soviet production cost over 400,000 rubles, up 30 percent from a decade before, and the trend continued.[106] However, expensive films were not necessarily popular ones, and filmmakers were producing fewer and fewer hits as the years went by. In 1960, thirty-nine Soviet-made pictures sold 20 million tickets or more in the first year of their release, whereas by 1964, only twenty-three could boast this level of success.[107] *Amphibian Man*'s 65.5 million tickets in 1962 stunned the cinematic community not only because it was the first Soviet film to surpass the 50 million *and* the 60 million mark but because its success was completely out of proportion to that of the rest of the industry. The average Soviet picture in the mid-sixties sold just *under* 15 million tickets.[108] The downward trend continued through the 1970s, and by 1984, one-half of new productions did not meet the 5 million-ticket mark for their first year on the screen.[109] None of the non-Russian Soviet republics had a film industry that covered its own costs in box-office returns; they were all (except Ukraine, which covered its own losses) dependent on direct subsidies from Moscow.[110]

The core mechanism of the Soviet cinematic system was the official rating assigned to every film for its "ideological-artistic quality" by a special Goskino commission of bureaucrats and cineastes. There were four levels. Studios received financing according to fiscal plans (and before films went into production); most people who worked in cinema earned regular salaries. But it was a film's rating

105. Evgenii Zhirnov, "Kak zakalialsia brend. Tselluloidnoe iskusstvo," *Kommersant-dengi,* 20 September 2004.

106. L. Furikov, "Analiz odnogo . . . analiza fil'ma," *IK,* no. 8 (1970): 108.

107. RGALI, f. 2936, op. 4, d. 1307, l. 97.

108. Ibid., l. 23.

109. Valerii Golovskoi, *Mezhdu ottepel'iu i glasnosti: Kinematograf 70-x* (Moscow, 2004), 68; Sergei Kudriavtsev, "Rekordy i mify sovetskogo kinoprokata," *Vremia novostei,* 2 August 2007.

110. Interview with Baskakov in Troianovskii, *Kinematograf ottepeli: Kniga vtoraia* (Moscow, 2002), 334.

that set the gears in motion for additional forms of compensation. A top-rated picture brought its studio a bonus of 15 percent of its budgeted cost, whereas a second-tier rating brought 10 percent and a third tier 5 percent.[111] Directors, too, received bonus payments based on ratings and regardless of whether they had met their fiscal plans.[112] In fact, from the perspective of a studio and its professionals, the longer and more expensive the production, the better. Since bonuses for production crews were calculated as a percentage of their total wages for the shoot, they had a built-in incentive to draw things out.[113] A picture that lost money overall still stood to make money for its studio and the people who made it. The forgotten *The General and the Daisies* (*General i margaritki*, 1963) failed to earn back even 70 percent of its costs (for production, copying, and distribution) in ticket sales yet still earned Mosfil'm a healthy 50,000-ruble bonus.[114] The key was the rating.

Ratings determined how many copies of a film were printed (its *tirazh*), and this made them especially important to screenwriters and composers.[115] Unlike other film professionals, these two groups had a right to royalties, calculated as a percentage of the gross take in theaters (*potirazhnye*). The range in film *tirazh* was very wide—anywhere from a dozen to a few thousand copies—and a high rating was no guarantee of high royalties.[116] Republic- and district-level authorities had a say in setting cinematic repertory in their areas, and in theory, a film with a top rating might not be selected widely. In practice, higher ratings

111. Cohen, *Cultural-Political Traditions,* 444. On the origins of the ratings system, see Kosinova, *Istoriia kinoprodiuserstva v Rossii,* 158.

112. Faraday's informant reported directors' bonuses of 8,000 rubles for first-category films, 6,000 for second, 2,500 for third, none for fourth, and 12,000 for *goszakaz*. These rates likely refer to the seventies and early 1980s. George Faraday, *Revolt of the Filmmakers: The Struggle for Artistic Autonomy and the Fall of the Soviet Film Industry* (University Park, PA, 2004), 59.

113. A 1972 *Pravda* article quoted in Cohen, *Cultural-Political Traditions,* 445. The system also encouraged longer-running films. The trend was for two-part films, running three-plus hours but shown in one seating. Viewers were said not to like them because of the length and because they had to buy two tickets. Steven Hill, "The Soviet Film Today," *Film Quarterly* 20, no. 4 (Summer 1967): 40; Chukhrai, *Moe kino,* 164–165.

114. Fomin, *Kinematograf ottepeli.* 78. *General i margaritki,* directed by M. Chiaureli, known for Stalin cult films. An official in 1966 cited different figures for the film (cost, 715,000r; sales, 190,000r; bonus, 36,000r) to make the same point. RGALI, f. 2936, op. 4, d. 1307, l. 46.

115. No doubt this is one reason why so many directors were credited as screenwriters as well. Some industry critics complained that the practice of directors writing or rewriting screenplays contributed to the gray-film problem. See Aleksei Kapler's letter to the CC in Fomin, *Kinematograf ottepeli,* 87–89. Fomin also published a 1969 KGB report on Kapler's complaints that directors were forcing writers to split screenplay royalties. Fomin, *Kino i vlast',* 92–94.

116. "Kak vziat' ot fil'ma bol'she?," *IK,* no. 7 (1966): 13.

almost always translated into larger print runs and widespread distribution. Actors also stood to gain materially from high ratings, although rarely at the level of screenwriters, composers, and directors.[117] Though most were ordinary salaried studio employees, actors who had been awarded state honors—"people's artists" (*narodnye artisty*), for example—brought home fatter pay envelopes and other perquisites as well. To participate in highly rated films with wide distribution was to increase the odds of collecting honors.[118]

Limiting distribution practically guaranteed limited audiences; the regime employed this strategy for controversial works throughout the postwar period. Tarkovskii's *The Mirror* (*Zerkalo*, 1975) was printed in only thirty copies for the entire USSR, to give one example.[119] Conversely, to grant a picture a high *tirazh* was to give it the biggest possible advantage on the Soviet market. This was the case with the so-called state orders (*goszakazy*), the most prestigious and potentially lucrative of all productions. Most filled the historical-revolutionary (1917 and the civil war) or military-patriotic (World War II) slots in studios' thematic plans, and all were lavishly funded, promoted, and distributed. *The Living and the Dead* (*Zhivye i mertvye*, 1964), a screen adaptation of the novel by Konstantin Simonov, was one example. With a whopping three thousand copies in Soviet theaters, it inevitably topped the box-office charts. The actor-director Sergei Bondarchuk made several films by goszakaz, including *War and Peace* (*Voina i mir*, 1966–67), a four-part extravaganza that gave new meaning to the cliché "a cast of thousands." Bondarchuk used his connections to muster an entire cavalry division for the film. The estimated cost: nearly 20 million rubles.[120] By way of comparison, the Filmmakers' Union reported spending a little over 2 million rubles over a five-year period in the seventies on housing projects for its members.[121]

A goszakaz film embodied the essence of Soviet cinematic production. In effect, the goszakaz filmmaker locked in top ratings, bonuses, honors, festival prizes, and foreign travel—the best the system had to offer if you played by its rules. He (and most were men) *guaranteed* Soviet cinematic success by successfully managing his relationships with people in power. Not every film could be a goszakaz, and not every film professional aspired to work on one.

---

117. Actors consistently complained about low pay levels. See, for example, comments at the 1981 Filmmakers' Union congress. *Chetvertyi s"ezd kinematografistov SSSR*, 111.

118. Other film professionals were also eligible for honors. Marina Raikina, "Patologicheskie narodnye," *Moskovskii komsomolets*, 14 May 1999. On the introduction of honors in 1937, see Maya Turovskaya, "The 1930s and 1940s: Cinema in Context," in Taylor and Spring, *Stalinism and Soviet Cinema*, 37.

119. Arkus, *Noveishaia istoriia*, 5:125.

120. "Kak vziat' ot fil'ma bol'she?" 9. The film was also reviewed in more than one hundred newspapers. Woll, *Real Images*, 153.

121. *Chetvertyi s"ezd kinematografistov SSSR*, 42.

Filmmakers often chafed against the demands of thematic planning and railed against the ratings system. But an overwhelming majority of productions received first- or second-category ratings; level-four productions were practically unheard of.[122]

If most Soviet films drew the highest ratings and funding levels while also failing at the box office, how did cinema rate as a profit-making sector of the Soviet cultural economy? Cinema-art did have a business model of a sort, and if we were to draw it, the best shape would be an inverted pyramid: a great block of middling and failing films balanced on a far smaller base of box-office hits. This model worked in large measure because the base of the structure was so solid and because moviegoing held a privileged place in Soviet social life well into the 1970s. It was the amphibian men plus strategic infusions of Bardot and Bollywood that filled Soviet movie houses and dominated the moviegoing experience of Soviet audiences. It was these films, in large measure, that bankrolled the industry.

In their public statements, Soviet officials were adept at stressing cinema's vitality in the USSR while eliding the issue of its basis—fudging their business model, in other words. But Soviet cineastes were also routinely excoriated for wasting the people's money and failing to meet the challenge of masscult infiltration. The attacks came in public speeches and published decrees as well as behind closed doors. Goskino's chairman told a group of filmmakers in 1963 that of the forty-two films he had recently screened, only five or six had a future. The rest, he said, "are doomed to lie in storage.... They will not be successful with viewers. They have nothing to offer from the perspective of cinematographic innovation. They have nothing to offer, period."[123] To be clear, these were not films the chairman planned to send to the shelf (though there were a few of those too, he said): they were "gray" films destined to fail on the market. At a 1966 conference on film distribution, the head of the film distribution agency took filmmakers to task for producing "large quantities of gray, boring, utterly uninteresting films that have no success whatsoever with viewers."[124] "Gray," of course, was not a neutral term but a cudgel in the hands of officials and filmmakers alike. One person's gray film was another's artistic experiment. A gray film was a lost opportunity to fulfill Soviet cinema's given mission—aesthetic, political, and ethical education of the masses. And if the masses then chose to spend time in the enemy camp with a film like *The Magnificent Seven,* this was a loss compounded and made potentially treacherous.

The "upper political leadership was always dissatisfied with cinema," said a former Goskino deputy, V. Baskakov, in a post-Soviet interview; in his view, the

122. RGALI, f. 2936, op. 4, d. 1307, l. 44.
123. RGALI f. 2944, op. 1, d. 19, l. 81.
124. RGALI, f. 2936, op. 4, d 1307, l. 13.

situation worsened as the sixties wore on, especially after 1968.[125] The ideological controversies around cinema were serious, and they have been skillfully documented by Fomin, Josephine Woll, and other film scholars. Yet for all that, we should recognize that nothing fundamentally altered the way filmmaking was organized in the Soviet Union after Stalin. Cinema was mass art, but small films (gray or artistic—much depended on your perspective) proliferated; *Amphibian Man* remained a rare exception; and generations of audiences packed the aisles for movies identified as ideological lightweights, if not pollutants.

As in other spheres of Soviet life, the question was not so much one of skill as one of self-interest, incentive, and inertia. Cinema's business model generated revenues for the state; the pyramid structure stood, and it was impressive in size and scope. Soviet filmmakers had very little incentive to alter its structure and produce audience-pleasing films. No doubt director Mark Donskoi spoke for many when he told distribution officials, "I think that if I have made a film, then it is your business to take care of putting it forward [*zanimat'sia ego prodvizheniem*]. I have never gone out to the movie theaters, and I do not feel comfortable selling my own films."[126] In terms of cultural capital, there was indisputably more prestige to be won by producing an artistically innovative, sophisticated work than by attracting mass audiences. Mass popularity could be damaging to one's reputation and sense of self; cinema's amphibian man, Vladimir Korenev, said he found his success embarrassing, and he refused romantic leading roles and eschewed entertainment-oriented films from then on.[127] The highest goal for any Soviet film professional was to join the canon, preferably the international one, which is where Soviet cinema-art saw itself as the natural leader. And though not everyone could be a Sergei Eisenstein, of course, there were few penalties for nursing those delusions, not even financial ones. The landscape was in fact strewn with incentives.

Cultural capital was a critical commodity for Soviet filmmakers on its own terms, as George Faraday has argued.[128] Film professionals publicly scorned "petit bourgeois materialism" (*meshchanstvo*), reflecting both Soviet ideology and the traditional orientation of the Russian intelligentsia. Antimaterialism was also a theme in many Soviet films, and we have no reason to question filmmakers' sincerity. Marlen Khutsiev, director of a controversial youth-theme film, *Ilich's Gate* (*Zastava Il'icha*), released as *I Am Twenty* (*Mne 20 Let*, 1965), recalled that after the film's first screening at the studio, Mikhail Romm came up to him

125. Fomin, *Kino i vlast'*, 135.

126. RGALI, f. 2936, op. 4, d. 1307, l. 98.

127. Elena Smirnova, "Zolotaia pora Ikhtiandra," *Rossiisskaia gazeta*, 21 June 2000; Tat'iana Khoroshilova, "Vladimir Korenev: Moi geroi byl naiven i chist," *Rossiiskaia gazeta*, 22 November 2003.

128. Faraday, *Revolt of the Filmmakers*.

and said, "Marlen, you have justified your existence."[129] Soviet cinema-art could not have been more serious to self-defined Soviet artists.

Nevertheless, the structure of the system was such that it was always impossible to isolate cultural capital from the political and material kind. Romm's opinion of *Ilich's Gate*—and, more broadly, mobilizing the cinematic community (so-called *obshchestvennoe mnenie,* or public opinion) in favor of your film— was essential. People at Goskino and the Central Committee were not certain to accept the currency, but sometimes they did. Cineastes knew too that cultural capital could be spent to improve their lifestyles: such was the way of the Soviet world. Tickets from the Filmmakers' Union to a rare movie screening went to your connection in the electronics shop who had promised you first pick from the next shipment of transistors, to your seamstress, to your doctor. If you were sent to Venice with your film and saved your per diem wisely, you just might be able to buy shoes for yourself and a raincoat for your daughter. Nearly every Soviet cineaste's memoir includes at least one story of this kind, and though most are gently self-mocking in tone, they also acknowledge the importance of these consumer boons in a system of chronic shortages. On a larger scale, to be acknowledged as a great Soviet artist (especially, but not only, by foreigners) could mean moving from a communal to an individual apartment or jumping the queue for a telephone or a car.[130] Cultural capital not only had real currency in the film community and among the intelligentsia, but it also counted "on the street" (with your hairdresser and mechanic) and most significantly, "upstairs" among the political-bureaucratic elites.[131]

In 1988, with the system unraveling at lightning speed, one Soviet director attempted to orient a reporter from the *New Yorker* magazine: "In most countries," he said, "you make either films that are high art or films for the general public— for people to enjoy. But in the political situation that existed here for so long the vast majority of films were of neither type. They were made to please the people in Goskino, and nobody watched them."[132] Fomin and other film scholars stress the same dynamic—filmmaker-bureaucrat or, better still, filmmaker *under* bureaucrat—and emphasize how damaging this was to the creative process because it induced people to play it safe. There were so many gray films in Soviet

129. Larisa Maliukova, "Cherno-beloe vremia Romma: Vladimir Dmitriev i Marlen Khutsiev govoriat o mastere," *Novaia gazeta,* 5 February 2001.

130. On networking and the lifestyles of the Soviet intelligentsia, see Maia Turovskaya, "Sovetskii srednyi klass," *Neprikosnovennyi zapas,* no. 1 (2002).

131. Here I part ways with George Faraday, who sees a "gulf between the creative intelligentsia and the nomenklatura" in terms of values. *Revolt of the Filmmakers,* 36. Not only did their ranks overlap (many members of the intelligentsia held nomenklatura rank), but their cultural values were broadly consonant.

132. James Lardner, "A Moment We Had to Grasp," *New Yorker,* 26 September 1988, 82.

cinema, the argument goes, because the bureaucrats, the party, the regime bled the color out of nearly every one.

The bleeding was real enough, no doubt. But determining just who ordered the operations and how they transpired is more difficult. Soviet cinema was a complex social formation. Although historians tend to trace bright lines separating film professionals from the "other side," if we look at the way the system was lived, we see that all lines of necessity overlapped. A filmmaker had to please people in power, but some of the most powerful people in Soviet cinema were fellow filmmakers—cinema's power brokers. Screenwriters and directors altered their work to meet the demands of their studios long before they went before Goskino. This was mutual censorship; there was also self-censorship. No doubt many people involved would have preferred not to do it—including some on the bureaucratic side. It is a point several former cineastes have made when prompted to recount their experiences with censorship. Khutsiev, for example, took exception to one interviewer's blanket statements condemning the authorities (*rukovodstvo*) in 2005. "Today people curse the editors, but they varied," he said, mentioning one studio editor who stood up for him. The interviewer persisted: "But there were 'supervisors' [*smotriteli*] at Goskino who saw sedition in the most innocent things." Khutsiev answered, "This is complicated too, because after all they were not free. They suggested that I get going on new projects."[133]

People had no choice but to work together across artist-bureaucrat lines, and given the importance of networking in Soviet life generally, they often socialized across lines as well. Many Soviet officials prided themselves on having friends in the arts and cultivated those ties. Actor Vsevolod Sanaev joked with a friend, "What do you think, why do the bosses include me in every film delegation traveling abroad? . . . Because they are bored! How do they relax there in the evenings? They sit in their hotel rooms and drink. And I tell jokes and cock-and-bull stories. . . . Thanks to this talent of mine, I have seen the whole world."[134] When director Georgii Daneliia went to Rome for the first time in 1963, he shared a hotel room with Baskakov, then new to Goskino. This would not have been his choice, he later wrote, but the two men got along better than he had imagined, and he sympathized with the deputy chair's difficulties on his maiden voyage abroad—his failure to anticipate needing more than two shirts, for example. Baskakov was the boss without a doubt (Daneliia handed over *his* shirts), but it was Daneliia who had experience in foreign situations, and it was Daneliia and his filmmaker colleagues who got Baskakov the invitation he coveted to a swanky dinner with Italian cinema's leading lights.[135] A film official had more power than filmmakers, but in some situations, he also had no power without them.

133. Larisa Maliukova, "Kul'turnyi sloi. Marlen Khutsiev: Vremia samo prostupaet na ekrane," *Novaia gazeta,* 3 October 2005, 24–25.

134. *Sergei Bondarchuk v vospominaniiakh sovremennikov* (Moscow, 2003), 476.

135. Daneliia, *Bezbiletnyi passazhir,* 182–189.

Figure 1.2. Connections: Minister of Culture Ekaterina Furtseva hobnobs with French star Leslie Caron and leading Soviet director Sergei Iutkevich, 1967. Boris Kaufman, RIA Novosti. Used with permission.

It was no minor point that filmmakers in the USSR were said to produce something defined as art—something that would uplift the masses at home and spread the good news about superior socialist culture abroad. Even in the context of an authoritarian system, Soviet filmmakers' status as artists always gave them a good deal more room for maneuver than the portrait painted for the *New Yorker* reader implies. Even films sent straight to the shelf still meant a paycheck for their producers. Some directors—Tarkovskii is the best example—saw their work all but banned at home yet screened and sometimes sold abroad. And even directors who were troublemakers from the regime's point of view, but did not enjoy international cachet, were usually able to secure financing for future projects. A fruitful, if painful contradiction. For all the real ideological pressures exerted on Soviet filmmakers, they were never compelled by the regime to make popular or even acceptable films. And this is because cultural capital was a meaningful commodity not only to them but to Soviet political elites as well.

REDEFINING CINEMATIC SUCCESS UNDER BREZHNEV?

The best demonstration of Soviet cinema's deep structure and values is the story of the Experimental Creative Studio, or ETK (Eksperimental'naia tvorcheskaia kinostudiia), a targeted test in applying the profit motive to film production that lasted from the mid-sixties to the mid-seventies. Although the formation of Goskino in 1963 was meant to put the cinematic house in order, the new men in the Kremlin were still dissatisfied and instituted another bureaucratic reorganization two years later. Goskino saw its status and staffing levels raised and also suffered a wave of firings.[136] More sweeping measures, however, still lingered in the air: one idea was to create a Ministry of Cinema, as had existed under Stalin; the Politburo also considered liquidating all the creative unions and replacing them with a single organization, the better to manage the intelligentsia.[137]

The new Filmmakers' Union worked actively in this period to forestall what it saw as drastic action, and together with Goskino, it put together a series of proposals for reforming Soviet cinema that were remarkable in their candor and often radical in their approach. Singling out the ratings system as, in the words of one 1966 proposal, "the source of the complete apathy of creative workers and studio directors regarding their films' performance in theaters," they advocated introducing limited material incentives pegged to box-office results.[138] It was an idea in step with the times: in 1965, the Kremlin had tipped its hat cautiously to the profit motive with the Kosygin reforms (named for the then chairman of the USSR Council of Ministers, Aleksei Kosygin). The reformist spark turned out to be fleeting, however, and the regime opted instead to ratchet up control by expanding and purging the film bureaucracy yet again and increasing party oversight. This process, which had parallels in other mass media, picked up momentum after 1968 and culminated in the 1972 reorganization of Goskino under Yermash. The Experimental Creative Studio was a lone survivor of the sixties reformist moment and lasted until 1976, when it was declared to have run its course.[139] Roughly ten years later, in the full flush of perestroika, cineastes would cite the ETK story as an example of how an incompetent and intolerant bureaucracy had stifled cinematic progress.

ETK's founder, Grigorii Chukhrai, was no run-of-the-mill Soviet cineaste, and the same could be said of Vladmir Pozner, his chief collaborator, a dynamic manager with a rare commodity in the Soviet film world: Hollywood experience. (Pozner was an émigré who had spent much of his adult life in the United States, where he had managed overseas film distribution for MGM.)[140] Chukhrai came

---

136. For Baskakov's view of the mid-sixties changes (which cost him his job), see Fomin, *Kino i vlast'*, 137.

137. Fomin, *Kinematograf ottepeli*, 60.

138. Ibid., 77; Kosinova, *Istoriia kinoprodiuserstva v Rossii*, 228–229.

139. Motyl', "Za derzhavu po-prezhnemu obidno." One historian reports that the CC approved plans for an ETK-like studio as early as June 1962. Kosinova, *Istoriia kinoprodiusertva v Rossii*, 229. Chukhrai described his initial meeting with Kosygin in *Moe kino*, 173–176.

140. Pozner was also the father of the future television star of the glasnost era, Vladimir Vladimirovich Pozner, who described his family's life in the United States in *Parting with Illusions* (New York, 1990).

to cinema a decorated veteran of World War II, and this, plus his international reputation (his films had won multiple awards, including Cannes) gave him unusual clout with the authorities. Moreover, though Chukhrai was a proud party man and socialist, he was also a self-styled maverick. With his intellectual and moral swagger, Chukhrai epitomized the *shestidesiatniki* (people of the sixties) spirit; he was a true believer. And it is in this context that we must examine his cinematic experiment in market socialism.

Chukhrai told *Soviet Screen* in 1966 that the problem with the Soviet cinematic system was that it "incessantly pushes people to lie."[141] The insight had come to him, he said, when he was working as a screenwriter, and a director asked him to add a few bogus shots in order to pad the budget. Chukhrai refused, but rather than blame the director, he concluded that the root of the problem was the system's fixation with meeting budgets regardless of performance or artistic merit.[142] The ETK was designed to reward people according to how well a film performed with audiences. Screenwriters, for example, earned twice as much at ETK as at other studios, *provided that* their films drew an audience of at least 30 million. The studio was also prepared to penalize failure: the same screenwriters who stood to gain from a hit got no bonus at all if their films failed to sell 17 million tickets, the average amount necessary to cover the cost of production and distribution.[143] It was a sink-or-swim operation: if they made unpopular films, it would fail, and its staff would be out of work.[144]

The ETK was thus the first and only Soviet studio since the 1920s to focus on crowd-pleasing productions. "The ETK shunned making films for an elite circle," said one of its most successful directors, V. Motyl'. "It was interested in genre films for mass distribution."[145] Many of these directors achieved terrific successes with their ETK productions, and on the whole the studio proved profitable. For the period 1966–71, ETK films on average drew 29.2 million viewers, compared with the overall Soviet average of 17.3 million.[146] Chukhrai boasted of their accomplishments in 1986: "Productivity increased sharply, and useless expenses dropped. In terms of profitability, our films surpassed our highest expectations."[147]

---

141. "Eksperiment vedet v budushchee," *SE,* no. 3 (1966): 1.

142. That this was not only an economic but a moral question for Chukhrai comes through even more clearly in his post-Soviet memoirs. "Workers were getting paid for money they did not earn. This suited them and at the same time corrupted them." Chukhrai, *Moe kino,* 168.

143. Fomin, *Kinematograf ottepeli,* 239.

144. "Eksperiment vedet v budushchee," 1.

145. Motyl', "Za derzhavu."

146. Fomin, *Kinematograf ottepeli,* 241.

147. G. Chukhrai, "Chto 'kormit' kinostudiiu?" *Pravda,* 14 February 1986, 3.

Although the ETK was brought summarily to an end in February 1976, Goskino's decree sounding the death knell also seemed to endorse the studio's business model.[148] Linking the "size of the material rewards for film crews" with their observance of shooting schedules and budgets had achieved "significant results," it said, and it recommended that the leading figures in ETK be rewarded for having "fulfilled an important governmental task."[149] The studio had passed all its periodic governmental audits with high marks, and in 1973, Goskino had gone so far as to establish a special commission to develop plans for expanding the experiment to the entire Soviet film industry. One year later, the head of Mosfil'm declared that his entire studio would shift to ETK's model of self-financing. The February 1976 decree itself claimed that Goskino and Mosfil'm had studied the results of the experiment and were "developing new, specific principles of planning and organizing production, providing economic incentives and increasing workers' material self-interest in creating films of high ideoartistic quality." None of this came to pass.[150]

It is hard to know why there were these confusing signals, but it should come as no great surprise that the ETK model was allowed to die on the vine. Following its principles would have turned the entire film industry on its head—precisely the kind of fundamental change that all bureaucracies, and not only the Soviet, resist. Yet why snuff out the studio itself, which was, after all, highly profitable? Valerii Fomin, who has enjoyed unusually broad access to the Goskino archive, reported that there is no paper trail to follow about the decision to close the studio; the 1976 decree is not accompanied by the usual supporting documents. Fomin speculated that Yermash, the Goskino chairman, was personally behind the disbanding of ETK because its success made him, and the entire industry, look bad.[151] Chukhrai told an interviewer in 2001 that the decision had "come from above" [Yermash]. "It was axed with the rest of the Kosygin reforms."[152] In 1986, he offered a few vague comments about people who saw the ETK as "a reproach and a threat to their well-being"[153] and elaborated more fully in his post-Soviet memoirs: Goskino economists and film professionals had opposed

148. The ETK's death was drawn out via two 1976 decrees. The first (February) ended the experiment formally and reconstituted the experimenters as a regular Mosfil'm working group; the second (May) dissolved this new unit. Fomin, *Kinematograf ottepeli,* 245–248.

149. Ibid., 245–247.

150. We have some signs of possible ETK influence, however. According to one recent history, films that passed the 19 million mark in the seventies could be reevaluated for higher ratings. Arkus, *Noveishaia istoriia,* 5:125. Golovskoy, a former Goskino employee who emigrated to the United States in the eighties, concurred. Golovskoy, *Behind the Soviet Screen,* 74.

151. Fomin, *Kinematograf ottepeli,* 249.

152. "Partinyi bilet za premiiu Fellini," *Novye Izvestiia,* 13 November 2001.

153. Chukhrai, "Chto 'kormit.'"

the model. On one occasion, he said, he was called in to the CC offices to explain how it was that Leonid Gaidai had earned 18,000 rubles for a single film. Apparently they had been hearing complaints from other people in the film world.[154]

Garden-variety jealousy? Yes, but given the rules of the game, opposing the ETK was also nothing if not logical. It seems telling that the ranks of ETK directors were filled with two extremes: the very young (E. Klimov, L. Shepit'ko, A. Smirnov) and the very well established (Chukhrai himself, G. Daneliia, L. Gaidai, P. Todorovskii).[155] Few people were interested in taking up the challenge. If the entire industry were to shift to an ETK model for production, then most professionals in the film world would be cut from the studios' payrolls and forced to compete for contracts. If bonuses were tied to box-office receipts, then some people stood to live without bonuses. The Filmmakers' Union was always interested in increasing its powers (and directors' powers too); the sixties proposals, in the full flush of a reformist moment, can be seen in that light. But the union was less supportive of competition (in 1960 it opposed and defeated a plan to award productions on the basis of contests), and a sink-or-swim approach had little to recommend it.[156] By the 1970s, the costs of filmmaking had risen substantially, and the overwhelming majority of Soviet productions were receiving high ratings. Bonuses were solid and dependable, and cineastes had even more reason to shun the risks of competition.

The other obvious possible source of opposition to the ETK is ideological. Konchalovskii, who worked as a screenwriter for ETK, claimed the studio was "a nest of revisionism, a hotbed of samizdat [and] seditious ideas."[157] The real ETK had ended as early as 1968, he wrote, when "tanks drove through Prague, showing the whole world how experiments end up." That year the studio, which had been independent, was attached to Mosfil'm. Certainly the atmosphere and ethos of the ETK were unique. Chukhrai and Pozner welcomed young professionals with dubious political credentials, and the studio was known to champion controversial projects as well. The 1976 decree has an undeniable whiff of ideological dissatisfaction: it faulted the studio for failing to create "large-scale pictures on contemporary and historical-revolutionary themes"—the two favored thematic categories for Soviet cinema-art.[158]

It is possible, as Konchalovskii suggests, that the ETK was shut down as a breeding ground of subversion, but the truth seems more prosaic. The studio inspired jealousy and had few defenders, and in a system that had for generations

154. Chukhrai, *Moe kino,* 183–184. The film was the comedy *Ivan Vasil'evich meniaet professiu (Ivan Vasil'evich Changes Careers)*—third place at the box office in 1973 with 60.7 million tickets.

155. Fomin, *Kinematograf ottepeli,* 237.

156. See V. Fomin, "God 1960," published at http://www.film.ru/sk-news.

157. A. Konchalovskii, *Vozvyshaiushchii obman* (Moscow, 1999), 53.

158. Fomin, *Kinematograf ottepeli,* 246.

relied on relationships and barter, this meant a great deal. But most important of all, the ETK was, in context, superfluous. It is true that it was profitable, but so was Soviet cinema in big-picture terms—inefficient, yes, wasteful, no doubt, but what of it? With a box office of 4 billion tickets, the bureaucrats at Goskino and the CC could still crow to their bosses *and* their foreign counterparts about Soviet cinema's might.

Chukhrai always spoke of the ETK as a model for modernizing Soviet cinema. (In his memoirs, he stressed that its planning experts had designed evaluation techniques analogous to those used in the American space program!)[159] Yet in many ways, by the late sixties and certainly the seventies, Chukhrai, with his socialist idealism, was already an old-fashioned figure on the scene. The Soviet cinematic sphere modernized without him, if by modernization we mean its increased complexity, differentiation, and resemblance to cinemas in the capitalist West. The notion of resemblance may seem counterintuitive, given the expansion of Goskino-party control mechanisms in this period and the increasingly complex choreography of social, political, and bureaucratic factors that came with it. Control was plainly never in question; there was no samizdat movie circuit in the USSR. What we do see, nonetheless, is a steady segmentation of the Soviet cinematic sphere into high/low, elite/mass, art-house/mainstream zones, with different films, different audiences, and even different venues. This was one facet of the broad process of sociological modernization in the postwar USSR that brought people more free time, disposable income, and cultural resources, as well as more clearly delineated phases in the life–cycle, and that therefore facilitated a variety of choice.[160]

Audience segmentation was an ideological live wire few people were willing to touch in public, certainly not in the fifties and sixties. Art, by definition, transcended individual taste and experience, and cinema was the "most important of the arts." A film about a construction worker might well appeal to construction workers more than to sailors or students, but its artistry (its "truth" as Soviet writers often put it) lent it universal import. Chukhrai's own work, to his mind, was *mass* art, and that was his goal for the ETK films as well. He was a traditionalist in this sense. But in the seventies the realities of the cultural marketplace very clearly pointed to self-segmentation of the Soviet audience and divisions within the filmmaking community too. And to some extent, these divisions were pursued and promoted by regime policies.

Goskino's new chairman, Yermash, was a vigorous proponent of Soviet-made genre productions, or films with an entertainment orientation, and an open admirer of capitalist models; one director even recalled his screening Hollywood

159. Chukrai, *Moe kino,* 179.

160. The connection between lifestyle changes, social differentiation, and the development of Soviet cinema is developed in D. Dondurei, "Gumanizm zhanra," *Kinovedcheskie zapisi,* no. 11 (1991): 82–86.

pictures at meetings as an example for cineastes.[161] However, the new emphasis on genre was never designed to supplant goszakaz films with ideological heft, nor was it advanced as Soviet cinema-art's organizing principle and dominant face to the world. Some former cineastes even praise Yermash today for having appreciated the value of aesthetically challenging projects and for supporting their development within the parameters of ideological correctness (unlike, it is said, his predecessor, Romanov). "He did not care about whether an individual picture covered its costs, but he did worry about the profitability of the sector as a whole," explained one historian.[162] In genre, he saw a mechanism for maintaining the movie industry's bottom line.

The Yermash policy had undeniable successes. Melodrama was a main beneficiary, and its most famous example, *Moscow Does Not Believe in Tears* (*Moskva slezam ne verit*, 1979) a sweeping Soviet-style rags-to-riches romance, not only conquered the Soviet market, selling 84 million tickets for each of its two parts, but won the Academy Award for Best Foreign Picture to boot. Cineastes also tried their hand at large-scale action films and thrillers during his tenure, including *Pirates of the Twentieth Century* (*Piraty XX veka*, 1979), another two-part extravaganza that pitted Soviet sailors against opium smugglers in a gripping if inevitably uneven battle. (The good guys won.) At 88 million tickets, *Pirates* was the number one Soviet film of the Soviet era and came close to besting the USSR's absolute record holder, the Mexican *Yesenia*. Yermash presided over an era of blockbusters. The overall audience for cinema in the USSR was in fact shrinking—people were going less and less often—but there was also a greater number of hit pictures than ever before in the seventies.

Meanwhile, in small, often out-of-the-way cinemas, clubs, and special screenings, cognoscenti audiences were watching what in the West would be called "art house" films—and this, too, must be considered an essential feature of the Yermash era. Some of these pictures were foreign-made, and others were productions that Goskino had decided to bury on the market by limiting their distribution, but many were films no one, including Yermash, had ever expected to reach a mass audience: films made to speak to an elite that did not call itself an elite. They were "people with developed taste," "aesthetically educated people." This sector, made possible by the remarkable boom in the movie industry after Stalin's death, expanded in the Yermash era; as it did, it took on a more distinctive cultural identity. By promoting a more robust entertainment sector in the industry, the regime also authorized a more forthright cultural elitism. Segmentation was still a tricky concept ideologically; the unified mass audience remained the ideal. Nonetheless, some critics and filmmakers now referred to elite productions and audiences proudly. As one cineaste said in the

161. Arkus, *Noveishaia istoriia otechestvennogo kino,* vol. 6.
162. Ibid.

perestroika period, "[T]he very existence of the Soviet arts depends on the fact that we can idle away year after year and then ingeniously hit the nail on the head."[163] It was this idling and ingenuity that the rejection of an ETK model protected, and with it a whole way of thinking about films, filmmakers, and audiences.

The postwar Soviet film industry always operated with a business model that used entertainment-oriented cinema, foreign and Soviet-made, to fill the coffers. The shift in the seventies under Yermash was not fundamental: it was one of degree and, to certain extent, of frankness about the model itself. In the eyes of many historians and some former Soviet cineastes, "cynicism" would be the more operative term. There is a tendency in the literature to present the policies of the Yermash era as antiprogressive, even reactionary. Some say masscult imports and Soviet-made genre films "deformed" audience sensibilities ("the public taste in entertainment turned 'bourgeois,'" wrote one historian). Others describe the growing segmentation of mass-elite cinemas in terms of loss ("the "destruction of audience cohesion"). Yermash is accused of trying to "enforce an entertainment orientation on the film industry."[164] It is an argument that echoes voices from the era, when Goskino's support for blockbusters was resented in many quarters as an assault on the notion of cinema as an art and on the position of the artist in Soviet society. At the Filmmakers' Union congress in 1981, several people, including the screenwriter for *Moscow Does Not Believe in Tears,* referred to the "snobbery" of the cineaste establishment faced with so-called box-office (*kassovye*) films; others defended their right and their duty as Soviet artists to ignore the box office. Yermash told the assembled filmmakers that the "economic factor" was "one of the most important [factors]" in their work. "Figures reflect the importance and the role of cinema in the life of the people."[165]

And yet, even at its most frankly commercial moment under Yermash, the Soviet film industry did not go so far as to adopt the ETK model; though economic viability may now have been touted as one of the most important factors, bureaucrats and political elites, cineastes and viewers all had more pressing factors in mind. For this reason, Faraday characterized the Soviet industry as "nonrationalized" in financial terms.[166] But Soviet cinema had its own terms. Mosfil'm had three times as many cameramen on staff as there were jobs in the seventies.[167] They knew the terms when they picked up their pay packets every

163. Lawton, *Red Screen,* 388.

164. "Public taste turned 'bourgeois,'" Anna Lawton, *Kinoglasnost: Soviet Cinema in Our Time* (Cambridge, 1992), 9; "destruction of audience cohesion," Graffy, "Cinema," 183; "enforce an entertainment orientation," Faraday, *Revolt of the Filmmakers,* 90. See also Golovskoy, *Kinematograf 70-x,* 75–76.

165. *Chetvertyi s"ezd kinematografistov SSSR,* 179.

166. Faraday, *Revolt of the Filmmakers,* 66–70.

167. *Chetvertyi s"ezd kinematografistov SSSR,* 98.

week, as did cineastes who defended their duty to pursue Soviet cinema-art, regardless of costs or revenues. And as for redefining cinematic success under Brezhnev, they saw no need.[168]

SOVIET FILMS ON FOREIGN SCREENS: CINEMA-ART AND THE CULTURAL COLD WAR

If the contradictions of Soviet cinema-art bore fruit domestically—for cineastes and the industry, for bureaucrats, and even for audiences in this golden age of moviegoing—what about the international context? Dependent though they were on masscult, Soviet officials always promoted their cinematic system as a world apart and a model for emulation. The Soviet minister of culture launched Moscow's 1958 International Film Festival by declaring, "[T]he days of Hollywood's domination of the world market are coming to an end."[169] Soviet cinema-art would lead the way. Nine years later the Soviets inaugurated an international festival in Tashkent for film from the postcolonial world that further promoted the image of Soviet cinema-art as both anti-Hollywood and the antidote *to* Hollywood.[170]

Success on the international screen was central to Soviet cinema's identity, and from some angles it did cut an impressive figure. In the Khrushchev era, Soveksportfil'm expanded its operations substantially to field offices worldwide (in over 50 countries as of the sixties); where it had no official representation (such as in the United States), its agents brokered deals via intermediaries.[171] In 1967, to take one year, the USSR boasted film sales in 108 countries, for a total gross revenue of over 4.4 million rubles (roughly 2 million from sales to the socialist bloc, 2.4 to capitalist countries.)[172] Certain films sold very widely. By 1963, Grigorii Chukhrai's *Ballad of a Soldier* (*Ballada o soldate,* 1959) had sold in 93 countries and *The Cranes Are Flying* (*Letiat zhuravli,* 1958) in 88.[173]

Raw figures, however, are often misleading. One major film could weight the scales: the rights to *War and Peace,* for example, sold for US$1.3 million, a sizable chunk of the total revenue from capitalist-country sales in 1967.[174] More important, a sale did not necessarily translate into widespread distribution. *The*

168. On similar phenomena in literature, see Dirk Krechmar, *Politika i kul'tura pri Brezhneve, Andropove i Chernenko, 1970–1985 gg* (Moscow, 1997).

169. "US Film Rule Scored," *New York Times,* 3 August 1959.

170. Rajagopalan, *Leave Disco Dancer Alone!* 84–85; S. Chertok, *Tashkentskii festival'* (Tashkent, 1975).

171. Fomin, *Kinematograf ottepeli,* 379–386. The situation for trade with the People's Republic of China was exceptional. See Tina Mai Chen, "Internationalism and Cultural Experience: Soviet Films and Popular Chinese Understandings of the Future in the 1950s," *Cultural Critique* 58 (Fall 2004): 82–114.

172. RGALI, f. 2918, op. 5, d. 511, ll. 10–11.

173. Fomin, *Kinematograf ottepeli,* 381.

174. RGALI, f. 2918, op. 5, d. 511, l. 14.

Cranes Are Flying was one of the films the United States bought via a 1958 U.S.-Soviet exchange, and though it got good play on the university and art-house circuit, it never entered the cinematic mainstream. The number of Soviets who watched *The Magnificent Seven* dwarfed that of Americans who saw *Cranes,* and the same might be said in comparing Soviet audiences for *Les Misérables* (1958) and French audiences for Chukhrai's *Ballad.*[175] The Soviets chalked this up to ideological warfare—audiences in the West were being denied Soviet movies for political reasons—and they protested; in 1963, a senior Soviet official announced that the USSR would stop buying U.S. films unless the American side could guarantee wide distribution for Soviet films.[176] No boycott ever happened, and in the seventies Soveksportfil'm was still struggling to broker deals with U.S. firms that would ensure not just sales but exposure for Soviet films.[177] The Americans, for their part, argued that Soviet pictures did not perform well, and they were not alone. The Indians were also reluctant to take on Soviet films, especially after 1960, when distribution moved from a cultural exchange format, via friendship societies and clubs, to a commercial one.[178] Even fellow socialists were far from enthusiastic; in the early sixties film distribution agencies in the people's democracies were refusing over half the Soviet pictures on offer.[179] A Soviet delegation to Poland in the summer of 1962 was dismayed to find Krakow's theaters showing only five Soviet films, but twenty-five capitalist ones.[180] The only sector that appeared to be expanding for the Soviets in the 1960s and '70s was the postcolonial one—Asia, Africa, Latin America, and the Middle East—but here too, despite Soviet attentions, the United States held an overwhelming advantage.[181]

The USSR lost the cultural Cold War in cinema in blockbuster fashion: the gap between Soviet cinema's reach and Hollywood's was colossal. It is true that in comparison with Western European countries and Japan, the USSR was very successful in protecting and developing its *domestic* industry. The Soviets, of course, did not see themselves as playing in the same league with anyone else

175. *Les Misérables* with Jean Gabin sold 46 million tickets in 1961. RGALI, f. 2329, op. 13, d. 138. On U.S.-Soviet film exchanges, see Yale Richmond, *US-Soviet Cultural Exchanges, 1958–1986* (Westview, CO, 1987), 65.

176. "Moscow to Halt US Film Imports," *New York Times,* 2 March 1963; I. Bol'shakov, "Sovetskie fil'my na ekranakh mira," *IK,* no. 9 (1959); Y. Vorontsov and I. Rachuk, *The Phenomenon of Soviet Cinema* (Moscow, 1980), 369–388.

177. See, for example, transcripts of negotiations between Soveksportfil'm and representatives of different U.S. film companies in 1973. RGALI, f. 2908, op. 7, d. 162, ll. 8–10, 13–15.

178. See Rajagopalan, *Leave Disco Dancer Alone!* chap. 2.

179. Fomin, *Kinematograf ottepeli,* 383.

180. Poland's cineastes had even more reason to be concerned: there were only two Polish movies on Krakow's screens! TsDAHOU, f. 1, op. 71, d. 261, ll. 6–21.

181. For Goskino concerns about Chinese cinema as a rising competitor in the developing world, see RGALI, f. 2981, op. 5, d. 283, ll. 81–89.

when it came to cinema for reasons of ideological superiority. But they also understood their innate material advantages: the Soviets were right not to compare themselves to, say, France, which, given its size, had little hope of supporting a large-scale, capital-intensive production and distribution operation along the lines of the Americans. (India, although it had both raw size and an extensive industry, lacked the capital.) The USSR was the only major industrialized country in the world with a domestic market big enough to drive an industry to rival Hollywood in its global reach. Arguably, the Union of Soviet Socialist Republics, a multiethnic, multilingual state, was in as good a position as the United States, and possibly a better one, to develop a cinema culture that could speak to a diverse global audience as well.[182]

The Soviets were always vociferous critics of Hollywood's bullying of the international movie marketplace, and for good reason. Yet as many critics also pointed out over the years, the USSR's export troubles had deep domestic roots. Soviet cinema was an industry that identified itself as an art but operated like a craft; it had a handmade quality that hindered its international competitiveness. As Hollywood and other cinemas went to color and wide-screen films, the Soviets lagged behind. More than that, they suffered baseline problems with equipment of all kinds. The production values in Soviet films often fell far short of international standards, and this was something cineastes talked about openly. Reform proposals from the Filmmakers' Union in the sixties flatly stated that Soviet films were not competitive on the world market because of their inferior production values. Film-stock quality was the most glaring issue. It was a problem universally acknowledged, repeatedly studied, and never solved.[183] The film industry also lacked adequate facilities for subtitling and dubbing films and so wound up spending hard currency for the services of foreign companies or, more often, doing without.

On the organizational side too, as we know, Soviet cinema suffered fundamental problems. An industry that missed its domestic production deadlines missed the international ones, too.[184] Indian film distributors complained about the lack of professionalism at Soveksportfil'm as agents dallied in selecting films

182. For an argument about Hollywood's competitive advantage internationally (including the question of the ethnic composition of the United States) and its relationship to the establishment of American "cultural hegemony" in Europe, see Victoria de Grazia, *Irresistible Empire: America's Advance Through Twentieth-Century Europe* (Cambridge, MA, 2005). For a different interpretation of the American challenge to European national cinemas, see Pierre Sorlin, *European Cinemas, European Societies, 1939–1990* (New York, 1991).

183. Soviet cinema suffered from the transfer of its industrial base to the Ministry of Defense Industries in the Khrushchev era. Yermash waged a successful campaign to change this in the 1970s and also had plans (never fulfilled) to buy a Kodak factory outright. Arkus, *Noveishaia istoriia,* 4:123–126.

184. RGANI, f. 5, op. 55, d. 51, ll. 638–666, 39–49.

and returned them damaged.[185] The Soviets also faced persistent rumors—well founded, as it turns out—that they illegally copied films sent to Moscow for consideration.[186] Many foreign cineastes who knew of the Soviets' high-handed attitude to intellectual property rights were reluctant to do business with them. Polish film officials complained to a visiting delegation in 1962 that the materials they got from Soveksportfil'm were of such poor quality that they could not use them to advertise Soviet pictures.[187] Similar problems hampered efforts to propagandize Soviet cinema through noncommercial (diplomatic and educational) channels. Though the only film projector bus in all of West Africa in the early sixties was indeed imported from the USSR, it sat rusting in a Soviet embassy compound in Senegal for years: the embassy claimed it had no money to operate it, and the State Committee for Cultural Relations with Foreign Countries refused to let it be presented as a gift to the Senegalese government.[188]

The other crucial question in Soviet cinema's fate on the world market was, of course, whether audiences wanted what it had to offer. The Soviet answer was always framed in terms of artistic and ideological caliber, as was true in evaluations of the domestic scene. The standard line was that Soviet films failed when they lacked depth and failed to take on important issues in contemporary life. I. Bol'shakov, the USSR deputy minister of foreign trade, fleshed out the portrait of failure for *The Art of Cinema* (*Iskusstvo kino*) in 1959: "[T]here are a lot of unnecessary details of everyday life [in these films]," he wrote, "and romantic troubles which do not touch the viewer, lots of little songs, dubious witticisms, and lightweight, openly entertaining scenes."[189] It is a formula that sounds rather promising from the point of view of genre, or entertainment-oriented, cinema. And of the films Bol'shakov listed that fit this bill—films therefore unfit for international distribution, in his view—a good number were crowd-pleasers on the USSR domestic market: for example, the spy drama *Case No. 306* (*Delo no. 306*), second place at the box office in 1956 with 33 million tickets, and *Girl with a Guitar* (*Devushka s gitaroi*), a musical comedy that sold 32 million three years later.

185. Rajagopalan, "Taste for Indian Films," 146–147.

186. Socialist bloc countries were also rumored to have copied capitalist films illegally and sold them to the Soviets. Philip Caputo, "The Soviets Veto the Hollywood Filmmakers' Box-Office Blockbusters," *Chicago Tribune,* 21 August 1977. Films sent for festivals were also illegally copied. This is how *Easy Rider* (1969), a noncompetition festival film in Moscow in 1971, entered the dacha circuit. "Director of Soviet Film Festival Rules Out the Publicity Seekers," *New York Times,* 21 July 1971; Stephen Solnick, *Stealing the State: Control and Collapse in Soviet Institutions* (Cambridge, MA, 1998), 97.

187. TsDAHOU, f. 1, op. 71, d. 261, ll. 6–21.

188. Sergey Mazov, "Soviet Policy in West Africa: An Episode of the Cold War, 1956–1964," in *Africa in Russia, Russia in Africa: Three Centuries of Encounters,* ed. M. Matusevich (Trenton, 2007), 303–304.

189. Bol'shakov, "Sovetskie fil'my na ekranakh mira," 123–124.

Soviet taste consistently fell within the international mainstream. Soviet hits, in theory, could be international ones too.

The USSR did market some domestic hits successfully—*Amphibian Man,* for instance. But bringing girls with guitars and amphibian men to the international viewer was never the ideal, as Bol'shakov made clear. And, more to the point perhaps, the Soviet film industry had few of these films to market anyway. Soviet cinema as a world cinema could not contravene the realities of domestic production—the great gray block of movies that few people cared to watch and the small clutch of films like *Ivan's Childhood* that, however important from an artistic point of view, also failed to attract mass audiences. Soviet cinema-art did not fare well on the open international market because it did not meet international standards for cinema entertainment. Surely it was galling that, as export officials reported to the CC in 1963, "we were unable to sell a single film at the Cannes Film Festival." It was unacceptable that even socialist countries turned up their noses at Soviet productions.[190] But the standards of the international market were not Soviet standards; they were, critics sneered, masscult in nature, cut from Hollywood's cloth. Soviet cinema-art doggedly sought refuge in its own values and sense of superiority.

As a strategy this had definite pluses: it provided a ready explanation for failure, and it played well for a time to pro-communist, and anti-anti-communist, elites. In the West, the fascination with the post-Stalinist USSR faded, and in the seventies in particular, intelligentsias set their sights on other sources of revolutionary chic (including, significantly, the cinema of the Soviet avant-garde of the twenties).[191] Tarkovskii and a few others remained influential, but in the eyes of fellow auteurs in the West, they looked more and more like exceptions to a rule of Soviet banality—a rule only confirmed by the Yermash-era run of homegrown genre hits. The influence of the Soviet cinematic model among educated elites in the postcolonial world developed somewhat later, and the USSR worked hard to promote it through material interventions such as the Moscow and Tashkent international film festivals. VGIK and other Soviet institutions also trained aspiring cineastes and contributed to the development of new, national cinemas. Despite the many problems of the Soviets' export business, audiences for Soviet films gathered in many postcolonial urban centers. The critic Kirill Razgolov maintained that "in a significant part of the world, primarily the 'developing' world, the doctrine was: the worst Soviet film is better than the most perfect Western one."[192]

190. Fomin, *Kinematograf ottepeli,* 383.
191. This was especially true of France in the aftermath of May 1968. For a brief discussion, see Richard Taylor and Ian Christie, eds., *The Film Factory: Russian and Soviet Cinema in Documents, 1896–1939* (London, 1994), 11–13.
192. Kirill Razlogov, "Vyvozu ne podlezhit," *IK,* no. 7 (2006): 64–70.

This may have been true, but we must recognize that in the postcolonial sphere, as in the West, the audience that preferred Soviet cinema to its capitalist rival was by and large an educated, elite audience. This is not to say that Soviet pictures never performed well internationally but rather that they consistently and dramatically performed worse than the Soviet model's sense of itself as world leader, and that this was important. At home, Soviet cinema made room for an elite/mass split in practice: it could accommodate a definition of cinematic success that relied on exploiting theoretically noxious or inferior productions (foreign and Soviet) to satisfy audiences while giving cineastes salaries and the all-important idling time for art. Internationally, however, in open market conditions, Soviet cinema had no way to implement this strategy, no way to fudge its business model and define its own way to success. Not only was the Soviet Union a net importer of cinematic imagery from its ideological archnemesis, masscult, but Soviet cinema, which defined itself as the world's leading cinema, was patently peripheral on the world screen. This was one contradiction that simply could never bear fruit.

THE NEW SOVIET MOVIE CULTURE

Soviet cinema-art was a particular kind of ideological construct, and at its heart was a particular model of a Soviet audience. It was, by definition, a gigantic audience, ceaselessly expanding, and unanimous in its appreciation for the work of Soviet cineastes. Each of these characteristics was essential. The size of the audience—not millions of tickets but *billions*—was living proof of Soviet cinema's success. And because film in the USSR was defined as art, a huge audience further demonstrated the cultural level of its people and their fundamental unity.[1]

Soviet cinema's model audience was forged in the 1930s, when *Pravda* had declared, "The Whole Country Is Watching *Chapaev!*" and in fact entire factories, military brigades, schools, and offices marched off to watch the 1934 civil-war drama en masse, as they did for other films instantly dubbed "classics" by the authorities. All Soviet viewers returned to these classics again and again, it was said, not only for recreation but also for inspiration and education, for *heroes*.[2]

The Soviet film world, bureaucrats and cineastes alike, invoked Soviet cinema's canon throughout the entire postwar period. *Chapaev,* especially, was summoned up as a symbol of unity—the unity of politics and art, of filmmakers and viewers, of the audience itself—and as a model for emulation. Yet in villages, towns, and cities across the postwar USSR, Soviet cinematic culture presented a rather different picture. Most obviously, if the whole country was watching anything in the years after World War II, it was likely to be the trophy film *Tarzan* or the first Soviet blockbuster, *Amphibian Man,* Bollywood's *Love in Simla* or the Soviet adventure story *Pirates of the Twentieth Century*—that

---

1. Cf. Stephen Lovell on Soviet book culture, *The Russian Reading Revolution: Print Culture in the Soviet and Post-Soviet Eras* (London, 2000).

2. On Chapaev and the canon, see Richard Taylor and Ian Christie, eds. *The Film Factory: Russian and Soviet Cinema in Documents, 1896–1939* (London, 1994), 334, 358–363; Richard Taylor, "Ideology as Mass Entertainment: Boris Shumyatsky and Soviet Cinema in the 1930s," in *Inside the Film Factory,* ed. Richard Taylor and Ian Christie (London, 1994), 211–213; Maya Turovskaya, "The Tastes of Soviet Moviegoers," in *Late Soviet Culture: From Perestroika to Novostroika,* ed. Thomas Lahusen and Gene Kuperman (Durham, NC, 1993), 95–107.

is, entertainment-oriented productions that violated nearly every standard for artistry, and most notions of heroic education, on Soviet cinema's books. But more than that, the very notion of the whole country united by any mass cinematic experience was increasingly outmoded in the media age. As everyday life was transformed in the post-Stalinist fifties, sixties, and seventies, cinema changed, too—both its sociology and its cultural footprint outside the movie theater. The reality and the ideology of the Soviet audience were very plainly diverging.

Compare the experience of cinema in the USSR in, say, 1965 with that of 1935. On average, every Soviet person went to the movies around twenty times a year in the sixties and under five times a year in the thirties; in the sixties, viewers could choose among well over one hundred new domestic productions and roughly the same number of imports; in the thirties, the selection was a quarter that size at best and nearly 100 percent Soviet. This explosion in choices was one factor enabling audiences to segment themselves as never before. Equally important, the culture *around* the movies—what I will call "movie culture"—in 1965 was a world away from what had been available to audiences in earlier decades. By the sixties, people in the USSR had many ways to engage with cinema outside the theater, from books and print journalism to movie-related merchandise like postcards and calendars to lectures, festivals, and TV and radio programming. Though most of these things had existed in some form in earlier decades, their scale had been incomparably smaller, and in the postwar forties and early fifties Soviet movie culture had nearly ground to a halt.[3] The USSR had only one regular publication about cinema in Stalin's final years, the monthly journal for professionals, *The Art of Cinema* (*Iskusstvo kino*).[4] There were no film clubs, no festivals, and no major delegations of foreign cineastes. The entire weight of film promotion bore down on the handful of Soviet productions selected for praise and reward.[5]

The fifties through the seventies represented a sea change in the Soviet cinematic experience. Not only did the culture around the movies revive and then grow to unprecedented dimensions, but in a new political environment, at home and abroad, and with the major sociological shifts and technological advances of the postwar era, this culture was transformed. Never before had people in the USSR enjoyed such large quantities of free time and disposable income to engage with cinema; never before had there been so many options

3. On the lively, diverse movie culture of the 1920s, see Denise Youngblood, *Movies for the Masses: Popular Cinema and Soviet Society in the 1920s* (New York, 1992), 23–24, 52–53.

4. The journal had a print run of roughly fifty thousand from the sixties until the Soviet collapse.

5. For late Stalinist cinematic publicity, see I. Makarova, *Blagodarenia* (Moscow, 1998).

at the theater, around it, and in the home. The Soviets' new media-age movie culture was not simply more expansive than anything that had preceded it; it was polyvalent and far more personal, and it facilitated an approach to cinema very much at odds with traditional Soviet values. Principally, the new movie culture helped develop consumerist attitudes among audiences and a culture of "stars" and "fans" that sidelined the traditional notion of Soviet heroism. While cinema had a strict functionality, according to the ideological play-book—modeling, educating, inspiring—the new Soviet movie culture opened cinema up to do many other things. Or, more to the point, the new culture opened doors for people across the USSR to do many other things *with cinema* as a cultural experience.

The changes afoot were especially evident among young people, the critical audience sector in the USSR not only in ideological terms (as young viewers were widely considered both more vulnerable to subversion and more recep-tive to education) but in sheer mass: the majority of the Soviet filmgoing public was under the age of thirty. Young people's taste for entertainment-oriented fare drove the Soviet market, yet many contemporary observers found their choices dismaying, if not alarming. For a cultural model that cast cinema in the role of great teacher, the popularity of films from outside the socialist orbit—and espe-cially films from the enemy camp, masscult—raised obvious questions. But so, too, did the situation with homegrown cinema.

The number one box-office draw for 1965 was a Soviet slapstick comedy called *Operation 'y' and Other Adventures of Shurik (Operatsiia 'y' i drugie prikliucheniia Shurika)*, whose "heroes" reveled in irresponsible drinking and petty crime.[6] "It should be perfectly clear to all of us that we cannot solve the problem of the people's moral education with this kind of film," said a 1969 Komsomol report on the state of youth cinema.[7] The auditor (a cineaste) was right on his own terms: *Operation 'y'* had little to offer in the way of worthy role models. What is more, although many Soviet films did fulfill this function, there was good reason to doubt that young audiences knew how to distinguish them in the crowd and, trickier still, that they were choosing their cinematic fare for the right reasons,

6. The film, directed by Leonid Gaidai, is a triptych of shorts, two featuring Georgii Vitsyn, Iurii Nikulin, and Evgenii Morgunov, popularly known as "ViNiMor," who special-ized in physical comedy and crude humor, often revolving around alcohol and petty crime. ViNiMor starred in other Gaidai films, all hits, and some post-Soviet commentators have read them as a subtly subversive commentary on Soviet society. Reviewers at the time cri-tiqued them for crudity and frivolity. For more recent discussions see Alexander Prokho-rov, "Cinema of Attractions versus Narrative Cinema: Leonid Gaidai's Comedies and Eldar Riazanov's Satires of the 1960s," *Slavic Review* 62, no. 3 (2003): 455–462; Elena Stishova, "Oblomok velikoi imperii," *Nezavisimaia gazeta,* 23 April 1998; Stanislav Rassadin, "Star-odum," *Novaia Gazeta,* 6 March 2000; Iurii Gladil'shchikov, "Balbes i Nebalbes," *Itogi,* 21 January 1997.

7. RGASPI-m, f. 1, op. 34, d. 352, l. 53.

leading to the right outcomes. *State Criminal* (*Gosudarstvennyi prestupnik*), a thoroughly correct KGB drama, was near the top of the box-office charts in 1965 as well, but as it also featured the star of *Operation 'y,'* Aleksandr Dem'ianenko, its popularity could raise questions. What if viewers flocking to the theaters were there to see *him* and not the admirable KGB-man he played? What if the messenger was outshining the message?

The question was more than academic, given the millions of fans then snatching up postcards with actors' images and thronging public appearances. Sociologists found that Soviet viewers were more likely to choose a film based on the participation of their favorite *actors* than on its subject matter, what critics said about it, or any other factor; the youth audience appeared to be particularly actor-oriented.[8] Sociologists also reported that young people were *least* likely among all age groups to favor Soviet-made pictures with young heroes targeted to youth audiences and most likely to choose foreign (nonsocialist) productions.[9] Some research suggested that young viewers were confused about or indifferent to the heroism concept generally. "All of them, and none in particular" was one sixteen-year-old's reply when asked to name his favorite screen hero. Other young respondents simply refused to answer.[10]

Nothing about cinema as a cultural medium dictates the existence of a culture around the movies, a movie culture, and certainly not a wide-ranging, personality-driven one. A movie culture is a matter of choices. And as was the case in other spheres of Soviet culture in the media age, these choices went forward because they made sense (personal, financial, social, political) to various people and institutions. Choices made cinema both a great success story for Soviet culture and, in many ways, its most thoroughly compromised ideological sphere.

A GOLDEN AGE OF MOVIEGOING

The 1950s through the 1970s were the golden age of Soviet moviegoing, and the essence of the golden age was expansion: more films, more theaters, more viewers, and for these viewers, more free time to go to the movies and options to engage in other ways. Never before and never again would such a large proportion of the population go to the cinema with such frequency. The peak years were 1968 and 1980, when annual movie ticket sales across the Soviet Union averaged out to nearly twenty per person. But the rates were nearly as high for

---

8. I. Lukshin, "Problemy reklamnoi informatsii i ee effektivnost'," in *Sotsiologicheskie issledovaniia kinematografa,* ed. I. A. Rachuk (Moscow, 1971), 94; L. N. Kogan, ed., *Kino i zritel': Opyt sotsiologicheskogo issledovaniia* (Moscow, 1968), 127–128; I. Levshina, *Liubite li vy kino?* (Moscow, 1978), 50–51.

9. Kogan, *Kino i zritel',* 180.

10. V. Volkov, "'Esli by chelovechestvo sostoialo iz Gusevykh,'" *Molodoi kommunist,* no. 3 (1965): 124. See also V. Volkov, "Vlianie kinogeroia," *Iskusstvo kino* [hereafter *IK*], no. 11 (1968): 63.

the entire period; by 1960, the Union average was already seventeen tickets per year. Only a decade before, it had been just six.[11]

Let us set aside for a moment the many regional and other variations masked by national averages: these figures translated into an enormous moviegoing public, and it was one made possible by major regime investments after the Second World War in the infrastructure for cinema. Soviet figures on film installations (*kinoustanovki*) included everything from the mobile units hauled by projectionists from village to village to small theaters in clubs and schools to movie houses and palaces of culture. In part because of the massive destruction wrought by war, the USSR faced a serious shortage of screens of all kinds when compared with other industrialized countries.[12] Agricultural regions were, as always, the most poorly served, but large urban areas were also left wanting. Minsk, for example, capital of the Belorussian republic with a population of about five hundred thousand, still had only one movie theater in 1955. Even Moscow was underserved: with its scant forty-nine theaters, or five seats for every thousand residents, the Soviet capital could not compare with New York (eighty seats per thousand) or London (one hundred seats per thousand)—facts underscored by the Ministry of Culture in a report lobbying for theater construction in 1955.[13] Rapid urbanization meant that theaters and clubs in Soviet cities were frequently unable to keep up with demand, at least for popular movies. Many urban venues in the mid-fifties had increased their number of daily shows from three to eight or more and were still failing to seat all potential viewers.[14]

But if in 1943, the vast USSR had fewer than 11,000 film installations of any kind, ten years later, the number stood at well over 50,000, and by the mid-sixties nearly 150,000.[15] Villages saw the biggest gains, not only in raw numbers (roughly four-fifths of the total) but in the overall improvement of their facilities.[16] Though the itinerant projectionist remained a familiar figure well into the seventies, stationary projectors were increasingly the norm, and by 1975, for the first time in Soviet history, the figures for film attendance in rural and urban areas equalized

11. M. Zhabskii, *Kino: Prokat, reklama, metodika, praktika* (Moscow, 1982), 16; I. Levshina, "Film idet k zriteliu," *Pravda*, 27 March 1967; D. Dondurei, ed. *Otechestvennyi kinematograf: Strategiia vyzhivaniia: Nauchnyi doklad* (Moscow, 1991), 22.

12. On pre–World War II limitations, see Jamie Miller, "Soviet Cinema, 1929–1941: The Development of Industry and Infrastructure," *Europe-Asia Studies* 58, no. 1 (January 2006): 103–124.

13. Cited in V. Fomin, *Kinematograf ottepeli: Dokumenty i svidetel'stva* (Moscow, 1996), 70.

14. "S tochki zreniia kinoprokata," *IK*, no. 10 (1956): 30.

15. The 1943 level was only two-thirds the prewar total. G. N. Goriunova, *Ekonomika kinematografii* (Moscow, 1975), 25, 28, 33.

16. Ticket prices were also lowered in 1954. On rural viewership in the fifties, see Mariia Zenzina, "Kinoprokat i massovyi zritel' v gody 'ottepeli,'" in *Istoriia strany, istoriia kino*, ed. S. S. Sekirinskii (Moscow, 2004), 401.

Figure 2.1. A movie theater palace in Krasnodar, 1967. ITAR-TASS. Used with permission.

at eighteen per year. In the Russian Republic, attendance in villages was actually higher on average than in urban centers as early as 1968.[17]

The postwar era was the heyday in the Soviet Union of the grand theater palace; most new theaters were far smaller, but the "thousander" (*tysiachnik*) was the gold standard of Soviet moviegoing in its golden age. A guide to the Moscow movie world published in 1969 listed theater after theater, either under construction or recently completed, with a thousand seats or more.[18] Many thousanders were multipurpose halls, like the Kremlin Palace of Congresses (six thousand-plus seats), Leningrad's Oktiabrskii, and Kiev's Ukraina (four thousand each).[19] Massive venues matched the ideal type of a mass Soviet audience united by experience and taste. Mass-scale building was also inextricably bound up with Soviet film distribution policies. As one official explained the system in a 1966 roundtable for *The Art of Cinema,* economic planners evaluated a film's performance based on box-office figures for the large urban movie theaters. There were roughly four thousand of them, and they accounted for 75 percent of the gross receipts for all urban movie screenings, which in turn comprised 75 percent

17. Z. G. Kutorga, ed., *Kino i zritel': Problemy sotsiologii kino* (Moscow, 1978), 50, 53.

18. M. Beliavskii and K. Andreev, *Moskva kinematograficheskaia* (Moscow, 1969), 121. Moscow added sixty-nine new movie houses in the period 1955–69.

19. B. A. Miasoedov, Strana chitaet, slushaet, smotrit (Moscow, 1982), 75; Zenzina, "Kinoprokat i massovyi zritel'," 400.

of gross receipts for the USSR as a whole. In order for a film to be considered successful in the distribution system, it had to be capable of filling these large-scale theaters consistently. Standards varied: one version had it that urban theaters had to sell 70–96 percent of their seats for all shows to meet their plans;[20] another set the level at 85–90 percent;[21] a third said Moscow theaters had to fill one-half of their seats, while regional houses were required to fill three-quarters of theirs.[22]

Critics of the system at the time depicted a hair-trigger response mechanism on the local level: the moment ticket sales for a film dropped below a set point, distribution officials and theater managers would replace it with another film—usually, but not always, a masscult production. In truth, this seems a highly unlikely scenario given what we know about the sluggishness of the planned economy as a whole. But critics insisted that Soviet cinema was a victim of relentless discrimination. Were it not for certain irresponsible figures, audiences would have the good Soviet cinema they needed and deserved. There were even hints of conspiracy. A 1965 The Art of Cinema article on the "secrets of success" pointed to the decisions, made "in semi-secrecy," of local officials.

The film Three Musketeers was imposed on viewers in the city of Vladimir—and now we know how it was done. 522,000 people watched it. A record. But this was the result of the activities of the film distribution office, and it does not represent the artistic demands of Vladimir's viewers. They watched what they were most often shown.[23]

The party set the tone for these complaints with its pronouncements on cinema repertoire in the late fifties and sixties. It, too, pointed fingers at the local level, and scapegoating, or blaming aberrant individuals and "commercial considerations" for systemic ills, is a pattern we will see many times in this book.[24] More realistic observers of the Soviet scene acknowledged that the very presence of masscult films was thanks to decisions made centrally, not locally, as was the structure of incentives around their use. They also recognized that audiences did not in fact agree to watch whatever was on offer (more on this below) and suggested replacing the mass-distribution system with a multidimensional one, making room for successful runs of small films and blockbusters alike.

In effect, what these Soviet critics were proposing was a form of audience segmentation—targeting different films to different audiences in smaller venues.

20. "Kak vziat' ot fil'ma bol'she?" IK, no. 7 (1966): 9.

21. I. Levshina, "Fil'm idet k zriteliu," Pravda, 27 March 1967.

22. N. Lebedev, "Fil'm i zritel'," IK, no. 6 (1964): 47.

23. Ia. L'vov, "Izuchaia sekrety uspekha," IK, no. 2 (1965): 90. The film was probably the 1961 French production Les trios mousquetaires: La vengeance de Milady.

24. See E. S. Afanas'eva et al., Ideologicheskie komissii TsK KPSS 1958–1964: Dokumenty (Moscow, 1998), 186–189, 257–262.

It was a technique Hollywood had embraced more than a decade before as the golden age of moviegoing ended in the United States, and giant movie palaces went empty. For Soviet critics, the apposite example was not Hollywood but Eastern Europe. A 1967 article in *Pravda,* for example, recommended that Soviet planners follow the lead of their Polish and Czechoslovak colleagues, who had designed special networks of smaller movie theaters for "films of high intellectual-artistic value, but not high operational [*ekspluatatsionnye*] value." In a nod to the concerns about cinema's financial health, *Pravda* assured readers that these Czech and Polish theaters were able to meet their plans for 70–90 percent attendance and turn profits.[25]

The Soviet Union never fully embraced this kind of audience segmentation despite sporadic official signals in that direction: the ideal of the unified, mass audience remained intact as a powerful marker of the anti-masscult approach to culture. The post-Stalinist boom gave audiences unprecedented opportunities to segment themselves, but it is important to recognize, too, that Soviet social realities had never matched the ideal: film consumption in the USSR was always a socially stratified activity. Urban/rural was the fundamental split, in cinema as in so many arenas of Soviet life. A world of difference separated an urban theater from a kolkhoz clubhouse or an al fresco movie night organized by a traveling projectionist. Although viewers in the countryside may not have had to wait on line for tickets, they stood a very good chance of waiting months, or even years, for new releases, only to find that the film copy they got was so worn out as to be nearly unwatchable. In Soviet cities, the downtown areas typically had more theaters, and more modern ones, than the outskirts. And the gulf dividing ordinary clubs and theaters from the world of special screenings was even wider.

Members of the top political elite watched movies in the comfort of their own homes, typically on weekends in their state dachas. The dacha circuit was the highest level of film consumption in the USSR, the cinematic "first circle," and like all film consumption, it expanded its scope greatly in the post-Stalinist period. Nami Mikoian (daughter-in-law of Soviet leader Anastas Mikoian) recalled that during summer holidays, her family and friends watched movies nearly every evening.[26] In the next circle there were special screenings organized by professional organizations—the Filmmakers' Union, the Writers' Union, the Academy of Sciences, and many other groups. Every major newspaper in Moscow had regular screenings of new films for its staff.[27] Although theoretically these were closed-door events, unaffiliated viewers gained admission to many of them through social networks and scalping. David Gurevich, a twenty-something film buff living in Moscow in the seventies, wrote that in his experience, the crowd

25. Levshina, "Fil'm idet k zritel'iu." Levshina also recommended the Polish example at the 1966 conference on distribution discussed below. RGALI, f. 2936, op. 4, d. 1308, l. 28.
26. Nami Mikoian, *Svoimi glazami* (Moscow, 2003), 173.
27. E. Riazanov, *Ne podvedennye itogi* (Moscow, 2000), 89.

at the Filmmakers' Union screenings consisted exclusively of "store managers, hairdressers, maitre d's—whoever filmmakers owed favors to." Films at special screenings needed no advertisement. Gurevich recalled trying to buy a ticket to *Last Tango in Paris* (1972): "[N]o one I knew had seen it, really, although someone knew a guy who had seen it in Hungary—well, a cut version.... But the rumors promised that you would leave the theater a new person—a complete spiritual rebirth."[28] Moscow was the best place to be if you were a film buff like Gurevich, but there were options in other cities, and patterns of access were much the same. A member of the Uzbek Central Committee staff or the Belorussian Writers' Union—or someone connected to him—was still in a better position to slake a cinematic hunger than most mortals on the streets of Tashkent or Minsk. Film clubs, too, flourished in the post-Stalinist era, and they were an important venue for limited-distribution films, foreign and Soviet, and instrumental in the growth of audience segmentation. A viewer from Saratov recalled that as a young woman in the Brezhnev era, she went exclusively to clubs, which showed "complicated, sophisticated films, not for ordinary viewers." They were "like food for us movie lovers," she said. "There was a lecture before each film. They chewed it for us, placed it in our mouths, and we only had to swallow."[29]

To say that cinema was popular in the Soviet Union is to state the obvious and yet to miss something even more obvious: it was moviegoing itself that was popular, for cinema was a vital form of Soviet sociability for everyone from nomenklatura wives to shop managers to rural teenagers.[30] The *Chicago Tribune's* James Sullivan reported that the atmosphere at one suburban Moscow theater in 1966 reminded him of Russian neighborhoods he had known in Chicago in the thirties. It was a matinee, and people had come early with their children and grandchildren to wait on line for tickets and enjoy cheap beer and sausage sandwiches before the show.[31] Urban theaters usually had a buffet in the lobby and sometimes an exhibit. The 1969 guide to Moscow's movie scene mentioned a photo exhibit called "The Image of Lenin on Screen" as an example, but content was not always so serious; very often exhibits focused on actors.[32] One film historian recalled that she and her childhood friends had made a sport

28. David Gurevich, *From Lenin to Lennon: A Memoir of Russia in the Sixties* (New York, 1991), 219–220.

29. Quoted in Donald J. Raleigh, ed. *Russia's Sputnik Generation: Soviet Baby Boomers Talk about Their Lives* (Bloomington, 2006), 207–208.

30. On the distinction between the popularity of movie-going and that of film(s) in the '30s, see Maya Turovskaya, "The Tastes of Soviet Moviegoers," in Thomas Lahusen with Gene Kuperman, eds., *Late Soviet Culture: From Perestroika to Novostroika* (Durham, 1993), 95–96.

31. James Sullivan, "Russ Enjoy Good Laugh, Even at Selves," *Chicago Tribune*, 3 June 1966.

32. Beliavskii and Andreev, *Moskva kinematograficheskaia*, 35.

Figure 2.2. Crowds at Moscow's Udarnik Theater, 1963. ITAR-TASS. Used with permission.

of stealing actors' photos on display at their local cinema.[33] In larger, more up-scale venues you might find a musical ensemble playing before the show. Many theaters hosted clubs: people went to their local cinema for, say, "chess nights" on Tuesdays.[34] Although it was not Soviet practice to offer a multipart program ("B" movie, "A" feature, and short films—the classic pattern in the United States and Western Europe in their cinematic golden ages), movie theaters did screen newsreels and sometimes cartoons.[35] Tickets were relatively cheap—25 or 30 kopecks on average (30 to 40 in the seventies), less for the undesirable seats and

33. D. Dondurei, ed., *Otechestvennoe kino: Strategiia vyzhivaniia* (Moscow, 1991), 70. This was in the thirties, but the actors' photo exhibitions were popular in later decades too.

34. Beliavskii and Andreev, *Moskva kinematograficheskaia*, 121.

35. Common newsreels included: *News of the Day* (*Novosti dnia*), *Foreign Newsreel* (*Inos-trannaia kinokhronika*), *Soviet Sport* (*Sovetskii sport*), *Pioneer World* (*Pioneriia*), *Soviet Serviceman* (*Sovetskii voin*), and *Around the USSR* (*Po SSSR*). The Soviets showed some interest in multipart presentations in the sixties, just as they were growing outmoded in

in humbler venues. It was not unusual for people in the golden age to go to the movies several times a week.

In small towns and cities, cinema was a major social event. The thousander theaters brought together huge crowds for films, and when the weather permitted, many places also had mass screenings in parks and football stadiums. This is how a quarter of a million people managed to watch the American *Roman Holiday* in a single Moscow summer (1960), including 30,000 in a single weekend.[36] Imagine thousands of people pouring out of the subway, lining up at the stadium entrance ways, and sitting in the stands. Imagine the hubbub in Karatau, Kazakhstan, when a local theater sold 14,000 tickets to Bollywood's *Ganga Jamuna* over a three-day period. With only 310 seats in the house, theater managers must have been running nearly round-the-clock screenings, as they often did.[37]

Cinema was also the mainstay of workers' clubs' cultural programming, and clubs were for many people the only places to meet outside work, home, and street. A brick factory worker described a typical situation in a 1958 letter to Goskino. His local club in Kaluga Province screened twenty films or more per month, and it was "so packed, they have to turn people away at the door." With no theaters in the region and the lone television just "sitting around" in one administrator's office or another, he said, people did not just love cinema—they depended on it. Many would go to see the same picture two and three times.[38] Even in the seventies a movie screening was an event in villages across the USSR. "In kolkhozes in richer parts of Central Asia," wrote one journalist, "the highlight of the summer was the arrival of the mobile projector-van and the rigging of the outdoor screen with its ear-splitting loudspeakers."[39] Georgii Daneliia's 1977 film *Mimino* shows cinema delivered by helicopter to a remote area in the Caucasus Mountains. The film is an Indian melodrama (as parodied by Daneliia); the audience watches by starlight, enraptured.

In any discussion of the Soviet audience, we must keep in mind the demographics of the USSR: about three-quarters of all cinema tickets were sold in the two most populous republics, the RSFSR and Ukraine.[40] Access was also very important. The Russian Republic had not only the largest population but the largest number of theaters per capita and the Union's most active moviegoers. The

———

the West. See Pierre Sorlin, *European Cinemas, European Societies, 1939–1990* (New York, 1991), 84–85.

36. *Roman Holiday* (1953; Soviet release 1960). Afanas'eva, *Ideologicheskie komissii,* 260; Osgood Caruthers, "30,000 in Moscow Warm to U.S. Film," *New York Times,* 22 March 1960.

37. *Ganga Jamuna* (1961; Soviet release 1965). Levshina, *Liubite li vy kino?* 62–63.

38. RGALI, f. 2329, op. 12, d. 75, l. 20.

39. Monica Whitlock, *Land beyond the River: The Untold Story of Central Asia* (London, 2002), 102.

40. Kutorga, *Kino i zritel',* 52.

density of theaters in Armenia was about half that of Latvia around 1960, and people in Armenia went to the movies about half as often as their counterparts in Latvia.[41] One sociologist in the seventies outlined four "zones" in the USSR for moviegoing behavior. The first zone, with the highest rates of attendance per capita, was the RSFSR and Kazakhstan; the second, Ukraine; the third, Latvia, Lithuania, Estonia, Belorussia, Turkmenistan, and Kyrgyzstan; and the fourth, Uzbekistan, Tadzhikistan, Georgia, Armenia, and Azerbaijan. The difference between the top of the list and the bottom was very wide—about ten trips to the cinema per capita per year in the seventies.[42]

Beyond simple access, gender and ethnicity also had an influence on moviegoing behavior, although given the very limited data on these questions, it is difficult to draw firm conclusions. According to one study from 1981, men and women were represented in equal numbers in the movie audience; given the large gender gap in the Soviet population (nearly 20 million more women than men), this would indicate that men were the more active moviegoers overall. The same study noted that the Union-wide figure could mask important ethnic differences: in Baku, for instance, the audience was over 60 percent male, whereas in areas of majority Russian ethnicity, levels of attendance balanced equally by gender. A special CC investigation in 1964 into the state of cinema propaganda in Azerbaijan found that, outside the larger cities, women in the republic seldom went to film screenings at all.[43]

The most important factor in moviegoing behavior across the board, though, was age. Precisely how young the Soviet audience was is difficult to say. The common estimate was that youth comprised 50 percent of the total viewing population, but some estimates ran even higher: *The Art of Cinema* in 1967 claimed that three-quarters of all visitors to movie theaters were "young."[44] "Youth" could mean under the age of twenty, as in a 1966 Komsomol report,[45] or under thirty, as in the Baku research cited above.[46] One study from 1978 claimed that schoolchildren bought over half of all tickets sold.[47]

41. *Narodnoe khoziaistvo SSSR v 1970 g.* (Moscow, 1971), 9, 676–677. See also Goriunova, *Ekonomika kinematografii*, 35.

42. Zones with the most active moviegoers prior to 1968 saw the fastest rates of decline afterward. Kutorga, *Kino i zritel'*, 52.

43. RGANI, f. 5, op. 55, d. 112, l. 28. Even in the eighties a Soviet journalist traveling in Tadzhikistan reported seeing almost no women in cinemas. V. Ivanova, *V zhizni i v kino* (Moscow, 1988), 63–64.

44. See "Ideal—na zemle," *IK*, no. 8 (1967): 27.

45. RGASPI-m, f. 1, op. 34, d. 1, l. 106.

46. Another seventies study (which put the youth audience at 57 percent) also used the under-thirty definition. Kutorga, *Kino i zritel'* (Moscow, 1978), 36.

47. Levshina in 1978 claimed that schoolchildren bought 2.5 billion of a total 4.7 billion movie tickets sold annually. Levshina, *Liubite li vy kino?* 29.

The dominance of young people corresponds with what we know about viewership patterns in the 1920s, the last period when sociological research was sanctioned in the USSR.[48] The youth audience in the post-Stalinist era was a teeming horde by comparison, though. One half the annual box office in the USSR amounted to 2 *billion* tickets. The youth market was also a thriving phenomenon in places that prior to 1950 had few if any theaters to speak of. Researchers working in the Urals region in the mid-sixties found that young people (in this case, those in their late teens and early twenties) went to the movies on average fifty to sixty times a year.[49] In the 1920s, it was only the young people of Moscow and a few other major cities who had an easy, everyday relationship with cinema of this kind, and this was still the case in the thirties. After the war and especially in the 1960s, cinema became broadly accessible, and moviegoing as a youth social activity became a different animal.

Urbanization was one crucial factor, and the mass expansion in education after World War II also meant an unprecedented number of Soviet young people outside the employment sector with free time to go to the movies. Young childless adults, another key segment of the audience, had more leisure time, too, as the regime reduced official working hours in these years. Finally, and especially important, the Soviet regime had chosen to make the large-scale investments in cinema's infrastructure we have seen and to fund and promote a powerful new Soviet movie culture.

The golden age of moviegoing gave Soviet viewers unprecedented scope to make bad choices from an ideological point of view—to choose the wrong movies for the wrong reasons. Yet bad choices were still choices, a luxury in the context of recent history. We might argue that this was simply the cost of doing business: that the Soviets achieved their golden age only fifteen years after the devastation of World War II was a significant achievement and a propaganda coup in the cultural Cold War as well. But then again, we might ask, if bad choices were the cost of doing business, what business was post-Stalinist Soviet cinema in? In other words, what was to become of the ideological model—cinema, the most important of the arts and the factory of heroic Soviet dreams—in a brave new world of (relative) postwar abundance?

POPULARITY AND THE SOVIET MARKET
By the 1960s, the Soviet film industry was producing well over one hundred new features per year, and the Soviet population was consuming cinema as never before. Yet we know most domestic pictures were not broadly popular: the performance gap between average productions and hits was very wide. Let us

48. Studies in the 1920s found that 45 percent of viewers were ten to fifteen years old. Youngblood, *Movies for the Masses,* 26.
49. Kogan, *Kino i zritel',* 180

Table 2.1. The Soviet Cinematic Hit Parade, 1955–1980

Year	Title	Studio	Genre	Ticket sales (millions)[a]
1955	Soldat Ivan Brovkin (Soldier Ivan Brovkin)	Gor'kii	Comedy	40
1956	Karnaval'naia noch' (Carnival Night)	Mosfil'm	Musical comedy	46
1957	Tikhii Don (And Quiet Flows the Don)	Gor'kii	Historical-revolutionary epic	47
1958	Nad Tissoi (Over the Tisza)	Mosfil'm	Spy drama	46
1959	Ch. P. (An Extraordinary Event)	Dovzhenko	Military adventure	48
1960	Prostaia istoriia (A Simple Story)	Gor'kii	Melodrama	47
1961	Polosatyi reis (Striped Voyage)	Lenfil'm	Comedy	46
1962	Chelovek-amfibiia (Amphibian Man)	Lenfil'm	Fantasy	66
1963	Optimisticheskaia tragediia (Optimistic Tragedy)	Mosfil'm	Civil war epic	46
1964	Zhivye i mertvye (The Living and the Dead), parts 1 and 2	Mosfil'm	World War II epic	Part 1: 42, part 2: 40
1965	Operatsiia "y" (Operation "y")	Mosfil'm	Comedy	70
1966	Voina i mir (War and Peace), part 1	Mosfil'm	Historical epic	58
1967	Kavkazskaia plennitsa (Prisoner of the Caucasus)	Mosfil'm	Comedy	77
1968	Shchit i mech (Shield and Sword), parts 1–4	Mosfil'm	Spy–World War II drama	68, 66, 47, 47 (parts 1–4, respectively)
1969	Brilliantovaia ruka (The Diamond Hand)	Mosfil'm	Comedy	77

Year	Title	Studio	Genre	
1970	Osvobozhdenie (Liberation)	Mosfil'm w/ DEFA (GDR), PRF'ZF (Poland)/ De Laurentis Studio (Italy)	World War II epic	56
1971	Ofitsery (Officers)	Gor'kii	World War II melodrama	53
1972	Dzhentel'meny udachi (Gentlemen of Fortune)	Mosfil'm	Comedy	65
1973[b]	A zori zdes' tikhie (Dawns are Quiet Here)	Gor'kii	World War II melodrama	66
	Vsadnik bez golovy (The Headless Horseman)	Lenfil'm	Adventure	69
1974	Kalina krasnaia (The Red Snowball Tree)	Mosfil'm	Melodrama	63
1975	Afoniia (Afonia)	Mosfil'm	Comedy	62
1976	Tabor ukhodit v nebo (Queen of the Gypsies)	Mosfil'm	Drama (gypsy)	65
1977	Nesovershennoletnye (Adolescents)	Gor'kii	Melodrama	45
1978	Sluzhebnyi roman (An Office Romance)	Mosfil'm	Comedy-melodrama	58
1979	Zhenshchina, kotoraia poet (The Woman Who Sings)	Mosfil'm	Musical melodrama	55
1980	Piraty XX veka (Pirates of the 20th Century)	Gor'kii	Adventure	88

Sources: http://www.nashekino.ru/ and the related publication *Domashnaia sinemateka: Otechestvennoe kino, 1918–1996* (Moscow, 1996); Sergei Kudriavtsev, "Lidery otechestvennogo kinoprokata," http://mega.km.ru/cinema/.

[a] Figures are rounded to the nearest million.

[b] Records for the number of tickets sold differ.

consider the all-Union "hit parade"—the most popular Soviet-made films for the years 1955 through 1980 (see table 2.1).[50]

Box-office performance is no science, as any Hollywood executive with his or her head on the block might tell us. In the Soviet case, we would also want comprehensive data on foreign films' performance in order to parse popularity, as well as republican (regional, city etc.) breakdowns in ticket sales. But even if we limit ourselves to the all-Union level, understanding what worked in the Soviet market means coming to terms with Soviet-specific market forces. Films were not on equal footing. And putting aside the special case of goszakaz filmmaking with its extraordinary advantages, the single most important aspect to consider in a film's performance was its geographic origin.

The Soviet hit parade was almost 100 percent Russian. The USSR was a multilingual, multiethnic state; Soviet cinema as a market (as opposed to an art form) was not. All the republics produced feature films, and some of them were box-office leaders on their home territory. But it was rare for a non-Russian production to win large audiences on the all-Union screen. Of the top seventy-five films for the entire Soviet period, only four were produced outside Moscow and Leningrad: the 1959 hit *An Extraordinary Event* (*Ch. P.* [*Chrezvychainoe proisshestvie*]) from Ukraine's Dovzhenko studio, two films from the Sverdlovsk studio (*Strong of Spirit—Sil'nye dukhom*—a war-adventure film from 1968, and *Trembita,* a comedy, from 1969), and a 1980 Uzbek-Indian coproduction, *The Adventures of Ali-Baba and the Forty Thieves* (*Prikliucheniia Ali-Baby i soroka razboinikov*).

How to explain this curious imbalance? After all, although the bulk of the moviegoing population did reside in the Russian and Ukrainian republics, not all were ethnically Russian or Ukrainian (nor native speakers of those languages). Besides, Russians, Ukrainians, and all the other peoples of the USSR showed tremendous interest in imported cinema; foreignness per se was not an issue for Soviet audience reception. What was to prevent an Estonian or Georgian production from taking the all-Union screen by storm?

Certainly many of the problems that hobbled the Soviet film industry's performance on the international market operated on the domestic scene as well. (Dubbing, for example, though not an issue for Soviet viewers, was a perennial problem for the industry.) But ideology was an even more important factor. With Russian designated as the lingua franca of the Soviet Union, the "second native language" of all non-Russians (to use Khrushchev's

---

50. Unless otherwise specified, all box-office statistics in this chapter are derived from the website Nashe kino, http://www.nashekino.ru/, and the related publication *Domashnaia sinemateka: Otechestvennoe kino, 1918–1996* (Moscow, 1996), and from Sergei Kudriavtsev, "Lidery otechestvennogo kinoprokata," http://mega.km.ru/cinema/.

formulation from the Twenty-second Party Congress in 1961),[51] non-Russian-language films were disadvantaged by design. In Ukraine, directors often shot their productions in Russian even when they were set in Ukrainian-speaking areas and starred Ukrainian-speaking actors; the films were then sometimes dubbed into Ukrainian—sometimes, but not always, much to the chagrin of many viewers in their republic of origin. The same was true in all the other republics.

Success on the all-Union screen spoke Russian, but more than that, it was channeled through Russia and *marked* Russian. "The national cinemas of the Union republics have not tended toward isolation or autonomy," crowed a 1979 textbook, "but on the contrary, toward the greatest merging [*sblizhenie*] among themselves and with the first among equals—Russian cinema."[52] The largest studios in the Union were in Moscow and Leningrad, as were the greatest re-sources, the best-connected power brokers of the cinematic world, and the all-Union media. Films from the republican studios seldom enjoyed the same print runs, distribution, and critical attention as productions from the two Russian capitals.[53] Moreover, republican films rarely benefited from the participation of actors with Union-wide reputations. Sociologists studying moviegoing behavior in the sixties and seventies found that Soviet viewers chose films largely on the basis of their attraction to particular actors, and many viewers paid attention to where the picture had been made (foreign or Soviet and if Soviet, which studio) as well. For republican studios, and republican actors interested in working in their home regions, this amounted to a vicious circle: actors grew famous and popular by starring in movies that succeeded on the all-Union screen; movies that succeeded on the all-Union screen almost always featured famous actors. Nearly all the films on the hit parade fell into this category, and many featured all-star casts. As a rule, the films of the hit parade were also large-scale produc-tions, hard to mount and beyond the scope of most republican studios. (For the earlier years, when most films were still shot in black and white, many were also color productions.) The perception of film officials in Moscow and, one suspects, in the republics, too, was that *all* audiences preferred Mosfil'm/Lenfil'm/Gor'kii studio productions and would not be interested in films made outside their republics.[54]

51. See Isabelle T. Kreindler, "Soviet Language Planning since 1953," in *Language Plan-ning in the Soviet Union,* ed. Michael Kirkwood (London, 1989), 46–63; Bohdan Kraw-chenko, *Social Change and National Consciousness in Ukraine* (New York, 1985).

52. R. Iurenev, *Kratkaia istoriia sovetskogo kino* (Moscow, 1979), 213.

53. Republican studio productions were also less likely to be promoted for export. See Gonul Donmez-Colin, ed., *Cinemas of the Other: A Personal Journey from the Middle East and Central Asia* (Bristol, UK, 2006), 201.

54. V. Troianovskii, ed., *Kinematograf ottepeli: Kniga vtoraia* (Moscow, 2002), 334.

It is clear that the deck was stacked against productions from the republics. Very few non-Russian pictures broke through, and those that did played a Russian hand. To take but one example, the Armenian studio's biggest hit in the Soviet era was the 1965 production *Emergency Mission* (*Chrezvychainoe poruchenie*), which sold about 31 million tickets in the USSR (300,000 in Armenia). The film featured a Georgian-born Armenian actor who lived in Moscow, Gurgen Tonuts, and a predominantly Russian cast, including a genuine star of Stalin-era cinema, the Ukrainian-born Boris Chirkov. The subject of the film was an episode in the life of the Armenian Bolshevik S. A. Ter-Petrosian. The language was Russian.[55]

Still, while certain productions on the Soviet market had the odds fixed in their favor, even this was not always decisive. Soviet cinema had its unexpected duds and surprise hits as well. Part 1 of *War and Peace* did top the charts in 1966, but its fourth and final segment sold fewer than 20 million tickets one year later—all in all, a rout for a film of its pedigree. Comedy was a neglected genre: there were always far fewer comedies on the market than other types of films. And yet perhaps the first thing that jumps off the hit parade list for the 1960s is the strong presence of comedy, with four out of ten films (and three of them made by the same man, director Leonid Gaidai). Military and espionage-themed films sat at the opposite end of the spectrum: they had an outsized weight in Soviet cinematic production overall. But even favored status cannot fully account for the huge success of a film like *Shield and Sword* (which, incidentally, inspired a young Vladimir Putin to offer his services to the KGB. Soviet cinema's hero-production model in action!)[56] Movies about World War II and spy themes were a dime a dozen, but few among them won impressive audiences.

The other thing that stands out clearly on the hit parade is the absence of works from the Soviet cinematic canon. Soviet critics and post-Soviet historians typically present a very different roster for important films from the era: not Gaidai but Grigorii Chukhrai and Andrei Tarkovskii, not *The Woman Who Sings* but *The Cranes Are Flying* (1957) and *The Color of Pomegranates* (1970). Some films on the Soviet hit parade did win awards at domestic and international film festivals. And some films identified by critics and historians as artistically important also won sizable audiences in the USSR, particularly in the Khrushchev era. *The Cranes Are Flying,* one of the most well known of postwar Soviet productions in the West, was in tenth place in ticket sales in 1957, with just over 28 million sold. But by and large, audiences in the USSR demonstrated a clear preference for genre filmmaking, or a cinema of entertainment.

When queried by sociologists in the sixties and seventies, Soviet viewers consistently identified their favorite genres as comedy, adventure, and melodrama,

55. K. Kalantar and E. Manukian, eds., *Armeniia kinematograficheskaia* (Yerevan, 1971), 41.

56. N. Gevorkian, A. Kolesnikov, and N. Timakova, *Ot pervogo litsa: Razgovory s Vladmirom Putinym* (Moscow, 2000), 24.

for both foreign and domestic productions. Sociologists also discovered that people would report choosing to see movies they thought were of poor quality. A group of high school students, for instance, when asked to name which films they thought "spread *poshlost'*" (banality), cited the very ones they also said they had already seen multiple times, including the French comedy *Fantômas*.[57] Similarly, research in Estonia found that movies with the highest rates of attendance, all Estonian productions, also received the *lowest* scores for quality from viewers.[58] When asked which films were the most worthy, many people identified the serious, important works endorsed in the media. Viewers knew what they were supposed to like, but that did not change their behavior. It was a phenomenon that journalist Marguerite Higgins noted while traveling in 1954: everyone she met derided the *Tarzan* trophy films, yet everyone had seen them.[59]

Indian imports were often identified as the "wrong" sort for viewers, and since they were by some measures the most successful of all foreign pictures in the Soviet market, they merit special attention. In cinematic circles, the idea that it was viewers from central Asia and the Caucasus who drove the Soviet market for Indian (and Middle Eastern) cinema was a commonplace. Soviet media tended to avoid the issue, stressing audience unity, but it did come up in various meetings where film policy was discussed and invariably criticized. At a 1957 Komsomol plenary session, an official from Azerbaijan expressed concern that many young people in the republic were better acquainted with Indian culture than with "the cultural achievements and interesting customs and traditions of the people of the Union republics."[60] (This is particularly interesting since 1957 was but a few short years after Indian film first landed on Soviet shores.)[61] When central Asian–Caucasian taste came up at a special 1966 Filmmakers' Union conference on distribution, it was as the butt of jokes—at least according to one speaker, I. Levshina, who took a rare position in its defense.

> We laughed to ourselves [earlier]: "Look how poorly they [distribution officials] are doing their jobs in the Caucasus." But really this isn't true. There are some things we don't want to understand. But we have to understand that

---

57. L. Furikov, "Zritel'skie otsenki kak pokazyvatel' osobennosti vospriatie film'ov iiunoi auditoriei," in *Sotsiologicheskie issledovaniia kinematografa,* ed. B. P. Dolynina (Moscow, 1973), 87–88.

58. K. Ianulaitis and E. Zelentsov, "Otsenka fil'mov zritelei i ego khudozhestvennyi vkus," in Rachuk, *Sotsiologicheskie issledovaniia kinematografa,* 81.

59. Marguerite Higgins, *Red Plush and Black Bread* (New York, 1955), 184. Also Harrison Salisbury, "Russia Re-viewed: Life of Soviet Common Man Is a Constant Struggle," *New York Times,* 25 September 1954.

60. RGASPI-m, f. 1, op. 2, d. 356, l. 161.

61. Indian films were shown in theaters in 1949 and 1951, but the big moment was a 1954 Indian film festival in Moscow, which sold millions of tickets and received broad media coverage across the USSR. Rajagopalan, *Leave Disco Dancer Alone!* 13–17.

the moral-political unity of our peoples does not in any way imply the unity of their aesthetic reception. Indian films are like native films for the Caucasus. They are related people, and Indian music, Indian ways of thinking—they're native, one's own [*rodnoe, svoe*].... Why should we hide these films from them?[62]

Without good comparative data, it is difficult to put the claims about central Asian and Caucasian audiences in perspective. A special CC investigation in 1964 found large audiences for Indian and Middle Eastern films in these regions, and anecdotal evidence points in the same direction. One journalist working in post-Soviet central Asia identified people who had grown up there in the Brezhnev era as "Shri children." "For millions of Tajiiks and Uzbeks, the 1970s are captured by the mingled sensation of ice-cream, sunflower seeds, and Raj Kapoor, superstar of the Bombay screen, belting out numbers from *Samgan* and *Shri 420* on a hot, black night," she wrote. "The ability to sing the showstoppers all the way through in Hindi without understanding the words became and remained a characteristic of the Central Asian Brezhnev generation."[63] Yet the CC's investigators found that in central Asia and the Caucasus audiences for movies from commercial European cinemas were as big as, or bigger than, those for Indian films. In Georgia, 53 percent of the population watched the French adventure film *The Three Musketeers* in 1963, and only 28 percent saw the Indian *Love in Simla*. (The canonical *Ballad of a Soldier*? 6.3 percent.) In Azerbaijan, the Indian and the French picture ran neck and neck.[64]

In the nineties, historian Sudha Rajagopalan conducted in-depth interviews with around fifty people in the former USSR, Russian and non-Russian, about their experiences with Indian cinema. Several of her non-Russian subjects commented on the films' special importance to them: an Armenian man recalled that the first Indian film he saw made a great impression on him because it was the first time he had seen leading actors on the screen who he thought looked like him; a Tadzhik viewer said he thought Indian movie music was popular in his region because it sounded familiar to people there.[65] Rajagopalan herself, however, did not single out any population in her analysis of Indian cinema's popularity in the USSR. (She also met plenty of Russians in Moscow eager to sing Hindi showstoppers for her.) With their exoticism and fairy-tale qualities, black-and-white morality, focus on family relations, and straight-laced yet swooning romance, Rajagopalan found that Indian movies appealed to a broad swath of the Soviet public.

---

62. RGALI, f. 2936, op. 4, d. 1308, ll. 17–18.
63. Whitlock, *Land beyond the River*, 102.
64. RGANI f. 5, op. 55, d. 112, l. 18, 30.
65. Sudha Rajagopalan, *A Taste for Indian Films: Negotiating Cultural Boundaries in Post-Stalinist Soviet Society* (PhD diss., Indiana University, 2005), chap. 1.

Statistics on the all-Union level bear this out. *Love in Simla* sold well over 30 million tickets in 1963, and only about 1 million of them were in Azerbaijan, with perhaps the same number in Georgia.[66] Even if every Azerbaijani and Georgian (Tadzhik, Armenian, etc.) living *outside* the region had bought a ticket to *Love in Simla,* it would not have accounted for the film's success. Millions of Russians, Ukrainians, and people of all ethnicities in the USSR were flocking to Indian and Middle Eastern films. Central Asia and the Caucasus were easy targets to scapegoat for perceived bad taste: they were regions with large rural populations (the natural habitat of cultural rubes everywhere, in the eyes of urbanites), and in the Soviet context they were also condescended to as regions with "exotic" and "colorful" local cultures that presumably drew them closer to people in the developing world. No doubt Levshina was right: some people in these regions did identify Indian and Middle Eastern films as "their own," and it is possible that they drew larger crowds proportionate to the population there than in other regions. But the popularity of Indian and Middle Eastern cinema was a Union-wide phenomenon, as was that of masscult like *The Three Musketeers* and the rare Soviet successes in genre movie-making like *Amphibian Man* and *Queen of the Gypsies.*

Several film scholars have situated Soviet cinematic taste in a continuum with prerevolutionary Russian cultural traditions. Neia Zorkaia, for example, connected popular cinema with *lubok* prints—cheap popular illustrations depicting fairy tales, historical figures, bandits, and other folkloric types. In Soviet (and post-Soviet) cinema, she argued, the key to a film's success was the presence of the "*lubok* element" (*ferment lubochnosti*), characterized by "utmost simplicity" and reliance on "easily identifiable image-archetypes," romance, humor, and unambiguous endings.[67] The kind of Indian cinema shown in the USSR (a subset of Indian production overall) fit this generic description quite well, as did the large majority of the films in the Soviet-made hit parade for 1955–80; most were productions offering straightforward rather than subtle narratives, lovable heroes and detestable villains, clear beginnings, middles, and ends.[68] Film distribution officials rarely published their opinions, but when they did, they offered a matter-of-fact assessment of popular taste: "Some people think that the best advertisement for a film is when the press says bad things about it.... [Our] audiences

---

66. Rajagopalan, *Leave Disco Dancer Alone!* 182.

67. Neia Zorkaia, "Sovetskii kinoteatr, ili chto tam bylo na samom dele v proshlye gody," *IK,* no. 11 (1995): 123. See also her *Fol'klor, Lubok, Ekran* (Moscow, 1994); Valerii Fomin, *Pravda skazki: Kino i traditsii fol'klora* (Moscow, 2001).

68. After the first few years of importation, when more self-consciously "artistic" cinema prevailed, the Indian films shown in the USSR were almost entirely Bollywood genre productions. Rajagopalan, *Leave Disco Dancer Alone!* 1. See also Zorkaia, "Sovetskii kinoteatr," 121.

happily go to purely entertaining, so to speak, 'lightweight'...pictures," wrote one in 1956.[69]

In its broad outlines, this portrait of Soviet cinematic taste correlates well with what we know about audience behavior in the teens and twenties, when the cinematic market was comparatively open and viewers thumbed their noses at the avant-garde. It also shows important continuities with the Stalinist era. Although audiences had little choice in the thirties and forties, certain films rose to the top of the heap, and they were not, as a rule, the artistically challenging works; they were genre productions stylistically, either Soviet-made or, after World War II, Western European and American productions (the trophy films). Critic Maya Turovskaya dubbed this the Soviet audience's "alternative taste" and argued that it was both broadly consistent across the decades and quite similar to that of audiences in other parts of the world. (In this, she saw a sign of viewers' "normalcy.")[70] The golden age of moviegoing and the new Soviet movie culture did not alter the basic pattern of audience taste. What they offered were many new opportunities to express that taste both in the theater and around it.

THE PROBLEM OF POPULAR TASTE: WHO IS TO BLAME?

Turovskaya's term "alternative taste" was one she coined after the Soviet collapse. In Soviet times, she explained, professionals in the film world spoke simply of "bad taste"—when they spoke of such issues at all. Turovskaya's colleague Zorkaia recalled:

> There was no sphere in Soviet cinema more closed off, hoodwinked, entangled in lies, forgery, illusions, blindness, stupidity, no sphere more vigilantly guarded and censored than film distribution [prokat], the relationship between cinema and Soviet viewers in the movie theaters. Take it from someone who was there, truly! It was easier to get through a line saying that Tarkovskii was a good director and a patriot...than to hint that viewers loved entertaining films, for example, Indian films.... For the authorities, you became a propagandist for ideological emptiness; for the elite, you became an agent of poshlost', a toady, and an enemy of the creative quest.[71]

It was imperative to assert that bad taste did not exist on a mass scale. "I do not believe that in our country only eleven million people wanted to watch *Tales of Lenin* [*Rasskazy o Lenine*, 1957], that is...six times fewer people than *Amphibian Man*!" fumed one critic in *The Art of Cinema*. "This cannot be!"[72] Bad

---

69. S. Trofimov, "S tochki zreniia kinoprokata," *IK*, no. 10 (1956): 27.

70. Maya Turovskaya, "The 1930s and 1940s: Cinema in Context," in *Stalinism and Soviet Cinema,* ed. Richard Taylor and Derek Spring (London, 1992), 49; Turovskaya, "The Tastes of Soviet Moviegoers," 105.

71. Zorkaia, "Sovetskii kinoteatr," 119.

72. Lebedev, "Fil'm i zritel'," 47.

taste could then be blamed on other factors: faulty distribution policies, venal local officials, and the immaturity of certain sectors of the viewing public (with young people, peasants, central Asians and Caucasians, and old women the usual suspects).

Readers of *Soviet Screen* (*Sovetskii ekran*), the USSR's main movie magazine, were well informed about the problem of bad taste from educational articles in which critics undertook to explain why, say, *Amphibian Man* was a rotten movie and harmful to their aesthetic development. Some viewers wrote in to express their solidarity with critics. A teacher from Moscow described her horror that "normal, good people" were charmed by Indian and Arab films. Her friends, she said, thought she was putting on airs when she talked about what she liked. "How should one act in this situation?" she asked. "How does one kindle in others a longing for beauty, for truth, for art? It really seems to me that the only method for educating taste is the ban [*zapret*]."[73] Other viewers wrote in to argue with critics and dispute their cultural authority. S. Rassadin, the man who had dared to pan *Amphibian Man,* later published an article quoting from the mountain of irate letters (around six hundred) he had received: "Your task is to reflect the opinions of viewers like a mirror," wrote one man. "But you write your own petty little opinions [*otsebiatinu*]!"[74] Aleksandr Lipkov criticized a Raj Kapoor film and heard worse: "Eh, if I got my hands on that Lipkov, I would slit his throat (excuse the vulgarity)."[75]

Although the existence of widely varying opinions in the enormous Soviet audience is not surprising, their presence on the pages of the leading Soviet movie magazine was one important sign of the changing cultural milieu.[76] Some consumers grew more daring in expressing their unorthodox taste, and the new movie culture was far more open to them, even if, as was almost always the case, the context for its expression was belittling by critics (i.e., bad taste was there to prove a point). Beginning in the 1960s, sociological research also provided important new information about audience behavior that contradicted the Soviet ideal type. Boris Firsov, himself a pioneering sociologist, remarked in 2001 that the main intellectual innovation of the new research was to show "that the cultural 'consumer' was a subject, and not the passive 'recipient,' of

---

73. "Odna problema—tri mneniia," *Sovetskii ekran* [hereafter *SE*], no. 10 (1966): 8.

74. S. Rasssadin, "Stoit li perezhivat'?" *SE*, no. 11 (1965): 13; S. Rassadin, "Krasota ili krasivost'?," *SE*, no. 5 (1962): 7; S. Rassadin, "Starodum: Mylo 'Elit,'" *Novaia gazeta-ponedel'nik,* 25 May 1998.

75. Aleksandr Lipkov, *Indiiskoe kino: Sekret uspekha* (Moscow, 1990), 6.

76. For a different approach to the development of taste communities in the Khrushchev era, see Susan E. Reid, "Destalinization and Taste, 1953–1963," *Journal of Design History* 10, no. 2 (1997): 177–207; Susan E. Reid, "In the Name of the People: The Manège Affair Revisited," *Kritika* 6, no. 4 (Fall 2005): 673–716.

cultural communication."[77] *Soviet Screen* readers who talked back to critics in their letters would surely have agreed.

Yet the buoyancy of popular bad taste was not something many filmmakers, critics, or cultural bureaucrats thought worth investigating, and even sociologists with a professional interest in the topic often betrayed their frustration with viewers. Sociologists of cinema were, in any event, few in number and circumscribed in their approach. It is significant—and telling—that culture was a low-status field in Soviet sociology; far more emphasis was placed on studies of labor and the working class.[78] As a result, the Soviets on the whole had a rudimentary understanding of cinema's audience (and skipping ahead, we might say the same for radio and television audiences). The broad outlines were established but little more. Even the parameters of ideology's idée fixe, the youth audience, were not well defined. Film scholars of postwar Western Europe tell us that the Italians favored family melodramas, whereas the British preferred comedy, and they also analyze patterns relating to ethnicity, class, gender, region, generation, and many other factors.[79] A Soviet Union of over 200 million people had many audiences, and it is precisely in this period that viewers first had the opportunity to segment themselves to a marked degree. But the framing of popular taste as bad taste in the USSR set in place a dynamic that blocked analysis and substituted stereotypes, scapegoats, and, in many quarters, defensiveness and paranoia. It really *was* true that Soviet theaters sold only 11 million tickets to *Tales of Lenin,* whereas 66 million went for *Amphibian Man* and 44 million for *Some Like It Hot.* The Soviet cinematic establishment managed this as a marketplace reality and, to some extent, as a sociological one, by condescending to viewers. Soviet cinema depended on both these realities—the first to fund the film industry, the second to project its elite status and tutelary role.[80] Ideologically, however, popular taste was indigestible and to some people, like the Moscow schoolteacher, quite troubling. Who was to blame?

The most glaring issue for a cinematic system tasked with providing role models, especially for young people, was the phenomenal success of foreign commercial imports. The limited protest directed toward trophy films in Stalin's final days was echoed and amplified many times as the USSR opened its doors to an increasing number of new foreign productions after his death. Most new imports

---

77. B. M. Firsov, *Istoriia sovetskoi sotsiologii 1950–1980-x godov* (St. Petersburg, 2001), 150.

78. See L. Kogan's comments in G. S. Batygin, ed., *Rossiskaia sotsiologiia shestidesiatykh godov v vospominaniiakh i dokumentakh* (St. Petersburg, 1999), 280–300. The main centers for the sociology of cinema were Sverdlovsk and the Baltic states.

79. Sorlin, *European Cinemas, European Societies,* 99–110.

80. Compare Reid on taste and status in "In the Name of the People." Like Reid's visual artists, Soviet filmmakers and critics did not enjoy stable cultural capital: their claims to status via superior knowledge were often challenged.

were socialist bloc in origin, yet Soviet media consistently devoted the lion's share of their attention to a handful of films from the capitalist world. They became bywords for the perils of what critics and officials termed "bourgeois cultural infiltration." Early in the sixties the chief bogeyman was *The Magnificent Seven*, an American Western linked in Soviet accounts to the growing problem of juvenile delinquency. The head of the Komsomol, Sergei Pavlov, informed Khrushchev in a 1962 letter that Soviet children had been forming gangs of seven in imitation of the film's "bandits and murderers" and "attacking passers-by...as if it were a joke."[81] Professionals in law enforcement wrote to the press to report that teenage criminals were confessing they had drawn inspiration from *The Magnificent Seven;* some called for a ban on films celebrating "banditism," as did some concerned parents.[82] The political scientist William Taubman, then a student at Moscow State University (MGU), found a young classmate who agreed: "We have enough troubles with *hooligany* without giving them more bad examples to imitate. Show them gangsters or cowboys and Indians and they start to play the parts in real life."[83]

The fact that elements from *The Magnificent Seven* had entered into slang and fashion was something that troubled some commentators as much as the film's violence.[84] The renowned literary critic Viktor Shklovskii wrote about spotting unusual headgear on boys in the subway and finally recognizing that they were homemade cowboy hats, fashioned from ordinary Soviet ones with the aid of a curling iron. Shklovskii recalled wistfully how boys in the thirties used to wear hats in the style of the film hero Chapaev. "I would like to see Soviet cinema create films whose heroes would be models for our boys," he wrote, "so that they acted, spoke, accomplished feats, and dressed like the heroes of *our* screen." *The Magnificent Seven* he dubbed "an alien film."[85] For Shklovskii, then, as for many others, the problem with foreign commercial cinema's popularity was not only that it conveyed harmful values—that it was *un*-Soviet—but also that it was foreign or *non*-Soviet; it alienated people from their own cultural and political traditions. At its core, this is a statement of the heroic model of cinematic identification and a simple calculus of cultural Cold War. As a distinguished director of the older generation put it at a special conference in 1966, "I got interested in the question: why hasn't America left the Western genre behind, but rather

81. RGASPI-m, f. 1, op. 32, d. 1066, l. 133.

82. V. Tikunov, "Chernoi maske vizy ne davat," *Izvestiia*, 28 May 1965, cited in RFE/RL Issledovatel'skie Zametki, 2 June 1965, in OSA, box 300-80-1-314.

83. William Taubman, *The View from Lenin Hills* (New York, 1967), 137–138.

84. For phrases from *The Magnificent Seven* that entered into teen slang, see Feodor Razzakov, *Dos'e na zvezd: 1962–1980* (Moscow, 1998), 406. Razzakov also reports that *The Magnificent Seven* was taken out of circulation ten months before its license expired (October 1966) because of the objections.

85. V. Shklovskii, "Shapka Chapaia," *SE*, no. 1 (1964): 4 (my italics).

developed it to the nth degree, and why have Poland, France, and Italy adopted it as a weapon?" His conclusion, he said, was that this was a "cunning and clever" decision on their part. "They don't have a Komsomol Central Committee, but they do have clever producers, and they have gone rather farther than manipulating their own youth—they are manipulating our youth."[86]

It was this understanding of film that fueled the calls to improve Soviet cinema by creating modern Soviet heroes and that lent them their sharp tones. Pavlov, too, invoked *Chapaev* in his letter to Khrushchev, underscoring that children had once imitated *him* and the heroes of another Stalin-era classic, *Young Guard* (*Molodaia gvardiia,* 1948), and not the bloodthirsty bandits of *The Magnificent Seven.* Concerns about bourgeois cultural infiltration and Soviet fecklessness were not limited to the political or cultural elites. Similar arguments could be found in letters to Goskino, the party and Komsomol administration, and the press. "I have come to understand," wrote a man from Kuibyshev in 1963, "that we have subordinated our film production to bourgeois culture. What good movies has our film industry given us recently? None. Where is *The Youth of Maxim*? Where is *The Great Citizen*? Where is *Lenin in October*?" After listing other classics from the Stalinist era, he continued,

> Why aren't there any public inspectors to monitor the behavior of teenagers on the street, day and night? After all, we are grooming our own successors; we are grooming the builders of communism. But everything is turning out the opposite. We are grooming gravediggers, rudeness, impudence, lack of respect for elders. And all of this happens to the accompaniment of jazz and screenings of low-brow [*nizkoprobnye*] movies. I am especially worried about the fate of my son, and other parents are worried about their children too. What in the world comes next?[87]

What came next was in most ways very familiar. The Soviet Union continued to import films identified as ideological pollutants. The maelstrom over *The Magnificent Seven* in the early sixties was recapitulated toward the end of the decade for the French *Fantômas,* though in later years, Soviet media allowed fans a stronger voice, sometimes publishing cycles of reader mail, pro and con, across several issues. "The time for cursing jazz and the 'Wild West' has passed," wrote one man from Tashkent. "Better to start talking about what needs to be done so that OUR films are interesting to watch!"[88] The 1970s press granted fans even more space to stand up for themselves and scold cineastes for failing to deliver

86. RGASPI-m, f. 1, op. 5, d. 1149, ll. 19–20.

87. RGALI, f. 2944, op. 1, d. 45, l. 16.

88. "Kakie my smotrim fil'my? Chitateli *Ogonka* obsuzhdaiut pis'mo 'Iadovitaia kinopishcha,'" *Ogonek,* no. 29 (1968), 31. On *Fantômas,* see also "Iadovitaia kinopishcha," *Ogonek,* no. 21 (1968): 11; and letters in numbers 32 and 42 (1968). *Ogonek* also ran related articles on the subject of foreign cinema's nefarious influence in numbers 27 and 33 (1968). See

what they wanted.[89] By 1975, *Soviet Screen*'s critic sounded almost despondent responding to the spectacular success of the Mexican melodrama *Yeseniia* and the huge numbers of letters the magazine had received defending it. "All this has already been written and spoken about a thousand times, and that's what keeps me from wanting to seize the educator's podium for the thousand-and-first to explain that the goal and mission of art is not showing pretty dresses and fateful passions, but the truthful, precise, and profound exploration of the world and of the person in it.... But here we are: I couldn't stop myself!" And so the critic went on to dissect the film, comparing its emotional effect to that of a carnival ride, and said he found viewers' ecstatic reactions "sad." "The most distressing thing is in fact those letters to the editor, because their authors sincerely believe that they saw a remarkable film, a work of art."[90]

Soviet movie culture thus grew more accommodating of the expression of alternative taste in the seventies, and the film industry, as we know, tried its own hand at genre filmmaking with some success. But just as the Yermash-era promotion of genre did not transform the structure of the industry and its core values, the terms of the discourse on cinema, audiences, and taste remained fundamentally the same. Again and again, political leaders warned about masscult's being used as a weapon against Soviet ideological integrity and about youth's particular vulnerability. The press printed letters from concerned parents and teachers and other authority figures calling for bans, better aesthetic education, new Soviet heroes. Paranoia about bourgeois cultural infiltration and calls for "a modern-day Chapaev" were the hardy perennials of Cold War Soviet culture.

In the end, it was not possible to assimilate ideologically either the presence in Soviet theaters of bad movies or the audience's bad taste for them. There were genuine explanations for these phenomena relating to the interests of industries, institutions, and individuals, and to the expectations viewers had brought to cinema for generations. The movie market in the USSR was a complex organism, and the audience was always far more diverse than the caricatures of Soviet discourse, connoisseur and rube. But Soviet mass culture did not make space for clear-eyed consideration of its internal dynamics. It looked to blame scapegoats at home and, most of all, enemy forces over the border.

Though the popularity of masscult was the most glaring issue for those who took cinema's ideological model seriously, it was not the whole of the problem with Soviet audiences. Rather, it is best seen as a subset of a more generalized pattern in audience attitudes influenced by exposure to foreign commercial models, but not limited to them. As it happened, Soviet viewers did not need bourgeois cultural infiltration to have bad taste or to engage in alien or un-Soviet

---

also the article "*Fantômas—Protiv nas*" and a follow-up article on readers' letters, "Protiv," in *Sem'ia i shkola*, nos. 1 and 6 (1969).

89. See Rajagopalan, *Leave Disco Dancer Alone!*, chap. 4.

90. Iulii Smelkov, "TK imeet uspekh," *SE*, no. 15 (1975).

modes of being a cinema audience. They had both Soviet tradition and a booming new Soviet-made movie culture upon which to draw.

"DRIVER, TURN ON THE LIGHTS!" SOVIET FANS AND THEIR STARS

In 1958, director El'dar Riazanov was mobbed by fans while trying to leave a premiere. In point of fact, it was not the director who was mobbed but rather his leading man, Nikolai Rybnikov, whom he had offered to drive home. But "around five hundred female fans" trapped the two men in his car. "All of the windows were covered with girls' bodies...and enraptured young eyes looked at us—rather, at him—from all sides," he recalled. The girls began to chant, "Driver, turn on the lights!" so that they could see their favorite, and Riazanov complied, realizing "once and for all," that he had chosen the "wrong profession."[91] (Let us note in passing, though, that though Rybnikov may well have gotten the girls, as Riazanov implied, the director was the one with the car.) Actor Oleg Strizhenov remembered being harassed by fans at home and once even cursing the minister of culture, E. S. Furtseva, on the telephone when he mistook her for one ("Go...yourself, you moron! If you call again, I'll catch you and rip your legs off!").[92] Vladimir Korenev recalled how the phenomenal success of his film *Amphibian Man* brought throngs of fans to his apartment building and a torrent of letters to his mailbox, "something like ten thousand in a year," including marriage proposals and erotic snapshots.[93] The Soviet Union's female stars were also showered with attention. The Amphibian's costar, Anastasiia Vertinskaia, said she received even more fan mail than he, about seventy letters per day.[94] Liudmila Gurchenko did too, and she also described how disorienting she found it to see carbon copies of herself on the street—young women with her exact hairstyle, clothing, and manner—after the release of her first film, *Carnival Night*.[95] Foreign stars visiting the USSR were the objects of equally rapt attention.

The term "star" refers both to an actual person and to a complex of cinematic and extracinematic information or, to use Richard Dyer's phrase, an "image in media texts."[96] In the capitalist context, star texts have been primarily connected to the marketing of films (advertising, publicity, and so on). Soviet cinema also used actors' images to promote individual pictures and, more generally, to propagandize Soviet ideals, but it rejected "star culture" as a capitalist perversion

91. E. Riazanov, *Eti neser'eznye, neser'eznye fil'my* (Moscow, 1977), 6.

92. Oleg Strizhenov, *Ispoved'* (Moscow, 1999), 167. Furtseva called back and convinced him it was really she on the line.

93. "Zolotaia pora Ikhtiandra," *Rossiskaia gazeta,* 21 June 2000.

94. Razzakov, *Dos'e na zvezd,* 403; *SE,* no. 6 (1964): 13.

95. Ludmila Gurchenko, *Aplodismenti* (Moscow, 1994), 302.

96. For the star as an image in media texts, see Richard Dyer, *Stars* (London, 1998), 10.

Figure 2.3. Gina Lollabrigida and fans at the Moscow Film Festival, 1973. RIA Novosti. Used with permission.

of cinematic art. The opposition to stars was thus a foundational principle for Soviet cinema-art; the essential contrast was stars versus heroes. In capitalism's culture of stars, the argument went, viewers were manipulated to form emotional attachments to actors as individuals and as a group. A culture of stars was also a culture of fans, or viewers seduced by beauty and glamour—subjugated to the ephemera of star imagery in the pursuit of profits. Soviet cinema, by contrast, claimed to elevate viewers by bonding them to heroes—characters who demonstrated exceptional daring, skill, and self-sacrifice (e.g., pilots, athletes, revolutionary martyrs) and who performed extraordinary feats of labor (e.g., Stakhanovites in mining, "hero-mothers" in reproduction).[97] And though Soviet heroes were also cultural constructs, in theory they had no fans, only imitators. It was not they, but rather their accomplishments, made possible by the socialist system, that were the locus of the culture. Every Soviet person was a "candidate hero"; cinematic consumption advanced one's candidacy.[98] Soviet actors,

97. The distinction between "heroes" and "stars" is delineated in a story (possibly apocryphal) about Stalin's awarding gold stars to heroic pilots with the words "Celebrated people abroad are often called 'stars.' So here we instituted this kind of award so that everyone could see our 'stars.'" Mark Kushnirov, *Svetlyi put, ili Charli i Spenser* (Moscow, 1998), 310.

98. On the "candidate hero" in Stalinist cinema, see Vitalii Troianovskii, *Kinematograf ottepeli: Kniga pervaia* (Moscow, 1996), 51.

no matter how worthy of respect, were *players at heroism* and so stood logically in the shadow of their heroic characters.

Like elite cultures throughout the West, prerevolutionary Russian culture harbored a certain disdain for acting as a manipulative, acquisitive, and distinctively "feminine" occupation, often likened to prostitution.[99] In the Soviet context, this negative view was reinforced by the cinematic avant-garde of the twenties and its rallying cry to banish the professional "bourgeois" actor from the screen. Directors were the masters of new revolutionary cinema, and even after the avant-garde was compelled in the thirties to alter many of its first principles, the taint on acting as a lesser form of artistry was never fully expunged.[100] For actors, success was measured by how well they effaced their own personalities and, under directorial tutelage, embodied the inspiring heroes viewers were thought to require. In the Stalinist era, Boris Babochkin was lauded for his transformation into Chapaev on screen; Liubov' Orlova's triumph was her oneness with the Soviet Cinderella characters she played. With little extracinematic information about these actors available to audiences, the risk of countering the identification was minimized. (Orlova's upper-class origins, for example, were never publicized.)[101] The idea—Soviet cinema-art's bedrock claim—was to promote heroes *without* stars and fans, healthy and productive idolization without dangerous idolatry.

Even in the 1980s, readers turning to a Soviet encyclopedia of film for a definition of stardom would have found a lengthy explanation of the star system in Hollywood from 1910 through the 1970s with no reference whatsoever to the domestic scene.[102] Soviet commentators identified the stardom-fandom dynamic as the keystone of masscult cinema, the critical mechanism for exploiting actors and controlling viewers. (So, too, have many Western film scholars).[103] For

99. See Beth Holmgren, "The Importance of Being Unhappy, or Why She Died," in *Imitations of Life: Two Centuries of Melodrama in Russia,* ed. Louise MacReynolds and Joan Neuberger (Durham, 2002), 79–98; James von Geldern and Louise McReynolds, eds., *Entertaining Tsarist Russia* (Bloomington, IN, 1998), 349.

100. For actors' critiques of the enduring legacy of this tradition, see comments at the organizing conference for the new Filmmakers' Union, *Vsesoiuznaia tvorcheskaia konferentsiia rabotnikov kinematografii: Stenograficheskii otchet* (Moscow, 1959), 263–265. The fact that many directors were former actors did not alter the overall hierarchy.

101. Orlova was widely acknowledged to be the most popular actor of her age, and she was one of the few Soviet actors of any era to be called a star—albeit rarely—by Soviet media. See Kushnirov, *Svetlyi put',* 309; S. Freilikh, *Besedy o sovetskom kino* (Moscow, 1985), 164–170; S. Nikolaevich, "Poslednyi seans, ili sud'ba beloi zhenshchiny v SSSR,"*Ogonek,* no. 4 (1992): 22–24; G. V. Aleksandrov, *Epokha i kino* (Moscow, 1976).

102. *Kino: Entsiklopedicheskii slovar'* (Moscow, 1986), 188.

103. See, for example, David Bordwell, Janet Steiger, and Kristin Thompson, *The Classical Hollywood Cinema: Film Style and Mode of Production to 1960* (New York, 1985); Thomas Schatz, *The Genius of the System: Hollywood Filmmaking in the Studio Era*

Soviet cinema, the goals were of course defined as ideological rather than commercial: inculcating socialist values, elevating aesthetic sensibilities, mobilizing the masses in the heroic work of building communism, and providing cultured leisure.[104] Nevertheless, Soviet cinema's devices have often been compared to those of commercial systems.

Film scholar Richard Taylor, for one, argued that Stalinist cinema should be considered a "red star system" analogous in many respects to "classic" Hollywood—and given the Soviets' keen interest in 1930s Hollywood in particular, a family resemblance makes sense.[105] Yet the differences between the two systems always outran the similarities if we consider both the content of star imagery and the ways it sought to structure relationships across the screen barrier. Tellingly, it was an American magazine, *Life,* that in the 1940s published the most revealing portrait ever of a Soviet actor. She was Liubov' Orlova, visited at her dacha by photographer Margaret Bourke-White. Although Orlova was the leading light of her day, no Soviet publication would have published images of her lounging at home—and even smoking!—with her husband and director, Grigorii Aleksandrov, or have listed the salaries of their maids, as *Life* did.[106] The "red star" image was nearly void of extracinematic content. By contrast, information considered personal was essential in constructing capitalist star imagery because it was said to forge direct and intimate connections between actors and audiences. And this made the capitalist star text far more unstable and multivalent than the Stalinist variant. No red star's divorce or alcoholism, no intimations of homosexuality or spousal abuse ever threatened to erupt into Soviet public space, as they did in the hothouse of Hollywood's star system. The cultural system around Stalinist cinema strove to put audiences on personal terms not with the actors themselves but with their heroic characters. The Soviet audience was, by definition, a group that embraced cinema as an art form and a school for heroism: an audience of connoisseurs and enthusiasts, not superficial fans.

(New York, 1988); Paul McDonald, *The Star System: Hollywood's Production of Popular Identities* (London, 2000); Hortense Powdermaker, *Hollywood, the Dream Factory: An Anthropologist Looks at the Movies* (Boston, 1950). For a book-length Soviet critique of stardom, see E. Kartseva, *Sdelano v Gollivude* (Moscow, 1964), especially 38–74, 181–196. Kartseva relied on the work of Powdermaker, among others.

104. Whether the capitalist star system has implicit ideological goals or ideological effects is not my question here. It is, however, a major issue for the scholarly literature on stardom in the West. See especially the work of Richard Dyer: *Stars* and *Heavenly Bodies: Film Stars and Society* (New York, 1986); Jackie Stacey, *Star Gazing: Hollywood Cinema and Female Spectatorship* (London, 1994); Christine Gledhill, *Stardom: Industry of Desire* (New York, 1991).

105. Richard Taylor, "Red Stars, Positive Heroes, and Personality Cults," in Taylor and Spring, *Stalinism and Soviet Cinema,* 69–89.

106. "*Life* Calls on a Russian Movie Star," *Life,* 1 December 1941, 118–119.

Soviet cinema after 1953 was still working within the framework forged in the Stalinist era. "The success of a film depends to a large measure on whether we are attracted to its heroes," explained a critic in 1963. "But when we meet people on the screen, we are meeting actors. The specificity of cinema as a spectacle, its authenticity, is that an actor achieves success only *when he lives the role and forces us to live it with him*: this links the screen image and the viewer."[107] Here was the Soviet model, and it would remain the model as long as Soviet cinema was *Soviet* cinema, self-defined as the anti-Hollywood, the most important of the Soviet arts. But the explosive growth of the cinematic sphere after Stalin's death, its increasing intercourse with the non-Soviet world, and fundamental changes in everyday work and leisure life in the USSR were also pushing the culture in very different directions. Viewers had more options at the box office (foreign and Soviet), more ways to engage with cinema outside the theater (the burgeoning movie culture), and more latitude to set the terms of their engagements as well. The door was opened to new attitudes to cinema—a new, personalized dimension that could burst the boundaries of the ideological model. One manifestation of this was the Soviet stardom-fandom dynamic.

The term "fan," like "star," reflects both a sociological phenomenon and a cultural construct. In the sociological sense, cinema fandom implies an extraordinary interest in moviegoing and, typically, in the lives of individual actors or actors as a group, expressed in a variety of behaviors. Soviet commentators in the fifties and sixties seldom used the standard translation for "fan" (*poklonnik/ poklonnitsa*) and, aside from photographs of crowds at film festivals and the like, Soviet media mostly refrained from reporting actual incidents of fan behavior. Riazanov's and Strizhenov's stories of importunate admirers would not have appeared in print at the time (they were published in *post*-Soviet memoirs) and even today, it seems, there is a marked reluctance on the part of former Soviet stars to discuss such things publicly. We might argue that to speak of fandom in the Soviet context is misplaced for this reason. Yet the basic facts of audience behavior are not difficult to glean from the sources: people were indeed writing letters in the millions, storming actors for autographs at public appearances, and so on—that is, fandom in the strict sociological sense is identifiable, if not quantifiable. More important still, fandom existed as a cultural construct in the Soviet Union even without a name: the fan was the antimodel, everything that a proper viewer, an admirer (*liubitel'*) or friend (*drug*) of cinema, was not. One viewer outlined the differences in a letter to *Soviet Screen* in 1964:

> Some people go the movies the way they go to the bathhouse on Saturdays— out of necessity or habit. Other people watch a film "for dessert," so to speak.

107. Anri Vartanov, "'Moi liubimye artisty kino…,'" *SE*, no. 3 (1963): 14–15 (my italics).

A third group collects actors' autographs and photographs and knows who is married to whom and all the other cinema gossip. In my opinion, this is warped....I go to the movies for advice, for knowledge about life and people....Cinema for me is a university for studying humanity. And I am a student there, an eternal student. And I am happy to be one.[108]

Soviet Screen was the prime locus for the image of the antimodel I am calling the "fan" and wasted no time in establishing it: the very first issue in 1957 featured a spoof about a young woman who sneaked into hotels to get stars' autographs, sometimes posing as a manicurist, and also collected their discarded cigarette butts and fallen strands of hair.[109] She (and it was almost always a "she") would become a familiar figure on the magazine's pages: the shallow, star-struck, self-indulgent fan. She was to be mocked and, if possible, educated. Critics often quoted her opinions in sneering reviews of popular films like *Amphibian Man* to illustrate the meaning of bad taste.

The magazine received vast amounts of reader mail, much of it addressed directly to actors asking for everything from autographs and photographs to loans and personal advice. Periodically, it chastised readers for pestering them.[110] "[I]f you give it some thought, you will honestly recognize that you have nothing special to write to an actress about," an editor chided one young woman.[111] In an article specifically about fan mail, one actor described her disappointment with the letters she received; they were often superficial, she said, and lacking the serious artistic evaluations of her work that she craved. The magazine's editors went further: "There is something insulting in that familiar tone and that superfluous boldness with which these people toss around their emotions."[112]

Soviet Screen also received stacks of letters from young people who dreamed of a life in show business; the "how do I become a film actor?" (*kak stat' artistam kino*) letter was the most common in the magazine's mailbag—so common that editors had preprinted response forms at the ready. *Soviet Screen* told its readers that they, like all Soviets, were already "in the movies" as "coauthors"

108. "Chto vy ishchete v kinoiskusstve?" *SE,* no. 3 (1964).

109. V. Ardov, "Muzei Kapy Tolokontsevoi," *SE,* no. 1 (1957).

110. In 1964, for instance, *SE* was receiving roughly six thousand letters per month. RGANI, f. 5, op. 55, d.112.

111. V. Orlov, "O groznoi Natashe i pape, kotoryi, 'vynudil,'" *SE,* no. 4 (1965), 12.

112. El'ga Gil'man, "Pochta aktrisy," *SE,* no. 6 (1964): 18–19. Another vein in the discourse criticized actors as willful and egotistical with hints—and occasional accusations—of moral debauchery. Writing of this genre was more likely to appear in the mainstream press rather than in *SE.* See, for example, "Vysoko nesti zvanie sovetskogo artista," *Sovetskaia kul'tura,* 7 June 1958. Even this critical discourse may have contributed to actors' glamour in a backhand way by depicting them as a breed apart.

of Soviet cinema-art[113] and tried to discourage dreamers by publishing statistics on the long odds of getting into VGIK.[114] It ridiculed them, too. When one young woman who complained of small-town life wrote that she "would really like to be in at least one film.... I want to live that life," *Soviet Screen* reminded her that a talented poet hailed from a neighboring town even smaller than hers. "Clearly, it is not a question of the size of the town where a person lives, but of her abilities, talents, and industriousness. And industriousness, clearly, is something Larisa lacks."[115] A 1965 article by critic Viktor Orlov used a pastiche of excerpts from readers' letters to demonstrate the shallowness of acting dreams. "What should a person who wants to become an actor but doesn't have any talent do?" he quoted one young woman. "There is nothing you can do, darling Natasha. Go to school or get a job.... Isn't that obvious?" To "a serious citizen from eighth grade" who wrote to ask whether it was "necessary to be beautiful, have a good voice and, of course, connections" in order to become an actor, Orlov replied, "Is it necessary to be beautiful? Yes, imagine that. But not in the sense that you think. The beauty of a perfume advertisement is not necessary. But real, inner beauty, significance, and a rich individuality are indispensable." A good voice was important, he added, but as for the question about "connections," Orlov found it "offensive" and declined to answer. Interest in acting he chalked up to simple vanity. "Would you like me to tell you one of the reasons you want to become movie actresses? It's very simple. You look in the mirror every day at your own face. You see that it is attractive (who isn't attractive in youth?) and you think it's a pity that no one but you ever will see it in 'close up.'"[116]

The gendered (and sexist) nature of these *Soviet Screen* commentaries flies off the page now, but it was par for the course at the time and common in other cultures as well.[117] Some former Soviet stars who reflected publicly on their careers confirmed the notion that young women were the most active fans, but others

113. Anri Vartanov, "200,000,000 khudozhnikov," *SE*, no. 6 (1963): 14–15. Compare with Reid's comments in "In the Name of the People" on the notion of coauthorship as popular among visual artists in the thaw. Although cinematic criticism was speaking in the same idiom, the hierarchy of correct/incorrect interpretation was, it seems to me, very rigid for cinema. Viewers were distinctly *junior* partners in this endeavor.

114. Ia. Segel', "Kem byt'," *SE*, no. 11 (1968): 20. *Komsomol'skaia pravda* gave even longer odds in 1965: four thousand applicants for fifteen spots in the actors' division. E. Topol', "Kak ustroit'sia v artisty," *Komsomol'skaia Pravda,* 15 May 1965.

115. Segel',"Kem byt'."

116. V. Orlov, "O neizvestnoi Aelite, mrachnoi Alene i Dzhul'ette Mazine," *SE,* no. 8 (1965): 20–21.

117. On female "irrationality" as a problem for post-Stalinist consumerism, see Susan Reid, "Cold War in the Kitchen: Gender and the De-Stalinization of Taste in the Soviet Union under Khrushchev," *Slavic Review* 61, no. 2 (2008): 220.

did not; most, if they mentioned fans at all, spoke in very general terms.[118] Without anything beyond anecdotal evidence (there are no statistical data on *Soviet Screen*'s mail), it is difficult to prove or disprove the stereotype. Soviet media culture portrayed young women as more apt than young men to be carried away with dreams of acting and more actively involved in certain kinds of fan behavior, such as writing love letters and collecting postcards.[119] The male fan image split in two. On the one hand, it was teenage *boys* who were said to be taking curling irons to their hats in order to mimic the heroes of *The Magnificent Seven* (or, ten years earlier, cutting their hair *tarzanets*-style). The young male fan had a somewhat feminized and pathologized image, one that overlapped with that of the style-hungry hipster, the *stiliaga*. (For a teenage boy to fuss over foreign fashion, or his looks in general, was represented as a troubling sign.) On the other hand were stories of young men lured into criminality by violent capitalist movies—a far more menacing image than that of a Leningrad cowboy. On both sides of this split screen, though, male fans' attitudes were legible ideologically: after all, any boy who mimicked screen heroes was enacting the Soviet model for how cinematic culture *should* work. It was the young women (and much less often men) who said they dreamed of acting who had truly jumped the tracks in ideological terms. Instead of being inspired to emulate heroes, they yearned to join the special ranks of those who portrayed them for millions—to separate themselves from ordinary folk and lead glamorous, bigger-than-life lives. And this was the Soviets' model of cinema and heroic identification in fun-house mirror form: cinema's fans in love with themselves (not heroes, not ideas) and casting *themselves* on the Soviet screen. For people convinced that progress depended on young people's casting their lots with new hydroelectric dam projects and hospitals, chemical fertilizer plants and architectural design firms, it was a red flag flying for a culture gone awry.

Scholars have elaborated ethnographies of fandom for many different cultural forms in the West, and one of the main themes of this literature is that people identified (or self-identified) as fans, far from being passive receptors, make their own meanings with the materials at hand.[120] Fan studies have a

---

118. Oleg Tabakov, *Moia nastoiashchaia zhizn'* (Moscow, 2000), 192–193; Strizhenov, *Ispoved'*, 162–173; Gurchenko, *Aplodismenty*, 299–309, 337.

119. In this way Soviet culture made the same connection between consumption, mass culture, and the feminine commonly advanced by anxious critics in Western Europe and the United States—not to mention prerevolutionary Russia and the Soviet Union of the twenties. See Andreas Huyssen, "Mass Culture as Woman: Modernism's Other," *Studies in Entertainment: Critical Approaches to Mass Culture*, ed. Tania Modleski (Bloomington, IN, 1986), 188–207; Anne Gorsuch, *Youth in Revolutionary Russia: Enthusiasts, Bohemians, Delinquents* (Bloomington, IN, 2000); Louise MacReynolds, *Russia at Play: Leisure Activities at the End of the Tsarist Era* (Ithaca, NY, 2003).

120. A helpful introduction to the main themes in the extensive literature on fandom (based on TV audiences but not limited to them) can be found in B. Casey et al., eds.,

strong populist and often celebratory tone. My goal is not to evaluate Soviet fan culture in these terms, as positive or negative, although I do see expanded options as typically a better thing for cultural consumers than limited ones. The very facts of what I am calling fandom—that someone in the USSR could experience a passion for an actor, Nikolai Rybnikov, for example, and choose to see all his films and collect picture postcards with his image, even fling herself across his car—signal the new personal latitude and the far richer cultural resources available to ordinary Soviet people. I see no reason to assume that it is always better to form emotional bonds with a historical figure than with a fantastical one (Chapaev vs. the Amphibian Man) or with a character rather than an actor (Rybnikov's working class heroes vs. Rybnikov as a star text), better to dream of being a scientist rather than a screen siren. I also agree in a general way with populist-oriented fan scholars that imaginative relationships with mediated images are not necessarily inferior to the material, face-to-face ones we choose to mark as real.

We know from memoirs and other kinds of evidence that people dreamed of actors and the acting world in the Stalinist "red star" era too, even if they had very little off-screen information for constructing star imagery. It is not that the behavior of fandom was new in the post-Stalinist era but rather that it was altered in scope, tone, and context. Soviet teenagers in 1970 could look back on the lives of their parents and imagine a time when comparatively few people had access to movie theaters, period, not to mention choice at the box office, a booming movie culture, and, at least as pertinent, the time and money to enjoy them. The stardom-fandom dynamic was a vivid marker of Soviet success in improving standards of living. But it also signaled important changes in the Soviet social environment. To immobilize a star's car in a parking lot, flaunt your frivolity (for that is how any authority figure would characterize such behavior), and press your demands ("Driver, turn on the lights!") showed a certain confidence, even nerve. Critics said as much at the time: "Who do these people think they are?" was the undercurrent of all writing about fans. Evidently they were people who thought they had a green light to do such things, much as the fans who wrote letters to *Soviet Screen* saw themselves as authorized to demand information, voice their opinions, and talk back to critics. And in fact, *Soviet Screen*, like all the new movie culture, was flashing green lights as well as red ones. Soviet movie culture trafficked heavily in the things it said it despised: charisma, glamour, intrigue. The very same culture that chastised people for their emotional engagement with actors and acting was also working very effectively to facilitate that engagement.

Television Studies: Key Concepts (New York, 2002), 89–94. The classic text on fans as meaning makers is Henry Jenkins's *Textual Poachers* (London, 1992).

FESTIVALS AND GLAMOUR

One of the first signs that the landscape for cinema was changing after Stalin's death was the revival of the film festival in the USSR. In 1954, first Moscow and then other cities began organizing special weeks of foreign cinema and hosting visiting cineastes, and in 1959 the grande dame of Soviet festivals, the Moscow International, was revived with great fanfare.[121] But the festival phenomenon was not only about international ties. An all-Union event was first inaugurated in 1958,[122] and there were scores of other festivals across the Union, sponsored by the Komsomol, trade union organizations, republic-level ministries of culture, the Filmmakers' Union, and cities and towns. The 1960s were the heyday of the Soviet film festival. Twenty years later, director Vladmir Men'shov evoked the excitement of the moment in the blockbuster *Moscow Does Not Believe in Tears*, showing his young protagonists in a crowd of festival fans outside the new Push-kin Theater Palace in Moscow.

Festivals count as a key element of the new Soviet movie culture, both in expanding access to film and in generating and circulating star imagery. Take the 1960 "Screen Image of the Contemporary Person" festival, for example, which brought more than a dozen Moscow-based directors and actors with their films to Riazan' Province (and since the festival ran concurrently in other regions, dozens more to other locations as well). Sponsored jointly by the Filmmakers' Union and the RSFSR Ministry of Culture, the festival was billed as an opportunity for the audience to meet its cineastes, ask them questions, and offer suggestions and critiques. This format, known as the "creative meeting," was widespread in Soviet culture and akin to other public events where people in positions of power were called to answer to the masses. Filmmakers had long participated in meetings of this type in other contexts.[123] The point to emphasize about the post-Stalinist festival revival is, again, one of expansion and of the ways in which expansion can transform the nature of a culture itself: not only were there now many more of these events, but with the explosive development of print and broadcast media in the postwar era, the circle of Soviets involved in them widened further still. In the case of the contemporary-person festival, at most a few hundred collective farmers watched director V. Dorman dance with a milkmaid when his group visited a kolkhoz outside Riazan', while perhaps a few thousand had packed theaters in the city to see him and his colleagues and to clamor for their autographs. *Soviet Screen's* coverage of the festival included reports on both events, as well as photographs. One shot showed a car entirely surrounded

121. M. R. Zezina, *Sovetskaia khudozhestvennaia intelligentsiia i vlast' v 1950-e-60-e gody* (Moscow, 1999), 237.

122. The all-Union festival became a regular biannual event only as of 1964 and shifted to an annual basis in 1972.

123. See, for example, "Studiia otchityvaetsia pered zritelem," *SE*, no. 4 (1961).

Figure 2.4. *Soviet Screen* covers Riazan' fandom, 1960.

with people peering into the windows, and its caption read, "What is this—an accident? No, it's the hospitable people of Riazan' who will not let their beloved film artists leave for a long time after meeting them."[124] Glamour is a currency that takes on added value with increased circulation, and so mass media meant

124. "V gostiakh u zritelei," *SE,* no. 15 (1960): 20.

more to the festival phenomenon than just an exponential increase in the number of people involved. A local festival was transformed into a national event. An ordinary creative meeting was made extraordinary.

Soviet media outlets were even more important for their publicity of international film festivals. In the 1960s, the Moscow International Film Festival was a biannual event that attracted cineastes of world stature and widespread coverage in Soviet print and broadcast media.[125] Not only did the general press (*Pravda, Moskovskii komsomolets, Ogonek,* and others) and publications related to the arts (*Sovetskaia kul'tura, Literaturnaia gazeta*) cover the Moscow festival but there were also articles in newspapers with no obvious connection to cinema, including *Sovetskii flot* (for the Soviet navy), *Lesnaia promyshlennost'* (on the forestry industry), and *Uchitel'skaia gazeta* (the newspaper for schoolteachers). *Soviet Screen's* coverage was the most extensive of any Soviet publication, and it was also the most visual. For the Fourth Moscow International in 1965, for example, the magazine did extensive reportage before and after the event and ran multiple pages of photographs: readers saw shots of Czech actor Olga Schoberova gazing intently at a painting in the Tretyakov Gallery, of Raj Kapoor wearing a hard hat during a visit to Moscow construction workers, of Sophia Loren accepting an award from a somewhat sheepish-looking director Sergei Gerasimov, and of American Susan Strasberg throwing her hands up in animated conversation with fellow actor Nina Drobysheva, to name a few.[126]

As its official slogan, "For humanism in cinematic art, for peace and friendship among peoples," emphasized, the Moscow festival promoted the notion of cinema as an international language that facilitated dialogue and extended the promise of mutual understanding. Soviet coverage of the festival drew an explicit contrast with film festivals in the West, which were said to be run purely and cynically for profit. Moscow, on the other hand, positioned itself as a defender of artistic integrity and a broker for peace. Images of Soviet cineastes in hugs and heart-to-heart conversations with their foreign counterparts—including, pointedly, those from developing countries—were essential in demonstrating Soviet cinema's progressive role. The comments of foreign guests reported in Soviet media often carried a subtext of envy toward their Soviet colleagues. This was an envy born of respect for the Soviet cinematic canon and the Russian theatrical tradition, both of which came in for ritualistic praise, and also of the supe-

125. The 1965 Moscow festival, for example, attracted Steve McQueen, Kim Novak, Marlon Brando, Gregory Peck, Jean-Luc Godard, Antonioni, Sophia Loren, and Audrey Hepburn. Western star power significantly dimmed in the seventies. Festivals could be lucrative; Moscow's 1964 festival took in a gross of over 1 million rubles in ticket sales and netted over 550,000 rubles after expenses. See V. Fomin, "God 1965," http://www.film.ru/sk-news.
126. *SE,* no. 16 (1965), front inside cover and 17.

rior work conditions for artists in the USSR—that is, the opportunity to focus on one's art alone and ignore the brutal demands of the market.

Yet though the superiority of Soviet artists to foreign stars was ever the moral of the story, both festival programming and coverage consistently blurred ideology's bright lines. Moscow's festival traded in Soviet star power—the personal allure and crowd appeal of the Soviet cineaste. How else to explain the attire of Soviet actresses who, although often more modestly dressed than their foreign counterparts, certainly did not wear practical clothes to major festival events? They did not appear in the work clothes of an actor (suits such as one might wear to a rehearsal, or costumes) but instead matched the uniform of a contemporary movie star in the West: floor-length gowns in shimmering fabrics and off-the-shoulder and backless styles, stiletto heels, eye-catching jewelry—all clothes associated with leisure, wealth, and ostentation. As most Soviet actors were not rich, and evening clothes were difficult to come by at any price, many struggled to outfit themselves; others had their finery requisitioned for them by the state, much like any work uniform.

Images of Soviet and foreign actors at gala events stimulated the us/them comparison that was the bread and butter of Soviet cinema's identity. But the glittery atmosphere of a film festival was more clearly "their" ideological turf than any other kind of event, and the Soviet choice to play on it was critical. Although no one acknowledged it publicly, it was the Moscow festival that strove to attract big-name foreign stars and to rival Cannes or Venice—and not the other way around. It is telling that only in the context of the Moscow International or festivals abroad did Soviet media refer to Soviet actors as stars.[127] It is as if journalists could come up with no other concept than star power to describe those scenes of high glamour and mass adoration that came with major festivals. Soviet media also showed unusual tolerance at these times for that other object of official cultural disdain: the besotted fan. Images of people packed together, straining for a glimpse of their favorites and beaming unself-consciously, and of actors thronged by autograph seekers were common fare in festival coverage. And in these images Soviet moviegoers bore little resemblance to sober connoisseurs of cinema art—the ideal type. With an international film festival in town, all the stars came out, and summertime Moscow in Soviet media took on shades of Cannes or Venice.

POSTCARDS AND CINEMA'S PERSONALIZATION

The glamour of the new Soviet movie culture was often bound up with that of postwar (especially 1960s) technological modernity—jet travel, broadcast

---

127. *Ogonek* referred to T. Samoilova as a star when she won best actress at Cannes in 1958 for her role in *The Cranes Are Flying*. A. Popova, "Zvezda festivaliia," *Ogonek,* no. 25 (1958): 15. The article included captioned photographs of Samoilova with Gina Lollabrigida and Sophia Loren and one of Samoilova and other Soviet film professionals with Pablo Picasso and Jean Cocteau.

journalism, the swift movement of people, images, and ideas through space—and this was certainly the case for festivals of all kinds, especially international ones. But as much as the new movie culture built on new technologies and their exciting imagery, it was not limited to them. If we are tracking cinema's biggest footprint in Soviet everyday life, we should turn first to the humble postcard printed with images of Soviet and foreign actors.

Like film festivals and clubs, cinema postcards were not new to the postwar period—consumers had bought them in earlier decades too.[128] But in the golden age of moviegoing, the publication of postcards took on unprecedented and truly mass dimensions, placing images of actors squarely in the mainstream of Soviet everyday life. The Filmmakers' Union reported sales of 66 million cards for 1960–61 alone.[129] *Soviet Screen,* by comparison, though it was the only mass movie magazine with Union-wide circulation, had a print run of 3–4 million in the mid-sixties. Books about cinema were printed in the tens or perhaps hundreds of thousands. A book about Oleg Tabakov had a print run of around fifty thousand, but the actor himself estimated that there were 6–7 million postcards with his image in circulation in the 1960s. Just one version of the Tabakov card (there were several) had a print run of 1 million copies.[130]

Soviet-made cinema postcards came in a variety of different types: there were small black-and-white photos (about half the size of the familiar postcard), larger color cards suitable for mailing, and sets of pictures, sometimes representing national cinemas (e.g., Actors of France, Cinema of India). Most cards were printed with studio photographs of actors, or "head shots," rather than movie stills. Many people collected them avidly, traded them, and kept them in special albums designed for the purpose. They were cheap—a few kopecks apiece—and never in adequate supply. *Soviet Screen,* in response to the many letters it received asking for cards or advice on where to find them, periodically published the address of a Moscow store where fans could look.

The postcard trade was a venture of the Filmmakers' Union, which—through its propaganda wing, the Office for the Propaganda of Soviet Film Art—produced and distributed the cards and collected the revenues. The union paid no royalties to actors for the use of their likenesses, but if they were Soviet actors, they, like all union members, stood to benefit from the perquisites the postcard trade funded, such as holiday homes and housing projects. Even at a net take of one kopeck per card after the costs of production and distribution—a conservative estimate—tens of millions of cards, year after year, added up to sizable sums.

128. See Joseph Brodsky, *On Grief and Reason* (New York, 1995), 10; Stanislav Safonov, "'Novyi lubok' v sovetskoi strane serediny dvadtsatogo veka," *Nezavisimaia gazeta,* 24 January 2003.

129. See Fomin, "God 1962," http://www.film.ru/sk-news.

130. Tabakov, *Moia nastoiashchaia zhizn',* 140.

Still, if the trade made all the sense in the world from a financial perspective, it was also roiling in ideological incoherence. Perhaps exploiting the images of foreign actors to fund the Filmmakers' Union could be justified as a kind of Cold War cultural realpolitik. But Soviet actors? Peddling their images for personal use tapped into attitudes that had little to do with Soviet cinema's artistic, moral, and political mission and everything to do with such things as charisma and glamour. By taking Soviet actors out of the movies and putting the spotlight on them as individuals, picture postcards helped uncouple the actor and the character and thus set cinema's ideological framework to one side. People did not collect images of heroic construction workers; they collected shots of Nikolai Rybnikov. The distinction here, though slippery, is real. Although Rybnikov did play construction workers, and his image was surely connected to the heroism of these characters, the postcard trade helped dissociate the two by selling him alone. And though this may have helped advertise film in the sense of bringing people into the theaters, it was not the same as propagandizing Soviet cinema-art and heroes. On the contrary, the picture postcard played into and stimulated values that worked against the notion of cinema as a school for art and valor. A picture postcard cut Soviet cinema down to size, mixed it up with the enemy ("I'll trade you Rynbikov for Jean Marais"), and sold it. This was a piece—a humble object, but one's own—of cinematic glamour, and it established a relationship with a specific individual, person to person. A postcard was an invitation to cinema's personalization and possession.

READING *SOVIET SCREEN*

Was this a problem? When a young reader from Georgia wrote to *Soviet Screen* concerned that her postcard collection was frivolous and harmful, the magazine enlisted Aleksei Batalov to set her straight. Batalov was one of the country's most famous actors: "In ten minutes of leafing through the [postcard] album," he wrote, "I once and for all came to hate actors' photographs and everyone who is involved with them."[131]

If postcards carried the contradictions of the new Soviet movie culture in crystallized form, *Soviet Screen* was their full flowering.[132] Other magazines and newspapers covered cinema, but *Soviet Screen* was both the locus of film journalism and one of the most popular of all Soviet publications. Like so many other aspects of the new movie culture, it was not new, technically speaking, but had been revived after a period of late Stalinist dormancy. Its first post-Stalinist issue in 1957 explained that the Ministry of Culture had reopened the magazine

131. "Konfetnyi mir," *SE,* no. 23 (1963): 14.

132. Another important factor in the development of Soviet movie culture outside the scope of this work was film journalism from socialist bloc countries, especially Poland. These magazines typically had higher production values than Soviet publications and more information on masscult cinema.

after sixteen years in recognition of cinema's "enormous role...in the ideological and political education of the working masses, particularly youth."[133] Four years later, Soviet Screen's print run was doubled to four hundred thousand, and oversight for the magazine was transferred from the Ministry of Culture to the Filmmakers' Union. The union had lobbied hard for the transfer, which, like the postcard trade, put revenues in its pockets. In 1962, it mounted a successful campaign to increase the print run to 1.6 million, but even this proved insufficient to meet demand and was soon increased to 2.6 million.[134] A reasonable estimate for the actual readership would run to four or five times that level, said the editors.[135]

Soviet Screen was a stand-out magazine in the run of Soviet publications, and this was particularly true in the late fifties and sixties; in these years, it established the main lines of Soviet movie culture journalism. It was a large-format magazine, comparable to Life magazine in size, with a modern, playful look. A standard twenty-page edition always included plenty of text, of course: there were reviews and articles on film history and aesthetics, satiric sketches, readers' letters, interviews, reportage, and all official pronouncements about cinema. When the party held a congress, or when Khrushchev traveled the globe, Soviet Screen ran reports to mark the moment, even when it lacked the pretext of a cinematic angle. But political material of this kind was usually limited to one or two pages, and the textual element in general was understated for a Soviet publication. An issue of Soviet Screen came filled with photographs, cartoons, and other engaging graphic design elements, many in color (and the use of color increased over the decades). Both its front and back covers were almost always full-page color photographs of Soviet film professionals—directors and, more often, actors—or movie stills. We know from anecdotal evidence (and can infer from the decor for contemporary movies) that people detached Soviet Screen photographs and hung them up, and the magazine's colorful covers seem almost designed for this use; back covers in particular, which usually had no text, were ideal for display.

The other signal feature of Soviet Screen was its positioning of Soviet and foreign cinema on the same page, literally and metaphorically. The magazine established itself from the start as an important conduit between Soviet people and the non-Soviet world. Opening the very first number in 1957, readers found a two-page spread on contemporary foreign cinema (covering films from Czechoslovakia, China, India, and Austria) and best wishes from Raj Kapoor, Silvana

133. SE, no. 1 (1957): 1.
134. See Fomin, "God 1958," "God 1961," and "God 1962," http://www.film.ru/sk-news; Kogan, Kino i zritel', 171. Golovskoy put circulation in the seventies at 1.9 million. Val S. Golovskoy, Behind the Soviet Screen: The Motion-Picture Industry in the USSR, 1972–1982 (Ann Arbor, MI, 1986), 64.
135. SE, no. 10 (1967): 21.

СОВЕТСКИЙ **20**
ЭКРАН 1960

Figure 2.5. Front cover of *Soviet Screen*, no. 20 (1960).

Pampanini, and other foreign actors. Future issues introduced readers to cinema from all over, with a marked emphasis on the capitalist sector (France, Italy, and the United States were especially well represented). Greetings from foreign cineastes became a standard feature, along with interviews and profiles. So, too, did reports of Soviet successes abroad—the prestige of Soviet cineastes among their colleagues and the gratitude of foreign viewers for Soviet-made films. The magazine made it plain that both the art of Soviet cinema and the screens of Soviet movie theaters were international by right.

Soviet Screen delivered standard ideological messages. The world of cinema was divided into camps: capitalist and socialist, reactionary and progressive, or, quite often, Hollywood, its "victims," and Soviet cinema. Films made in countries like India and Egypt could fall into either the progressive or the reactionary camp, depending on their perceived "quality," which was, needless to say, an ideologically determined category. All good cinema was art, and art was anticommercial; that is, though it might be produced in market conditions, its creators and its values always struggled against them. In this way, even a picture made in the belly of the beast, Hollywood, might just qualify as progressive, and Soviet Screen did champion some capitalist productions. But the more common tack was to critique the capitalist *mode* of production and to defend art and artists against it.

The exploitation of actors by a soulless masscult movie machine was one of Soviet Screen's favorite themes. To take one typical example, a 1960 survey of Bette Davis's career described her lifelong battle to "create realistic works of art" and her abandonment by heartless studios executives in later years. "Such is the fate of many talented Hollywood actors, because the only thing that always brings success in Hollywood is money" the article concluded (its author was an American—not unusual for the genre).[136] Soviet Screen frequently gave voice to foreign actors who complained that they were never offered serious and challenging roles, and it protested on their behalf. This was a common thread, for example, in the many articles on Marina Vlady, a French actor who received significant coverage in the sixties (in part, no doubt, because she was of Russian émigré origin).[137] The magazine also ran countless stories about actors caught in the snares of business dealings. One 1962 piece ran under the headline "Producer-Plantation Driver, or Contracts of Enslavement" and backed Italian Claudia Cardinale's efforts to break with her studio, which, it said, gave her no choice of parts and no time off and forbade her from marrying.[138] Directors, too, were often shown fighting to pursue their artistic vocations— something the magazine made plain would have been their birthright as Soviet professionals. Marcel Carné's decision to shoot a film on Alexandre Dumas was a tragedy, said the magazine, because the French director was interested only in contemporary subject matter. "How can one speak of 'artistic freedom' when one of the most prominent directors is forced either to do something for which

136. Dzhaims Kelli (James Kelly), "Bett Devis," SE, no. 15 (1960): 16–17.

137. See, for example, Iu. Sher, "Marina Vlady," SE, no. 17 (1962): 18–19. Vlady married the actor-singer-cult figure Vladimir Vysotskii in 1969.

138. "Prodiuser-Plantator, ili Kabal'nye Kontrakty," SE, no. 9 (1962).

he has no heart, but which the producers will pay for, or to find himself once again unemployed?!"[139]

As a rule, *Soviet Screen* made more room on its pages for foreign masters, maligned and mistreated, than for foreign (commercial) productions. Masscult cinema was of course inferior by definition; its main defects—moral degeneracy, which covered both sex and violence, and frivolity—were inevitable by-products of a capitalist mode of cultural production. In *Myths of Western Cinema,* a 1963 series, critics dissected capitalist moviemaking genre by genre in typical fashion. Comedy, for instance, was marked as "a means for distracting people from the urgent problems of real life and 'a great pacifier,'" thereby remaining primitive to the extent of naïveté from an artistic point of view."[140] Horror movies, thrillers, and films about war were said to inculcate a taste for violence in audiences and blamed for rising crime rates in the West.[141]

Sympathy for the oppressed and championing of the righteous, the innate superiority of the Soviet cultural system, and the treachery of its rival were the warhorses of Soviet propaganda. No less a publication than *Izvestiia* ran a piece about Marilyn Monroe's suicide, "The Tragedy of a Movie Star," pronouncing her death "unequivocal proof" of masscult's depravity. "Marilyn Monroe was Hollywood's victim. Hollywood gave birth to her and murdered her."[142] What distinguished *Soviet Screen* was not its performance of these familiar ideological notes but rather their unusual harmonics. The same article on Bette Davis that lamented her fate as a cast-off star also described her work, almost entirely unknown to Soviet audiences at the time, and offered seven photographs of her (one studio portrait and six movie stills); the overall size of the visual material on Davis significantly exceeded that of the text. Most *Soviet Screen* articles on foreign cinema followed a similar pattern. Only two films with Monroe, *All About Eve* and *Some Like It Hot,* were distributed in the USSR, but that did not prevent the magazine from both writing about her and exploiting her image. It was also on the pages of *Soviet Screen,* and not the movie screen, that most people in the USSR encountered the French New Wave, James Bond—indeed, most trends in contemporary foreign cinema. For all the hoopla about bourgeois cultural infiltration, the range of foreign films shown in the USSR was actually quite small, a fraction of overall production. Reading *Soviet Screen* offered viewers a kind of secondhand consumption

---

139. "Frantsiia," *SE,* no. 5 (1961): 20.

140. A. Kukarkin, "Mify zapadnogo kino," *SE,* no. 12 (1963): 18.

141. This was a particularly popular theme for American and West German cinema, accused of supporting the forces of fascist revival (another trope of Soviet Cold War propaganda). See, for example, "Revanshizm i ego 'iskusstvo,'" *SE,* no. 6 (1965): 21.

142. *Izvestiia,* 7 August 1962. A. Adzhubei recalled that his decision as editor of *Izvestiia* to publish a more extensive article on Monroe's career and death "shocked the orthodox public." A. Adzhubei, *Te desiat' let* (Moscow, 1989), 125.

experience, drawing them into an international cinematic imaginary otherwise unavailable.[143]

That this information was set in a Soviet ideological framework goes without saying. But the magazine's heavy use of visual material opened the door to uses outside this frame; any reader could well admire and display images from movies held up for condemnation in Soviet media. It is also clear from its presentation of anti-Western critiques that *Soviet Screen* got more mileage from them than mere moralizing and aesthetic education. The magazine was not above putting ideology into the service of intrigue and mild titillation.

An extensive 1960 piece, "Cinema of the 'Free World,'" ostensibly analyzing the inundation of poor little Belgium (in its terms) by Hollywood productions, was a laundry list of horror, thriller, and romantic film titles strung together for effect. "They say that a film's title is its 'visiting card,'" the piece began. "Let's start to read the list then. I will forewarn you, reader, that you will feel your Nerves on the Edge....I ask you not to be frightened when A Murderer Talks to You....If you'd like, you can watch The Kiss That Kills or you can find yourself In the Net of a Sadist, see Blood on the Street, and at the sight of this Die from Pleasure." The article went on in this provocative fashion for two full pages and even mimicked the graphics for horror films in its title banner, as any reader could note by comparing it with the images from American film publicity that were also included.[144]

A 1962 review of a new French book, *Hollywood Babylone,* explained that the "cult of stars" was a cynical ploy on the part of businessmen to capitalize on the "unhealthy interests" of the audience. (The review itself was titled "The Business of Blood and Dirt.") At the same time, it teased readers by hinting at the kinds of information they too would have, if they were ever to sully themselves with a book like *Hollywood Babylone.* They would not, as everyone knew; such books were not published inside the USSR. But the review offered readers a glimpse all the same: "The book gives a graphic picture of the corrupted morals of Hollywood, that 'factory of dreams' with its harems, producers' escapades, drunkenness, debauchery, and all possible means of perversion and drug abuse!" Or, "The book presents photocopies of love letters, authentic and fabricated, of bank checks used to pay for love or crimes, and snapshots of these crimes." And to top off the tease, the article included an image from the "business of blood and dirt": the cover of an American movie magazine, *Confidential,* featuring

---

143. E. Kartseva's *Sdelano v Gollivude* (Moscow, 1964) is a classic example of this kind of secondhand consumption, discussing (with many stills) a host of movies few Soviets would ever see, including *Psycho, Citizen Kane,* and *Rebel without a Cause.* It had a respectable print run of seventy thousand. Kartseva also wrote regularly for *SE* in the same vein; see, for example, "Kogda zvezdy gasnut," *SE,* no. 6 (1962): 18–19, and "Mushketery s kol'tami za poiasom," *SE,* no. 15 (1962): 18–19.

144. Iu. Sher, "Kino 'svobodnogo mira,'" *SE,* no. 24 (1960): 20.

Jayne Mansfield, bare-shouldered and vamping for the camera in a slinky black dress.[145] For *Soviet Screen* readers who knew English, there was also the headline "Jayne Mansfield's Wacky Weekend in the Mountains" to contemplate.

Gossip about gossip was a vital genre for the new Soviet movie culture, providing both new information and a new kind of cultural experience. American actor Deanna Durbin had once been a darling of moviegoers in the USSR, but few people knew anything about her personal life. *Soviet Screen* ran an article about Durbin in 1965, describing how she was being hunted in her retirement by paparazzi outside Paris. This was a disgrace, a sign of the debased morals of capitalism, "the price of glory," as one header for the piece put it. Yet *Soviet Screen also* published a paparazzi shot of Durbin. "You probably recognized her too?" the magazine asked its readers. "No comment" (a trope for these gossip-about-gossip pieces) ran the second header.[146] The magazine was working both sides of the aisle and working them very well. Precisely what was the main information here, we might ask: the image of a middle-aged Durbin or its ideological gloss? The crucial point to recognize is that consuming *Soviet Screen* required no definite answer. The magazine's approach allowed its readers both cheap thrills (albeit in measured doses) and a sense of moral superiority. Look how dowdy (or lovely, old-looking, etc.) she is now! Look how horrible it is that she is hounded by those money-grubbing photographers! In this sense, the ideological message of gossip about gossip was not beside the point; it was an integral part of the point and of people's experiences of Soviet movie culture.

Once again, though *Soviet Screen* was not the only publication to provide information about foreign cinema, it was the Soviet viewer's main source, and it was also particularly important because it placed the foreign and the Soviet toe-to-toe. One goal of the juxtaposition was to burnish the reputation of the Soviet side. But opening up the pages of the leading film magazine to foreigners, no less than opening screens to foreign productions, might also corrode the idea of Soviet superiority and exceptionalism. On the one hand, juxtaposing images of foreigners and Soviets allowed for direct comparisons, and these might not always run in the Soviets' favor. How *did* Anastasiia Vertinskaia stand up as a beauty next to Audrey Hepburn and Sophia Loren? *Soviet Screen* was a cultural product that practically demanded such comparisons. On the other hand, jumbling together foreign and Soviet images might actually flatten out the differences between the two. Though the Soviet film industry claimed it made no stars in the Western sense, the images of Soviet and foreign actors in *Soviet Screen* and other publications often looked similar, and they were probably used in the same way: some people cut out the photo portrait of Vertinskaia; others preferred Hepburn. The place of the actor's image in everyday life crossed ideological barriers.

145. A. Goncharov, "Biznes krovi i griazi," *SE*, no. 16 (1962): 20.
146. "Tsena slavy," *SE*, no. 6 (1965): 21.

Figure 2.6. Glamour without borders: *Soviet Screen*, 1959. Soviet and American cineastes at the U.S. premiere of *The Cranes Are Flying*.

Soviet Screen did, however, spill a great deal of ink striving to maintain the barriers, and not only in its criticism of foreign cinema cultures. The bulk of the magazine by far was devoted to Soviet cinema-art, which it depicted as a comradely realm of hardworking people—a socialist production process in ideal form. That one would find similarly talented and dedicated people working together in laboratories and construction sites and collective farms throughout the country went without saying; cinema's very role was to depict this truth for millions. The standard *Soviet Screen* approach to writing about an actor was to focus on his or her work and its development over time. Many a "creative portrait" (*tvorcheskii portret*), as the genre was known, began with tales of an actor's arduous training at VGIK and apprenticeship to one of cinema's masters. Regular features on the school also emphasized the heavy workload and included photographs of aspiring young actors studying weighty tomes in literature and mathematics.[147] Interviews often adopted as serious tone. Soviet actors discussed how they prepared for their roles with intensive reading, struggling to reveal the essence of their characters, and how responsible they felt toward their viewers and their art. From time to time, readers would encounter complaints about condescending and tyrannical directors who thwarted an actor's growth as an artist, but for the most part the magazine endorsed the cult of directorial mastery.

147. For example, the photo-essay "Kogda idut ekzameny," *SE*, no. 15 (1963): 10–11.

A director was almost always a heroic figure on its pages, the true heir to the glorious Soviet artistic tradition. And perhaps more than anything else, this attention lavished on directors signaled the magazine's overall orientation toward cinema as labor, duty, and artistry.

Yet as was true of its coverage of foreign cinema, *Soviet Screen* had both a rigid ideological frame and a wealth of information that spilled right over its edges. For as much as the magazine pressed the point that moviemaking was serious, socialist work as well as an art, it also presented a world of special personalities with a singular relationship to the rest of society. Personal information about film professionals did splash the pages. A 1962 article on actor Liudmila Kasatkina quoted her saying that all her successes were less important to her than her son, Aleshka. "Gosh, I don't want to brag, but you can see for yourself what a wonderful little boy he is!" she said, and *Soviet Screen* handily published a candid shot of Kasatkina and her son with their arms outstretched as if about to embrace.[148] The same issue had other actors chatting about their everyday lives and photos of them at home—Liudmila Shagalova with her stamp collection and in action with her hula hoop, Lidiia Smirnova cross-country skiing, Svetlana Kharitonova cooking and walking her dog. The caption on Smirnova's photo told readers it had been taken "an hour before work," and the hula hooping was explained with reference to how important it was for an actor to stay in shape. But these were tenuous connections at best; the principal focus of the material was on the actors' lives outside work. In *Soviet Screen* viewers also learned that Nikolai Rybnikov's parents had objected to his choice of profession (they had wanted him to become a doctor) and that he liked to ski and fish and go to hockey games in his spare time.[149] Innokentii Smokhtunovskii told the magazine that he suffered from shyness more than anything else in life.[150] *Soviet Screen*'s reporters also gave the star treatment to master directors, many of whom were photographed in their homes. There was even a shot of director Sergei Gerasimov and his wife and collaborator, Tamara Makarova, making soup together; both were wearing aprons.[151]

The amount of this kind of material in *Soviet Screen* was always quite limited and subdued in comparison with the coverage in a magazine like *Confidential*. Though there were many star couples in Soviet cinema, fans had no photo spreads from their weddings, no inside accounts of their divorces.[152] To judge

148. "Liudmila Kasatkina," *SE,* no. 5 (1962). This issue celebrated International Women's Day.

149. "Nikolai Rybnikov," *SE,* no. 2 (1957).

150. G. Medvedeva, "Nash korrespondent v gostiakh . . . u Innokentiia Smokhtunovskogo," *SE,* no. 19 (1964): 10–11.

151. A. Sergeev, G. Ter-Ovanesov, "Nash korrespondent v gostiakh . . . u Tamary Makarovoi i Sergeia Gerasimova," *SE,* no. 3 (1964): 10–11.

152. Overall, there seems to have been a greater willingness to provide information and imagery about the lives of foreign actors than about Soviet ones. Some sources indicate

from anecdotal evidence and the censorious remarks of critics about shallow fans, people found ways to gossip about such things nonetheless. And *Soviet Screen* offered periodic openings—one might even say invitations—to do just that: to mull over cineastes' off-screen lives and to use them in their own. With its heavy use of naturally posed photographs and its covers designed for display, the magazine succeeded in personalizing cinema for audiences even when it made no direct reference to personal matters. It built on and promoted people's interest in a world of individual personalities—not only heroes and stories, and perhaps not heroes and stories at all.

Soviet Screen and Soviet film journalism in general portrayed actors as people in demand, special people one wanted to learn about and build a relationship with; these were also people one might have a piece of at home (an image on the wall, an autograph) without ever making their acquaintance. The closest parallels to actors in Soviet culture of the day—athletes and cosmonauts—were also media idols. But no Soviet actor, however many images of him one might find in magazines and kiosks, was ever officially lionized for his work the way Iurii Gagarin and colleagues were for their achievements in space. An actor, after all, should aspire to *play* a Gagarin. What did he stand for individually outside the frame of cinematic work? What was an actor outside a role? Soviet culture's first answer to this was simple and adamant: an actor was an artist, and a Soviet actor was a socialist artist whose work was to educate and inspire audiences; strictly speaking, the only reason to know an actor outside a role was to understand his or her creative process. But it was precisely the extracinematic, personal information about actors that Soviet culture was now also offering in unprecedented volume and inviting people to personalize, domesticate, and possess.

TELEVISION AND THE DOMESTICATION OF CINEMA

Television technology was the only altogether new element in the new post-Stalinist movie culture and arguably the most potent. It is true that cinema and TV were competitors for viewer attention, and given the high percentage of Soviet airtime devoted to screening films, including many new features still showing in theaters, the competition was in some respects even more pronounced in the USSR than in other countries.[153] In the 1970s, as TV access reached saturation levels, overall box-office figures declined, and most contemporary observers concluded that there was a direct causal link between the two phenomena: television was cinema's assassin. However, though the long-term trend in the USSR was clearly toward an increase in watching TV rather than going to movies,

---

that regional media provided more personal information from interviews with visiting Soviet actors than did central sources like *Soviet Screen,* but this is not something I have been able to verify.

153. For more on the competition between television and cinema, see chapters 4 and 5.

Figure 2.7. Aleksei Kapler chats with French cineastes on *Kinopanorama*, 1972. RIA Novosti. Used with permission.

this tells us more about changing patterns of leisure than about people's actual engagement with cinema and cinema culture. In the bigger picture of Soviet media culture, television can be seen as bolstering cinema, and not only because so much of TV programming was, in fact, movie programming. Television also promoted cinema by showcasing the industry and its professionals, and in the process it greatly expanded the range of information and experience open to viewers. If the hallmarks of the new movie culture were personalization and domestication, Soviet TV broadcasting offered both in powerful new forms.

Take, for example, *Kinopanorama,* one of the most popular Soviet TV programs of all time.[154] Introduced on Central TV in 1962, *Kinopanorama* was a regular monthly show of 90–120 minutes entirely devoted to cinema, and it ran straight through to the collapse of the USSR (and beyond). Picture a host and a guest or two, sitting in armchairs, smoking, drinking tea, and chatting about the world of cinema. The host would be a film professional (and some of Soviet cinema's most illustrious names sat in the chair over the years); the guests would be Soviet directors, screenwriters, actors, and critics, along with the occasional

154. *Kinopanorama* was not the first show on Central TV devoted to cinema. For earlier programs, see A. Iurovskii, *Televidenie: Poiski i resheniia* (Moscow, 1983), 126; A. Iu. Rozov, ed., *Shabolovka, 53: Stranitsy istorii televideniia* (Moscow, 1988), 116–117.

visiting foreigner. Like all Soviet programming, *Kinopanorama* was well orchestrated and controlled; in the sixties, when it broadcast live, editors vetted topics for conversation ahead of time and scripted and rehearsed some segments as well; the transition to prerecorded broadcasts in 1970 probably lowered editors' blood pressure levels but not levels of control. Nevertheless, *Kinopanorama* managed to strike an unusually informal and intimate tone for Soviet programming, and although it steered clear of overtly personal topics, it personalized the world of cinema for audiences in critical ways. Tea drinking and smoking on camera were part of it, to be sure. (Remember Liubov' Orlova, the "red star" who performed the role of casual interlocutor only on the pages of *Life* magazine? Soviet movie culture had room for the performance now.) Also important were the show's own efforts to establish connections across the screen divide. Viewers wrote to *Kinopanorama,* as they did to many popular TV programs, and *Kinopanorama* incorporated many of these letters into its programming. In one instance, a viewer wrote asking what had become of a young actor who had appeared years ago in a film written by the show's host from 1964 through 1971, Aleksei Kapler. (The film was the 1939 classic *Lenin in 1918.*) Kapler read the letter on the air and since he did not know the answer, asked viewers to contact the show if they had any information. Twenty minutes later, with the program still running, he told viewers he had just had a telephone call in the studio from the actor's neighbor; she now lived at such-and-such an address in the city of Noginsk. And a short while later, *Kinopanorama* brought her to Moscow to talk about her youthful career as an actor playing in one of the Soviet classics.[155]

Soviet viewers had other options for reaching out to actors. Many wrote to *Soviet Screen,* to Mosfil'm and other studios, and even to Goskino. But TV broadcasting held the potential for a more personal connection—or the sensation of a more personal connection—because only on television could viewers see and hear how actors responded to them. And television made this possible by programming shows like *Kinopanorama* and employing hosts like Aleksei Kapler, whose affability and preference for personal and colloquial language ("Oh Lord, I forgot the title! I had it written down here somewhere, but now I can't find my notes.") facilitated the experience of contact for viewers.[156] Another key example of this dynamic was the genre of shows known as the "television café" (*televizionnyi kafe*).

In the early sixties, with the Komsomol promoting cafés as a solution to the problem of cultured leisure, Central TV launched a television version known as

155. S. Muratov and G. Fere, *Liudi, kotorye vkhodiat bez stuka* (Moscow, 1971), 99–100.

156. Quotation from Kapler as recalled by *Kinopanorama* director K. Marinina in Rozov, *Shabolovka, 53,* 180–181. For more on Kapler's on-air personality, see M. Krasnianskaia, "Mnogie khoteli 'skorrekirovat' ego ubezhdeniia," *Nezavisimaia gazeta,* 15 October 2004; interview with M. Krasnianskaia, Moscow, July 2002 (Gosteleradiofond Oral History Project).

Little Blue Flame (*Goluboi ogonek*), which became staple evening entertainment for tens of millions and spawned copies on regional stations throughout the Union.[157] (It is safe to say that many more people knew TV cafés than physical ones.) The approach was similar to *Kinopanorama*'s in that viewers were set up to "meet" interesting guests in a comparatively informal and social setting, but here the setting was a mock café: *Little Blue Flame*'s set had a stylized backdrop of the Moscow TV tower, Shabolovka, a performance stage, and little round tables for the guests, who ran the gamut from cineastes, opera singers, and ballerinas to prize-winning athletes and miners, military men, cosmonauts, and crooners.[158] Hosts circulated among the tables and engaged in pleasing banter with the guests in between performances. Contemporary America's most famous TV critic, Jack Gould, described the broadcast he saw in 1965 (a thirty-minute fragment on the ABC network) enthusiastically:

> There was a corps of chorus girls who could have come straight from the Jackie Gleason show. A puppet band did a pantomime to the Glenn Miller hit, "In the Mood." Edith Pyekha was the vocalist who knew the nuances of effective salesmanship in putting over a song. There was also a fine juggler, Cossack dancers and a wisp of the Bolshoi Ballet.[159]

In the days of live TV, *Little Blue Flame* and other café shows were typically more tightly scripted and rehearsed than an interview program like *Kinopanorama*. Intentional deviations from the set program were rare. In 1962, for instance, the poet Andrei Voznesenskii caused an uproar by reading a poem on Central TV's *Little Blue Flame* that he had not cleared with the show's producers ahead of time.[160] Still, the absence of teleprompters and the near-certainty of some kind of technical glitch arising on glitch-prone early Soviet TV added elements of unpredictability. Hosts and guests had to rely on their wits and sometimes speak extemporaneously. Viewers were even treated to some genuine spontaneity, as in the case of one show when a bewildered guest, a collective farm chairwoman, tried to crawl under the table at the end of her chat with the

---

157. The "blue" in *Blue Flame* refers to the informal name for television, the "blue screen" (*goluboi ekran*). The first hosts were actors and singers, but the studio soon turned to TV personalities instead. Launched in 1962, the program ran more or less monthly and then, as of the late sixties, exclusively on major holidays, most notably, New Year's Eve. Fedor Razzakov, *Dos'e na zvezd: Tainy televideniia* (Moscow, 2000), 113–115; Sergei Muratov, "Kofe i liudi," *Sovetskaia kul'tura*, 1 April 1965, published in Muratov, *Televidenie v poiskakh televideniia* (Moscow, 2001), 44–51; A. Makarov, "Vstrechi v kafe," *Teatr*, no. 2 (1963): 83–88.

158. Other café-style shows focused solely on actors (e.g., *Teatral'nye vstrechi—Theatrical Encounters*).

159. Jack Gould, "TV: Soviet Variety Fare," *New York Times*, 25 February 1965.

160. GARF, f. 6903, op. 1. d. 766, ll. 8–9.

host. The director had told her to "tell us a little about yourself and then move off-screen," and she had decided diving for the floor was the best solution.[161]

Viewers "went" to a TV café ostensibly for the performances, but the format also invited them to indulge in a mild form of voyeurism or to imagine that they, too, were guests sitting side–by side with the country's leading lights. In this sense, the prizewinning milkmaids and miners who participated, though not the stars of the program, were proxies for people on the other side of the screen. Alternatively, viewers might imagine themselves as hosts who, thanks to the wonder of TV technology, had invited these talented guests into their very own homes. This was the concept advanced at the time by TV professionals and critics, who delighted in the café shows.[162] "*Little Blue Flame* wins the viewer over with intimacy, informality, and a pleasing sensation of human equality with people we have long been accustomed almost to bow down to," said one reviewer.[163] A TV café was no place for gossip or scandal; viewers heard precious little talk of personal life on these programs. But one does not need a discussion of the personal to have a personal experience, and this was the essence of Soviet TV's contribution to the new movie culture. Like *Kinopanorama,* a TV café program held out the potential for viewers to experience new forms of intimacy with film professionals. After all, broadcasting delivered its sights and sounds in a setting a priori more intimate than a movie theater, say, or a creative meeting in a factory club. Though this was true of films shown on television as well, *Little Blue Flame, Kinopanorama,* and similar programs were distinguished by being marked as "real"—and, we might add, the sensation of real-life interaction was all the stronger given that the programs were broadcast live. Television served up actors out of character, along with an opportunity to engage with them as individuals. ("What in the world is she wearing?," the viewer asks. "How different his voice sounds than in the movies!" "She fidgets a lot." "He's left-handed, just like me.")

The personalization and domestication dynamic did not inhere in TV technology per se, any more than a Soviet-made picture postcard required a glossy head shot of an actor or a magazine about cinema demanded photographs of women in tulle gowns and gossip about gossip. They were choices, the results of manifold decisions that made up post-Stalinist movie culture. In television, the decision to site the technology in individual homes was critical, but so too was the choice to offer certain kinds of programming.

Kinopanorama's stated mission was to educate viewers about cinema-art, and this was also Kapler's goal, however informal he may have been on the air. In 1971, he told an interviewer about a recent visit to a high school with one of his

161. Razzakov, Dos'e na zvezd: Tainy televideniia, 114.
162. See, for example, Sergei Muratov, "Razmyshleniia u teleekrana," Sovetskoe radiove-shchanie i televidenie, no. 11 (1964); Muratov and Fere, Liudi, kotorye vkhodiat.
163. Makarov, "Vstrechi v kafe," 83.

cineaste colleagues. The other man, a character actor, told the students he had been in the film *Operation 'y.'* "Oooh!" shouted the kids. *Operation 'y'* was a genuine blockbuster. But when the actor went on to say he had had a small role as a police officer, they lost interest. Kapler was dismayed: "I would like to be able to tell TV viewers about a man who gave all his life to cinema and who in essence does the same thing on screen as, let's say, some mediocre player of hero-studs," he said. "But all the girls are in love with that guy, and no one knows the legitimately talented actor."[164]

The pattern is now familiar. Kapler was straining against the gusts of Soviet star culture, and they were gusts of his own making. The language of his interview comments is interesting in this regard. "I would like *to be able to* tell TV viewers about a man who gave all his life to cinema." Did something or someone prevent him from doing so? Soviet TV programs did not live or die by ratings— far from it. Soviet television ran scores of programs that it suspected were unpopular. *Kinopanorama* did not need to prove its worth by winning audience approval.

Kapler died in 1979, and we cannot ask him why he chose to continue interviewing the men who played "hero-studs." His own biography, however, provides food for thought. Aleksei Kapler (born Lazar Kapler in 1904) began his career as an actor in Kiev and went on to write some of the leading films of the cinematic canon in the Stalinist era, including two Stalin-Prize winners (*Lenin in 1918* and *She Defends the Motherland—Ona zashchishchaet rodinu*, 1943). After a brief romance with Stalin's daughter, Svetlana, provoked the dictator's ire, Kapler was convicted on trumped-up charges of being a British spy and spent ten years in a forced labor camp. In 1954, he was released, returned to cinema, and wrote two movies on the Soviet hit parade for the fifties and sixties, a zany comedy called *Striped Voyage (Polosatyi reis,* 1961) and the blockbuster *Amphibian Man*.[165] Kapler knew Soviet cinema as few people did, in other words; he knew the heights of Stalinist success and the depths of Stalinist repression; he knew haute ideological drama, melodrama, and comedy; his success in producing box-office hits demonstrates that he knew a great deal about Soviet audience taste, too. Kapler not only interviewed the players of hero-studs but also wrote their roles. And as much as he may have wished that viewers would show more interest in the actors he thought truly talented, Kapler, it seems, valued his connection with them as a screenwriter and TV host. We could parse this as a form of self-interest or cynicism. But television was no road to riches in the sixties, and beyond that, Kapler's life shows him as someone who identified with Soviet cinema. Its successes were his successes. *Kinopanorama* did not need to

---

164. Muratov and Fere, *Liudi, kotorye vkhodiat,* 98.

165. The relationship with Svetlana, though not official public knowledge, was well known in elite circles. See Svetlana Allilueva, *Dvadtsat' pisem k drugu* (Moscow, 1990), 134–140.

be popular with audiences to survive, but Kapler, I suspect, wanted it to reach as large an audience as possible. The goal of promoting Soviet cinema and educating viewers could be advanced with hero-studs across the table in the studio and star-struck girls in the audience.

Or could it? This was the question posed by the new Soviet movie culture.

THE PARADOX OF THE NEW SOVIET MOVIE CULTURE

In the 1961 film *Dima Gorin's Career* (*Kar'era Dimy Gorina*), Aleksandr Dem'ianenko is Dima, a young and nerdy loner striving to make a career in a bank. Fate sends Dima on a business trip to the taiga, where he encounters a group of heroic Soviet youths who welcome him into their collective and teach him the value of labor and comradeship. Dima is transformed from a pampered and selfish *meshchanin* (petit bourgeois, philistine) into a real Soviet person. He abandons the bank and takes a job with the collective stringing high-tension wires across the taiga, and everyone lives happily ever after.

Dima Gorin's Career is a classic Soviet coming-of-age story in many respects.[166] Its good and bad categories are neatly flagged for the viewer—nature/lucre, collective energy/petty individualism and, of course, Komsomol/non-Komsomol (Dima does not join until he finds himself in the woods with the model youth). And one sure sign of Dima's initial shallowness is his obsession with images of movie stars. An early scene in the film shows Dima alone in his room in his pajamas with his two collections: stamps and film magazines, both of which mix Soviet and foreign "specimens." After peering at the stamps for some time, Dima is seized by an idea, and the musical score shifts to a perky tune. Wielding a pair of scissors, Dima goes through his magazines, cuts out his favorite parts of various female star images—best nose, best mouth, and so on—and pastes them together to construct a new image. Dima makes his own star, a hybrid Soviet-foreign face and, once satisfied by his handiwork, he sits back in his chair and smiles at her dreamily. When he arrives in the taiga, he meets the very woman he has created and falls in love with her. She is Galia, a crew forewoman (played by Tat'iana Koniukhova) and part of the young collective that educates him to be a real Soviet person.

Much in the manner of the moralizing criticism in *Soviet Screen, Dima Gorin's Career* is a film that talks back to the star culture in which it participates.[167] The

---

166. For the bildungsroman as the master plot of socialist realism, see Katerina Clark, *The Soviet Novel: History as Ritual* (Bloomington, IN, 2000), and "Socialist Realism *with* Shores," in *Socialist Realism without Shores,* ed. Thomas Lahusen and Evgeny Dobrenko (Durham, NC, 1997), 27–50.

167. The scene also has interesting echoes of Soviet montage theory from the 1920s and, in particular, of Lev Kuleshov's famous experiments. Kuleshov paired different images (a plate of soup, a coffin) with identical close-ups of an actor's face in montage sequences. Audiences invariably interpreted each close-up as a response to the first image they had

dichotomy between real Soviet women and movie stars is as clear in the film as are all the other good/bad binary oppositions, and it too is resolved expediently. Just as we understand that Dima the bank employee could not have been a Komsomol member, we know that Dima the forest worker will have no truck with glossy photos of movie stars. The film's happy ending proves that Soviets do not in fact need these images; the ideal woman was there along, and it only took Dima's liberation from his petty world to find her. But even as *Dima Gorin's Career* resoundingly rejects star culture, it also undermines its own argument by suggesting that the culture can be useful. The film directs viewers to do violence to the imagery that surrounds them—to cut it up into pieces—and then to make use of its components and their own imagination to create something new and personally meaningful.[168] Star imagery itself is a means to an end, the movie indicates; it can lead viewers to the beauty and heroism of everyday Soviet life. After all, would Dima have recognized beauty and been able to envisage his ideal if he had not had the stuff of movie magazines before him? And if he had not fallen in love with Galia, would Dima have made the all-important decision to stay in the taiga, the decision that led to his reeducation, his redemption as a real Soviet person, and his happiness?

Dima Gorin's Career's ambivalent message about star culture and Soviet viewers is emblematic of the dilemma faced by Soviet movie culture as a whole. Publicizing star images was an effective method, in the USSR as elsewhere in the world, for attracting people into theaters and communicating with audiences. But communicating what? Any Soviet viewer knew that Dima did not find an ordinary Soviet young woman in the taiga; he found Tat'iana Koniukhova, a renowned beauty of the day. The non-star Dima had created was very much a recognizable star for Soviet audiences. And Dima himself was not only Dima but Aleksandr Dem'ianenko, who was in the midst of his own highly successful career playing, for the most part, nerdy, decent, love-struck young men. Dem'ianenko was also a Soviet movie star. And as Soviet stars were, by and large, people with extraordinary looks and personal appeal, focusing on them ran the risk of deflecting attention from image to image maker, message to messenger.

Soviet culture had no doubt always run this risk. Iurii Lotman argued that although in the theater it is possible and even necessary for the audience to forget about the actor, film is too semiotically dense a medium and too closely tied to everyday life to allow for the total identification of actor and role. For this

seen on the screen (an expression of hunger or sorrow, for example). Thus, the actor's performance was nothing more (or less) than a montage element wholly subordinate to the director's manipulation. Dima's montage project similarly puts him in total control.

168. The violence of Dima's act is underscored by the fact that he pastes his new star portrait on top of a magazine cover with imagery taken from what appears to be one of Goya's "black" paintings (*Saturn Devouring One of His Sons*).

reason, he maintained, the film actor always exists as both "the player of a given role" and "a sort of cinema myth."

> Such concepts as "Charlie Chaplin," "Jean Gabin," "Mastroianni," "Anthony Quinn," "Aleksej Batalov," "Igor Il'linskij," "Mareckaja," and "Smokhtunovskij," are a reality for the audience and are much more influential on audience perception of the role than is the case in theater. The cinema audience deliberately and consistently connects films having a central actor into one series and views them as a text, a kind of artistic whole.[169]

Lotman's work considered the "mythologized persona of the actor" an inevitable component of any cinema culture and a problem only insofar as it had the potential to thwart creativity. But the mythologized persona held destructive potential for a Soviet culture that counted on cinematic images to inspire heroism and respect for labor, art, and Soviet tradition. If the screen delivered heroic images that matched and reinforced one another, and there was nothing in the culture to counter them, then cinema might deliver a powerful, unified message—the actor and the heroic image forcibly united in a conceptual whole. Arguably, Soviet culture came closest to this ideal of managing audience perception in the 1930s and early 1940s, when there were few points of comparison for Soviet cinema and little in the way of extracinematic culture. Yet even then it seems likely that many viewers also built personal relationships with actors based on perceptions of their individual personalities, looks, and other subjective factors (not least their memories of cinema in earlier times) separate from their understanding of the characters they played. Soviet culture may have done its best to keep attention squarely focused on Chapaev and his heroic message rather than on Boris Babochkin, the actor who played him, but the fact that people wrote to the actor asking for advice and special favors alone indicates that no merging process is ever complete.[170]

The post-Stalinist 1950s through the 1970s saw a transformation in Soviet cinematic experience that had political, sociological, and cultural dimensions. The tremendous growth in the number of films and in viewers' access to them facilitated the connections between roles that Lotman underscored. There were also critical changes outside the movie theater. From postcards to festivals, film journalism to television, cinema reached further into Soviet everyday life than ever before. The fact that some of this movie culture conveyed images and ideas from the Soviets' ideological opponents was considered by many contemporaries an obvious problem. But homegrown images and experience could be equally important. The new Soviet movie culture opened up spaces for viewers to build

169. Jurij Lotman, *Semiotics of Cinema,* trans. Mark E. Suino (Ann Arbor, MI, 1976), 90–91.

170. See N. B. Babochkina, ed., *Boris Babochkin—Vospominaniia, dnevniki, pis'ma* (Moscow, 1996).

new relationships with actors and movies and to contemplate them outside their didactic function. Like the "silly girls" who wrote to *Soviet Screen* with their requests for photos and autographs and their dreams of becoming actors, Dima Gorin, the young bank clerk, was portrayed as a pathetic and unworthy figure. But Dima did have imagination, and he had a fantasy life fueled by images from Soviet movie culture. On screen, the fantasy naturally drew him straight to the truths of Soviet life—labor, self-sacrifice, and the collective spirit. Movie culture helped Dima blossom into a real Soviet hero. Off screen, millions of people went on collecting those star images and relating to them in their own private ways. As midwife to stardom and fandom, Soviet movie culture offered viewers the opportunity to bypass the Soviets' culture of heroes and, like Dima Gorin, to sit at home alone in their pajamas and create their own ideals. One need not imagine that these ideals were anti-Soviet in any way to understand the fundamental clash between this relationship to the movies and the Soviets' official model of cinema as a primary moral and aesthetic educator, particularly for youth.

The solution most often proposed was to create compelling new young heroes and to boost publicity for the heroic classics. In the sixties the film industry refurbished and rereleased many classics of the Stalin era. *Chapaev,* in particular, was treated to a mass promotional campaign in 1964 as 1,800 copies of a new print were distributed and premiered throughout the country. But by that time, the figure of Chapaev had entered the realm of Soviet folklore and many—perhaps most—young people were more likely to share off-color jokes about him than buy a ticket to see the original film. A good number of them would have seen *Chapaev* on television, as the film was, and would remain, a staple of Soviet broadcasting.[171] But *Chapaev* as something to be sampled while eating dinner, arguing with relatives, or waiting for a date to come to the door was a world away from the *Chapaev* of the thirties, when it may well have been the only film in the local theater for six months—indeed, for many Soviets, the only film they would have ever seen.

The sea change in the cinematic sphere after Stalin's death—in production, infrastructure, and movie culture—pulled cinema in the Soviet Union far from its ideological framework in many important ways. And yet it is essential to recognize that all these changes also helped make cinema a stunning success story for Soviet culture in the media age. Four billion tickets a year at the box office, *Chapaev* or *Kinopanorama* over dinner, the postcard album on the sofa, must be recognized for the achievements they were. This was the paradox, the successful failure, of the new Soviet movie culture.

171. An official celebration of the film's thirtieth anniversary was held at Moscow's Rossiia Cinema on 6 November 1964. *SE,* no. 12 (1964). On the Chapaev joke phenomenon, see Seth Graham, "A Cultural Analysis of the Russo-Soviet Anekdot" (PhD diss., University of Pittsburgh, 2001), esp. chap. 5.

WHAT WAS SAID WHEN THE MUSES WERE HEARD

FOREIGN RADIO IN SOVIET CONTEXTS

When the Everyman Opera Company brought its production of *Porgy and Bess* to the USSR in 1955, a young Truman Capote went along, too, as a reporter for the *New Yorker*. Capote called his account "The Muses Are Heard," a phrase he had heard many times talking to a solemn official from the Soviet Ministry of Culture. "When the cannons are silent, the muses are heard," the official said, and this was, in truth, a historic moment: no American theater company had visited the USSR since the 1920s.[1] But although *Porgy and Bess* stunned the selected few in Moscow and Leningrad, other foreign voices had enjoyed mass Soviet audiences for years—not muses, said the Soviet authorities, but sirens from the British Broadcasting Corporation (BBC), Radio Liberty (RL), the Voice of America (VOA), Deutsche Welle, Vatican Radio, and many other organizations that had begun broadcasting to the USSR soon after World War II.[2] The Soviet regime had countered at once with a defensive strategy of jamming, or broadcasting signals to block out the "enemy voices," as they were known. It was a losing battle. By 1955, the USSR was spending more on jamming than on broadcasting its own programs, and officials at the radio administration were discussing the possibility that, given both the amount of interference they were throwing up and the impossibility of precision jamming, they would soon paralyze the domestic radio network entirely.[3] Television, the wunderkind of postwar Soviet modernity, was also under threat in some areas: in 1958, Lithuania's minister of communications implored Moscow to suspend radio jamming in the

---

1. Truman Capote, "Porgy and Bess in Russia: The Muses are Heard," *New Yorker,* 20 October 1956, 27 October 1956.

2. The British Broadcasting Corporation (BBC) began its Russian service in 1946, the Voice of America (VOA) in 1947, and Radio Liberation (later, Radio Liberty) in 1953. The best overall account is Michael Nelson, *War of the Black Heavens: The Battles of Western Broadcasting in the Cold War* (London, 1997). Broadcasting from Soviet bloc countries did not figure in the category "enemy voices" (a term derived from VOA), although it was troublesome to the Soviet authorities at different times (e.g., Polish radio in 1956, Czechoslovak radio and TV in 1968). For simplicity's sake, I use the term "foreign broadcasting" to refer to non-Soviet bloc countries (including, as of 1964, the People's Republic of China).

3. GARF, f. 6903, op.1, d. 488, ll. 158–159.

evenings so people could watch Vilnius TV.[4] Meanwhile, outside the downtown areas of a few major cities, foreign broadcasters had little trouble evading the jammers. The cannons were silent, and the voices were heard.

Much of what we know about foreign radio in the USSR is what we have heard from former broadcasters themselves, and it is a chorus of celebration.[5] Former Soviet citizens have chimed in too: for some, foreign radio was a vital source of information about events within and beyond Soviet borders; for others, a resource for Western popular music and a portal to a different way of life. To this day, the guest book on BBC presenter Seva Novgorodtsev's website is awash with well wishes from Soviet-era fans grateful for his popular music program in the 1970s and '80s; Novgorodtsev, like the VOA's Willis Conover, another musical host, is a widely acknowledged cultural icon of the postwar era.[6] Yet for all the extravagant praise these figures, and the radios in general, have received, there has been very little analysis of their relationship to *Soviet* cultural politics and practices. What does the history of the foreign radio phenomenon have to tell us about Soviet culture in the media age?

We might begin by reminding ourselves that the very success of the foreign voices in the USSR was predicated on the scope of Soviet cultural ambition and achievements. It was the commitment to culture as a linchpin of the socialist idea that delivered broadcasting to most Soviet homes by 1960. At the same time, however, the phenomenon of foreign radio in the USSR pointed to endemic Soviet blind spots and weaknesses. The great irony of this Trojan horse is that it was built in large measure by the conquered people's hands: Soviet industry produced the shortwave sets that carried enemy voices (even as the regime was also pouring millions into a futile effort to shut them up).

This was, from one perspective, a stunning failure and as good an example as any of Soviet policy incoherence on the macrolevel. Yet there is another

4. LYA (Lietuvos ypatingasis archyvas- Lithuanian Special Archive), f. 1171, ap. 194, b. 10, ll. 4–6, http://www.radiojamming.info/.

5. Arch Puddington, *Broadcasting Freedom: The Cold War Triumph of Radio Free Europe and Radio Liberty* (Lexington, KY, 2000); Gene Sosin, *Sparks of Liberty: An Insider's Memoir of Radio Liberty* (University Park, PA, 1999); George Urban, *Radio Free Europe and the Pursuit of Democracy: My War within the Cold War* (New Haven, CT, 1997); James Critchlow, *Radio Hole-in-the-Head/Radio Liberty: An Insider's Account of Cold War Broadcasting* (Washington, DC, 1995). For a helpful review essay, see Marsha Siefert, "Radio Diplomacy and the Cold War," *Journal of Communication* 53, no. 2 (2003): 363–373.

6. See Seva Novogodtsev's site, http://www.seva.ru. For comments on foreign radio, see V. Aksyonov's *In Search of Melancholy Baby* (New York, 1989), a touchstone text for all discussions of the influence of Western culture on postwar Soviet youth. In Russian, a similar role is played by Aleksei Kozlov, *"Kozel na sakse": I tak vsiu zhizn'...* (Moscow, 1998). See also Andrei Konchalovskii, *Nizkie istiny* (Moscow, 2000), 75–76; Liudmila Alexeyeva and Paul Goldberg, *The Thaw Generation: Coming of Age in the Post-Stalin Era* (Boston, 1990), 181–182.

perspective to consider, one where powerful bureaucratic and ideological logics worked to propel radio development in the Soviet Union *and* frame it as a success story for various individuals and institutions. It is within this framework that the specific problem of foreign broadcasting slipped on and off the official radar screen. We must also consider the various ways in which foreign broadcasting to the USSR might have worked to the regime's advantage. After all, a narrative of audio invasion had a lot to offer to the Soviet authorities. It confirmed their worldview (the historic struggle with the forces of capital and their leading role in it) while helping explain some obvious flabby spots on the domestic ideological body (the younger generation, in particular, seduced by the siren song of masscult). The phenomenon of foreign broadcasting to the USSR was also a ringing testament to its modern, technologically advanced society and a backhanded compliment to its international importance. In the period 1963 to 1968, the USSR lifted jamming almost completely, even as Soviet media continued to rail against the enemy voices. To some observers it looked as if the Soviet authorities had settled in for a hostile, useful peace.

They had not, because though the ideological category of enemy voices had its uses, to be sure, the reality of foreign radio broadcasting to the USSR did pose genuine, intractable problems. What the authorities objected to on the most basic level was information.[7] Jamming practices varied over time, but by and large the Soviets did not attempt to jam broadcasts with purely musical content, nor did they typically jam programs in foreign languages not native to peoples in the USSR, such as English. The programming deemed most offensive had to do with Soviet domestic affairs. This could be news of natural disasters or readings of literature banned inside the USSR; it could be first-person accounts from émigrés about historical events such as collectivization or analyses of Kremlin politics. In 1968, it was news of the Czechoslovak heresy of "socialism with a human face" and the subsequent crackdown that triggered the resumption of full-scale jamming. Evidence suggests, however, that the authorities were already moving in this direction in 1965–66.[8] Foreign broadcasting delivered information that the regime did not want people to have, period, and this made jamming, however ineffective, its natural stance.

Yet arguably, it was the very fact of foreign broadcasting inside the USSR, and not the informational content of its programs, that spoke loudest of all. By

---

7. That a large proportion of broadcasts were *not* informational in content did not mitigate Soviet objections, as articulated repeatedly in the press and diplomatic exchanges. Radio Liberty (which posed as a private organization but was unmasked as a CIA front in 1967) was considered particularly noxious and was most consistently jammed.

8. M. Lisann, *Broadcasting to the Soviet Union: International Politics and Radio* (New York, 1975). Lisann based his conclusion on a close reading of Soviet media sources. See also Gerhard Wettig, *Broadcasting and Détente: Eastern Policies and Their Implication for East-West Trade* (London, 1977), 7.

breaking the Soviet regime's media monopoly, foreign broadcasting shattered the regime's hold on the modes and meanings of cultural consumption in Soviet everyday life.[9] It is true that in the first decade after World War II, the regime's cultural monopoly was already being challenged by foreign cinema, as the famous trophy films dominated movie screens across the Union. But *Tarzan* and *The Girl of My Dreams* were presented in a controlled and very public Soviet framework; they were war booty, a decadent reward for a long-suffering population, and so limited by definition. Foreign broadcasting, on the other hand, offered an unauthorized, private experience without limits and with designs on everyday life. Its very presence in Soviet space was an anthem to the regime's impotence; its very popularity suggested that Soviet culture was substandard, replaceable, even irrelevant.

Foreign radio succeeded in changing the terms for broadcasting itself by introducing Soviet audiences to new models for media. Although no doubt many listeners found intimacy and entertainment in Soviet radio programming, and they could also tune in for something called *The Latest News (Poslednye izvestiia)*, these experiences were not the pith of the Soviets' broadcasting enterprise on its *own* terms. Radio in the Soviet context was designed to educate, inspire, and organize collectives; entertainment always took a backseat to edification, and information was to be provided on a need-to-know basis in line with longer-range political agendas. Broadcasting, in other words, was part of planned cultural economy that had little to do with popular taste or timeliness. By contrast, foreign broadcasters went out of their way to present themselves as the Soviet audience's intimate friend and a champion of its rights to information and satisfaction. Programming on foreign stations often mixed formats (news and music) and cultural registers (high and low, serious and silly)[10] and promoted entertainment for entertainment's sake in a way directly counter to Soviet cultural hierarchies and to the idea of uplift.[11] Finally, foreign radio modeled a very different relationship to time than what was to be found in Soviet media; it was, in a word, timely, and as it delivered not just news but "breaking news," foreign radio told Soviet listeners that they wanted, needed, and perhaps even had a right to be up-to-date in a modern world.

None of this would have mattered much had listeners spurned the advances of the enemy. But they did not, and the popularity of foreign radio

9. Cf. Thomas Wolfe, *Governing Soviet Journalism: The Press and the Socialist Person after Stalin* (Bloomington, IN, 2005), esp. 126–142.

10. Cf. the comments of the BBC Russian service's programming director in the sixties in Asa Briggs, *The History of Broadcasting in the United Kingdom*, vol. 5 (Oxford, 1995), 687.

11. Behind the scenes, people in charge of broadcasting to the Soviet bloc often defined the political stakes of radio entertainment in very different terms. See Hixson, *Parting the Curtain: Propaganda, Culture, and the Cold War, 1945–1961* (New York, 1997). On Radio Free Europe's use of Western popular music, see Puddington, *Broadcasting Freedom*, 135–141.

with Soviet audiences was an embarrassment to the regime both at home and abroad. Foreign broadcasting threw Soviet media culture on the defensive and then forced a conversation the culture did not wish to have and, more to the point, was utterly incapable of sustaining. By the early 1960s, a number of people working in radio and in the party apparat had concluded that the only solution was to beat the enemy at its own game; in 1964, agitation for media reform led to the creation of a round-the-clock news and entertainment station based broadly on foreign models and known as *Maiak* (the lighthouse or beacon). But popular as the new station was with listeners, it did not succeed in its primary goal of inspiring them to renounce the sirens of foreign radio. Worse still, *Maiak* managed to look like both a watered-down version of Soviet broadcasting ideals (in terms of its political and cultural mission) and a second-rate imitation of foreign broadcasting. And this was not just an embarrassment for Soviet culture in the media age; it was a political liability for a Cold War Soviet regime.

THE IRONIES OF *RADIOFIKATSIIA*

The USSR had already made significant progress in spreading radio technology in the 1920s and '30s. Like "electrification" (*elektrifikatsiia*), "radiofication" (*radiofikatsiia*) was a keyword of socialist modernity: with radio, it was said, the cultural gulf between the city and the countryside would collapse. Bring radio to the village and watch the backward past vault into the radiant future, now. This vision inspired local enthusiasts in radio clubs all over the Union.[12] It also helped motivate significant regime investment in set production (which ranked high on world charts) and, in the thirties, in establishing a centralized network based in Moscow. Although there were freestanding radio sets (*priemniki*) in the USSR, for the most part Soviet radio operated via a system of radio diffusion exchanges (*radiouzly*) that picked up signals (via long-, medium-, and short-wave broadcasts) and relayed them to wired units (*radiotochki*).[13] By 1941, there were roughly 7 million radios, nearly 6 million of them wired public amplifiers of one sort or another, and Soviet broadcast signals reached almost every corner of the USSR.[14]

12. Aleksandr Sherel', *Audiokul'tura XX veka* (Moscow, 2004), chap. 1.

13. Technically, the term "broadcasting" should apply only to the nonwired radio network. I use it in a more generic sense. The Soviets defended wired radio as providing better reception at lower cost and offering greater security than aerial broadcasting. See Alex Inkeles, *Public Opinion in Soviet Russia: A Study in Mass Persuasion* (Cambridge, 1958), 243–244.

14. James von Geldern, "Radio Moscow: The Voice from the Center," in *Culture and Entertainment in Wartime Russia,* ed. Richard Stites (Bloomington, IN, 1995), 45. A 1971 Soviet publication gives slightly different figures for 1940: 5,852,700 wired and 1,122,500 sets. *Problemy televideniia i radio* (Moscow, 1971), 201.

Figure 3.1. Radio as collective experience: kolkhoz farmers listen to Molotov, 1941. ITAR-TASS. Used with permission.

Though radio was already a mass phenomenon in the thirties, it was the experience of World War II that solidified its place in Soviet culture.[15] It was during the war that millions of people learned for the first time to rely on broadcasting as an essential feature of daily life. In 1941, the regime had confiscated all freestanding radios for military use (and also, it seems, for the purpose of walling off the population from foreign broadcasters),[16] and this meant that even more than in the thirties, the locus of the Soviet radio experience was the wired public set. People gathered around these radios to get the latest news, but they also came together to hear Soviet literature's leading lights recite poetry and read the Russian classics (including all of *War and Peace*). They assembled for symphonies and stirring popular melodies and countless speeches at the "radio meetings" then convened by everyone from soldiers' mothers to Belorussian scientific workers; they tuned in for daily readings of personal letters written to and from frontline soldiers, and they did so even when they were not hoping for news of their loved ones. Radio was the voice of Moscow as supreme

15. On the 1930s, see Stephen Kotkin, "Modern Times: The Soviet Union and the Interwar Conjuncture," *Kritika* 2, no.1 (2001): 119–127; Richard Stites, *Russian Popular Culture: Entertainment and Society Since 1900* (New York, 1992), 81–83; Sherel', *Audiokul'tura XX veka*, chap. 3; P. S. Gurevich, *Sovetskoe radioveshchanie: Stranitsy istorii* (Moscow, 1976).

16. Sherel', *Audiokul'tura XX veka*, 73.

political and military authority; it was a conduit for high culture and its values. And along with this, Soviet wartime radio was a space of comfort and inspiration and, within the confines of censorship, a kind of people's forum as well.[17]

Radio's performance during the war heightened popular esteem and expectations while also raising its profile in the eyes of the Soviet authorities. As early as 1944, work began on rebuilding the wired network in territories formerly occupied by the Germans, and in 1945, the regime declared a national holiday for radio, May 7. Radio Day honored the wartime contribution, and it also celebrated the invention of radio by A. S. Popov fifty years earlier.[18] Radio thus acquired a heroic, nationalist genealogy in the USSR that extended from its birth in the mind of a "progressive" Russian scientist to a remarkable Bolshevik childhood in the twenties, a dynamic role in the building of socialism in the thirties, and finally its trial–by fire and moment of greatest triumph, the Great Fatherland War.

In its first postwar decade, the USSR made a major push for radiofikatsiia. By 1955, Soviet industry was pumping out several times more sets *per year* than had been produced in the entire prewar period.[19] Annual sales of sets were ten times higher in 1950 than in 1940; five years later, they reached twenty-two times the 1940 level.[20] On the ground, this brought the total number of radios in 1955 to 33 million, a nearly fivefold increase over the 1940 level. Ten years later, the number of radios in the USSR would more than double again, to about thirty-two radios for every hundred people.[21] This was impressive growth, reflecting a major financial commitment on the part of the Soviet regime, much of it at a time when basic postwar reconstruction was laying claim to resources. But there was a devil in the details: an ever larger proportion of these new Soviet radios were not the wired variety of tradition—the loudspeaker on the corner, the box on the wall in the kitchen; they were freestanding sets. In 1950, there were still far more wired receivers than freestanding radio sets; in 1955, the numbers for

17. See M. S. Gleizer and N. S. Potapov, eds. *Radio v dni voiny: Sbornik statei* (Moscow, 1975) 106–113; Sherel,' *Audiokul'tura XX veka,* 76; James von Geldern, "Radio Moscow: The Voice from the Center," in Stites, *Culture and Entertainment in Wartime Russia,* 50–54. Cf. Stephen Lovell on wartime radio as the "apotheosis of the Stalinist model of radio," "Radio and the Making of Soviet Culture," paper presented at the American Association for the Advancement of Slavic Studies Conference, Washington, DC, November 2006).

18. See D.G. Nadzhafov and Z. S. Belousova, eds., *Stalin i kozmopolitanizm: Dokumenty Agitpropa TsK KPSS, 1945–1953* (Moscow, 2005), 145–147.

19. "K novym uspekham sovetskogo radio," *Radio,* no. 4 (1955): 9.

20. Radio bested other basic consumer items, including bicycles and sewing machines. E. Iu. Zubkova, ed., *Sovetskaia zhizn', 1945–1953* (Moscow, 2003), 98.

21. *Problemy televideniia i radio,* 201. All the émigrés interviewed by MIT's Comcom project (who left between 1956 and 1966) reported having had access to radio, 93 percent of them at home. Rosemarie Rodgers. "The Soviet Audience: How It Uses Mass Media" (PhD diss., MIT, 1967), 104–106.

both were quite close (13 million wireless to 19.5 million wired); and by 1963, the relationship had been reversed altogether: there were more wireless radios in the Soviet Union than wired receivers (35 to 34 million).[22]

This shift from wired to wireless radio had far-reaching implications that went almost wholly unrecognized at the time. For one thing, it meant that what had been a predominantly collective and public activity was now moving into the realm of private experience and was thus far less simple to quantify, monitor, and control—indeed, it was beginning to look less and less like a traditional Soviet phenomenon altogether. (Groups of listeners gathered to join a radio rally or attend a performance of radio theater were doing something that fit easily into the category of a Soviet activity, whether social, cultural, or political. But could the same be said of the solitary listener at home?) A second, even more critical issue about the wireless radios—and one that only served to heighten their potential un-Sovietness—was the fact that large numbers of these sets could receive shortwave broadcasts. In fact, according to a 1949 report to the party's Central Committee from the radio administration, nearly *all* the free-standing radios being produced by Soviet industry had shortwave capacity. And as A. Puzin, the head of the radio administration, or Glavradio, pointed out, this meant they were "designed for receiving not just Soviet, but also foreign radio programs" devoted, in his words, to "the foulest slander of the Soviet Union and the people's democracies." Puzin recommended curtailing shortwave production almost completely.[23] Nine years later, in 1958, the CC did its own investigation and found that production had not only continued but flourished: the USSR had produced more radios with shortwave capacity since 1949 than all the countries of the world combined. This meant that there were now roughly 20 million radios in the USSR ready and able to tune in to foreign slander. At the time Puzin raised his alarm, there had been a mere half a million.[24]

What had happened? How was it that Soviet radio, with its proud collective tradition, seemed set early in the postwar era to become a phenomenon of private experience? Stranger still, how had the USSR, which claimed to be the historic homeland of broadcasting, managed to make modern Soviet radio a medium for non-Soviet, and even anti-Soviet, material? Though there is no single answer to these questions, it is possible to identify a series of factors that made such things possible in radio development, as well as a kind of developmental momentum that tended to overwhelm and overshadow other considerations.

Once again, it was the World War II experience that proved critical. Early in the war, the Soviets evacuated their major broadcasting facilities to the interior of the country and converted to shortwave, which is better suited for

22. *Problemy televideniia i radio,* 201.
23. Nadzhafov and Belousova, *Stalin i kozmopolitanizm,* 438–439.
24. RGANI, f. 5, op. 33, d. 75, l. 165.

long-distance transmissions. To be clear, shortwave need not mean freestanding sets with individual users at the tuning dial, and during the war, Moscow used short-wave as part of a mostly wired system, broadcasting to radio diffusion centers that then transmitted via wire. But what about peacetime? In theory, the Soviets' wired system was ideal for broadcasting to large numbers of people, but it worked best, as during the war, when radio use was concentrated in urban areas and in specific target zones (which is why wartime radio's impact is belied by the modest number of sets in use). Wiring the vast expanses of Soviet territory for broadcasting, however, was an immense undertaking, even if the goal was to connect diffusion centers to loudspeakers and not individual homes. Radiofikatsiia using the wired system required three things in chronic short supply in the Soviet countryside: equipment, expertise, and perhaps most important of all, electricity.[25]

The village had always been the Achilles' heel of the Soviet radio system. In 1947, rural areas, where roughly 65 percent of the population lived, had less than 20 percent of the country's total radio equipment, according to Glavradio Puzin; most collective farms had no radios at all.[26] A late 1940s radiofikatsiia campaign criticized industry and the Ministry of Communications for dragging their feet and rallied young radio buffs to bring their expertise to the village. And though wired systems were still very much on the menu, this campaign also called for wireless sets: they were a simpler option technically (radio hobbyist journals published blueprints) and, often battery-powered, a better choice for the many thousands of villages still waiting for the long-promised *elektrifikatsiia*. Puzin made the case in *Pravda* in 1947, estimating that it would take more than a decade to meet the needs of the countryside (20–25 million radios, he thought) using the wired system. "It is clear that the village cannot wait upon such a tempo," he argued. If Soviet people put their minds to producing wireless receivers, they could "reduce by several times the period required for the mass radiofication of the countryside."[27]

The challenges of a wired system go some way to explaining the increased production of wireless receivers in the postwar period. It is also worth emphasizing that people wanted to buy them. Radio was one of the fastest-growing sectors for consumer investment in this period, and from a consumer's perspective, there were definite advantages to having a freestanding radio in the home.[28] But

25. Telephone lines could also be used for radio transmission, obviating the need for special wiring, and the Soviets did use this method in some areas. But villages were even less likely to be wired for telephone than for electricity.

26. A. Puzin, "Zadachi razvitiia sovetskogo radio," *Pravda,* 8 May 1947.

27. Ibid.

28. Freestanding sets offered greater personal control over such things as volume and, in many areas, access to more than one station, whereas most wired sets offered access to only one until the late sixties. Sherel', *Audiokul'tura XX veka,* 94. After 1962, freestanding

what about shortwave production? The initial rationale for shortwave use during World War II—its superiority for long-distance broadcasting—was far less important after the war. Most stations, including central broadcasting in Moscow, had long since returned to medium- and long-wave frequencies, and though some areas still used shortwave broadcasting, it did not necessarily follow that these regions had the highest density of shortwave sets. Quite the opposite was true. According to the CC's 1958 investigation, "up to 85 percent" of shortwaves were to be found in the European zone of the USSR—a region where, as the CC noted, there were no Soviet broadcasts on shortwave, and "the *only* thing to listen to" was enemy radio.[29]

It was an earful, too: by the late fifties, as many as sixty different foreign stations were broadcasting to the USSR at certain times of the day. Jamming was worse than futile. By their own estimations, Soviet signals for jamming typically exceeded foreign broadcast power (in kilowatts) by a factor of three and, often, by ten or even twenty times. The costs of this effort were enormous, running into "hundreds of millions of rubles," said the CC, and amounting to more than what the USSR was spending on domestic and international broadcasting combined.[30] Nonetheless, the enemy voices could be heard with little trouble in most areas outside the centers of Moscow, Leningrad, and a few other large cities. Worse still, jamming operations made tuning in to republic and all-Union radio impossible in many areas: the Soviets were jamming themselves. With enemy radio the only thing to listen to, some kolkhozniki were reportedly choosing to run the VOA and the BBC on their local wired networks.[31]

The problems with shortwave broadcasting were not news in 1958. As early as 1949, the USSR Council of Ministers had ordered a halt in the production of short-wave sets; it repeated the order in 1953, when *Pravda* also forwarded concerned letters to the CC from Soviet citizens demanding that their government silence the voices. A pensioner from Sarapul (Urdmurtia, more than a thousand kilometers from Moscow) complained about the "distressingly nasty, rasping, hysterical cries [that] rouse indignation and ruin people's moods and nerves. The USSR Ministry of Communications is taking 'some measures' *to muffle and only muffle—no more*—this disgusting Anglo-American hysteria. *But surely more can be done? Surely measures can be taken to jam, completely jam, these*

---

sets were also exempted from license fees, while wired sets were not—more evidence of the regime's discriminatory policies against the traditional wired network. Researchers in the state administration for radio and television thought the fee policy had helped retard the wired radiofication of the countryside. GARF, f. 6903, op. 3, d. 433.

29. RGANI, f. 5, op. 33, d. 75, ll. 164–165 (my italics).

30. Ibid., d. 106.

31. For complaints about jamming in Ukraine in 1958, see ibid., d. 75, l. 105. For VOA-BBC wired kolkhozy in 1957 in Latvia and Moldavia, see GARF, f. 6903, op. 1, d. 538.

nasty Voice of America and BBC programs?"[32] The USSR Council of Ministers, taking the same view, announced an acceleration in the construction of jammers in 1953.[33]

Initially, this defensive approach to the radio problem would not have seemed far-fetched given how few wireless sets of any kind there were in the USSR (3.6 million in 1950).[34] People at the VOA and BBC in the late forties worried that Soviet jamming would be too effective, and there were debates in the West about whether to continue broadcasting to the Soviet bloc.[35] But rather than scrap their programs, the United States, Great Britain, and other foreign broadcasters increased their strength and devised techniques to outwit their opponents, such as changing frequencies midprogram, using "clippers" to intensify the higher and more penetrating tones of announcers' voices, and "cuddling," or broadcasting on wavelengths so close to those used by Soviet domestic radio as to make precision jamming nearly impossible.[36] The Soviet regime responded with more, and more powerful, jamming stations.

It was a war of escalation, and although the Soviets appeared to hold their own for a few years, by the mid-fifties they were losing badly. At meetings radio officials openly expressed their frustration with jamming. "It seems to me that we're hiding our heads in the sand," said one at a 1955 discussion on radio's future. Even given "limitless" funds, he thought, it would be impossible to seal off Soviet territory from foreign broadcasting, and currently they were in danger of paralyzing their domestic broadcasting network with jamming. The head of the radio administration called again at this meeting for restrictions on shortwave sales.[37] But like those earlier bans on production, this proposal was dead in the water, and the voices of foreign radio only grew stronger.

Tuning in to foreign radio was not itself an illegal activity. In fact, using shortwave to increase your knowledge of foreign cultures and languages could be parsed as a progressive, internationalist activity, provided, of course, that the listener chose wisely. It was the choice that posed the problem, as the boundary between good and bad foreign culture was often blurred. Anthropologist Alexei Yurchak has emphasized how useful this gray area could be for listeners, arguing that it made tuning in to the enemy voices "at least during late socialism, seem perfectly acceptable"; people listened "quite openly" all over

32. RGANI, f. 5, op. 16, d. 645, l. 59 (emphasis in the original).

33. Nadzhafov and Belousova, *Stalin i kozmopolitanizm,* 437; A. Fateev, *Obraz vraga v sovetskoi propagande, 1945–1954 gg.* (Moscow, 1999), 189.

34. *Problemy televideniia i radio,* 245.

35. Nelson, *War of the Black Heavens,* 22–24.

36. The Talk of the Town, *New Yorker,* 4 June 1949.

37. GARF, f. 6903, op. 1, d. 488, ll. 160, 162. Officials presented radio paralysis as a national security risk in case of war as well as a cultural problem.

the USSR, he maintains.[38] Yet the historical record is more textured. First, the political climate of late socialism—the 1950s to the 1980s, in his definition—varied greatly, as did the Soviet people's relationship to mass media. Whereas listening to the voices may have been unremarkable in, say, 1975, especially among the educated, urban population that Yurchak focuses on, it would not have been taken lightly by most Soviets in the Khrushchev period, when the foreign radio phenomenon was still novel to many, the political situation was in flux, and the USSR's new openness to the non-Soviet world was a source of delight and anxiety both. Second, who was listening to what mattered enormously: Estonians tuning in to Finnish radio were in a very different (as a rule, better) position than Tadzhiks listening to religious broadcasts from Iran or Siberians getting reports of the Cultural Revolution from Radio Beijing. And more generally, listening to something defined as *enemy* voices, however socially acceptable, was never altogether beyond suspicion in the eyes of the Soviet authorities.

People called in by the KGB for questioning and "pastoral care" (so-called prophylactics) or charged with "anti-Soviet activities" under the Criminal Code were likely to be probed about their listening habits. (The KGB also intercepted letters addressed to enemy broadcasters.) Both Article 58-10 of the code—"propaganda or agitation containing appeals to overthrow, undermine or weaken Soviet power or for individual counterrevolutionary crimes"—and Article 190 (as of 1966)—"knowingly spreading false conceptions, defaming the Soviet state and social structure"—could be interpreted to include repeating content heard on foreign radio.[39] The 1957 police record for a young Ukrainian plumber arrested under Article 58, to give one example, charged that he had "been recounting programs from foreign radio and anti-Soviet poetry to workers since summer 1956."[40] (Other records from 1964 concluded with the observation "listened to VOA, BBC.")[41] Then again, a man who in 1968 managed to flood an entire Estonian beach with VOA—the radio he was listening to was, unbeknownst to him, connected to a loudspeaker system—saw his case dismissed.[42] The situation was never clear-cut, and the truth is that we have a great deal yet to learn about how and why people in the USSR of different eras, ages, regions, and ethnicities used foreign broadcasting.

38. Yurchak, *Everything Was Forever Until It Was No More: The Last Soviet Generation* (Princeton, 2005), 176, 179.

39. V.A. Kozlov and S.V. Mironenko, eds., *58-10: Nadzornye proizvodstva prokuratury SSSR po delam antisovetskoi agitatsii i propaganda: Ananotirovannyi catalog, mart 1953–1991* (Moscow, 1999), 11; Sergei Arustamian, "On i dnia ne sluzhil v armii, a byl general-polkovnikom...," *Novoe vremia*, 15 December 2005.

40. Kozlov and Mironenko, *58-10*, 265.

41. Ibid., 654.

42. Ibid., 691.

The Soviet authorities never knew with any certainty what percentage of the population was tuning in (nor did broadcasters themselves).[43] Officials in Estonia were probably the first to have any survey data because Estonian media professionals were among the first in the Union to have developed a research division for studying their audiences. In 1966, the Estonian CC estimated that at certain hours of the day "up to 70 percent of radio listeners" were tuning in to Finnish and other foreign stations.[44] A study of university students in nearby Lithuania one year later found that 35 percent reported listening to the voices.[45] When the research division for Central Radio studied the question in 1968, it found close to 50 percent of people surveyed in urban areas across the Union acknowledged tuning in to foreign radio at least occasionally.[46] Finally, in the mid-1970s, the KGB cited a USSR Academy of Sciences study that gave a figure of 80 percent for Moscow's university students and 90 percent for those in high school and technical schools; another study of students in Omsk reported close to 40 percent.[47]

In thinking about these figures, we should reflect again on the useful role that the projected audience played in the Soviet political and cultural imagination. One former apparatchik in the CC's international department told Radio Liberty in 2003 that he thought both foreign radio's audience size and its influence had been purposefully inflated. "They were exaggerated for the simple reason that in order to impart . . . a sense of the great effectiveness of your own work, for a start you must exaggerate the activities of your opponent," he explained.[48] Given this reasoning, it was not only the KGB that had a stake in the image of a massive Soviet audience in thrall to the voices—so too, in a broader sense, did the entire Soviet political elite, for whom the external threat served both to validate their power and justify their failings. Even broadcasters and sociologists had good incentive to emphasize the strength of the ideological opponent when promoting their own work.

The exact size of the Soviet audience was and will remain elusive, but evidence of foreign radio's influence abounds. Foreign broadcasting was plainly instrumental in the revival of jazz and the popularization of contemporary

43. For foreign broadcasters' attempts to gauge audiences, see Kristin Roth-Ey, "Mass Media and the Remaking of Soviet Culture, 1950s–1960s" (PhD diss., Princeton University, 2003), chap. 4.

44. RGANI, f. 5, op. 58, d. 25, l. 99.

45. Lisann, *Broadcasting to the Soviet Union,* 127.

46. GARF, f. 6903, op. 2, d. 501.

47. The 1976 KGB report is published in the *Soviet Archives at INFO-RUSS* project, http://psi.ece.jhu.edu/~kaplan/IRUSS/BUK/GBARC/pdfs/dis70/ct37b76.pdf.

48. Viktor Tolz, "Rodina slyshit: Chast' piataia: Skol'ko i pochemu?" Radio Svoboda, 7 August 2004. Cf. Amir Weiner, "Déjà Vu All Over Again: Prague Spring, Romanian Summer and Soviet Autumn on the Soviet Western Frontier," *Contemporary European History* 15, no. 2 (2006): 160.

Western popular music in the Soviet Union.[49] In the very center of Moscow circa 1960, consumers buying new radios in the country's flagship department store, GUM, would be approached by people offering to alter them for shortwave reception for a price. The practice was common in other areas as well and was inadvertently promoted by the official encouragement of radio hobbyists and tolerance of black markets for parts and services.[50] Party and Komsomol officials found that foreign radio had a hand in the widespread student unrest in 1956 and 1957—as it did, they noted nervously, in the far more consequential events in Poland and Hungary.[51] There were incidents of students posting reports they had copied down from slow-speed BBC broadcasts on the walls of their institutes.[52] Some students detained for "anti-Soviet" activities in 1956 told the authorities that they had developed their ideas by listening to foreign radio.[53] When party and Komsomol officials sat down for question-and-answer sessions the following year, they often found themselves having to refute or explain something VOA or some other station had said the night before. And many people did not apologize for tuning in. "What's shameful about a person listening to the BBC?" one student wanted to know. "Who is interfering with radio broadcasts from foreign countries, and why?"[54]

In closed-door meetings and in public settings, including in mass media, Soviet authorities regularly attacked foreign radio for corrupting listeners. The official list of corrupting influences from abroad grew long in the post-Stalinist era—foreign tourists and exchange students, films and literature in translation, visiting exhibitions and cultural groups, the magazine *Amerika,* chewing gum, the twist.... But arguably, enemy radio had a place of honor in the official imagination. There were multiple divisions in the bureaucracy for transcribing and analyzing foreign broadcasts, and their reports, sometimes quite sophisticated, went to the in-boxes of party elites on a regular basis. Jamming, although no longer a matter for public discussion by 1960 (it was on Glavlit's, the main

49. The most famous music program was Willis Conover's *Music USA* on VOA (1955–1996). See S. Frederick Starr, *Red and Hot: The Fate of Jazz in the Soviet Union* (New York, 1983), 243–244; Hixson, *Parting the Curtain,* 117; Kozlov, *Kozel na sakse,* 70–71; Reinhold Wagnleiter, *Coca-Colonizaton and the Cold War: The Cultural Mission of the United States in Austria after the Second World War* (Chapel Hill, NC, 1994), 210–212.

50. Amanda Wood Aucoin, "Deconstructing the American Way of Life: Soviet Responses to Cultural Exchange and American Information Activity during the Khrushchev Era" (PhD diss., University of Arkansas, 2001), 199; Yurchak, *Everything Was Forever,* 177.

51. Foreign radio, notably Radio Free Europe (RFE), was strongly criticized after the Hungarian revolt for having given false hopes of Western military support. See Urban, *Radio Free Europe and the Pursuit of Democracy,* 211–247; Nelson, *War of the Black Heavens,* 69–84; Puddington, *Broadcasting Freedom,* 89–114.

52. Nelson, *War of the Black Heavens,* 90–91.

53. RGASPI-m, f. 1, op. 46, d. 192, l.8.

54. Ibid., d. 207, ll. 67–68.

censorship agency, list of taboo subjects),[55] was no secret, and people in radio and the party-state administration were well aware of how ineffective and injurious it was.

Soviet leaders, Khrushchev in particular, made periodic attempts to use the issue of jamming in diplomatic gamesmanship. The Soviet approach was to seek assurances from the main government-run broadcasters, VOA, BBC, and Deutsche Welle, that they would cease "offensive" (perceived anti-Soviet) programming in exchange for an end to jamming. The Soviets also tried to bargain for reductions in the broadcast power directed toward the USSR and attempted to play VOA against the more objectionable Radio Liberty—if the U.S. government agreed to rein in RL, then the USSR would suspend jamming VOA.[56] Jamming was first lifted as a good-will measure during Khrushchev's trips to Britain in spring 1956 (to be resumed during the Hungarian uprising that fall) and to the United States in September 1959 (until the Soviet Union shot down an American U-2 spy plane in May 1960). The Soviets lifted jamming again in June 1963—a reprieve that lasted until the invasion of Czechoslovakia in August 1968 (with an additional blackout period during the Six-Day War between Egypt and Israel in 1967)—and then from September 1973 to the declaration of martial law in Poland in August 1980. But even in these periods, the idea of open airwaves was to a large extent illusory. Moscow continued to jam BBC, VOA, and Deutsche Welle programs selectively and to block Radio Peking, RL, and several other broadcasters entirely.[57]

Foreign broadcasting and the Soviet response were always identified as problems. Yet somehow, Soviet industry continued to pump out shortwave radio sets in the millions, and jamming, though periodically lifted, remained in a real sense the default mechanism for handling the enemy voices through the Cold War. This was a situation that defied logic in big-picture political terms; it was, as one observer put it, a case of the USSR "shooting themselves in both feet."[58] Without

55. GARF, f. 9425, op. 1, d. 1051.

56. Although mostly unsuccessful in modifying content, Soviet bargaining did result in the temporary closure (1963–1968) of a massive broadcasting transmitter in Munich, especially objectionable to the Soviets because it used frequencies assigned by international accords for Soviet domestic broadcasting. When the facility went off-line in 1963, the Soviets immediately took over the frequencies for jamming. On the technical history of jamming, see Rimantas Pleikis, "Radiotsenzura," http://www.radiojamming.info/ (Vilnius, 2002–2003).

57. See Lisann, *Broadcasting to the Soviet Union,* 8–17; Wettig, *Broadcasting and Détente;* Nelson, *War of the Black Heavens,* 91–106.

58. The Soviets did make one important change: as of 1958, industry stopped producing shortwave sets with higher frequency bands, best for long-distance reception during daylight hours. Nelson, *War of the Black Heavens,* 93. Listeners then used lower-frequency "evening" bands. Hence the well-known saying (a rhyme in Russian): "The custom in Russia is to listen to the BBC in the evening." (*Est' obychai na Rusi—noch'iu slushat' Bi-bi-si.*)

imposing a false coherence on the Soviet position, I suggest that there were two logics at work that facilitated shortwave development and foreign radio penetration in direct and indirect ways. The first has to do with the nature of the Soviets' planned economy and bureaucracy and of career-making in the Soviet system; the second, with the all-important international context for Soviet radio broadcasting.

OF PLANS AND PORTUGUESE SPEAKERS

Let us begin by asking, who was in charge of radio and the foreign radio problem in the postwar Soviet Union? The question is simple, but given radio's straddling of technological, sociocultural, and political spheres, the answer is not. Soviet broadcasting had its official home in the Soviet state administration; as of 1957, it was the State Committee for Radio and Television (with analogous structures in all the Union republics) that was responsible for production and programming.[59] Nearly all of postwar radio broadcasting was prerecorded (by 1946, 95 percent), and censorship was exercised primarily at the level of production, by professionals within radio's editorial groups (*redaktsii*) and then by Glavlit censors.[60] Technical issues such as relay-cable systems and station construction were theoretically under the control of the USSR Ministry of Communications and its republic-level analogues. But in practice, developing and exploiting a modern communications infrastructure was a complex business that naturally involved broadcasters themselves and a host of other state actors as well: Gosplan and the Ministry of Finance on investment and planning, the ministries of Light Industry and Trade on questions of radio set production and distribution, the border police and civil defense authorities on illegal ham-radio operation ("radio hooliganism")[61] and jamming, and the Ministry of Foreign Affairs on diplomatic

---

See also G. A. Sheveleva, ed., *Pozyvnye trevog i nadezhd: "Maiak," sorok let v efire* (Moscow, 2004), 413–414.

59. From 1946 to 1949, the state body was the All-Union Committee for Radiofication and Radio Broadcasting of the USSR Council of Ministers. A 1949 reorganization split it in two: the Committee of Radio Information (for domestic broadcasting) and the Committee for Radio Broadcasting (for foreign broadcasting), both under the USSR Council of Ministers. This structure lasted until 1953, when radio responsibilities were given over to the USSR Ministry of Culture (the Main Administration for Radio Information for the domestic service and the Main Administration for Radio Broadcasting for the international.) With the 1957 creation of the State Committee for Radio and Television of the USSR Council of Ministers, foreign broadcasting oversight was temporarily granted to the State Committee for Cultural Ties with Foreign Countries. In 1959 it reverted to the State Committee for Radio and Television.

60. Sherel', *Audiokul'tura XX veka*, 79.

61. A Komsomol Central Committee report in 1963 estimated that there were eleven thousand amateur radio operators. "Radio hooligans" often acted as DJs for Western popular music, but because they reportedly used frequencies set aside for military

questions related to Soviet broadcasting abroad and the foreign radio problem at home, to name but a few. In keeping with standard Soviet practice, the State Committee for Radio and Television reported to the Central Committee apparat— in this case, to its Department of Propaganda and Agitation, radio division.

The KGB had a particularly important role to play in the matter of the enemy voices, and not only in terms of "educating" wayward Soviet listeners. TASS, the Soviets' main news agency, monitored the voices as part of its overall reporting on foreign media to the Soviet authorities, and some republic broadcasting committees set up their own monitoring operations as well,[62] but this work was a true KGB specialty; KGB staff produced arguably the most incisive analyses of foreign radio content, packaged in regular reports to the CC and for use by party and Komsomol activists.[63] The KGB also monitored where and when the voices were audible on a macro (Union-wide) level. It reported on new foreign efforts and proposed policy responses: in 1959, for instance, it was the KGB that sent news to the CC of round-the-clock broadcasts in Russian, Azerbaijani, and Armenian from powerful stations along the Soviet-Iranian border and recommended formal protests to the Iranian government.[64] Finally, the KGB used its own, unpublicized methods of fighting the enemy voices: counterespionage (there were KGB plants at Radio Free Europe/Radio Liberty and presumably other broadcasters), assassinations, and disinformation campaigns.[65] Needless to say, the KGB had operatives working inside Soviet radio as well.

Radio in the Soviet Union was, then, a kitchen with many cooks, and relations among them could be tense. Broadcasters accused the USSR Ministry of

---

broadcasting, they raised national security concerns. RGASPI-m, f. 1, op. 5, d. 925, l. 48. The problem seems to have been exclusive to Russia and Ukraine. For the situation in Ukraine between 1959 and 1964, see TsDAHOU, f. 1, op. 24, d. 4947 (1959); TsDAVO, f. 4915, op. 1, d. 2198 (1959); TsDAHOU, f. 1, op. 70, d. 2447 (1960); TsDAHOU, f. 1, op. 31, d. 1679 (1961); TsDAHOU, f. 1, op. 24, d. 5786 (1963); TsDAHOU, f. 1, op. 70, d. 2533 (1963); TsDAHOU, f. 1, op. 31, d. 2562 (1964).

62. TASS's full name was the Telegraph Agency of the Soviet Union (Telegrafnoe Agentstvo Sovetskogo Soiuza). TASS's secret fourth department prepared reports for top leaders based on information from its correspondents and foreign telegraph agencies and media (with radio broadcasts taped, transcribed, and translated into Russian). Viktor Tolz, "Rodina Slyshit: Chast' pervaia: Stalin slushaet 'golosa,'" Radio Svoboda, 27 June 2004; "Rodina Slyshit: Chast' chetvertaia: Novye slushateli v Kremle i novye temy," Radio Svoboda, 31 July 2004.

63. For one of countless examples (from 1966), see RGANI, f. 5, op. 58, d. 25, ll. 127–173.

64. RGANI, f. 5, op. 33, d. 106, ll. 108–109.

65. Nelson, *War of the Black Heavens,* 98–99; Puddington, *Broadcasting Freedom,* 225–252. The KGB established a new "fifth department" in 1967 specializing in ideological deviance, including foreign radio. Arustamian, "On i dnia ne sluzhil v armii." Its head claimed in post-Soviet memoirs that Soviet leaders ignored the KGB's repeated advice to take a more aggressive stance refuting foreign propaganda. F. D. Bobkov, *KGB i vlast'* (Moscow, 1995), 38–40.

Communications of incompetence and high-handedness;[66] republic-level communications ministries and radio committees complained that they were starved for cash;[67] Central Radio in Moscow criticized local radio for substandard programming; local radio committees faulted Moscow for giving them too little support; different groups working within the radio administration found fault with each other; everyone complained about jamming and about being undervalued and underfunded. The CC apparat was in charge of adjudicating all these issues and more, and it did: a letter to the CC generally triggered an investigation of some kind and a report. At the same time, it was the CC that was responsible for coordinating overall Soviet media development (to wit, the decrees "On Improving Soviet Radio Broadcasting," "On Measures for the Further Improvement in the Work of Radio Broadcasting and Television," "On Measures for the Improvement of Propaganda to Foreign Countries," and so on). CC work in media, as in other areas, ran the gamut from small bore to great guns, taking in administrative, legislative, and executive functions.

With this situation in mind, let us consider a brief conversation about the shortwave radio problem at the CC Presidium in 1963:

> Khrushchev: Let's . . . figure out a solution so that we produce radio sets that
>   work only for the reception of our stations.
> Kosygin: Without shortwave.
> Ponomarev: Hobbyists will adapt them fast, and practically, it's a hard thing
>   to do [to stop production].
> Khrushchev: They won't adapt all of them.
> Il'ichev: They'll adapt them as along as we continue to produce shortwaves.
>   We ourselves are giving them the chance.
> Brezhnev: We put out 9 million of them.
> Khrushchev: *Why did we do this?*
> Il'ichev: There was a decision, but people didn't follow up on it. The biggest
>   objection came from the Ministry of Trade: consumers won't buy [sets]
>   without shortwave, they figured. They won't buy them, and there will be
>   a surplus.
> Khrushchev: But we have to cut down on production.
> Kosygin: When there's nothing else available, they'll buy them.[68]

66. For example, GARF, f. 6903, op. 1, d. 538, 808.

67. For official complaints from the Ukrainian Ministry of Communications to the Ukrainian CC about underinvestment in the republic in 1964, see TsDAHOU, f. 1, op. 31, d. 2562; for complaints about administrative neglect of broadcasting investment at the republic level and calls for increased central control in 1970, see GARF, f. 6903, op. 1, d. 1054.

68. A. A. Fursenko et al., *Prezidium TsK KPSS, 1954–1964*, vol. 1 (Moscow, 2003), 714 (my italics). The meeting was held on 25 April 1963. Aleksandr Iakovlev claimed that the Ministry of Communications attempted to shield the top Soviet elite from the shortwave

Nothing came of this conversation, just as nothing had come of the earlier decisions to stop production. Yet it would be too pat to conclude that the Presidium was toothless, or the apparat of which it formed the apex simply dysfunctional. It is true that the CC was not well staffed in the media sector: there were only four people devoted to broadcasting at the time of this meeting. Khrushchev himself brought this up at another point in the conversation, mentioning not only radio but also film, theater, and other sectors of what he called the "ideological question." "Four people here, four people there... it's all scattered and inadequate, and that's why it's also uncontrollable [*neupravliaemoe*]."[69] But there was more to it than that. Khrushchev proposed forming a new commission with representatives from the center and all the republics to steward the ideological ship, but as his colleagues pointed out, the CC already had an ideological commission in place. The problems were well known, and there was no shortage of proposed solutions.

In a system of overlapping responsibilities and competing interests, different interests were able to promote—and block—initiatives at different times but not to enact a coherent, unified policy. The dynamic was typical of Soviet bureaucracy writ large.[70] In the case of radio, both consumer and producer (or plan-fulfilling) interests managed to exert influence effectively. If we look back at the CC's 1958 investigation, we find an explanation for the shortwave boom similar to the one mooted by Khrushchev and his Presidium colleagues in 1963: "commercial considerations" had hijacked radio affairs, they said. This was, on the one hand, a routine bit of bureaucratic scapegoating. (It should bring to mind the figure of the venal film distribution official from chapter 2 who was said to have discriminated against Soviet pictures in favor of masscult.) And on the other hand, commercial considerations is an explanation well worth exploring.

Soviet consumers did want shortwave radios, and factory managers (and many other functionaries in the production and distribution process) wanted to fulfill their plans. It goes without saying that Soviet consumers wanted a great many things that industry failed to produce; and there were also many ways to meet planned targets on paper that did not involve production at all.[71] This is no simple love story, "Supply Meets Demand." Still, it is not difficult to imagine how demand for a product (a radio set) and for perks associated with

---

problem by installing high-power jammers in their home neighborhoods. Iakovlev, *Omut pamiati* (Moscow, 2000).

69. Fursenko, *Prezidium TsK KPSS, 1954–1964*, 1:708.

70. The locus classicus on the bureaucracy is Merle Fainsod, *Smolensk under Soviet Rule* (Cambridge, MA, 1958). See also Moshe Lewin, *The Soviet Century* (London, 2005), esp. 342–360; Stephen Solnick, "Revolution, Reform and the Soviet Telephone System, 1917–1927," *Soviet Studies* 43, no. 1 (1991): 157–176.

71. Paul Gregory, *The Political Economy of Stalinism: Evidence from the Soviet Archives* (New York, 2004).

quantifiable success (in numbers of sets produced and sold) kept shortwave in play. Shortwave had momentum—never an easy thing to redirect in the planned economy—and it served many specific interests, even as it was said to violate more general and abstract ones, such as the "ideological health" of the Soviet people. Party and state officials also had a strong interest in being able to report that their regions had been successfully "radiofied." Seventy million Soviet radios in the mid-sixties did mean 70 million radios, no matter where they were and what they broadcast; this was success of a sort easily grasped and publicized, and its charms could not be ignored.

The second major factor in the shortwave phenomenon—the international context for Soviet broadcasting—also involved the logic of numbers on a page and the imagery of Soviet success, but set in an even broader ideological framework. What we must understand is that even as the USSR was railing against the invasion of enemy voices, it was also engaged in a massive international broadcasting effort of its own. Radio Moscow, as it was known, had a history stretching back to the 1920s, but like domestic radio, it gained significant momentum during World War II. In the postwar era, the international service was further emphasized, and throughout the sixties Radio Moscow expanded at a faster pace than did Soviet domestic broadcasting.[72] This was true in terms of the overall volume of broadcasting (in hours) and in the number of languages Moscow spoke to the world—from twenty-one at the war's end to forty-five in 1958 and over sixty-five in the late sixties.[73] Soviet domestic radio expanded, too, and it was also famously multilingual, itself boasting over sixty broadcast languages for audiences within the USSR in the sixties. However, raw numbers could be misleading.

The name of the game in Soviet domestic media development was always centralization, and this meant ever-increasing doses of Moscow's Central Radio and of republic-level radio as well. Central Radio spoke Russian exclusively, and though the republic-level stations did broadcast in titular languages (i.e., languages of the national groups for which the particular republics were named) and usually several more, they also carried programming from Central Radio. The net result was overall Russian-language dominance but also very limited service for speakers of minority languages. Most of the USSR's Korean and German speakers would have had a better chance of hearing their languages on Radio Moscow than on the domestic network.

Even in the sensitive western borderlands regions, support for multilingual broadcasting—and broadcasting period—was not always robust. In Latvia, the

72. Gurevich, *Sovetskoe radioveshchanie,* 190. Soviet international broadcasting counted for roughly 35 percent of the total in 1940, 50–60 percent in the period 1955 to 1965. *Problemy televideniia i radio,* 207.

73. Gurevich, *Sovetskoe radioveshchanie,* 289; *Problemy televideniia i radio,* 203; RFE Reports in OSA box 300-80-1-685.

local CC noted the implications of Latvian radio's carrying Central Radio at peak times for foreign broadcasts—the local, non-Russian-speaking population was tuning in to the enemy—but argued for the status quo in 1959. It was "impossible" not to broadcast Moscow because it would "leave the majority of radio listeners who do know Russian without the summaries from *Pravda* and [Central Radio's] *Latest News*." Jammers were the only solution, the Latvian authorities said.[74] Neighboring Estonia took a different tack, and it was sometimes successful in its bids to increase Estonian-language broadcast time, perhaps because its leaders made the argument that the capitalist Finns were tuning in to their programs, too.[75] But in Ukraine, the local authorities frequently came up short, in terms of both securing resources to build up the republic's broadcasting facilities and expanding multilingual programming. In 1964, for example, we see Ukraine's radio officials lobbying the CC to increase "Moldovan" language broadcasts in Chernivtsi oblast to a piddling forty minutes a day.[76] They were successful, but at this rate, Radio Moscow had them beat in multiple languages, including Assamese, Gujarati, Kannada, and Orija: four languages of India that Moscow started speaking in the late sixties to the tune of seven hours a week.[77] Even in the midst of the Prague Spring in 1968, Ukrainian leader Petro Shelest had reason to complain that broadcasting was being neglected in his republic. In July, he confided his concerns about western Ukraine to his diary: "[Official] radio and television practically don't work at all [and] residents are listening to Western radio stations and watching Western television." Ukrainian officials had approached Moscow's CC, the Council of Ministers, and Gosplan multiple times "in the hope of getting suitable technical equipment for the republic," as had he, and all to no avail.[78] Six months later, the Ukrainians were still complaining that they had yet to receive the resources they had been promised to build up broadcasting (specifically, television) in

74. RGANI, f. 5, op. 33, d. 106, ll. 8–9. The Latvians did win authorization from the center that year to boost Latvian-language programming to Western Europe. Ibid., ll. 14–16.

75. For conversations at Gosteleradio about increased funding to Estonian broadcasting related in part to Finnish audiences in 1963, see GARF, f. 6903, op. 1, d. 801, ll. 33–44; for a request from the Estonian CC and Council of Ministers to the center for funding in 1966, again with reference to Finnish audiences as well as to competition from enemy radio, see RGANI, f. 5, op. 58, d. 25, ll. 99–103. The Estonians still got less than half of the amount they asked for (234,000 of 485,000 rubles).

76. They also pitched to increase Hungarian shows in Zakarpats'kii oblast from forty to sixty minutes a day. TsDAHOU, f. 1, op. 31, d. 2408, ll. 117, 129–130.

77. Z. Nagorski, Jr., "Soviet International Propaganda: Its Role, Effectiveness, and Future," *Annals of the American Academy of Political and Social Science* 398, no. 1 (1971): 135.

78. Translated in Mark Kramer, "Ukraine and the Soviet-Czechoslovak Crisis of 1968: New Evidence from the Diary of Petro Shelest," *Cold War History Project Bulletin*, no. 10 (1998): 236; for Shelest's July 1968 letter to the CC in Moscow, see RGANI, f. 5, op. 60, d. 28, l. 66.

the western borderlands.[79] This was not a question of plain incompetence, although incompetence was surely a factor: the center may have flubbed on Ukrainian broadcasting, yet it did manage to launch a massive radio campaign to Czechoslovakia in 1968, boosting broadcasts from under 20 to over 160 hours a week.[80]

Foreign broadcasting enjoyed a special status in the Soviet media system, and Radio Moscow was itself a unique professional milieu. Its staff was dominated by a highly educated group of Soviets with the requisite language skills—people such as Joe (Iosif) Adamov, the legendary announcer for the North American service—and by foreign émigrés and their children. (There was probably more than the average share of KGB operatives in the mix as well.)[81] Because it was seen as competing with foreign media, Radio Moscow gave its journalists comparatively good resources, including access to foreign publications, and allowed them to pursue different techniques for relating to audiences. The international service ran contests with prizes, for example, and announcers like Adamov were able to develop much stronger on-air personalities and cultivate far more personal relationships with listeners than was possible on domestic radio, which, aside from a few outsized figures (Iurii Levitan being the most important), was famously allergic to stars.[82]

Radio Moscow also emphasized timely, efficient news reporting early on and cultivated a notion of journalistic professionalism that would turn out to be highly influential. Vladimir Pozner, Vlad List'ev, Aleksandr Liubimov, Evgenii Kiselev, and many others who went on to make their names on Soviet TV (not to mention Evgenii Primakov in the political world and numerous literary lights) all got their start in the foreign service.[83] In the Brezhnev era, Radio Moscow was also reportedly the only division in all of Soviet broadcasting permitted to

79. TsDAHOU, f. 1, op. 25, d. 20, l. 21.

80. Nagorski, "Soviet International Propaganda," 137.

81. Oleg Kalugin, Radio Moscow correspondent in New York City in the early sixties, is among the more famous of these journalist-spies. Oleg Kalugin, with Fen Montaigne, *The First Directorate: My Thirty-two Years in Intelligence and Espionage against the West* (New York, 1994).

82. Radio Moscow's prizes to international listeners could be expensive (e.g., cameras or watches). U.S. State Department Report, "The Soviet Bloc Exchanges in 1957," January 1958), 12.

83. Although Radio Moscow was subject to stringent censorship, its journalists are said to have enjoyed a bit more breathing room than their counterparts on the domestic network, if only because very few people understood the languages they worked in. See Vladimir Pozner, *Parting with Illusions* (New York, 1990); "Legenda teleradiozhurnalistiki, laureate TEFI Iurii Fokin: 'Mne peredali pros'bu glavy pravitel'stva "uspokoit" narod,'" *Vek,* 31 August 2001; Georgii Zubkov, "Razmyshleniia bez mikrofona," in Sheveleva, *Pozyvnye trevog i nadezh,* 28–38.

edit speeches of top-ranking Soviet officials and Politburo announcements for broadcast.[84]

Although the special status of Radio Moscow was never set down in black and white, it was obvious enough to engender resentment among domestic radio staff. In 1957, staff at a meeting convened to discuss recent CC criticisms complained that radio journalists posted in Berlin, London, and Paris worked for Radio Moscow only, while domestic radio struggled to get permission to send correspondents abroad.[85] The head of Kazakh radio complained a few years later that in his republic, the priority of foreign broadcasting translated into a situation in which two-thirds of the local population was cut off from the domestic network. The problem was that Kazakhstan had only two long-wave stations, and all the rest were shortwave, given over to broadcasting to foreign countries like Canada and Brazil. "I don't understand why we are paying the Ministry of Communications such enormous sums of money when Kazakhs cannot listen to our programs, but foreigners can."[86]

A reasonable question, on the face of it, but one that missed the bigger picture. Radio Moscow commanded such important resources, financial and administrative, because the context for discussing radio in the USSR was not just domestic, but also international, or internationalist in the Marxist-Leninist sense; and given the ideological postulates of the regime, these two contexts were indivisible. That is why at a special conference on youth in 1964 a representative from the radio and TV administration could outline the dangers of the voices in the darkest of tones and yet conclude by reminding his audience, "We are not unarmed. We also conduct powerful radio broadcasting abroad."[87] This was a war, in other words, where the USSR was not the only battleground and the ears of Soviet listeners not the only prize.

In February 1957, the CC Presidium discussed plans for enhancing the effectiveness of Soviet foreign propaganda, and the Council of Ministers approved a decree on the matter the following month. The recent Hungarian crisis was an evident catalyst. "Our propaganda was not up to the task," read the proposed decree. "The press, radio, cinema, and other organs of Soviet propaganda aimed abroad were unable to counter the flood of slander against the Soviet Union and communist parties with reasoned information and analysis of the events in Hungary." One problem was propaganda's material base, including radio, and the decree set out a host of improvements in Soviet broadcasting power: new transmitters, cable- and radio-relay lines, and equipment—even pricey

---

84. "Inoveshchaniiu—75 let!" Radio Maiak, 29 October 2004, http://old.radiomayak. ru/interview/04/10/29/32855.html.

85. GARF, f. 6903, op. 1, d. 525, l. 30.

86. Ibid., d. 808, l. 46.

87. RGASPI-m, f. 1, op. 5, d. 976, l. 118.

foreign-made equipment, if necessary—and a boost to the Ministry of Communication's budget to the tune of 650,000,000 rubles (in the proposed decree) to cover the costs. Also included were plans for improving connections with Latin America, Southeast Asia, and the Far East, reflecting the Soviet Union's growing interest and involvement in the postcolonial world.[88]

The Soviets saw radio as an especially potent tool for use with postcolonial populations because of their high illiteracy rates—and saw their own history with the medium as proving the point. A particular *Soviet* model of radio culture was also touted to postcolonial audiences as the antithesis of Western, and especially American, culture (which Moscow could also handily define along the way, for those audiences who lacked firsthand knowledge, as crass, racist, etc.) Radio was a terrific candidate for "showcase diplomacy," demonstrating the superiority of the Soviet model to capitalism for potential junior players on the socialist side.[89] Khrushchev lectured a specially convened "Meeting of Third World Journalists" in Moscow on this point in 1963: "Whereas the colonialists earlier relied only on the whip and the bayonet, now they are ideologically masking their activities, so to speak, adroitly using the press, radio, television, religion and other means of ideological influence." The only solution, he told them, was the socialist one, where the means of cultural production were in the hands of the people: "[S]ocialism alone makes the press a popular one." The only model for third world media was the Soviet model, as embodied by Radio Moscow and hammered home at events such as the Moscow meeting.[90] In the 1970s, the Soviet Union expanded on this point by leading a coalition of allied postcolonial and nonaligned States against Western efforts to promote the idea of access to a "free flow of information" as a human right rather than a governmental prerogative. The Soviet position was that the "free flow" argument was but another smokescreen for capitalism's ruling classes bent on asserting power over new markets. Where Soviet broadcasting was a gift to third world audiences, Western broadcasting was an attack on their national sovereignty and a threat to their future development.[91]

In fact, despite its comparatively privileged status, the Soviets' international broadcasting program suffered from many problems similar to those that plagued their domestic service. Here, too, the shortwave devil reared its head: the bulk of Soviet broadcasting abroad was shortwave, but in many countries, consumers

---

88. See "O merakh po uluchsheniia sovetskoi propagandy na zarubezhnye strany," in *Prezidium TsK KPSS, 1954–1958*, vol. 2, ed. A. A. Fursenko et al. (Moscow, 2006), 575–581; RGANI, f. 5, op. 33, d. 106, l. 72.

89. On "showcase diplomacy," see Karen Dawisha, "Soviet Cultural Relations with Iraq, Syria, and Egypt, 1955–1970," *Soviet Studies* 27, no. 3 (1975): 420.

90. "Beseda tovarishcha N. S. Khrushcheva s uchastnikami tret'ei vsemirnoi vstrechi zhurnalistov 25 oktiabria 1963 goda," *Pravda*, 27 October 1963.

91. For more on the Brezhnev era and "free flow of information" argument, see chapter 5.

had made the switch to medium- and long-wave sets long before. Soviet jammers inadvertently blocked out Radio Moscow as they did the domestic service.[92] And even though the international side relied on large numbers of foreign-born staff, its programming was, by and large, one size fits all: understanding the tastes and needs of different audiences was no more a priority for foreign audiences than it was for domestic ones. One professional who worked for many years in Radio Moscow's Africa division said that the cultural gulf between Soviet broadcasters and their listeners was acknowledged but ignored. "Folk songs and melodies from classical opera and ballets mixed with ideological commentary took up the bulk of the broadcasting time," he recalled. "[T]he leaders of the State Committee for Radio and Television thought that the problems could be solved by flooding our listeners with information on our achievements in culture and arts."[93]

Nevertheless, with its raw size and scope, Radio Moscow played effectively to Soviet leaders' vanity as world revolutionaries. Moscow's international voice was served up regularly as a matter of pride for domestic Soviet consumption as well. World-class powers, it was understood, had world-class cultures, and they spoke to the world. Few Soviets had the opportunity to assess whether people in India or Indonesia were actually listening to Radio Moscow, but the message from domestic media was clear. "Postal workers in every country in the world know the address 'Moscow. Radio'. . . . For millions of foreign listeners, the voice of Moscow is the voice of reason, the voice of truth, the voice of conscience," said *Pravda*.[94] The very fact of Soviet cultural reach—the sounds of Pushkin, the story of Stalingrad, news of the Moscow theater season, and all in places you could scarcely find on a map!—was presented as proof of Soviet power and prestige. In this way domestic and international propaganda bled into one another, and more than that, they were, at least in theory, mutually reinforcing phenomena. Radio Moscow, as the Soviet Union's voice to the world, had domestic propaganda functions; media inside the USSR were models for world emulation. A shot on one front was heard around the world.

This is the context in which the problem of shortwave and the enemy voices could slip on and off the official radar screen. Taken on its own, developing shortwave capacity inside the USSR did not make sense from the regime's perspective—and it made little sense to various observers along the line who recommended putting an end to production. But the shortwave problem was never a stand-alone issue. Rather, it came bundled with other concerns, such as how to

92. For these and other problems, see the 1959 report prepared by the former deputy head of the State Committee for Cultural Ties with Foreign Countries to the CC, RGANI, f. 5. op. 33, d. 106, ll. 57–71

93. Quoted in Sergey Mazov, "Soviet Policy in West Africa: An Episode of the Cold War, 1956–1964," in *Africa in Russia, Russia in Africa: Three Centuries of Encounters*, ed. M. Matusevich (Trenton, NJ, 2007), 303.

94. "Bez bumagi, bez rastoiianii," *Pravda*, 8 May 1968, 3.

meet production plans and make careers, how to find more qualified Portuguese speakers for broadcasts to Brazil, and how to increase power to reach bigger audiences in Egypt. At the same time, the shortwave situation, coming in under the overall rubric of "radio," was wrapped up with many things that looked like sure signs of success: so many millions of radios produced in the USSR and so many millions of listeners to Soviet broadcasts, not only at home but on the far ends of the earth. On a macrolevel, Soviet radio policy was inconsistent, even self-destructive, as many observers within the bureaucracy pointed out at the time. It also had proven strengths. Shortwave radio production had constituencies and momentum, and although it was periodically flagged as a problem, in the absence of a consistent opponent, it carried on and on.

COMPETITION AND THE LIMITS OF REFORM

By 1960, with nearly 60 million radio sets in use, the Soviet authorities at last found themselves with a country they could call radiofied—though not, perhaps, on the terms they might wish. Radio in the postwar period had taken a definite turn away from the Soviet tradition of collective cultural consumption toward the realm of private experience. Radio listening appeared less identifiably Soviet as a practice, and this raised questions about its role in people's lives and in the broader project of socialist construction. Gathering around a public loudspeaker for a radio meeting, a reading of Vladimir Maiakovskii's poetry, or a medley of mass songs left no doubt about what radio listening was. (Though listeners' personal, interior experiences may well have burst the bounds of prescribed political mobilization or cultural uplift, the basic questions—what they were listening to and why they were listening—were easy to answer in theory.) Bring the radio indoors and behind closed doors, though, or on the road in the form of a transistor, and all bets were off: What *were* people experiencing as they tuned in privately? This was a question for radio's younger sibling, television, too—and, in some respects, television was more troubling for many observers because it seemed to have such a dramatic impact on people's physical behavior (immobilizing them, in effect). Radio listening acquired its own disturbing undertones as of the late 1940s because of its association with foreign broadcasting. Radio was already moving in the direction of private consumption in the postwar USSR. Foreign radio, the enemy voices, pushed the point and could make all of private listening seem more intimate and illicit.

The Soviets' ideological stockroom had plenty of shopworn explanations for why people listened in. The taste for what foreign radio had to offer was a "holdover" (*perezhitok*) from the bourgeois past, it was said. Enemy radio targeted young people, who were naturally vulnerable to foreign seduction (and contemporary young people all the more, because unlike earlier Soviet generations, they had not been tempered by revolutionary struggle and war). Foreign broadcasting looked straightforward, but it was actually an ultrasophisticated form of psychological warfare in which the West was investing untold millions;

Figure 3.2. Radio as personal companion: transistors, 1973. Maksim Blokhin/
ITAR-TASS. Used with permission.

ergo, the fact that the USSR had not yet conquered it was, if not acceptable, then
at least understandable.

It was these rationales that Soviet officials pulled off the shelves at every
meeting on the problem of bourgeois cultural infiltration. (Terms like "USIA" and
"Ford Foundation" entered the Soviet lexicon via this discourse in the 1960s.[95])
Yet as logical as the situation may have been in ideological terms, there was no
getting around one very troublesome thing: the popularity of enemy radio made
Soviet radio look bad. And as competition heated up in the 1950s and '60s, you
would not have to look far to find both officials and radio professionals declaring
that it *was* bad.

Let us pause briefly to consider what Soviet radio's main station had to offer
on one Monday in 1963.

6:30 a.m.	*Zemlia i liudi* (Land and People)
8:45	*Dlia tekh, kto doma—Rasskaz Iu. Iakovleva "On ubil moiu sobaku"* (For Those Who Are At Home—A short story by Iu. Iakovlev, "He Killed My Dog")
9:45	*Pisateli u mikrofona* (Writers at the Microphone)
10:00	*Detskaia opera "Ivan-bogatyr"* (Children's Opera, "Ivan-bogatyr")

95. For one of countless examples, see "The Threat of Western Ideas Is Topic of Agit-
prop's Talk," *Digest of the Soviet Ukrainian Press* 12, no. 7 (July 1968): 1–7.

11:10	*Kogda serdtse poet. Kontsert* (When the Heart Sings. A Concert)
12:20 p.m.	*Za mir na zemle—Muzykal'no-literaturnaia kompozitsiia* (For Peace on Earth—A Musical-Literary Composition)
1:10	*My liubim poeziiu. Peredacha po zaiavkam radioslushatelei* (We Love Poetry. A Radio-Listener Request Program)
1:35	*V dobryi chas. Kontsert pesni* (A Good Time. Concert of Songs)
2:00	*Schet minutam. Peredacha o Tashkentskom ekskavatornom zavode* (Minute by Minute. A Program about the Tashkent Excavator Factory)
3:00	*Estradnyi kontsert* (*Estrada Concert*)
4:10	*Dlia detei. A. Musatov and M. Liashenko. Glavy iz povesti "Berezhki"* (For Children. A Musatov and M. Liashenko. Chapters from the story "Birch Trees")
5:00	*Pochta radio* (Radio Mailbag)
5:15	*Uchenye u mikrofona. Chelovek peredelyvaet prirodu* (Scholars at the Microphone. People are Remaking Nature)
6:30	*Radiokompozitsiia "Ural'skii bogatyr" i kontsert po zaiavkam kollektiva Ural'skogo zavoda tiazhelogo mashinostroenniia.* (Radio-Composition "Bogatyr of the Urals" and Concert of Requests from the Urals Heavy Machinery Construction Factory)
8:05	*Iul'skii Plenum TsK KPSS i zadachi ekonomicheskoi nauki—Beseda akademika K.V. Ostrovitianova* (July Plenum of the CPSU and the Tasks of Economic Science—A Conversation with Academician K.V. Ostrovitianov)
9:20	*Kontsert "Nad selom opuskaetsia vecher"* (Concert "Evening Falls on the Village")
10:30	*Dekada pol'skogo muzykal'nogo iskusstva. Vystuplenie masterov iskusstv* (Ten-Day Festival of Polish Musical Art. Performances by Masters)

If we compared this Monday with the next, we would find some differences—perhaps an evening slot for sports reportage, a radio forte well into the seventies, or an opera (Central Radio put on nine or ten full-length operas, with explications, every week in the sixties), or an afternoon political speech. But because Soviet programming was so consistent by design, even a single day's schedule can tell us a great deal. First, we should note the predominance of music. Soviet radio had always devoted substantial airtime to music, but the proportion rose substantially in the postwar period: over 50 percent of airtime on Central Radio was given over to musical programming as a rule (and republic-level stations provided roughly the same proportion).[96] Second, we might ask, where is the news? In fact, listeners would have heard periodic news bulletins every day, but their absence from the official schedule—and

96. Sherel', *Audiokul'tura XX veka*, 93.

the dearth of current events material in general—tells us something about the position of news in the programming hierarchy. Next, we can see radio's continued emphasis on the collective experience and audience participation (here in the form of listener request programs). And finally, there is the overall tone of the program: thoughtful and purposeful, with no personalities on display and no games to play. This radio, the schedule announces, takes itself and its listeners seriously.

In the late fifties and early sixties, Soviet broadcasting was a target of brutal official critiques. Along with a series of secret directives on the specific problem of foreign radio, the Central Committee published two decrees outlining the sins of Soviet radio (in 1960 and 1962). Programming was "clumsy" and "banal," it said, full of "bland readings," "fake-sounding reports," and "affected" musical accompaniment; it "exuded boredom and apathy." No wonder, then, that listeners did not show "great interest" in Soviet radio. The CC concluded that radio workers were the root of the problem: many of them simply failed to understand what they had in their hands—the "most powerful means for educating the masses"—and they lacked initiative.[97]

While published criticism of Soviet radio could be extremely harsh, it never called into question the overall superiority of the Soviet model for broadcasting. In closed-door sessions of radio officials and party media managers, though, and in more or less every internal report on the state of radio as well, Soviet inferiority to the West was a dominant theme. Glavradio Puzin browbeat his engineering staff in 1955 for their failure to close the technology gap with the West: "Steal foreign designs," he exhorted them. "Comrades, you have to steal, and we're not stealing."[98] Two years later, at an all-Union meeting on how to improve broadcasting, radio workers put invidious comparisons to foreign radio right on the table, alongside complaints that they were not being given the resources to do their jobs. "We've heard that the BBC has four hundred people working in their news division, and we've only got twenty to thirty people on news in Central Radio," sniped an official from Moldavia.[99] Radio workers often used the threat of foreign competition to lobby for higher salaries and more staff and for hard currency infusions to import equipment and publications. News was a particular sore spot, and radio professionals complained bitterly of being treated as second-class citizens in the Soviet information system. They were right. TASS, the major newspapers, and even Radio Moscow all had foreign correspondents, while the domestic service was left to pick up scraps. As late as 1959, the main offices of radio and television administration in Moscow did not even have a direct

---

97. *KPSS o sredstvakh massovoi informatsii i propagandy* (Moscow, 1987), 533–539, 545–551; Gurevich, *Sovetskoe radioveshchanie,* 250–252.

98. GARF, f. 6903, op. 1, d. 475, 1.68.

99. Ibid., d. 538, l. 43.

telephone line to the CC offices. Radio and TV offices in Kiev and many other republic and regional capitals did not have so much as a teletype.[100]

Radio on the republic and regional level was in a worse position than Central Radio overall, given the cardinal principle of all Soviet broadcasting: "Moscow first." No story with Union-wide implications—and in practice, this meant more or less any important news item and certainly anything with an international angle—was supposed to air on republican radio before Central Radio had covered it. What if VOA reported on an accident in *your* area or a public statement made by *your* republic's first secretary on a trip to Germany? No matter: Moscow still had priority. The principle posed particular problems in border regions, where the reception of enemy voices was at least as good as, and often better than, that of Soviet radio.[101] The center could and did take its own sweet time. Estonian radio officials in 1967 said they themselves sometimes turned to Finnish radio to get the basics on major political speeches out of Moscow because TASS was so slow in forwarding them the information.[102]

Under pressure from foreign broadcasting sallies, the situation for news reporting on Soviet radio did see some improvement. Beginning in the late fifties, there was a steady increase in the amount of time given over to news broadcasts on Central Radio (and because the center set the standards, on regional radio as well).[103] The 1960 decree officially designated radio as first in the information food chain—TASS reports were to go to radio first, print media second—and stressed the importance of timely reporting, as did its 1962 follow-up. The head of the radio and television administration in the early sixties was Mikhail Kharlamov, a member of Khrushchev's informal "press group" headed by Aleksei Adzhubei and so associated with the notion of media modernization.[104] In closed-door sessions with radio professionals, Kharlamov did not mince words about the need to compete with foreign radio on its own terms. Jamming was no solution, he told a group in Kiev in 1963:

> We expended so many resources and so much energy on it, and if we had spent the same on broadcasting, we wouldn't need jamming....Why do people

---

100. For Moscow, see GARF, f. 6903, op. 1, d. 578, l. 148; for Ukraine, see TsDAVO, f. 4915, op. 1, d. 2201, ll. 58–60. A number of regional and republic-level reports responding to the 19 July 1960 decree "O merakh aktivnogo protivodeistviia vrazhdebnoi propagande" noted recent (or planned) teletype connections to Moscow. RGANI, f. 89, d. 373–379, 380–385, 399, 400.

101. On the Taimyr region, see GARF, f. 6903, op. 1, d. 808, l. 50.

102. Ibid., d. 944, l. 85. For Ukrainian broadcasting's pleas for the Ukrainian Ministry of Foreign Affairs news bulletin in 1965(!), see TsDAHOU, f. 1, op. 70, d. 2577, l. 70.

103. Sherel', *Audiokul'tura XX veka*, 88.

104. On the press group, see A. I. Volkov et al., *Pressa v obshchestve, 1959–2000: Otsenki zhurnalistov i sotsiologov, dokumenty* (Moscow, 2000); Aleksei Adzhubei, *Te desiat' let* (Moscow, 1989).

listen to VOA and the BBC? We're the guilty ones here.... Now that many of our listeners have become more literate, educated, they want to know a lot of things, and we hide a lot of things and, in this way, we artificially arouse their interest in programs from foreign countries.

Kharlamov went on to say that the solution to the problem was timely reporting: "[T]here should not be a single event we report later than America, at the very least. Because the person who steps in first to analyze an event is the winner."[105]

Such was the substance of pep talks to broadcasting professionals, but day to day the situation remained quite different. At issue was not only TASS (which continued to lag),[106] but also the nature of all Soviet media as tools for education and mobilization. Certainly the work of republican and regional broadcasters remained circumscribed by the Moscow-first imperative. A common theme in their reports on compliance with another CC radio decree from 1960, this one specifically on combating enemy voices, was their success in providing *more* of Moscow's content, especially during peak hours. This meant direct feeds ("[C]urrently, we are broadcasting all discussions on international themes broadcast by all-Union radio," crowed Azerbaijan) or recorded translations of Moscow's programs in local languages.[107] But it also meant providing listeners with print media content: as report after report from the regions spelled out, listeners needed to *hear* the central press. The reform efforts of the early sixties may well have decreed radio as first in line for new information, but they did not dislodge *Pravda* as the center of the Soviet media universe. And, indeed, no media reform ever would.[108]

Mikhail Nenashev, among many others, described the heart of Soviet governmental power, the CC apparat, as a milieu fixated on the written text. Nenashev would go on to head up Soviet television during perestroika, but in the Brezhnev era he was one of the many bees in the CC hive, where, he recalled, "all the department workers were continually writing something."[109] Although much of this content was for internal use only and never made its way into the pages of the central press, the most prestigious writing projects did—speeches of Soviet leaders, policy statements, and so on. These texts were never attributed to men like Nenashev. The "right to be named" was reserved for those of rank, including CC secretaries and, of course, top Soviet leaders.[110] In this cultural and political context, with these organizational structures and values (and the setup was

105. TsDAVO, f. 4915, op. 1, d. 3430, ll. 238–239.

106. Lisann, *Broadcasting to the Soviet Union*, 54; TsDAVO, f. 4915, op. 1, d. 3717, l. 189.

107. RGANI, f. 89, d. 373.

108. Cf. Jeffrey Brooks, *Thank You, Comrade Stalin! Soviet Public Culture from Revolution to Cold War* (Princeton, NJ, 2000), esp. prologue.

109. Mikhail Nenashev, *An Ideal Betrayed: Testimonies of a Prominent and Loyal Member of the Soviet Establishment* (London, 1995), 30–31.

110. Ibid., 28.

replicated at lower levels), it goes without saying that any person who stepped in first to analyze an event was no winner. These were the structures and values that ruled all Soviet media operations.

The crown jewel of Soviet news reporting, like bureaucratic report writing, was never the fact per se, but the "attitude to the fact" (*otnoshenie k faktu*). Few journalists disputed this approach; the reality was that calibrating attitudes was a politicians' game, not a journalistic one.[111] Kharlamov, who traveled abroad with Khrushchev, criticized the Soviet press corps for lacking the drive of their Western counterparts; once a Soviet reporter had been published a few times, Kharlamov quipped, he considered it "not quite decent to run" in pursuit of a story.[112] Perhaps this was true, but one can well imagine a Soviet journalist thinking, "Why bother?" In 1965, radio's Delhi correspondent earned an official reprimand for putting the cart before the horse, the fact before the attitude: he had recorded—not broadcast, but simply recorded—an interview with India's prime minister without first securing permission from Moscow, and his mistake was important enough to make its way to the offices of the Central Committee.[113] When the staff at Central Radio's propaganda *redaktsiia* put together a hard-hitting response to a program that had aired on VOA (a speech by an American pastor), it took twenty-three days to get through the approval process.[114]

Soviet radio was forced to be "timid," as one staffer put it at a party cell meeting. He was from Central Radio's literary and drama redaktsiia, not propaganda, and it is essential to recognize that the problem was always broader than the news. There were many instances of poems and stories rejected for broadcast that later made it into print.[115] And if this seems logical, consider the following: radio staffers could also land in hot water for airing work that had already been published.[116]

Standards for musical programming were no clearer, though music was perhaps the most vital arena for East-West cultural competition. It was no mystery that one of foreign radio's attractions—and perhaps its primary attraction for the youth audience that so preoccupied the authorities—was contemporary popular music from the West. And Soviet broadcasters knew from listener mail how thorough the frustration with their own programming could be. In the late fifties, Central Radio actually reduced the amount of opera it was broadcasting in

111. Sheveleva, *Pozyvnye trevog i nadezhd,* 35. On the Soviet concept of the news, see Ellen Mickiewicz, *Media and the Russian Public* (New York, 1981); Thomas Remington, *The Truth of Authority: Ideology and Communication in the Soviet Union* (Pittsburgh, 1998).

112. TsAOPIM, f. 2930, op. 1, d. 32, ll. 17–18.

113. RGANI, f. 5, op. 55, d. 129, l. 9.

114. TsAOPIM, f. 2930, op. 1, d. 33, ll. 108–109.

115. Ibid., ll. 17–18.

116. Ibid., d. 21, l. 50.

response to a flood of protest letters.[117] All the various directives on combating the enemy voices demanded more "light" music at peak hours, and Soviet radio tradition was well in line with this approach. Entertainment, typically framed in terms of creating a "positive mood" for listeners, was very much part of its brief, and though relaxing to arias and overtures was surely the ideal, this kind of "cultured leisure" was not to be expected from most listeners, at least not yet. But as broadcasters began to program more Western popular music and especially more homegrown (or Soviet bloc) soundalikes in the sixties, they were routinely chastised for it. The CC's harsh 1962 decree, for example, faulted radio workers for pandering to "philistine tastes" with "modernist and jazz music" and reminded them pointedly of their role in aesthetic education.[118] The head of Central Radio's music division framed the problem as one of Soviet leadership in the Cold War: "It needs to be said that our comrades abroad really need our light music," he told his colleagues at an all-Union conference of radio workers in 1957. "They say that in order to do battle with American jazz and the American influence, we need to put up something against it."[119] *Something,* but what?

In 1964, the head of the Komsomol, Sergei Pavlov, gave a hair-raising report to his Central Committee on the state of affairs in Czechoslovakia. The Czechoslovaks, he explained, were under assault from not only foreign radio but also TV, and although their Komsomol organization was trying to "beat off young people's interest in Western culture," it was failing miserably. Pavlov described a proliferation of local "big beat" groups modeled on the Beatles and their unruly fans. On May Day, he said, a police intervention at an outdoor concert in Prague had led to a serious public disturbance: hundreds of people had stopped traffic and, he reported, "anti-Sovietism started—anticommunist and anti-Soviet slogans." And the roots of this, said Pavlov, were in a Czechoslovak media policy lacking in ideological mettle, a policy of "splitting hairs." "Oh, you have jazz, and we have jazz," he mimicked the Czechoslovaks. "Let's not have them listen to Radio Luxembourg; let them listen to Czechoslovakia." Pavlov warned, "[T]his changes little, because at the end of the day, there is no difference."[120]

Sergei Pavlov was famously hard-line, but in fact the views he shared with his Komsomol colleagues differed little from what they might have read in the press that morning. Soviet radio, like all Soviet culture, needed to be offensive rather than defensive, was the argument, and to achieve this it had to be different—to offer images, experiences, and values of its own rather than adapt or respond to the enemy. There could be no splitting hairs. It was, in many ways, an unavoidable conclusion for anyone who took seriously the ideological battle with the West.

117. GARF, f. 6903, op. 1, d. 542, l. 49.
118. *KPSS o sredstvakh,* 546.
119. GARF, f. 6903, op. 1, d. 538, l. 58.
120. RGASPI-m, f. 1, op. 5, d. 1004, ll. 10–11.

The problem was not, as some have suggested, that jazz and rock 'n' roll spoke the language of freedom and individuality and so were innately incompatible with Soviet-style cultural administration.[121] The history of Western mass culture teems with tightly managed, even manufactured, success stories. In the Soviet world, the overwhelming bias toward high culture forms and chronic border conflicts between "healthy" entertainment and philistinism made taking this route far more problematic than in the West. High-culture biases were of course widespread in *bien pensant* circles in the United States and Europe, too. But attitudes and systems are different things: in the USSR, the high-culture bias was both extensively institutionalized and enshrined at the heart of the system's political identity. Light music was an unlikely—some might say foolish—path for any Soviet musician aspiring to a career in the Composers' Union or to creating Art, with a capital "A," because the Soviet cultural system presented these two goals as mutually reinforcing.

What happened on the Soviet music scene after Stalin's death was an eruption of activity *outside* the official channels and a pattern of fitful official accommodation. By the mid-fifties, according to S. Frederick Starr, every town in the Soviet Union had a jazz band.[122] Moscow's International Youth Festival in 1957 catalyzed change in Soviet popular music and not only because it brought Polish jazzmen, English skiffle players, and American rock 'n' rollers to the USSR: since festival organizers had also approved Soviet groups for participation in the competition, the months before the big event saw homegrown jazz ensembles performing in local run-up festivals across the Union. The Composers' Union, indignant at the spectacle, accused the Komsomol (in charge of the festival) of promoting "lowbrow" music; the party's Central Committee investigated, and it agreed, but no systematic crackdown ensued.[123] In the sixties and beyond, jazz and rock 'n' roll could be heard performed at university and factory clubs, hotel restaurants, festivals, and even on radio and television. Soviet media continued to fulminate against bourgeois cultural infiltration, and the authorities continued to resort to prohibition at times, literally pulling the plug on performances, as David Gurevich recalled happening at a high school dance in 1966 when the band launched into the Beatles' "Can't Buy Me Love."[124] But pop-music-fueled socializing had become part of "cultural work" for the Komsomol and other organizations, where it had fans and—perhaps even more important—it generated revenues.

Still, even if jazz and rock 'n' roll had been swallowed up in the Soviet Union in institutional terms, ideologically speaking, nothing about the situation could

121. David Caute, for example, made this point in *The Dancer Defects: The Struggle for Cultural Supremacy during the Cold War* (New York, 2003).

122. Starr, *Red and Hot,* 251.

123. RGANI, f. 5, op. 36, d. 46, ll.55–56.

124. David Gurevich, *From Lenin to Lennon: A Memoir of Russia in the Sixties* (New York, 1991), 129. On the vicissitudes of jazz, see Starr, *Red and Hot,* 270–290.

be easily digested. Where were the new and distinctively *Soviet* forms? In typical Soviet style, committees were convened and reports written. The Moscow press in 1964 said the Central House of Folk Art was investing "huge sums" in inventing new dances—the "Enthusiasts' Dance," for example, was developed by a dance specialist, a professor of therapeutic gymnastics, and a pentathlon coach(!) and promoted in youth magazines and clubs.[125] According to the Komsomol's own reporting, most young people ignored the new dances and the bans on foreign ones (only two, the East German lipsi and the cha-cha, were on the Ministry of Culture's approved list at the time) and did as they liked.[126]

In music, the effort to move beyond accommodation to innovation was some-what more successful. Soviet culture did generate its answer to Western bands as of the mid-sixties. They were known as VIA, or "vocal-instrumental ensembles," and though they could be youthful, electrified, even shaggy-haired, they were not, pointedly, rock bands: "rock" in official discourse, at least until the 1980s, applied exclusively to the West. VIA, by contrast, were Soviet institutions, legally registered and regulated by "artistic committees," and they were supposed to play a strict Soviet repertoire: songs from the Composers' Union or variations on traditional folk tunes plus a limited selection of their original compositions and the occasional song in English. Within a decade, there were over 150,000 registered groups, and for a few, VIA status brought not only gigs and electric guitars but also Union-wide celebrity.[127] The most popular VIA (Poiushchie gitary from Leningrad, Veselye rebiata from Moscow, Pesniary from Minsk) in the late sixties and seventies toured the Soviet Union, won airplay on the radio, and appeared in film and on television.

Considering the sheer numbers of people involved, as performers and audi-ences, we can say that VIA worked on many levels as Soviet cultural policy. But the proliferation of officially sponsored groups did not equal the end of unofficial ones; many musicians shunned the controls that came with VIA status and con-tinued to work on the margins. Nor did the success of VIA mean the Soviet ro-mance with contemporary Western pop and rock was over—far from it. Despite the emphasis on Soviet repertoire, some groups achieved their greatest suc-cesses with Russian-language covers of English-language originals. And more pertinently, what VIA most resembled, in sound and style, were rock bands, masscult. Pesniary specialized in folk songs, but with their electric guitars and long mustaches, none of their fans would have mistaken them for a traditional

125. *Vechernaia Moskva* as reported in "Soviet Is Seeking Twist Antidote," *New York Times*, 16 March 1964.

126. RGASPI-m, f. 1, op. 34, d. 1, l. 60.

127. L. K. Bubennikova, "VIA i rok-gruppy," in *Samodeiatel'noe khudozhestvennoe tvorchestvo v SSSR: Ocherki istorii. Konets 1950-kh—nachalo 1990-kh,* ed. L. P. Solntseva and M. V. Iunisov (St. Petersburg, 1999), 81; Polly McMichael, "The Making of the Soviet Rock Star: Leningrad, 1972–1987" (PhD diss., Cambridge University, 2007), 41–47.

Figure 3.3. Rocking in Georgia: the Tkibul'sk Miners' VIA, 1978. G. Gersamiia/ ITAR-TASS. Used with permission.

Soviet folk ensemble. That was the point. Sergei Lapin, head of radio and television in the 1970s, got the point and reportedly demanded that they shave and change their costumes before they appeared on Central Television.[128]

Let us be clear that we are not speaking here about the realm of individual experience. Soviet rock *was* derivative, but that does not mean it was inauthentic in the eyes of the people who made it and used it. For self-defined Soviet rockers of the 1980s, borrowing from the West was a deliberate and creative act.[129]

128. The year was 1971. *Za zheleznoi maskoi. Sergei Lapin,* TV documentary produced by the station RTR-Planeta (2008). Lapin famously commented that estrada star Alla Pugacheva's success was "not a Soviet one." Olga Partan, "Alla: The Jester Queen of Russian Pop Culture," *Russian Review* 66, no. 3 (2007): 488.

129. McMichael, "The Making of the Soviet Rock Star," 24.

Soviet fans of Western popular music—and its domestic offshoots—heard something that spoke to *their* experience, and something not perforce incompatible with an ideal of socialist culture.[130]

Yet ironically, perhaps, what worked for rockers and their audiences was never going to work for the Sergei Pavlovs and Sergei Lapins of the world, and on the issue of Soviet cultural competition with the West, it was these men who had the sharper eye. Soviet rock, parasitic as a concept if not as an experience, was never viable in ideological terms. What Soviet culture needed in order to be Soviet culture—by its own definition—was something irrefutably, distinctively Soviet, something that would make people forget they had ever heard the alien words "jazz" or "rock 'n' roll." The popular music that dominated the Soviet scene in the postwar era was, as cultural conservatives constantly warned, very much the reverse.

MAIAK

It is no accident that the main initiatives on improving radio dated to the Khrushchev era, the high tide of postwar optimism about a socialist lift-off, like Sputnik from the launch pad, into the radiant future. What Soviet media policy lacked in coherence in this period it made up for with bravura. Every year there were more radio sets, more stations, and bigger audiences; every year Soviet media expanded their reach across the USSR and around the globe. Expansion itself could go a long way toward inspiring optimism about the culture and its ability to compete. One way to read the change in jamming policy in 1963 is as a sign of this optimism.[131] The same energy and a rising sense of professional pride also motivated many people working in radio, and in the early sixties they created a series of new shows that would dominate the programming schedule for the next twenty-five years. (A similar phenomenon pertained to TV.) Some programs, like *Iunost'* (*Youth*), won an audience of millions, and *Iunost'*'s staff even boasted at party meetings about letters from fans who said they had lost their taste for the enemy voices thanks to their broadcasts.[132] But the true innovation of the period was the restructuring of the all-Union network in 1964 to create a round-the-clock news and entertainment station, Maiak. The concept was simple: twenty-five minutes of varied and predominantly light music followed by five minutes of the latest news, every half hour, nonstop, and on an all-Union basis.[133] With this, Soviet radio changed more than its structure; it tampered with its own first principles.

Aleksandr Iakovlev, then of the CC's Department of Propaganda and Agitation, later claimed paternity for Maiak, along with a deputy chairman at the

---

130. Yurchak, *Everything Was Forever,* 185–193.

131. Lisann, *Broadcasting to the Soviet Union,* 154.

132. TsAOPIM, f. 2930, op. 1, d. 147, l. 161 (1964).

133. *Maiak* took over the second station, previously used for broadcasts to European Russia and the Urals, and expanded it into a twenty-four-hour and all-Union enterprise.

radio administration, and this is true in terms of who put the project on paper and shepherded it through the bureaucracy. Maiak's progenitor on a deeper level, though, was foreign radio. As Iakovlev recalled, it was the popularity of the enemy voices that forced the issue of reform: "[P]eople preferred to listen to foreign radio because ours was churning out 'bubble gum' and 'exalted nonsense.'"[134] What is more, the main models for Maiak were two spheres of Soviet broadcasting that had long been in competition with foreign radio in a direct and self-conscious way: Radio Moscow, the international service, and Estonian radio. The deputy chairman, Enver Mamedov, was for many years the head of Radio Moscow, which saw itself as a world-class service and cultivated an idea of journalistic professionalism. When Mamedov moved to the domestic side, he brought the unique sensibility of Radio Moscow and urged staff there to follow its example. The five-minute news block—disciplined, efficient, reliable—was very much in the spirit of Radio Moscow. Maiak also drew directly on Radio Moscow staffers, a number of whom had been transferred to the domestic service's news division after the 1960 decree and were pushing for reform.[135]

The other main model for Maiak, Estonian radio, went unacknowledged by Iakovlev but was possibly even more important. In Estonia, geography, the similarity of the Estonian and Finnish languages, and very high levels of wireless radio (and TV) ownership had created a perfect storm for the infiltration of foreign media. The Estonian situation represented the closest approximation to market conditions for culture anywhere in the Union and, crucially, local media professionals did not duck the challenge: Estonian media chose (with at least partial support from local political elites) to experiment with competitive strategies, and they conducted audience research, virtual terra incognita in the USSR at the time, to guide their work.[136] The head of Estonian radio reported on their efforts at a 1963 all-Union conference in Moscow, explaining that once they had determined from listener surveys that people were tuning in to the VOA's eleven o'clock show, for instance, they began scheduling their most popular features, like sports and news, at eleven.[137] Around this time, and with the same goal of seducing audiences out of enemy radio's arms, the Estonians also set up a mixed news and entertainment radio program that used what would soon become

134. Iakovlev, *Omut pamiati,* 143.

135. Lisann, *Broadcasting to the Soviet Union,* 26; on the transfer of Radio Moscow staff, see Sheveleva, *Pozyvnye trevog i nadezhd.*

136. Pseudomarket conditions stimulated innovation in other areas too. Estonia was the only republic where the authorities took a (qualifiedly) positive attitude to rock music, including even the local Composers' Union. A. Troitsky, *Back in the USSR: The True Story of Rock in Russia* (London, 1987), 75–80. On Estonian exceptionalism more generally, see Weiner, "Déjà Vu All Over Again."

137. GARF, f. 6903, op. 1, d. 808, l. 54.

known as the Maiak format: "5+25" (that is, five minutes of news and twenty-five minutes of varied music).

Estonian radio professionals were widely recognized in media circles for their innovative approach, but in many ways they were doing what they were supposed to be doing, in line with party directives: taking an "active, fighting" position in the battle against bourgeois cultural infiltration. In August 1964, Central Radio went on the offensive too; there is no question that Maiak was designed to draw listeners away from foreign radio, and within a few years, media professionals would even refer to this factor openly in trade publications. Yet as logical as this development was, getting Maiak on the air was a struggle. One technical specialist sent by the CC to investigate the influence of foreign radio in Estonia remembered being told by his superiors to keep mum back in Moscow about the local innovations because they were too controversial.[138] The CC rejected the Maiak concept at first, and Mamedov aside, higher- ups in the radio administration were opposed too. Iakovlev recalled that it was only when he came back with the idea of broadcasting Maiak on the same frequencies used by the enemy voices—using Maiak to jam, a proposition he said he knew then was phony—that the CC came on board, and only then with the proviso that he win over the people at Central Radio.

What was so objectionable? Iakovlev's explanation highlighted entrenched interests: once word of the proposal got out, the CC's offices were "strewn" with protest letters from staff at radio's second station.[139] As for Estonian radio, it is likely that the entertainment portion of its new 5+25 format had something to do with the controversy. The specialist sent from Moscow noted that the Estonians were putting on "rather daring" music. In 1963, all Estonian media suffered an official dressing down at the hands of the Komsomol's CC for making "entertainment" rather than "progressive ideological content" (*vysokaia ideeinost'*) the main goal of youth programming. Radio was said to be overloaded with jazz and jokes, and when a highly ranked staffer was asked to explain its programming, he said that the redaktsiia "oriented itself toward Finnish radio, which did very engaging shows."[140]

Here, in a nutshell, was the problem with the Maiak idea: How do you produce a new cultural product close enough to your competition to attract its fans but distinctive enough to stand on its own two feet? How do you make something derivative look original, independent, and proud? Staff at Central Radio who objected to Maiak were no doubt protecting their own interests, but the

138. Sheveleva, *Pozyvnye trevog i nadezhd,* 415–416.

139. Iakovlev, *Omut pamiati,* 144. Iakovlev claimed Kharlamov opposed Maiak actively and recalled a showdown with him at Gosteleradio's party cell meeting. The cell records do not record this. Kharlamov spoke in favor of Maiak at a cell meeting in October 1963. TsAOPIM, f. 2930, op.1, d. 42, l. 134.

140. RGASPI-m, f. 1, op. 32, d. 1125, l. 21.

reluctance to embark on this route also makes perfect sense. This was change inspired by the threat of foreign radio and bringing foreign practices into play, but was it really Soviet radio?

Although in many ways Maiak furthered developments already under way in Soviet radio—the growing emphasis on news and light music—it also introduced new challenges. The sheer quantity of news reports involved put the new station in a different category from all other Soviet media at that time. The news division had been preparing daily newscasts in the single digits for Central Radio before Maiak (and TV had even fewer); now the news came every half hour, around the clock, for forty-eight different newscasts a day.[141] The new format meant gathering more information from more sources, and Maiak's staffers cast their net wider than anyone in domestic radio had before (they were loath to repeat the news from segment to segment, a solution considered unprofessional).[142] The format also made pinning down the all-important "attitude to facts" a much more rushed affair and increased the risk of mistakes, especially given the round-the-clock schedule. As one staffer recalled, one of the first, very basic problems to work out was who would sign off on the texts to go on air. Censors did not work nights.[143]

Maiak was a new animal for Soviet broadcasting, and it demanded that radio professionals develop new approaches. Even so, a hard, high wall still stood between them and fundamental change: the Soviets' informational hierarchy. While Maiak was timelier than anything Soviet media had ever seen, it could not possibly compete with foreign broadcasters like the BBC or VOA. There was no way to scoop a story when you were waiting for approval from Moscow, even if you were *in* Moscow. Reading the reminiscences of former Maiak staffers, one is struck by how much they emphasize the reliability of their reporting as a service to listeners (every half hour, without fail) and its literary value; they were not out in front of the international press pack and did not mean to be. Throughout the sixties and beyond, Soviet radio, Maiak included, continually found itself in a position of responding to information that the enemy voices had gotten out first—or, as was more often the case, not responding for fear of drawing more attention to those voices and to the information itself. The new station, in other words, while providing new experiences for journalists, did not itself spell a cardinal change in Soviet media practices.

And yet Maiak did represent a radical shift for Soviet culture, and to appreciate this, we must look to the other side of the radio set and at the ways the new station structured listeners' relationships to time and to cultural consumption as an activity. Soviet radio was traditionally distinguished by its combination

141. Gurevich, *Sovetskoe radioveshchanie.*
142. Sheveleva, *Pozyvnye trevog i nadezhd,* 36.
143. Ibid., 57.

of extreme textual rigidity and baggy scheduling. Although it was incredibly important what was said on the air, and heads could roll for saying the wrong thing, no one expected a talking head to say her piece at exactly the same time every week or even at the scheduled time (a few minutes late would do). A show was a cultural event, a political event, maybe even a social event—shows like *Iunost'* could combine all three—and it went on air when it was ready and ran as long as it ran. Ideally, the listener went to the radio to move beyond time, to be magically transported to the past or future and to other parts of the world. Maiak did something very different. With its strict schedule and nonstop rhythm, it put listeners in the here–and now and indicated that right now, or at the most in twenty-four minutes, there were things they needed to know. With Maiak, radio was no longer about the program or about anything per se: it was a service, a necessity for modern living, "an extension of man," to use Marshall McLuhan's famous phrase of the same era.[144]

Nowhere was this clearer than in Maiak's approach to music—and musical programming, let us remember, comprised over 80 percent of what the station offered. Unsurprisingly, Maiak stepped into the ongoing controversy about Western pop, but it was also criticized in the press more broadly for violating cultural hierarchies and abandoning or even subverting what should have been its main goal: aesthetic education. In 1965, the editor of the journal *Soviet Music* (*Sovetskaia muzyka*) summarized the opponents' positions in a letter to the CC's Ideological Commission. Maiak's program was dominated by light music, "often copying Western styles," she said, and whatever "serious" music it offered went on the air at inconvenient hours for listeners. Adding insult to injury, Maiak played serious works without so much as mentioning their titles or the names of their composers or performers. And quite often, shockingly, the station cut them off in the middle.

> Not long ago, for example, I heard them put on after the news without any sort of announcement a recording of a concerto for voice and orchestra by R. Gliere performed by N. Kazantseva.... This kind of practice reduces music to the role of a sort of "aural background" that is neutral in terms of its ideological-aesthetic content.... This kind of practice does not instill in listeners the habit of listening attentively to music and contemplating it; it does not inculcate respect for music as a great, deep, and rich art.

The editor, E. Grosheva, told the CC that the journal had received numerous letters from music lovers about Maiak. She printed one, accusing the station of "amputating Prokofiev," among other sins, and this earned her a trip to the offices of none other than Aleksandr Iakovlev, who defended Maiak and even

---

144. Even Maiak, however, had trouble sticking to its schedule. Ibid., 417. Marshall McLuhan, *Understanding Media: The Extensions of Man* (New York, 1964).

refused, she said, to acknowledge the distinction between serious and light music.[145] Grosheva was writing to the CC higher-ups, convinced that Iakovlev "was extremely far from understanding these questions," and although the CC backed him up in the end, her point of view was not unusual and cannot be ignored. If, as every Radio Day editorial claimed, one goal of Soviet broadcasting was cultural uplift, then where *was* the elevation in Maiak's breezy round robin of arias, folk songs, and pop? What was elevated was the listener's mood, or so the redaktsiia hoped, and it is true that this was also one of Soviet radio's official goals. But like the never-ending news cycle, a nonstop entertainment model created a very different listening experience. It catered to a cultural consumer, not to an aesthete or aesthete in the making. Make no mistake: there was quite a lot of high-minded, serious music on Maiak. What Grosheva and like-minded critics wanted to know was how listeners would ever learn to love it and ultimately prefer it to the lighter fare if Soviet radio did not teach them. Maiak was not teaching. Its format said the station's main purpose was to have people listening, period.

In 1965, the radio and TV administration's recently organized research bureau ran a series of surveys on Maiak (primarily of listeners in the RSFSR) and found that the new station had already won a very large audience. Overall, 70 percent of listeners reported that they were listening to Maiak at least some of the time, and 36 percent described themselves as "constant listeners." In Moscow and several other regions where radio ownership levels were high and reception was clear and reliable, listener rates for the new station were close to 100 percent.[146]

But if Maiak could be considered a clear success in terms of attracting audiences, the same could not be said of its goal of distracting them from the charms of the enemy voices. A 1968 survey by radio and TV's research bureau found that 47 percent of people identified themselves as listeners to foreign radio (openly, the researchers noted); just under 10 percent described themselves as "regular listeners," while another 15 percent said they did not tune in themselves but heard about foreign radio broadcasts secondhand. The study was limited to urban regions, but unlike the Maiak survey, it covered multiple republics. It also gathered some interesting information on the tastes of listeners and their social profiles. The largest group of self-reported listeners was in the sixteen- to thirty-year-old category; more men listened than women (52 percent to 41 percent), and most people listened at night. However, there was no clear-cut correlation between educational levels and listening practices: aside from those in the lowest level (who had markedly lower rates), people of varying backgrounds reported listening to the foreign voices in rather similar numbers. Interestingly, when asked what they listened to on foreign radio, they split into two roughly

145. RGANI, f. 5, op. 55, d. 129, ll. 64–65.
146. GARF, f. 6903, op. 3, d. 325, ll. 3–4.

equal camps. About 45 percent said they tuned in only for music, and roughly the same number said they listened only to the news; 10 percent described themselves as tuning in for both.[147]

Soviet researchers drew a direct connection between the inadequacy of domestic radio and the success of the enemy voices. "The sluggishness and narrowness [*neoperativnost' i uzkost'*] of the programs on Soviet radio, including on the First Station and Maiak, lead to a situation where a part of the audience is switching over to listen to foreign stations on either a regular or an episodic basis." Listeners reported that they tuned in to foreign radio not only for what was unavailable from Soviet media sources but also for its timeliness. Here the researchers referred to an earlier study of Maiak to demonstrate just how far off the mark the station was: fewer than 1 percent of the news segments covered events that had happened within the previous few hours, and almost none were live, on-the-scene reports (0.5 percent of the total); about 35 percent of the airtime was given over to discussion of events or ideas with no clear time reference at all.[148]

The solution was to speed things up, they argued, but we know this was easier said than done. Kharlamov's successor at the radio and TV administration, Nikolai Mesiatsev, wrote in his memoirs that he approached his "comrades in the Politburo" about pushing the pace. "I tried to convince them that every piece of news can be divided into two parts: the first part is the actual delivery of the fact, while the second part, which comes after the first, and need not come immediately, comments on that fact—that is, after I quickly put the fact on the air, the higher authorities would have time to say . . . how exactly we wanted to comment on that fact."[149] Mesiatsev, let it be said, had impeccable credentials (World War II, Komsomol, and KGB service, a reliable, behind-the-scenes participant in the 1964 ouster of Khrushchev)—he was not the problem. It is not clear from his account whether he approached his comrades after 1968's Prague Spring, which we know was interpreted as an object lesson in the dangers of loosening control on mass media. But even prior to 1968, it is doubtful Mesiatsev would have found many supporters at the top. In 1965, he had seen his proposal to hire three special political commentators (two for radio, one for TV) shot down. Mesiatsev argued that continuing to rely on the political correspondents from *Pravda* and *Izvestiia* to go on air was crippling the Soviets' ability to respond to enemy radio; the CC concluded that Soviet broadcasting did not need in-house commentators.[150]

147. The survey was conducted in Ukraine, Belorussia, Estonia, Kazakhstan, Azerbaijan, Moldova, and the RSFSR between May and August 1968—a very particular historical moment, to say the least, but not one the researchers chose to comment on. One thousand three hundred eleven people were surveyed via a network of 118 interviewers. The results were never released. GARF, f. 6903, op. 2, d. 501, ll. 1–35.

148. Ibid., ll. 34–35.

149. N. N. Mesiatsev, *Davnoe perezhitoe* (Moscow, 2000), 84.

150. RGANI, f. 5, op. 33, d. 227, ll. 49–51.

Delegating authority to a greater number of people in the informational hierarchy would have helped Soviet media combat their natural sluggishness. But this was never a priority for the people at the top. Preserving the hierarchy was a priority—and not only for perceived security reasons (the specter of rogue media) and for vanity's sake. Soviet media culture was by definition a top-down, educational enterprise (teaching political, cultural, and social values). Sluggishness, well, what was a little sluggishness when enduring values were at stake? It took a team of apparatchiki like Nenashev days and sometimes weeks in a dacha to write a single speech for a Politburo member. This was not a culture designed for responsiveness or change.

Meanwhile, with the latest news and hit songs, foreign broadcasters were thrusting another cultural model—a disposable, in-the-moment culture, without a clear direction—into Soviet everyday experience and doing it successfully. Mesiatsev recalled feeling oppressed by the knowledge that foreign radio was winning: "it 'hung' over me constantly like a reproach against our powerlessness," he wrote. Maiak was the Soviets' one best effort to compete with the enemy voices, but what it amounted to was a halfway house. Maiak said that news mattered by programming it every half hour and sticking to its schedule, yet it failed to deliver breaking news. In music, it validated the entertainment model of Western radio by playing light music and, more important, by presenting all music, even serious music, as a soundtrack to personal experience. This was Soviet culture stripped of its bran. And though a lot of people evidently used it—Maiak, after all, was popular—it could not hope to draw people away from enemy radio.

HEARING THE MUSES

Alex Inkeles and Raymond Bauer, keen contemporary observers of the Soviet media scene, put it best: "[T]he nature of the Soviet Union is such that the communications behavior of citizens must be regarded as one of the dimensions of their relations with the regime."[151] Foreign broadcasters to the USSR and their supporters tended to take this idea and draw a straight line between listening to the enemy voices and opposition to the regime. There is no question that foreign radio was significant for many people because of its ideas, including the foundational idea of the free flow of information. But a muse is a muse and not a marching order, and it is always difficult to know what attracts people in any cultural experience and where inspiration will take them. Foreign radio listening did not equal dissent, nor can we say that it necessarily generated dissent.

The story of the Soviet entanglement with foreign broadcasting is more ambiguous and interesting. Consider the spectacle of Khrushchev and his comrades

---

151. A. Inkeles and R. Bauer, *The Soviet Citizen: Daily Life in a Totalitarian Society* (New York, 1968), 165.

scratching their heads in wonder at the shortwave radio boom. "Why did we do this?" Khrushchev asked, because, as anyone could see, it was counterproductive in the extreme. (Khrushchev went on to hold up the Americans as an example because they had been clever enough, he thought, to seal off their population from Radio Moscow by banning shortwave production.) The Soviets' Cold War media empire had no coherent media policy; what it had was Soviet culture, and this meant tremendous growth in the radio sector, domestic and international. It helped make careers and was a source of pride and prestige; its success was of a kind useful and comprehensible to many people. And it is in this context that we must consider the development of foreign radio listening in the USSR.

The gut reaction of the Soviet authorities to the enemy voices was always to expand their own broadcasting, especially internationally, and to jam: maintain the informational hierarchy at all costs, generate more and more information that serves your interests, spread it wider, say it louder. This response reflected the core values of Soviet political culture and also the Soviet idea of culture, twinned as they were. It was the political agitator on the factory floor with a megaphone (perhaps reading a newspaper with the authoritative spin from on high); and it was also a performer on a stage and an audience sitting quietly, eyes upturned. It was not about speed or stylishness or the latest thing, or about personal pleasure. This was what made sense to the Soviet authorities as a media experience, and while millions of people in the USSR voted with their tuning dials for a different concept of the media age, the authorities proved incapable of conceptualizing their radio problem in these terms. The success of foreign broadcasting was in changing the terms for media experience within the USSR. Foreign radio made Soviet radio look bad—frumpy, hidebound, cautious, not modern, not with it, not *good enough.* This was a common phenomenon in Soviet life: BMWs made Ladas look lousy too. But riding in a BMW (or, what was more realistic, seeing one on film) was not an intimate, daily experience; radio listening was. More important still, though there was no reason to think that you needed a BMW to be a modern, up-to-date, fully cultured person in the Soviet context, there was every reason to think you needed, and could reasonably demand, good radio.[152] Radio was Soviet culture; culture stood at the heart of the promise of Soviet socialism. And that made accepting the terms of cultural competition with the West only to fall flatly short of them a ringing political failure for the Soviet regime.

152. Lewis Siegelbaum's recent work on automobile culture suggests that this attitude to cars was beginning to change in the Soviet Union's final years as increasing numbers of people had (frustrated) expectations about car ownership. Seigelbaum, *Cars for Comrades* (Ithaca, NY, 2008), chap. 6.

FINDING A HOME FOR
TELEVISION IN THE USSR

In the 1970s, Moscow's massive Ostankino television tower was known in nonconformist circles as the "needle" for its supposed role in injecting propaganda into the supple veins of the Soviet masses.[1] By that time, Soviet TV was a vast enterprise employing tens of thousands throughout the Union, broadcasting on multiple channels across eleven time zones, and reaching into the homes of the overwhelming majority of the population. From the perspective of the regime's opponents inside the USSR and beyond its borders, there was an ineluctable logic to the medium's growth: TV was naturally at home in a Soviet media system predicated on mass indoctrination and pacification.[2] Inevitably, though, television's trajectory in the postwar period was far more chaotic, and far more fraught with political, social, and cultural tensions, than Ostankino's thrusting lines suggest.

TV technology put tremendous new opportunities on the table, and in the words of Raymond Williams, the "moment of any new technology is a moment of choice."[3] Strictly speaking, TV was not a *new* technology for the Soviets in the postwar period; there had been experimental TV broadcasts in Moscow and Leningrad in the 1930s, and the central press regularly reported on the new medium's progress.[4] Nevertheless, it was not until after the war, and really not until the second half of the 1950s, that the technology first took hold in the USSR; by the 1970s it had developed into the massive political, cultural, and social

1. Scott Shane, *Dismantling Utopia* (Chicago, 1994), 153. "Ostankino syringe" as a critique for Soviet TV also appeared in Vladimir Kuprin's story "Sorokovoi den'," *Nash sovremennik* no. 11 (1981): 72–117. *Nash sovremennik* was reprimanded for publishing Kuprin's story, among other materials. See Dirk Krechmar, *Politika i kul'tura pri Brezhneve, Andropove i Chernenko 1970–1985 gg.*, trans. M. G. Ratgaus (Moscow, 1997), 136–137.

2. The needle reference is reminiscent of the "hypodermic effects" model, a major early theory of mass communications. See Todd Gitlin, "Media Sociology: The Dominant Paradigm," *Theory and Society* 6 (1978): 205–253. Ellen Mickiewicz also discusses the parallel in *Split Signals: Television and Politics in Soviet Society* (New York, 1988), 181–183.

3. Raymond Williams, *Television: Technology and Cultural Form* (New York, 1975), xv.

4. A. Iurovskii, *Televidenie: Poiski i resheniia* (Moscow, 1983), 29–39; A. Iurovskii, "Pervye shagi," *Problemy televideniia i radio* (Moscow, 1971), 95–108; V. A. Urvalov, *Ocherki istorii televideniia* (Moscow, 1990), 89–146.

Figure 4.1. Heart of the Soviet TV empire: Ostankino, 1967. ITAR-TASS. Used with permission.

institution known as Soviet TV. That this was a complicated and often messy process, not easily slotted into standard historical periodization (e.g., Stalinism and post-Stalinism, Khrushchev's thaw and Brezhnev's stagnation) and not susceptible to silver-bullet explanations, is too readily overlooked. As Williams explained in his analysis of broadcasting's development in the West, we are all so accustomed to seeing television as a major institution and to TV's basic forms that we tend to view both as "predestined by the technology." But if, like Williams, we move in for a closer look, the patina of inevitability fades, and we can see the people of the past and the important choices they made.[5]

In the Soviet Union of the 1950s and '60s, many people in diverse political, social, and cultural locations understood that there were choices on the table when it came to television. Some were apprehensive, others unmoved and apathetic, and not a few looked at TV technology and were deeply inspired. Moscow's top-ranking official for television in 1956 was still known as Glavradio, the head of radio, so little status did TV have then in the Soviet media system. But he rallied local studio directors together in Moscow for the first time that year and told them they were "blazing totally new trails in this area, different from those established in other countries."[6] Soviet TV broadcasting, the province of the self-described "enthusiasts" we will meet in chapter 5, was then in flux in almost every conceivable way. The question of TV's relationship to the Soviet political tradition and to methods of mass mobilization was very much up in the air. So, too, were the new medium's rights and responsibilities vis-à-vis the arts and its role in a modern Soviet way of life. Who and what belonged on the screen, who was responsible for programming and safeguarding the airwaves, who should watch, and when and why they should watch—all were issues that were not settled in any definite sense until television reached its institutional maturity in the 1970s. That TV became the single most important source of official political information and culture for the Soviet population, massively promoted, tightly controlled, and a bedrock institution of Soviet life seems as predictable now as the anchor's "Good evening, comrades" on *Vremia* (*Time*), the nightly news program. But once we strip the paint of predestination, a far more mottled and interesting picture emerges.

One aspect is clear-cut: the Soviet regime made an unambiguous choice when it came to investing in television technology across the decades. For much of the postwar period, TV and related technologies were on the cutting edge of communications internationally, and they offered a potent symbol of Soviet scientific prowess to observers at home and abroad. As an industrial product promising knowledge and pleasure to millions with the flick of a switch, television also provided a fitting emblem of the socialist "good life" and proof of Soviet competitiveness on the Cold War's home front. In practical terms, TV broadcasting

5. Williams, *Television*, 17.
6. GARF, f. 6903, op. 1, d. 499, l. 5.

promised an audience of unprecedented size and, given the foreign radio problem, one that could also be walled off from the non-Soviet world—or so it seemed in the years before satellite, when television's reach was limited by its reliance on relay stations and cables to carry signals. In fact, even without the superior reach of satellite, millions of people living in the western borderland regions of the USSR had access to foreign TV broadcasts. But this was a relatively contained problem, and even in the 1970s, when satellite broadcasting was well established, television was always a far more secure medium, from the regime's point of view, than radio. In short, both symbolically and practically, television technology presented tremendous opportunities, and the Soviet regime did not hesitate to invest in its development. With the Soviet press cheering heartily off-screen, people across the USSR learned that a modern socialist marvel called Soviet television was fast becoming an ordinary feature of Soviet life.

Yet what seemed so clear on the pages of *Pravda* and the latest plan often presented a fuzzier picture on the ground in the 1950s and '60s. Choosing to invest in a technology was not the same as deciding how to use and administer it. And in this respect, as even Soviet scholars acknowledged, the leaders of the "propaganda state" were at first disorganized, uncreative, even detached.[7] This indecision at the top opened a door to initiative at lower levels, and in the 1950s especially, we see consumers, scientific hobbyists, and local political elites all playing important roles in pushing TV development forward. But here again, enthusiasm for the technology did not translate into effective management, nor did it address critical questions about how the Soviets should use TV. What were the answers? One obvious tack was political communication. Yet well into the 1960s, local political elites, while pushing hard to bring TV technology to their regions, seemed largely indifferent to its propaganda potential and kept their distance from the camera. Another tack was cultural uplift, and the Soviet press bubbled over with enthusiasm about television's matchless ability to deliver culture directly to the masses. At the same time, though, many professionals in the established arts—theater, film, literature, dance—were turning a very cold shoulder to the new medium. Television was in the paradoxical position of being celebrated and denigrated, pampered and ignored in its first formative postwar decades.

American social scientists pioneered the study of television in the Soviets' system of political communication.[8] This chapter builds on their insights as well as

7. Iurovskii, *Televidenie,* 106; see also his *Televizionnaia zhurnalistika* (Moscow, 1998), 71. For the concurring views of Western scholars, see Ellen Mickiewicz, *Media and the Russian Public* (New York, 1981), 18; Kristian Feigelson, *L'URSS et sa télévision* (Paris, 1990), 58; Mark Hopkins, *Mass Media in the Soviet Union* (New York, 1970), 251; Reino Paasilinna, "Glasnost and Soviet Television" (YLE–Finnish Broadcasting Co., research report, May 1995), 94.

8. Mickiewicz was the most important: *Media and the Russian Public; Split Signals; Changing Channels: Television and the Struggle for Power in Russia* (Durham, NC, 1999).

on new archival materials and other sources to sketch out a fresh interpretive framework for TV's trajectory from wunderkind to bedrock Soviet institution in the postwar USSR. The approach here is perforce not comprehensive, yet it strives to be multidimensional, interrogating not only political but also cultural and social factors in TV's development—and pointedly so. My argument is that it is only by examining the history "in 3D" that we can grasp the nature of the problem of television in the Soviet context. The cultural education that Soviet TV provided (or failed to provide) and the social phenomenon of TV watching were political questions in the Soviet context; similarly, the reaction of political elites to the opportunities and challenges of a new medium had a great deal to do with how they defined such things as art and leisure—that is, they were inflected with cultural and social understandings.

If initially the Soviet regime did a better job propagandizing and funding television than figuring out how to use the sets, that is because, in many ways, TV looked better in the Soviet context as a symbol than as a reality. Home-based broadcasting was the modern standard worldwide after World War II, but it was an uneasy fit at best with political, cultural, and social practices in the USSR. Indeed, even in the controlling hands of the Soviet state, television opened the door to new practices and raised many troubling new questions, particularly when it came to its mode of consumption.

The individual home, signpost of Soviet achievement in the postwar era, was also a conundrum. How would propaganda and cultural uplift operate when mediated by a glowing box in the corner? Who knew for sure if viewers were snoozing their way through symphonies and lectures on Lenin, or laughing at lecturers and gossiping about their hairstyles, or not tuning in for important political and cultural programming at all? And if people were at home in front of the set, was this not drawing them away from concert halls and movie theaters, amateur sports, and civic activism? Did TV watching fit the profile of a people who, as Nikita Khrushchev promised, would "catch up and overtake" the West and achieve communism in their lifetimes? Where Soviet tradition was geared to mass political and cultural mobilization, TV looked like immobilization; where Soviet tradition privileged collective, public settings, TV broadcasting reached individual and anonymous viewers in their homes. Never had the Soviet regime

See also Kendall Bailes, *Soviet Television Comes of Age: A Review of Its Accomplishments and a Discussion of the Tasks Facing It* (New York, 1968); Rosemarie Rodgers, "The Soviet Mass Media in the Sixties: Patterns of Access and Consumption," *Journal of Broadcasting* 15, no. 2 (1971): 127–146; Gayle Durham Hollander, *Soviet Political Indoctrination: Developments in Mass Media and Propaganda since Stalin* (New York, 1972); David E. Powell, "Television in the USSR," *Public Opinion Quarterly* 39, no. 3 (Autumn 1976): 287–300; Jonathan Saunders, "A Very Mass Media," *Television Quarterly* 22, no. 3 (1986): 7–27; Thomas Remington, *The Truth of Authority: Ideology and Communication in the Soviet Union* (Pittsburgh, 1988).

had a medium for reaching so many people with its messages, and never had a medium appeared so potentially out of sync with the messages it was to deliver.

In the end, TV technology did find a home in the Soviet system, despite the ambivalence that it met as it first came through the door. The dynamism of local broadcasting and its tremendous popularity with consumers helped force television to the fore, and over time the Soviet central authorities began to make clearer choices about using the technology—and more explicit demands on political and cultural elites about their involvement. Television was effectively centralized, standardized, and mobilized to become the Soviet people's leading source for propaganda, culture, and entertainment in the 1970s. Ostankino, the world's largest TV center with the world's tallest TV tower, was its proud emblem. But just as Ostankino was not built in day or a year, the institutionalization of TV technology in the USSR was a process, a "set of particular social decisions, in particular circumstances," as Raymond Williams put it. The symbolism of a TV set in every Soviet apartment as proof of socialism's ability to deliver the good life had made an irrefutable case for the technology. The challenge was bringing this symbolism to life as Soviet politics, Soviet culture, and a Soviet way of life.

INVESTING IN TELEVISION

Many foreigners who visited the USSR in the first years after Stalin's death were struck by the presence of TV technology in a country evidently still struggling with the basics of quality food, clothing, and shelter. American journalist Marguerite Higgins reported "one of the strangest sights in Russia" was that of television antennas atop wooden houses on the outskirts of Moscow. "Although the houses are so dilapidated they literally sag sideways into the mud, each of the two families crammed into the tiny space possesses a set of its own," she marveled.[9] This was in 1955, when there were perhaps 1 million such households in the Soviet Union, most of them in Moscow. By 1960 that number would rise to nearly 5 million, doubling again by 1963 to 10.5 million and reaching roughly 25 million by the end of the decade.[10] These were modest figures in comparison with those in the contemporary United States, where two-thirds of families bought a TV set between 1948 and 1955. But the United States was in a league all its own when it came to TV development. In total number of sets, the Soviet Union bested all of continental Europe and ranked fourth in the world in the late fifties. The Soviets naturally fell in standing once their population size was taken into account, but even so, they fared relatively well when compared with fellow socialist countries

9. Marguerite Higgins, *Red Plush and Black Bread* (Garden City, NY, 1955), 40.

10. *Narodnoe khoziaistvo SSSR v 1970 g.* (Moscow, 1971), 466; *Problemy televideniia i radio* (Moscow, 1971), 210, 246. TV ownership varied greatly by republic, with the RSFSR in first place by a wide margin and Ukraine a distant second. The proportion of RSFSR sets declined over time (from 78 percent of the total in 1958 to 63 percent in 1965).

in Eastern Europe.[11] And comparisons aside, Higgins's larger point remains: the Soviets were choosing to produce and purchase TVs at a blistering pace.

There is no disputing the USSR's strong financial commitment to television technology. The head of Soviet broadcasting from 1964 to 1970, Nikolai Mesiatsev, contended that "the government spared no expense on the development of mass broadcasting," and this "despite the fact that the country lived rather poorly."[12] In 1960, the year the Soviets broke ground on the Ostankino complex, approximately 30 percent of collective farms (and this according to *official* statistics) were still operating without electricity, and millions of urban families were living in cramped communal apartments.[13] Television, though, was never treated as a luxury, despite its terrific expense. It cost an estimated 10 million rubles to set up a one–thousand-kilometer stretch of radio-relay cable in the early 1960s, 20 million for coaxial cable; by 1982, the USSR had laid *ninety* thousand kilometers.[14] The initial estimates for the Ostankino project alone ran to 127 million rubles. It is true that, according to Aleksandr Iakovlev (then head of the radio-TV division in the CC apparat), the Politburo refused to approve such a large lump sum, and so the monies were doled out incrementally.[15] But the financial commitment was clear, and it distinguished television from many other technologies that the Soviets bypassed for major investment in the postwar period. In 1960 there were only 4.3 million telephones in this country of over 200 million people, and more than half were public phones.[16] Overall automobile production topped out that year at around 525,000, and the authorities used a variety of methods to discourage individual car ownership.[17] Yet the Soviet regime constantly expanded production and promoted consumption of television; more important still, it chose to promote an individualized, domestic

11. The top three were the United States, Canada, and Great Britain. Irving R. Levine, *Main Street, USSR: Selections from the Original Edition* (New York, 1960), 66. UNESCO reported 13.9 sets per hundred inhabitants for the Federal Republic of Germany (FRG), 10 for Czechoslovakia, 9 for the German Democratic Republic (GDR), 7.5 for France, 3.3 for Poland, 2.7 for Hungary, 0.3 for Bulgaria, and 3.2 for the USSR. Their USSR total—7 million sets—is significantly lower than the 10 to 11 million figure found in Soviet sources, however. See *World Communications: Press, Radio, Television, Film* (New York, 1964).

12. Interview with N. N. Mesiatsev, Moscow, July 2002.

13. *Narodnoe khoziaistvo SSSR v 1970 g* (Moscow, 1971), 378. Plans to build a new TV center in Moscow with a record-breaking tower dated back to 1956. Construction was then repeatedly delayed because of technical problems. Iurovskii, *Televidenie,* 42.

14. For 1960s costs see GARF, f. 6903, op. 1, d. 808, l. 65; for 1982 kilometer totals, see Iurovskii, *Televidenie,* 46.

15. A. N. Iakovlev, *Omut pamiati* (Moscow, 2001), 142–143.

16. *Narodnoe khoziaistvo,* 466.

17. S. Frederick Starr, "New Communications Technologies and Civil Society," in *Science and the Soviet Social Order,* ed. Loren Graham (Cambridge, MA, 1990), 19–50. This figure included trucks and buses as well as cars.

version of TV. When prices on luxury consumer items were raised in 1959, not only were TVs excluded, but the price of sets was lowered.[18] Two years later the USSR Council of Ministers announced a further boon: an end to the license fees levied on TV owners. These fees, collected quarterly, were a major revenue stream—95 million rubles in 1961 alone, a sum nearly equivalent to that year's total budget for investments in television *and* radio (102 million). License fees were a common means for funding state broadcasting systems, and most countries, including the people's democracies of the Soviet bloc, maintained their licensing systems into the 1970s. The Soviet regime's willingness to forgo these funds and push on with development is as good an indication as any of its strong commitment to promoting TV technology at the consumer level.[19]

The Soviet people also proved to be eager investors in the new technology. There were waiting lists across the Union for would-be set buyers, and throughout the fifties and sixties factories struggled to keep pace with demand.[20] Judging from the reports of various foreign correspondents, a new TV set would cost anywhere from 850 to 2,600 old (85 to 260 new) rubles in the late fifties and about the same in the mid- to late sixties.[21] These prices put a new set at several times the typical monthly salary, even for urbanites: senior engineers working in television in 1963 made 140 rubles a month, typists, 55.[22] A Soviet consumer willing and able to spend such a hefty sum was usually getting a set with a screen the size of a postcard and, more important, a set almost certain to break down.[23] By the government's own admission, the majority of new sets in the late fifties failed at least once within their first six months of use.[24] The press in this period frequently ran letters from readers describing the frustration of bringing home a new set only to have it sit idle in the corner; not only was their TV defective, but the parts needed to repair it were nowhere to be found.[25] Consumers who

18. Wilson Dizard, "Television in the USSR," *Problems of Communism*, no. 12 (1963): 39.

19. GARF, f. 6903, op. 7, d. 542, l. 10. In 1962, the license fee was technically replaced by a one-time tax included in the price of the set. Poland, Czechoslovakia, the GDR, and Hungary all maintained their licensing systems. See Burton Paulu, *Radio and Television Broadcasting* (Minneapolis, 1974).

20. Higgins reported a ten-month wait in 1955. Higgins, *Red Plush*, 42.

21. Levine, *Main Street, USSR*, 66; Joseph Evans, *Through Soviet Windows* (New York, 1957), 60; Higgins, *Red Plush*, 42; Hopkins, *Mass Media*, 253; M. Likhachev, "Sovetskie televizory dolzhny byt' luchshie v mire," *Ekonomicheskaia gazeta*, 18 July 1961.

22. GARF, f. 6903, op. 7, d. 551, l. 15. TV sets were also among the goods that consumers could buy on installment plans.

23. The first mass-produced set, the KVN-49, went into production in 1949 and had a screen measuring just eighteen centimeters diagonally. Magnifying lenses were often attached to sets for this reason.

24. V. Kuibyshev, "Nuzhdy telezritelei," *Izvestiia*, 26 October 1958.

25. V. Bezgulyi, "Za ekranom televizora," *Izvestiia*, 17 July 1960; L. Shumov, "Bel'mo na televizore," *Ogonek*, no. 48 (1960); "Posle vystupleniia *Ogonka*: Kogda zhe prozreiut

Figure 4.2. The TV hearth: a worker's family, 1964. ITAR-TASS. Used with permission.

invested their money and time on TV would have done so for the pleasure of a few hours of viewing a day: in the late 1950s, Central TV in Moscow, by far the country's most developed station, was offering four hours of programming daily (as of 1956 on two channels); in the rest of the country, many stations broadcast less regularly and for fewer hours. Finally, judging by the many letters of complaint in the press and recollections of former TV professionals, the technical quality of broadcasts was often abysmal. Viewers complained about wavy, unclear images and whistles and hisses, and about fingers and other extraneous objects that made their way onto the camera; television made their eyes water and their heads ache.[26] Given the conditions, it is a wonder many TV studios put out any programming at all. Riga's first studio in the fifties, for example, was so small that only one person at a time could fit on camera. It was also terrifically hot (42 degrees Celsius), as were most Soviet studios because of the low

televizory?" *Ogonek,* no. 6 (1961). Locating the right parts was complicated by the large number of different models (eighty-seven by 1965). Urvalov, *Ocherki istorii televideniia,* 152.

26. TsDAVO, f. 4915, op. 1, d. 2394, l. 2.

quality of their lighting technology.[27] As was true of early television the world over, early Soviet TV consisted (cinema aside) almost entirely of live broadcasts, and viewers watched the toddler medium fall flat on its face repeatedly.

Nevertheless, as *New York Times* reporter Harrison Salisbury observed as early as 1954, Muscovites were "frankly wild about television," and they were not alone.[28] Sociological research in the sixties found no direct correlation between a person's decision to buy a TV set and either salary level, professional activity, or educational background; people of all social groups were buying.[29] For the same amount of money (and assuming these products were available—an admittedly broad assumption), a consumer might have purchased other household appliances that were then promoted in Soviet media as part of a modern lifestyle: a vacuum cleaner perhaps, or a small refrigerator, or both. And surely many people did. Yet just as surely, millions of consumers chose TV sets instead (or first), despite the costs, their well-earned reputation for breaking down, and what many viewers derided as low-quality programming. If the moment of any new technology is a moment of choice, Soviet consumers chose television with gusto.

LOCAL CHOICES AND THE CENTER'S PREROGATIVES

As the production and consumption of TV sets increased dramatically in the 1950s and '60s, so too did the infrastructure for broadcasting. Figures for the number of TV stations in the USSR tell a dramatic story: in 1955, there were just 9 stations, in 1958, 12. But by 1960, the number had rocketed up to 84, reaching 121 in 1965.[30] Accordingly, the number of people employed by the new medium ballooned from four hundred to nearly eighteen thousand in the same period.[31] Figures like these would seem to indicate a well-orchestrated campaign from the center to develop TV technology. But in fact, at least until the early sixties, the explosive growth of Soviet TV owed its momentum in large measure to local initiatives.

Who were these local boosters for television? In Vladivostok, they were Viktor Nazarenko and his comrades, a group of engineers, who built the first studio in 1956.[32] An analogous group in Dnepropetrovsk convinced the local mining institute to let them use a tower in their building for broadcasting.[33] In Kazan,

27. GARF, f. 6903, op. 1, d. 499, l. 92.

28. Harrison Salisbury, "What Russians See on TV," *New York Times,* 11 July 1954.

29. Researchers did find that families with children were more likely to buy a set than families without; married couples had more TVs than people living on their own. B. M. Firsov, *Puti razvitiia sredstv massovoi kommunikatsii* (Moscow, 1977), 114–115.

30. Iurovskii, *Televidenie,* 43. One study estimates 275 stations in operation in 1960, with numbers continuing to rise in the early sixties. Urvalov, *Ocherki istorii televideniia,* 150, 146.

31. Iurovskii, *Televidenie,* 43, 108.

32. G. Khaliletskii, "Goresti mestnogo televideniia," *Literaturnaia gazeta,* 27 August 1957.

33. Ivan Mashchenko, *Telebachennia Ukraini,* vol. 1 (Kyiv, 2004), 52.

Kharkov, and many other cities, ham radio clubs, typically run by civil defense organizations, were the new medium's pioneers.[34] Given Soviet culture's emphasis on scientific knowledge, many people had the motivation and the skills to develop television in their own communities. The surprising thing is how little their activities were regulated. Certainly no studio could have taken shape without the approval of local party and state officials; often enough, the regional party secretary was the first person in town with a TV set in his apartment and a main instigator in getting a local station up and running. But it was not until 1957, when the TV audience already numbered in the millions, that the party's Central Committee put together a group for managing TV, a division in its Department of Propaganda and Agitation (the division headed by Iakovlev); and it was not until 1957 that the industry won firm footing in state structures as the State Committee for Radio and Television, or Gosteleradio, under the USSR Council of Ministers.[35] Prior to that, the Ministries of Culture and of Communications shared oversight over television, with Communications responsible for technical issues, including new studio construction, and Culture supervising programming. Or so matters stood on paper. In practice, there were Viktor Nazarenkos and party secretaries who liked their TV in many localities, and even after the 1957 administrative reorganization, the central authorities could not say with any precision how many TV stations the country had.

In 1958, the head of Gosteleradio lodged an official complaint with the Central Committee about "so-called 'amateur TV centers'" that had cropped up alongside official studios "with the foreknowledge and the protection of local organizations" (a reference to regional party structures). These centers, fumed Gosteleradio, had been "built in a slipshod fashion using funds given by local organizations, without the permission of the Council of Ministers . . . and without taking into account the basic conditions for TV programming." In some instances, "local organizations" were moving their homegrown studios to neighboring towns once an official center opened in the area, while in others, the amateurs were now petitioning for official status and funding.[36] This "disorganized state television," said Gosteleradio: it stimulated TV sales in the wrong areas and caused shortages

34. "Na ekrane televizora—dosaafovtsy," *Sovetskii patriot,* 13 September 1961, in GARF, f. 6903, op. 3, d. 175; Mashchenko, *Telebachennia,* 91; *Pechat', radioveshchanie i televidenie Tatarii, 1917–1980: Sbornik dokumentov i materialov* (Kazan', 1981), 176.

35. The State Committee for Radio and Television (Goskomitet po radioveshchaniiu i televideniiu pri Sovete Ministrov SSSR) was not officially known as Gosteleradio until 1972, when "television and radio" switched order in the name, as discussed below. I use Gosteleradio throughout as a generic term. After 1957, all Soviet republics (excluding the RSFSR) developed analogous committees in their state administrations. CC departments and divisions were also analogous on the republic level.

36. GARF, f. 6903, op. 1, d. 543, l. 79; TsDAHOU, f. 1, op. 70, d. 2447, ll. 11–13. Some amateurs were capable of broadcasting their own programs, while others were mere relay stations. The RSFSR and Ukraine had the highest density of stations of all types.

in the right ones—that is, in nearby cities with official centers—and robbed the state of revenues (since viewers who watched the amateurs were failing to pay their TV license fees).[37] But Gosteleradio's chief complaint about the amateurs was that they provided a substandard service. Here is how its deputy chairman described the situation at a meeting of Ukrainian studio heads in 1963:

> Whoever made a better case to the Ministry of Communications, or was more convincing, or had more nerve, that's where a studio sprang up. So, not long ago, they opened a studio in one place... and it turned out there's no theater in the area, no [musical] ensembles. And you have to work... you have to put the equipment to use. So every night there they put two soloists on the air: one on the balalaika, the other on the accordion.[38]

The fact that Gosteleradio was still complaining about amateur studios as late as 1963—and, back in Moscow, threatening to sanction local party secretaries who refused to come to heel—speaks volumes about early Soviet TV development.[39] The disjuncture between investment and effective administration was colossal.

Soviet television's centralization in Moscow was never in question. Radio, its closest kin in technical and administrative terms, provided a ready model for a centralized network, but more than that, the phenomenon was in the bones of the cultural and, indeed, political system.[40] Moscow TV *was* Central or All-Union TV (*Tsentral'noe* or *Vsesoiuznoe televidenie*) as a matter of principle; it was only a question of time and technical development for principle to become reality. In the early 1950s, the Soviets began working on connecting local studios to Moscow and, as a second order of importance, to each other using cables and relay stations. Centralization then took a giant leap forward with the use of satellite technology, which linked far-flung regions in Siberia, the Far East, central Asia, and the far north to Moscow (as of 1967), and with the completion of the massive Ostankino complex as Central TV's hub.[41] By the decade's end, the voice and the image of the center stretched across the eleven time zones of the Soviet Union.

What this meant in practical terms was that many stations built by local enthusiasts were closed within a few years of opening, and those that remained

37. GARF, f. 6903, op. 1, d. 543, l. 80.

38. TsDAVO, f. 4915, op. 1, d. 3438, l. 5.

39. At a 1963 meeting, Gosteleradio's chief directed his staff to write the regional party organizations as follows: "[T]he CC is demanding that we straighten things out, otherwise there will be a thousand TV centers in the country, and each one will offer its own programs. We in Moscow are not satisfied with your programs." If Gosteleradio were unable to "come to an agreement" with them, he said, then they would "punish via the CC Biuro." GARF, f. 6903, op. 1, d. 783, l. 109.

40. In the 1950s, the centralizing impulse meant proposals to cut *all* local (regional and city level) radio centers. See GARF, f. 6903, op. 1, d. 474, ll. 51–52.

41. The Molniia-1 satellite for TV transmission was first launched in 1965 and went into operation two years later. V. V. Egorov, *Televidenie: Teoriia i praktika* (Moscow, 1993), 11.

open found their programming shunted aside to make room for Moscow once the cable (or later, the satellite feed) had been established. In many areas, then, TV's development spelled a critical linguistic shift, as Central TV's Russian-language First Channel replaced programming in local languages. (It was also possible for a region to be linked directly to Moscow and not to the republic-level TV studio; such was the case until 1970 in parts of Zaporiz'ka oblast in southern Ukraine, on the Moscow-Tbilisi radio-relay line.)[42] In the 1960s and '70s, most of the larger republican and regional studios developed two- and sometimes three-channel systems, which theoretically allowed them to offer both their own programming and the Moscow feed.[43] But a good deal of Moscow-based programming—for instance, *Vremia,* born soon after Ostankino in January 1968—was mandatory on all channels in all regions nonetheless.[44] Moscow primacy was a bedrock principle of all Soviet broadcasting.

The history of how centralization played out across the vast USSR has many dimensions, and any detailed discussion is beyond the scope of this book. One important point to highlight, though, is that centralization was a force operating at the republic level as well, and if republic-level broadcasting officials did sometimes object to Moscow's primacy, they were also likely to ally themselves with the center in the name of providing a better service. Let us take Ukraine as an example. Ukraine prided itself on having the third TV station in the Union (and the first outside Russia) and an impressive rate of growth. When its Kiev Studio first went on the air in late 1951, the audience numbered in the low thousands; ten years later *Pravda Ukrainy* was claiming a TV audience of 12 million for the republic (out of a total population of roughly 40 million).[45] A large number of these viewers were no doubt watching balalaika players at this time, but it is essential to understand that Kiev was no more tolerant of amateur operations than Moscow. The Ukrainian authorities set their sights on a republican network: centralized, professional, and worthy of the name Ukrainian TV (Ukrains'ke Telebachennia—UT—announced officially in 1965). Local rogue stations were a sign of weakness, not strength. As late as July 1964, we find the Ukrainian

42. I. Mashchenko, *Telebachennia de facto* (Kyiv, 1998), 50, 149.

43. A 1960 Gosteleradio report set a goal of providing a bilingual soundtrack for central programming in all republics by 1962. GARF, f. 6903, op. 1, d. 655, l. 16. Such a soundtrack did exist in ten of the fifteen republics in 1965, although it is not clear how widely available it was. Paulu, *Radio and Television Broadcasting,* 75, 88.

44. Moscow was on a two-channel broadcasting system as early as 1956. The Second Channel was for the Moscow region only. A third, educational channel was added in 1964, and a short-lived fourth in 1967.

45. This figure smacks of wishful thinking, but the speed of television's penetration was impressive nonetheless. "Ukrainskomu televideniiu-10 let," *Pravda Ukrainy,* 11 Nov 1961, GARF f. 6903, op. 3, d. 175, l. 14.

Central Committee reprimanding local officials for "giving priority to local interests [*mestnichestvo*] ... in the telefication of the republic" and ordering immediate closures.[46]

Relations with Moscow were not without tensions, to be sure. In 1966, to give one example, the head of the Ukrainian radio and television administration, Mikola Skachko, fired off an indignant letter to Gosteleradio about the interruption of a UT soccer broadcast (a Kiev-Odessa match). Moscow had demanded, without warning, that the cable running westward through Kiev be freed up for a special Central TV broadcast on Intervidenie, the socialist bloc TV consortium. "Who is responsible for this cavalier violation of local studio programming?" Skachko demanded to know.[47] Yet the Ukrainian head could also be a tireless cheerleader for Central TV. At a meeting of radio and TV officials from all over the Union in the early sixties, Skachko told his peers that his administration's main goal was "to give Soviet Ukraine's radio listeners [and TV viewers] the opportunity to hear the voice of their native [*rodnaia*] Moscow." And to that end, their plan was "to *increase* the overall proportion of all-Union broadcasts" on all their programs.[48] Lower-ranking media professionals from Ukraine could also be very vocal in their support for central broadcasting. One official from Vinnitsa told a 1959 gathering of radio and TV workers in Kiev that it was "abnormal" that some people in Ukraine could not listen to Moscow. He was referring to radio in particular, but it is worth hearing out his explanation for the attitude it conveys toward local media overall. "There are many radio stations in Ukraine," he said, "but none of them has its own artistic profile. They're broadcasting Kiev all the time, and it seems to me that's why radio listeners are listening to foreign broadcasts." The solution, in his words, was the "voice of the heart of the fatherland," Moscow.[49] In a similar vein, the head of the Donetsk TV studio told his counterparts in 1963, "We orient ourselves toward Central Television because they do a better job. Central TV is better."[50]

All these statements may sound like solos in a sycophants' choir, but they also speak to fundamental facts on the ground. Ukrainian TV was provincial TV; it never got the resources it needed for the highest-quality broadcasting—not

46. Egorov, *Televidenie*, 132. For local-republic center conflicts, see TsDAHOU, f. 1, op. 31, d. 2562, ll. 134–135, 137–138; TsDAVO, f. 4915, op. 1, d. 3708, ll. 139–141. Local initiative in Ukraine was overwhelmingly a phenomenon of the east and south—urban industrial regions with resources for building stations.

47. TsDAHOU, f. 1, op. 70, d. 2590, l. 11.

48. GARF f. 6903, op. 1, d. 808, l. 39 (my italics). It is clear from the context that Skachko was speaking about both radio and television.

49. TsDAVO, f. 4915, op. 1, d. 2367, l. 20.

50. GARF, f. 6903, op. 1, d. 806, l. 92.

from Moscow and, importantly, not from Kiev, either.[51] And so Ukrainian-made television was widely acknowledged as inferior across the board. The rise of a centralized Soviet network in Moscow could surprise no one working in the industry, given both the radio precedent and the economics of broadcasting. It is unquestionably cheaper to produce one program and deliver it to dozens of locations than to produce dozens of separate programs, especially if you can film or tape your product and distribute copies. In the sixties, some Soviet officials understood this and saw their future in terms of video and a central fund of Russian-language TV programs to be used again and again. In theory, there was no reason a regional studio could not supply programs for the central fund, and arguably a republic like Ukraine, with a high percentage of Russian-speaking TV professionals, was in a better position than any to step up to bat. The key was to produce high-quality programming worthy of all-Union distribution via Moscow. Gosteleradio's deputy chairman made the case to Ukrainian studio heads in 1963:

> To be frank, there has never been a real network for central broadcasting. . . . Essentially, the word "central" was appropriated illegally by Moscow television. There were no grounds for calling the Moscow program "Central Television" because other cities and areas had practically no representation on that program until recently. What kind of Central TV is that? . . . That's why we need to think about how to make this program a truly all-Union one that would reflect the interests of the enormous number of people who get television from Moscow.[52]

These were the parameters for Ukrainian TV and other republican-level services as Central TV, the all-Union network, took shape in the 1960s. It was Moscow that dominated the horizon for people working in the industry. For many an ambitious TV professional, the dream was to have your programs picked up by Moscow for the all-Union network or to get hired away by Moscow. Many a studio head hoped to raise his studio's status by getting more programming on Central TV: studios were ranked, and higher status meant higher salaries.[53] Local TV officials also saw access to the best programming of Central TV as the surest way to provide a quality service—and, not incidentally, to fend off audience criticism. When the head of Donetsk TV said his station oriented itself

---

51. Skachko and other Ukrainian officials pressed repeatedly and fruitlessly for additional funding. For an example see TsDAHOU, f. 1, d. 31, d. 2562, ll. 61–62.

52. TsDAVO, f. 4915, op. 1, d. 2394, ll. 3–4.

53. The decision to rank all TV and radio stations and differentiate pay scales accordingly dates to 1960. Radio and print media were similarly ranked, and there were frequent protests over the rankings. See, for example, TsDAHOU, f. 1, op. 70, d. 2447, ll. 38–40.

toward Central TV because Central TV was better, he added that it had hell to pay from viewers when it did not.[54]

Soviet TV development owed a great deal to local initiatives, but the heyday of the balalaika player was very brief. As of around 1959, the authorities in Moscow ratcheted up both their scrutiny of the new medium and their demands. Boris Firsov, future head of the Leningrad studio and then a rising star in the Komsomol apparat, suggested that Khrushchev's 1959 trip to the United States was instrumental in the shift because it demonstrated to the Soviet leader the potential power of TV and the need to control it.[55] In a similar vein, Aleksandr Iakovlev linked the new attention to TV around 1960 to the development of satellite technology and concerns that it would soon bring a foreign TV invasion. Once scientists determined it would prove impossible to wall off the population from satellite broadcasting, Iakovlev said, Moscow decided that its best defense was a good offense, in the form of better, Soviet-made TV.[56]

Both explanations are plausible, but in a more general way we can point to the perceived threat of foreign radio broadcasting as a key factor in Soviet TV development (as in domestic radio). Although jamming remained the default policy, there was a growing recognition of its futility and, in the late fifties— right around 1959–60, in fact—the Soviets experimented with lifting jamming. Television, it was thought, could redirect people's attention. A 1959 CC decree on the foreign radio problem, "On Enemy Propaganda," was explicit on this point: "[T]he development of television and improvement of its programming are important means of limiting the population's access to enemy propaganda."[57]

Soon enough the authorities would find that TV, too, posed problems in many border regions, notably Estonia, where high rates of TV ownership, the similarity of the Estonian and Finnish languages, and geographical proximity created ideal conditions for broadcasting penetration.[58] Czechoslovakia's Prague

54. For complaints in Ukraine about local broadcasting and demands for better access to Central TV, see TsDAVO, f. 4915, op. 1, d. 2394, d. 3377.

55. According to Firsov, Khrushchev was greatly concerned about the possibility of hostile outsiders seizing the airwaves, and a new security system (with guards and ID cards) was introduced at all the country's TV stations within a few days of his return. Interview with B. M. Firsov, St. Petersburg, June 2002. Khrushchev's son, Sergei, who was also on the 1959 trip, did not agree with this interpretation and did not recall his father's taking any particular note of television in the United States or commenting on Soviet TV. Interview with Sergei Khrushchev, Providence, RI, June 2007. Mikhail Kharlamov, head of Gosteleradio from 1962 to 1964 (and a close associate of the Khrushchev family), was part of the entourage for Khrushchev's 1959 trip to the United States.

56. Iakovlev, *Omut pamiati*, 142.

57. RGANI, f. 5, op. 33, d. 106, l. 26.

58. For the situation in Estonia in the 1980s, when Finnish radio and TV were even more widespread than in the fifties and sixties, see Mickiewicz, *Split Signals*, 20–21. Finnish broadcasting also reached Leningrad oblast (sometimes more clearly than Soviet

Spring triggered grave concerns about foreign TV watching all along the USSR's western border and particularly in western Ukraine. But by and large, television technology in this period did not allow for the penetration of uninvited foreign broadcasts; and even in the era of satellite in the seventies and eighties the situation was never as acute (taking the official perspective) as the official paranoia. Television, unique among Soviet mass media, was in a position to develop more or less unchallenged on its home turf.

In 1960, the Central Committee released its first major statement on television—a decree unusual both for its harsh tone and for the publicity that attended its release.[59] In it, the men in Moscow slammed Soviet television broadcasting as substandard, and they laid the blame squarely on TV staffers, whom they accused of rank incompetence, and on local officials, who, they said, had failed to monitor and nurture TV. The pot calling the kettle black? In a sense, yes: many local officials had shown far more interest in television by 1960 than had their counterparts in Moscow. And when Khrushchev sat down for his first televised interview from the Kremlin in 1957, it was for none other than CBS's *Face the Nation;* Soviet TV had been invited as an afterthought and was lucky to squeeze its own cameras in for piggyback coverage.[60] In truth, local and central Soviet authorities were very similar in their approaches to television broadcasting in these early years. Both groups had been interested in the new technology primarily as a symbol (of regional status, of Soviet modernity) and so set great store by numbers (of sets, stations, staff, and programming hours). Getting involved in the day-to-day business of broadcasting—not simply building but working out how actually to use TV—never ranked high on either group's list of priorities.

TV AND THE SOVIET TRADITION OF
POLITICAL COMMUNICATION

We may marvel at the reluctance of professional propagandists to seize on TV, but we should remember that they did not come to the medium empty-handed. On the contrary, party secretaries from Tomsk to Tashkent, First Secretary Khrushchev included, came armed with a powerful tradition and an extensive apparatus devoted to direct oral agitation—lectures, rallies, question-and-answer sessions,

---

broadcasting), as reported by concerned local officials in 1962. RGANI, f. 5, op. 33, d. 207, l. 102.

59. L. S. Klimanova, ed., *O partiinoi i sovetskoi pechati, radioveshchanii i televidenii* (Moscow, 1971), 536–541. According to Mark Koenig, only two other post-Stalinist decrees on propaganda (1979 and 1983) rivaled the 1960 decree for publicity. Mark Koenig, "Media and Reform: The Case of Youth Programming on Soviet Television (1955–1990)" (PhD diss., Columbia University, 1995), 93.

60. Daniel Schorr, *Staying Tuned: A Life in Journalism* (New York, 2002), 99–102.

and so on.[61] By comparison, television and all mass media are anonymous, fluid means of conveying messages. An individual person watching TV, listening to the radio, or reading the press can easily tune out—fall asleep, flip the dial, use the paper to wrap sandwiches. But as sociologist Alex Inkeles noted in his classic study of public opinion in the Stalinist era, the physical presence of an agitator has distinct advantages: it "gives the party additional assurance that its message will get across" and eliminates the need for complicated research techniques; direct agitation also means that "the audience does not have to be attracted or mobilized to act—since the agitator comes to the audience, and not the other way around."[62] It was common Soviet practice to combine methods of communication (in organized radio listening, for example), and theoretically at least, the personal contact with a skillful agitator plus peer pressure would reduce the risk of audiences' disengaging. In reality, plenty of people tuned out all the same. Party and Komsomol workers knew this. Yet they demonstrated an enduring preference for the older methods, as *Kommunist* complained in 1959:

> Publishing a pamphlet in 10,000–15,000 copies is sometimes considered more important than broadcasting a television program on the same theme. Reading a lecture on television to some people seems not a terribly important affair, while appearing in a hall seating 300–500 people seems so much more responsible: after all, you can count how many people were there and how many questions were asked.[63]

Kommunist blamed the force of "habit" for the "bean-counting" approach, but there was more to it than that. The persistent orientation toward direct agitation and group settings was rooted in many traditional attitudes of party elites—doubt about rank-and-file Soviets' ability to understand political messages, suspicion of individual rather than group activities, and trust in monitoring, measuring, and control. It also made good career sense. In the mid-sixties central Komsomol authorities were still urging local leaders to take an interest, calling on them to "transform the youth divisions of radio and television into their direct instruments."[64] Yet as Stephen Solnick has explained, focusing on an increase in the membership rolls or in attendance at mass rallies was the safest

61. Technically, agitation and propaganda differ (propaganda delivers many ideas to a few people, whereas agitation communicates a few ideas to the masses). I follow Peter Kenez's lead in *The Birth of the Propaganda State: Soviet Methods of Mass Mobilization, 1917–1929* (Cambridge, 1985), 8, and use the terms interchangeably. For a discussion of the tensions between the Soviet propaganda tradition and broadcast technologies, see Mickiewicz, *Split Signals,* especially chap. 5.

62. Alex Inkeles, *Public Opinion in the Soviet Union* (Cambridge, MA, 1958), 122.

63. G. Kazakov, "Televidenie—Moguchee sredstvo kommunisticheskogo vospitaniia," *Kommunist,* no. 8 (1959): 68.

64. One practical suggestion was to include radio and TV *redaktory* (editor-producers) in the ranks of their nomenklatura. RGASPI-m, f. 1, op. 32, d. 1168, l. 21.

route to career advancement for aspiring young *apparatchiki* in the center and the regions alike.[65] Why involve oneself with television—potentially explosive, or just plain embarrassing—when a meeting would do?

The Khrushchev era in fact saw a significant expansion not only in mass media, but in traditional political agitation activities as well. There were 4.6 million people on the books as participating in local meetings to discuss the party's draft program in 1961.[66] Enrollments in the formal political education system increased from 4 million to 35–36 million between 1953 and 1964.[67] And in a more general sense, the Khrushchev era saw a push to engage people in a renewed vision of socialist community through group activities such as work brigades, civic policing (*druzhinniki*), the amateur arts (*samodeiatel'nost'*), and comrades' courts. Like political education classes, propaganda lectures, and film screenings, all these group activities had the pleasing quality of being quantifiable.

Television did attempt its own forms of bean counting. As sociology revived in the 1960s, Gosteleradio established an audience research division that ran surveys about specific programs and viewing habits more generally. It was, however, chronically underfunded and largely ignored by creative types and administrators alike (see chapter 5). The favored method for assessing audience size was always to examine the mailbag. TV workers counted the number of letters sent in by viewers—the greater the number, the larger the presumed audience and the more influential the program—and tallying letters quickly became as much of a fetish for TV workers as it was for their colleagues in radio and print media. (It was also a mandated requirement.) Yet letter counting never matched the seeming solidity of a headcount at a lecture or even of box-office receipts. What is more, the message from letters—and from sociological studies, too, for those who looked—was prone to displease: as judged by these sources, the most popular and influential programs were, by a crushing margin, entertainment shows. Political education programs similar to traditional lectures were clearly not liked and, suspicion was, probably not watched. Bean counting did not necessarily work to television's advantage.

The CC's 1960 decree ordered local officials to take an active role in television and specified that they would have to make regular on-air appearances; the same order was repeated in 1962.[68] But one year later, an assessment team found that Kharkov's leaders had such a "bad attitude" to TV that the local station had

65. See Stephen Solnick, *Stealing the State* (Cambridge, MA, 1998), especially chap. 4.

66. William Taubman, *Khrushchev: The Man and His Era* (New York, 2003), 510.

67. David Wedgwood Benn, *Persuasion and Soviet Politics* (Oxford, 1989), 135; Ellen Mickiewicz, "The Modernization of Party Propaganda in the USSR," *Slavic Review* 30, no. 2 (June 1971): 257–276.

68. In addition, every TV studio was to "regularly broadcast at a set day and time a program with answers to questions from the population by leaders from the ministries and administrations, as well as local party, Soviet, and social organizations, and people's

even struggled to find someone to commemorate the forty-fifth anniversary of socialist Ukraine. Some people, like the secretary in charge of propaganda for the region, admitted to auditors that they were "afraid to go on the air,"[69] while in other cases, political figures found themselves butting heads with TV staff over issues of style and presentation. Journalist G. V. Kuznetsov recalled one such clash with the minister of the press, who was to make a taped appearance on his program, a weekly news magazine, in the mid-sixties. Kuznetsov first tried to convince the minister that it would make for better TV if he agreed to be interviewed about his topic, an international book fair, than if he simply lectured. The minister balked and commanded the camera operator to start shooting. Kuznetsov recalled, "He took out a volume of Lenin's works from his bag, raised it to the level of his face, and started lecturing. He then put the book on the table and bent over for the next one, disappearing from the frame. There were a lot of books. The camera operator barely managed to change the tapes."[70]

Holding forth with volume 5 of Lenin's collected works half obscuring your face was not a stylish or effective mode of presentation in the eyes of Soviet TV's newly minted professionals. It was a political style, all the same, and it was the one with which most Soviet authorities felt comfortable. TV broadcasting put them, like all political elites at the time, on unfamiliar terrain and demanded they adapt. Many other contemporary figures—Richard Nixon and Charles de Gaulle, for example—also balked at first but went on quickly to become the medium's adepts.[71] By the mid-sixties a Soviet minister might have grudgingly accepted the necessity of a televised appearance; indeed, he might even have given rousing lectures, in person, about the importance of television in political education. But he was not about to abandon his bag of Lenin's works for a tête-à-tête with a journalist or take advice on how to pitch his message. Paradoxically, for all the investment it attracted and the energy directed toward its development, Soviet political elites remained ambivalent about television; when it came to their *personal* involvement, they kept it at arm's length, and there was very little incentive for them to move in closer.

The same 1960 decree that sent leaders to the studios also directed newspapers to write more about TV, a directive they did not fully embrace. The major all-Union dailies covered television infrequently; they were far more likely to

---

deputies." Klimanova, *O partiinoi i sovetskoi pechati,* 539. For the 1962 decree, which also covered radio, ibid., 542–548.

69. TsDAVO, f. 4915, op. 1, d. 3430, l. 34.

70. Kuznetsov decided to scrap the minister's tape and run his own commentary. Although the head of Gosteleradio authorized the change, his party superiors objected, and Kuznetsov was temporarily banned from the screen. G. V. Kuznetsov, "Zapiski lishnego cheloveka," in *Televizionnaia mozaika,* ed. Ia. N. Zasurskii (Moscow, 1997), 38–39.

71. See Jerome Bourdain, *Histoire de la télévision sous de Gaulle* (Paris, 1990); Wilson Dizard, *Television: A World View* (Syracuse, 1966), 141–147.

discuss mass events (speeches, parades) and also cinema and literature than TV. Newspapers did not even print daily programming schedules until 1959 (by which time, let us remember, there were nearly 5 million television sets in the USSR).[72] In a system that prided itself on a highly differentiated press, there was no popular mass publication for television and radio until 1966 (when the TV audience topped 60 million), and it was discontinued within a year.[73] TV was, in many respects, a second-class citizen in the world of Soviet political communication.

TV AND SOVIET CULTURE'S "TABLE OF RANKS"

If the Soviet propaganda tradition was one factor in TV's paradoxical position, another was its relationship to the idea of art and, more specifically, to Soviet cultural elites. As was the case in other countries, early television in the USSR was on an uneasy footing with the performing arts and cinema. On the one hand, TV relied on them for content and won praise precisely for that. Television was "aesthetic education's most widespread and flexible instrument...a powerful tool for the propaganda of the beautiful," glowed *Kommunist* in 1965.[74] Yet throughout the fifties and into the sixties, people who worked in TV complained of being snubbed by the creative establishment and forced to feed the air with second-rate productions. Celebrated comedian Igor Il'inskii was unusual in taking a strong stance against this resistance to television on the pages of *Literaturnaia gazeta*: "How can we give the people the worst examples of art instead of the best and...spread them out to a huge audience?" he browbeat fellow artists. "Who are we, after all? Business people, or policymakers?"[75]

Part of the problem, as Il'inskii noted, was hostility to competition. In the film industry, some people kept a worried eye on the example of the United States and Europe, where TV's rise was often followed by drastic declines in ticket sales for films. As early as 1951, when there were only three studios operating in the country, the Ministry of Cinematography lobbied for limiting television to broadcasts of documentary films and cartoons—in effect, for banning feature films on TV.[76] The campaign was unsuccessful; the concerns did not go away. Minister of Culture N. Mikhailov complained to the CC at the end of the decade that the press was going too far in its criticisms of television on this score. "Showing feature films on television soon after their release would do unquestionable harm

72. *Pravda* first published daily schedules for radio and television on 5 April 1959. Other central Soviet newspapers followed suit on 1 January 1960.

73. An illustrated weekly called *RT* (*Radio-Televidenie*), carrying information on programming, reviews, and a viewers' forum, was closed in 1967, reportedly by M. A. Suslov. *Ocherki po istorii rossiisskogo televideniia* (Moscow, 1999), 139.

74. Iakovlev, "Televidenie," 74.

75. Igor Il'inskii, "Razmyshleniia u televizora," *Literaturnaia gazeta,* 12 May 1956.

76. RGASPI, f. 17, op. 133, d. 339, ll. 75–77.

to the fulfillment of the plan," he argued. The CC agreed and called newspaper editors in to its offices for instruction.[77] In 1966, screenwriter E. V. Braginskii told an audience of his peers, "When people say 'It doesn't matter, the viewer will always go to the movies,' I feel like sending a telegram to TV saluting them for the fact that they do a bad job, and people still do go.... But if they start to do more talented programming, we'll be completely out of work."[78] Many theater managers had similar concerns, and they experimented with strategies for self-defense. In Kharbarovsk, for instance, one theater decided it would open its doors to TV cameras only if the local station agreed to buy out any empty seats in the house.[79] Kharkov's theater companies closed their doors entirely, prompting the local TV studio to invite troupes from Poltava and Orel.[80] And even the Bolshoi Theater for a time limited broadcasts to performances by visiting foreign companies. (Central TV countered by inviting Bolshoi talent to perform in its Moscow studios.)[81]

Protective policies such as these won sharp official rebukes, and most were short-lived.[82] Soviet TV's access to recently released films was remarkable by Western standards (with waiting periods between theatrical release and broadcast as short as one month), and in the sixties it was also possible for a regional studio (Riga) to broadcast a city's *entire* theater repertoire. Still, there remained an implicit hierarchy in Soviet culture—a "table of ranks," as *Kommunist* put it, alluding to the hidebound tsarist bureaucracy. Television, the upstart, ranked low.[83] Many established creative professionals continued to approach the new medium with indifference, condescension, or even light contempt—attitudes shared, as we know, by many in the party elite.[84] TV's association with radio, also low in the cultural ranks, did not help. But its status also had something to do with two factors unique to the medium: TV production as a cultural milieu and TV consumption as an activity.

Early Soviet television was in many respects the terrain of young creative intellectuals manqués. In the fifties most people educated to be theater and film

---

77. RGANI, f. 5, op. 33, d. 105, ll. 26–27.

78. RGALI, f. 2936, op. 4, d. 1308, l. 93.

79. Norman Sklarewitz, "Themes and Variations: TV—Soviet Style," *Wall Street Journal,* 1 September 1964.

80. V. Ardmatskii, "V poiskakh novykh form," *Literaturnaia gazeta,* 2 April 1958.

81. For Gosteleradio's letter protesting Bolshoi policy in 1958, see GARF, f. 6903, op. 1, d. 542, l. 49.

82. The 1960 CC decree directed the film industry, theater, music, and sports to cooperate with TV. Gosteleradio complained to the CC later that year about a continuing lack of compliance. GARF, f. 6903, op.1, d. 623, l. 148. TV's editor for literature and drama in the sixties claimed that many Moscow theaters still rejected cooperation at the end of the decade. Interview with V. N. Kozlovskii, February 2002 (Gosteleradiofond Oral History Project).

83. Iakovlev, "Televidenie," 71.

84. Although notable cultural figures (such as Kornei Chukovskii and Irakli Andronnikov) did participate in early TV, they were exceptional, particularly in the 1950s.

directors, actors, journalists, cameramen, and the like did not go into television if they had a choice of employment. Established professionals in these fields, although they might (and did) participate as guests, rarely moved to TV. One important reason was no doubt the low pay scale for television compared with that for other spheres (a sure sign of its lowly status).[85] TV's young workers were often forced to be jacks-of-all-trades as a result: the same person might write and edit the script, design and construct the scenery, and shoot the program or read the voice-over. The rough-and-ready environment of early TV made for an exciting workplace, but it also led to a lot of rough-and-ready broadcasts and, unsurprisingly, to the continuing derision of many creative professionals. One of Estonian TV's pioneers recalled, "Deciding to devote yourself to television in those years required a certain amount of courage, and not only because it meant starting from scratch, so to speak. Mistakes, blunders, and sometimes professional incompetence gave representatives of the established arts, especially cineastes, grounds to laugh their heads off at us."[86]

In the long run, Soviet television did find a partial solution to its prestige problem by improving its performance. With the professionalization of its staff and technological advances (especially video), TV was able to develop its own program genres and so win a measure of cultural clout.[87] But arguably, television never broke through to the top on Soviet culture's table of ranks. Genre filmmaking met a similar fate; there was little to be gained, in financial or social capital, from producing a box-office hit seen as frivolous. Yet even a genre filmmaker was also an artist in the Soviet context; a movie faulted for frivolity was failed art. A journalist for a mass-circulation newspaper, too, while not producing art on a daily basis per se, was a writer, and perhaps had a major work, a *book,* on the way. Television, despite a clamorous campaign on the part of its enthusiasts, was rarely acknowledged as art—the highest honor. It was, on the contrary, rapidly assigned to the realm of *byt:* everyday, domestic life but also, and significantly, everyday personal needs and desires. This association with byt played a crucial role in establishing television's status in Soviet culture and helps further explain the ambivalence with which party and cultural elites approached the new medium.

85. Low rates of pay applied to freelancers as well as staff, making it difficult to attract talented outsiders. See GARF, f. 6903, op. 1, d. 542, ll. 1–4, for letters from Gosteleradio pleading to the CC to raise the rates in 1958. The host of *Muzykal'nyi kiosk* reported earning 4 rubles per show plus 5 rubles per script in the sixties. Interview with E. V. Beliaeva, 2002 (Gosteleradiofond Oral History Project).

86. T. Elmanovich, *Obraz fakta: Ot publististiki k fil'mu na Estonskom televidenii* (Moscow, 1975), 4–5.

87. See chapter 5. Professional training for TV dates to 1958, with courses at the Journalism Faculty of Moscow State University. Iurovskii, *Televidenie,* 109. On professionalization, see Mark Koenig, "Media and Reform."

TV AND BYT

Although statistically speaking, it was not until 1970 that a majority of Soviet homes had a TV set, Soviet journalists had begun referring to television as a vital mass phenomenon years before.[88] Already in 1956 and 1957, press accounts routinely used the term "necessity" for the new medium and made the phrase "television immediately became a part of everyday life" (*televidenie srazu voshlo v byt*) an instant cliché. For the central press, this was perhaps understandable: any phenomenon that touches the city where a newspaper is published, and especially one that concerns its elites, is typically bigger news than what happens in peripheral regions. (We can imagine that many editors and their friends in Moscow were buying *their* first TV sets around then.) But *Literaturnaia gazeta* also labeled TV in faraway Vladivostok "a fact of everyday life" in 1957. The central press delighted in reports of television in distant regions and unlikely places—atop an ice floe, for example, or on a shipping vessel or with a family on a picnic.[89] And local papers ran articles and letters testifying to the importance of TV as well. Often, as in the report from Vladivostok, the press backed up consumers frustrated with the state of TV technology and demanding action. One group of viewers from Magnitogorsk complained about the construction of the local TV center, which had "really been dragging on too long. Please tell us when we will finally get the opportunity to relax in a cultured manner in a domestic setting in front of the TV."[90] A viewer from Kirov wrote, "Some time ago, we had made peace with our position as 'provincials.' Now we don't want to make peace because times have changed many things. The lives of millions of workers who live in distant cities and regions can be just as rich and full as those of Muscovites: there is TV, and there is film stock. The only thing is, it makes no sense—why don't they shoot the best performers and the best companies?"[91]

Although TV was not a part of everyday life for most people in a literal sense, it did enter Soviet official culture and the realm of cliché with remarkable speed and a distinctive cast. The cast was domestic and demanding. When the press had TV travel to remarkable places like ice floes, the hook for the story was the very incongruity of the locale: TV was understood to be an essentially home-based phenomenon. It was also presented as something that took over the domestic world in an elemental and somehow urgent way.[92] Vladimir Sappak, the

88. Firsov, *Puti razvitiia*, 111.

89. *Izvestiia*, 27 November 1957; "Televizory v more," *Ogonek*, no. 20 (1959); "S televizorom v avtomobile," *Ogonek*, no. 25 (1965).

90. *Magnitogorskii rabochii*, 10 December 1961, in GARF, f. 6903, op. 3, d. 175, l. 7.

91. *Sovetskaia kul'tura*, 4 January 1962, in GARF, f. 6903, op. 3, d. 175, l. 19.

92. It is worth noting that sets were often placed in a corner near the window, considered the best spot in a room. The location, plus the tendency to drape sets with lacy cloths, put TVs in the place of icons in traditional Slavic dwellings. Svetlana Boym, "Everyday

era's most influential television critic, presented TV's power in a lyrical, almost mystical light:

> It is often difficult to tear ourselves away from that tiny little screen. Why this is so, even we can't really explain. If I turn on the TV by chance and see that there's a movie or a theatrical performance on, I can turn it off right away with a fearless hand, as they say. But all it takes is for me to see those announcers we all know so well now reading the news, or a soccer field with bustling players, an English lesson, or kids in white shirts and pioneer scarves reciting poetry written for the occasion in their ringing voices, and my hand involuntarily hesitates on the off switch. Here [is a place] where you can look at any time and without thoroughly investigating the heart of the matter; you can just observe the *movement of life* for a moment, and let the idler inside you wake up and gawk at how the birds are flying, how the grass is growing.... And your hand will not make a move to stop this living life on the screen, to turn it off, to cut it short.[93]

As depicted here, the television set is a forceful and, one might say, intoxicating presence in the home. With its ability to convey "the movement of life," the tiny screen takes on the qualities of a dynamic being; television itself is alive. Another of the era's most influential voices on TV, Sergei Muratov, cast the medium in a more ironic and vaguely threatening light: "Once you've acquired a Rubin or a Temp [a Ruby or a Tempo brand TV set], you very quickly start to notice that the tempo of your life . . . has changed in a fundamental way. And you can hardly estimate the loss of time in rubies. The blue screen dictates its terms and imposes its programming. *You thought it belonged to you, but, in fact, you belong to it.*"[94]

On the pages of the contemporary press, the TV set was a commanding presence, and viewers were often represented as demanding and needy: complaints about faulty sets and boring or slapdash programming were never-ending. Soviet media had a long history of airing consumer grievances, and there was also a surge in the genre under Khrushchev.[95] But television was not just an industrial product (a set) but a complex of cultural products (programming) and a sociological phenomenon to boot (TV watching). These were complaints and demands of a different order. Soviet media had consistently portrayed television as a necessity with the power to change people's lives. Once consumers

---

Culture," in *Russian Culture at the Crossroads,* ed. Dmitri N. Shalin (New York, 1996), 174. I am grateful to Susan Reid for sharing her observations on this.

93. V. Sappak, *Televidenie i my* (Moscow, 1962), 42.

94. Sergei Muratov and Georgii Fere, "Telepanorama—Oktiabr'," *Sovetskaia kul'tura,* 4 November 1965, 3 (my italics).

95. See Susan Reid, "Cold War in the Kitchen," *Slavic Review* 61, no. 2 (Summer 2002): 211–252.

became viewers, they refused to make peace with the privations of pre-TV life any longer.

If TV—good TV—was suddenly a necessity of daily life, it was also something the viewer had earned through hard work. In this sense, television was something quite close to a right, as expressed in the aphorism "the Soviet person has the right to relax in front of the television after a day's work," attributed to none other than Leonid Brezhnev.[96] Soviet official culture was at times capable of acknowledging the joys of spending an evening alone ensconced in an easy chair:

> The whistle blows. Your working day is over. The day's labor is finished, and the evening's relaxation begins. People usually say: cinemas and theaters are open to you, parks of culture and dance pavilions are at your disposal, exhibits and libraries are there for you. To this stock phrase I would add: six to eight hours of TV programming awaits you.
>
> At work you were stern and reserved, but now you will laugh like a child; during the day you were restrained and tense, but in the evening, by the television set, you'll abandon yourself to having a pleasant time. All in all you are going to have a glorious time, a 100 percent time, as they say.[97]

In this vision of TV watching, the viewer is alone in his own world and awash in his own pleasure.[98] This is television as a retreat into byt. Note that the content of the programming is not clear and not terribly important: it is the medium of television itself that generates these startling effects. And what distinguishes the medium most of all is its social location in the home; being at home is what facilitates the transformation of active Soviet person into passive and childlike viewer, from worker into what Soviet media derided in other contexts as a person enmeshed in byt (obyvatel'). But in a context that privileged the notion of well-earned relaxation (otdykh), there was at least some room as well for a celebration of something rather like a Soviet couch potato.

Although the right to otdykh was not a new concept in Soviet culture, it did take on new forms and momentum in the fifties and sixties, thanks in part to official reductions in working time and to the post-Stalinist revival of sociological research. Soviet consumers had long cited their right to otdykh in appeals for more light music on radio and more comedies and musicals at the movies. But TV as otdykh was different because in the Soviet context, watching TV carried distinctive connotations. Going to the movies was in step with the traditional ideal of otdykh as something collective, active, and educational. There was a

96. *Ocherki po istorii rossiiskogo televideniia,* 143.

97. The article goes on to calculate the viewer's actual enjoyment factor at "6–7 percent." Viktor Slavkin, "Sem' protsentov vessel'ia," *Sovetskaia kul'tura,* 9 September 1965, 3.

98. I use "his" advisedly, considering the wide disparity in viewership rates for men and women discussed below.

history of people attending movies in organized groups from their workplaces. Watching TV, by comparison, though it certainly denoted education, also implied isolation and passivity. To watch TV required no one else and no particular engagement with the physical world (no travel, no planning); a solitary viewer simply switched on the set at home and sat down. Somewhere in between going to the movies and watching TV stood listening to the radio. Though like TV it might entail passive reception, radio did not demand stasis (people often performed other activities while they listened), and it was also strongly associated with dancing, a social activity much like moviegoing.[99] Despite the similarities in the technology, radio was not as linked to solitude as television was. Tellingly, the one form of radio listening that did often figure in Soviet propaganda as a solitary activity was tuning in to foreign broadcasts—represented as an antisocial behavior and a sign of emotional instability.

For Soviet sociologists studying otdykh, the question was how "rational" and "cultured" people were in budgeting their free time, and the findings, to their minds, were often discouraging. A large-scale 1965 survey of *Komsomol'skaia pravda* readers concluded that there was "still a segment of the population with an undeveloped culture of leisure, insufficiently developed tastes and desires, and inadequate knowledge of how to organize their free time."[100] In the terms of the study, these were people who shied away from such activities as concert- and museumgoing, amateur arts, reading, and sports. Other studies found that it was these people—people identified as having immature taste—who logged the most hours in front of their TV sets. In Leningrad, where roughly 85 percent of families had a set by the mid- to late sixties, sociologist Boris Firsov created a typology for TV viewership, identifying four distinct groups of viewers based on how much they watched. The most important factor distinguishing the top of the scale—an impressive twenty-seven hours per week—from the bottom—a more moderate three—was education: the lower the educational level, Firsov found, the more hours in front of the set.[101] Gender was an important secondary factor, as there were many more men than women among the active viewers.[102] Subsequent studies found rural residents to be the most active viewers of all, despite the lower density of TV sets in the countryside. Overall, 1970s research showed rates of TV viewership steadily on the rise for all groups.[103]

99. There is an interesting distinction to be drawn here between the conception of TV watching as isolating and actual social practice. In reality, most people watched TV in groups.

100. "Kak vy provodite svobodnoe vremiia," *Komsomol'skaia pravda,* 24 February 1966.

101. Firsov, *Televidenie,* 118–119. This is the same Boris Firsov who headed up the Leningrad studio in the sixties.

102. Other studies from the period confirmed the gender gap. Firsov, *Puti razvitiia,* 118.

103. Mickiewicz, *Media and the Russian Public,* 19–23.

Soviet sociologists were not antitelevision, but they did object to what they saw as excessive interest in the medium, connected directly, in their eyes, to the "insufficient development of a person's cultural needs."[104] The paradox of Soviet television was that in its programming it was oriented toward developing precisely those needs—uplifting its audiences culturally and propagandizing all the "rational" leisure-time activities—and also providing a broadcast version of many of them. Soviet TV transported its viewers to the activities and sat them down in countless concert halls, theaters, sports arenas, and so on. But though television brought culture to the masses and exhorted active participation in cultural and social life away from the set, it did not, of course, require it. TV participated in a discourse of the traditional ideals of otdykh while at the same time challenging this discourse as a social practice.

The status of television in the broader culture was thus mutable and ambiguous. TV watching was clearly taken by many at the time to be an individual and comparatively easy or even lazy form of leisure. Print media poked fun at and sometimes criticized the TV-obsessed. One columnist joked that archeologists a thousand years in the future would discover evidence of "the hypnosis of television" and conclude that it was a "religious ritual" for people of the twentieth century.[105] In cartoon images from the mass magazine *Ogonek,* people watching TV are often alone in a space or unaware of others around them. One cartoon, for example, shows a man and woman sitting akimbo and watching two sawed-off halves of a single set, an image that emphasizes the solitary character of TV watching (see fig. 4.3).[106] Cartoonists showed viewers—always male, in this case—so relaxed as to be sleeping, but they also showed viewers of all kinds enraptured before the set (see fig. 4.4).[107]

Numerous cartoons represented TV watchers as so wholly absorbed in the screen image that they failed to notice something important happening around them. One depicts two happy thieves who have outwitted a guard by giving him a TV set; once he is hypnotized by the screen image, they can slip past to rob a safe (see fig. 4.5).[108] Another pictures a family crowded around a TV screen oblivious to the water flooding their room from an overflowing sink in the distance; on screen is an image of a sinking ship (see fig. 4.6).[109] On occasion, the press would even print photographs of people with their backs to their new TV sets, an interesting iconography that managed to celebrate the arrival of the technology in the home while subtly emphasizing people's independence from it.

104. B. M. Firsov, *Televidenie glazami sotsiologa* (Moscow, 1971), 124.

105. V. Slavkin, "Chto by my delali bez televideniia?" *Sovetskaia kul'tura,* 11 November 1965, 4.

106. *Ogonek,* no. 34 (1960).

107. For one of many "sleeping husband" images, see *Ogonek,* no. 1 (1959).

108. *Ogonek,* no. 36 (1965).

109. *Ogonek,* no. 22 (1966).

Споров больше не будет.   Рисунок И. Массины.

Figure 4.3. "No more arguments." *Ogonek,* no. 34 (1960).

In the 1960s the press offered darker representations of TV, speaking of its "hypnotic effect" and the problem of "TV gluttons," or people who watched indiscriminately (a particular worry about children). The most sinister images were of television in the West, not Soviet TV, and they often picked up on and amplified Western critiques of the medium. One example, a 1969 piece headed "The Home Screen: Friend or Foe?" described an "uncontrollable 'information explosion' that is steadily pushing people to critical stages of stress" and encouraging a "defensive reaction" of retreat into private life. "In the conditions of capitalism, the revolution in communications media... strengthens the alienation between members of an antagonistic society and the estrangement of the individual," warned the author.[110] But there is reason to wonder how effective critiques such as these were in quarantining problems to the West—or whether that was indeed their objective. It seems likely that for at least some authors, this was also an effective method to introduce Soviet audiences to critical thinking about the medium in general. "The Home Screen," although ostensibly about the West, was accompanied by an image of *Soviet* television (a photograph of

110. Iu. Sheinin, "Domashnii ekran: Drug ili vrag?" *Literaturnaia gazeta,* 29 January 1969.

— Раньше, когда у нас не было телевизора, муж страдал хронической бессонницей.
Рисунок О. Калласа (Таллин).

Figure 4.4. "Before we got the television, my husband suffered from chronic insomnia." *Ogonek,* no. 1 (1959).

a soundstage at Ostankino). Similarly, Firsov's pioneering sociological study featured a ringing endorsement of "humanist" Soviet TV but also managed to familiarize readers with contemporary critiques of television via a discussion of Western media sociology. Firsov also took an entire chapter to dispute the existence of *telemania* in the USSR.[111] The relevance of these examples lies less in whether there was a code in use than in the end result: the circulation within Soviet culture of a skeptical, even critical vocabulary about television as a social practice.

111. Firsov, *Televidenie,* chaps. 2–5; for the discussion of "telemania," see chapter 10.

— Это была гениальная
мысль — подарить старику те-
левизор.
Рисунок Б. Боссарта.

Figure 4.5. "It was a stroke of genius to give the old man a television." *Ogonek,*
no. 36 (1965).

In the 1970s, under the watchful eyes of Sergei Lapin, Gosteleradio's powerful new head, criticizing television in any fashion grew far more difficult.
Lapin publicly rebuked one journalist for suggesting in print that a woman
who complained of her family's TV addiction should stop watching. "Let her
turn off her own television," Lapin lectured, "but why teach other people to
do the same?"[112] Aesthetic TV criticism, a field only just finding its sea legs
in the 1960s, was also effectively closed down under Lapin, along with the
audience research division at Gosteleradio.[113] The only arena for critical discourse to have remained relatively open through the 1970s concerned TV's
impact on children. Sociologists continued to probe the question and participated in a public discussion involving parents, teachers, and health professionals. The great worry was that TV watching had displaced reading,
music, and sports as the number one leisure activities in childhood; many
people also fretted that it drew young people away from their studies and

112. "Zapreshchaetsia zaplyvat' dal'she vsekh!," *Zhurnalist* no. 8 (1988): 25.
113. See chapter 5.

Без слов.　　　　**Рисунок Б. Боссарта.**

Figure 4.6. "No comment." *Ogonek,* no. 22 (1966).

disrupted their sleep.[114] Available statistics were in fact quite striking: an early 1970s survey of over forty thousand children in the RSFSR found that up to 75 percent of school-age children were watching two to two and half hours of television a day. The researchers diagnosed another group of more active viewers (up to five hours in a row on weekdays and eight on Sundays) as suffering from "so-called television sickness," with symptoms including "irritability, anxiety, sleeplessness, loss of appetite, headaches, deterioration of the eyesight" and even "convulsions and fits." The only cure, suggested researchers, was a ban on watching: within two to three weeks away from the screen, children's symptoms of television sickness disappeared.[115]

Discussions of TV addiction in the Soviet context always took pains to point out that it was only the uneducated and unprepared who were in any real

114. See G. Galochkina, ed., *Televidenie priglashaet detei* (Moscow, 1976); V. Zhuravleva and G. Al'tov, "Sila telepritizheniia," *Sovetskaia kul'tura,* 29 May 1965, 1. Cinema's effects on children aroused similar fears in the 1920s.

115. *Televidenie i deti* (Moscow, 1974), 20–21. See also V. S. Korobeinikov, *Goluboi charodei: Televidenie i sotsial'naia sistema* (Moscow, 1975), 125; GARF, f. 6903, op. 3, d. 343, ll. 6–10.

danger, and children were the prime candidates in this category. The solution for everyone was to develop people's cultural interests more broadly and to teach them how to watch selectively. Press reports offered examples of parents who "saved their children from the captivity of television" by force of example and planning.[116] And in a general sense, all viewers, not only children, were encouraged to be active, discriminating, and well organized in their relationship to television—in effect to make TV watching a "rational" form of otdykh. *Pravda* quoted a collective-farm worker declaring, "It's a good gadget, a television set, but it's better [to watch] with another person," because that way, people can discuss what they see.[117] By promoting collective and engaged viewership, official culture worked to inscribe the new medium, television, into traditional ideals of Soviet sociability and otdykh.

TV TECHNOLOGY AND THE COLD WAR HOME

If a home-based medium presented such an obvious challenge to traditional ideals, how did television find itself in the Soviet home to begin with? After all, as Raymond Williams stressed in his study of TV's development in the West, there is nothing inherently domestic about the technology itself. Although it is hard to imagine now, in the 1930s and '40s, there were many people, even in the United States and Great Britain, who questioned whether television would ever be suited to home use. Some assumed TV technology would always be too expensive to reach the mass of ordinary consumers. Others looked at the tiny screens of early home sets and the tremendous popularity of radio and concluded that the new medium could never complete. TV's future, they imagined, would have to be in theaters specially equipped with projection screens.[118] Nazi Germany established a system of public viewership, as did postwar Japan for a time (under commercial auspices), and there was nothing to stop the USSR from doing the same.[119]

The evidence for the Soviets' plans for television is mixed. Although Soviet industry produced very few TVs in the prewar period, they included sets designed for both home use and public settings, like workers' clubs.[120] In the fifties

116. Korobeinikov, *Goluboi charodei*, 128.

117. Iu. Koginov, "Krest'ianin vernul'sia s raboty," *Pravda*, 2 January 1967.

118. Williams, *Television*, 17–25. See also Mickiewicz, *Media and the Russian Public*, 40. Anthony Smith, ed., *Television: An International History* (Oxford, 1995), 110.

119. The decision to locate TV in public spaces was a source of interministerial conflict in Nazi Germany. See William Uricchio, "Television as History: Representations of German Television Broadcasting, 1935–1944," in *Framing the Past: The Historiography of German Cinema and Television,* ed. Bruce Murray and Christopher Wickham (Carbondale, IL, 1992), 167–196. On Japan, see Shunya Yoshimi, "Television and Nationalism: Historical Change in the National Domestic TV Formation of Postwar Japan," *European Journal of Cultural Studies* 6, no. 4 (2003): 459–487.

120. *Ocherki po istorii rossiiskogo televideniia*, 37; Egorov, *Televidenie*, 7.

and sixties there were many public sites for TV watching in Soviet cities, from clubs to parks, museums to children's homes. As early as 1951, Moscow's Sokolniki Park was showing TV in an open-air pavilion seating two hundred to three hundred people, while a Zhdanov district park had a special hall outfitted with nine TV sets and charging two rubles at the door.[121] When television came to the countryside, it was very often in the form of group viewings, sometimes organized by traveling brigades from regional studios. Tomsk and Kiev TV workers, for instance, went on the road in the fifties to propagandize TV to skeptical kolkhozniki, and Tomsk TV was also running what it called "collective auditoriums of TV viewers" in town, sometimes for a fee. The Tomsk studio head told colleagues in Moscow that there were now "fewer amoral acts and police detentions" in the railway district where they had five such auditoriums. "Seven o'clock comes around and the kids are sitting in front of the TVs."[122]

It seems clear that there was at least some experimentation with organized group viewing in TV's first decades, motivated by a mix of practical considerations (how to reach the most kolkhozniki), social concerns (how to control youth after dark), and financial interests. And given the Soviet emphasis on collective activities—an overall ideological orientation that Khrushchev was trying to reanimate at this very moment—one might have expected a lot more. But the main thrust of TV's development in the postwar USSR was indisputably domestic. Soviet consumers played an important role in this dynamic, as we have seen: had it not been for their overwhelming enthusiasm, TV could not have entered the home as rapidly as it did. However, this enthusiasm was authorized by a centrally planned Soviet industry that produced sets primarily for individual, rather than group, consumption, and by financial incentives (pricing policies, the end to licensing fees) that made owning a TV broadly accessible.

The head of Soviet TV in 1956 may have rallied his staff with the idea that they were "blazing totally new trails,"[123] but of course, Soviet television was not sui generis; on the contrary, Soviet TV, like all Soviet culture, was embedded in an international context that was an essential factor in its development. It mattered, in other words, that TV technology burst on the scene just as the USSR was challenging the West, and more particularly the United States, to a contest over which system could best build rockets and provide a satisfying, modern lifestyle for rocket scientists and everyone else. In the iconic moment of this duel at the 1959 American Exhibition in Moscow, Vice President Richard Nixon used a gleaming "miracle kitchen" to make the case for capitalism's superiority. But television also had a role in the Kitchen Debate: no less than a refrigerator, a TV set served as powerful symbolic marker of the Cold War nexus between scientific

121. RGASPI, f. 17, op. 133, d. 339, l. 75.

122. For Tomsk, see GARF, f. 6903, op. 1, d. 499, ll. 17–20. For Kiev, see GARF, f. 6903, op. 1, d. 500, l. 37; TsDAHOU, f. 1, op. 70, d. 2447, ll. 28–37.

123. GARF, f. 6903, op. 1, d. 499, l. 5.

progress and the good life. Just prior to entering the exhibition's now-famous kitchen, Nixon drew Khrushchev's attention to a few color TV monitors, which reportedly irked the Soviet leader. Color TV was nothing special, he insisted, adding that the USSR would soon overtake the United States economically, "waving bye-bye" along the way. Though Nixon conceded that the Soviets were ahead in space technology, he pushed the point about American superiority in TV. No, Khrushchev insisted, the United States was not more advanced there either.[124]

Khrushchev was playing fast and loose with the facts (color broadcasts, for one, were nearly a decade away), but his prickliness about TV at the exhibition was indicative of a broader sensibility: from the beginning, television had been identified by the Soviets as *Soviet,* as Soviet as Sputnik, and the regime was not about to be outdone by the capitalist West in the development of mass communications any more than in rocket science. Home-based communications were plainly the modern, international standard in the 1950s. At this time, the Soviet home was also developing into a highly potent symbol of the regime's commitment to raising living standards, as Khrushchev declared that every family would have an individual apartment by 1980. The Soviet press made it clear, in photo spreads and descriptions of new housing, that these would be "modern" homes with "modern" furniture and, pointedly, with television sets. Even planners joined in the chorus identifying domestic TV as a modern staple: "normative consumption budgets" for urban families identified only two electronic appliances as essential—refrigerators and TVs.[125]

Soviet culture had anointed television as fundamental to a modern lifestyle and as a symbol of Soviet science's power to deliver that lifestyle and draw together people from across the USSR. Print media had comparatively little to say about programming: they were far more likely to discuss mass events like parades, books, or even cinema than TV shows. What the press did cover was TV technology—both its failings and, even more, its conquest of time and space. In articles with titles such as "Another 1,000,000 Viewers," journalists celebrated the end to "blank spots" in the television network, as ever more regions were connected to one another and to Moscow via coaxial cables, relay stations, and as of the mid-sixties, satellite. Every newspaper crowed on May 7, Radio Day, that Russia was the birthplace of broadcast technology, and the USSR, with its

124. Karal Ann Marling, *As Seen on TV: The Visual Culture of Everyday Life in the 1950s* (Cambridge, MA, 1994), 272; William Taubman, *Khrushchev: The Man and His Era* (New York, 2003), 416. When the exhibition was winding down, RCA, the company that had supplied the TV equipment, offered to sell it to the Soviets at an advantageous price; the Soviets turned them down. RGANI, f. 5, op. 33, d. 95, l. 3.

125. Reid, "Cold War in the Kitchen," 219. A 1960 Gosteleradio report also promised every family a set within twenty years. GARF, f. 6903, op. 1, d. 655, l. 17.

expertise in satellite technology, the best steward of its future development.[126] In 1967 there was a clamorous campaign celebrating the new Ostankino complex as a triumph of socialist technology and administration and "a gift of almost cosmic proportions" to the Soviet people.[127] Awe-inspiring in size, stridently superior to all foreign competitors, and built in Moscow, as per Soviet cliché, with materials and labor from the entire country, Ostankino became synonymous with Soviet television.[128] As celebrated in official culture, Soviet TV—millions of people in millions of rooms keeping company with glowing boxes—was an essentially collective phenomenon and an essential one as well: Soviet TV was proof of socialism's superiority.

TELEVISION AT HOME IN THE SOVIET SYSTEM: THE LAPIN ERA

Taken as a whole, television's trajectory in the USSR has an air of inevitability—the proud product of socialist science, administrative skill, and financial commitment (or of the drive to control minds, depending on your perspective) symbolized by the needle tower at Ostankino. But TV took many years to find a home in the Soviet system. Consumers showed an instant affection for the new medium, and their personal investment was an important factor driving development. So too was the enthusiasm of the people who established studios in the early years, both technology buffs and local political actors. The men in Moscow, by contrast, were initially sluggish in their response: the leading Soviet-era expert on the subject, A. Iurovskii, attributed the "serious errors" in establishing TV's infrastructure in the fifties to "an underestimation of its propaganda potential."[129] Perhaps, but Moscow's response was logical given the Soviets' tradition of political communication. No less important, many in the Soviet elite nursed a quiet contempt for TV as a cultural milieu and anxiety about its social effects. Television's success would always be haunted by the image of millions of homebound viewers, stuck in the petty personal cares of byt.

The taint on TV broadcasting was never fully expunged, as Soviet culture's table of ranks held strong until the collapse of the USSR. Soviet leaders would continue to boast that their people were the world's most avid readers (samyi

126. V. Danilov, "Eshche 1,000,000 zritelei," Pravda, 3 May 1968; "Moguchee sredstvo kommunisticheskogo vospitaniia," Pravda, 7 May 1960. The "birthplace" claim referred to A.S. Popov's invention of radio.

127. R. Boretskii, "When There Are Many Channels," Sovetskaia kul'tura, 11 September 1965, 2–3, in Current Digest of the Soviet Press 17, no. 39 (1965): 13.

128. Iurovskii, Televidenie, 42. Soviet media made much of the all-Union nature of Ostankino at the time, as did N. Mesiatsev in his memoirs, Davnoe perezhitoe (Moscow, 2000), 27.

129. Iurovskii, Televidenie, 106.

chitaiushchii narod) and even moviegoers, never TV watchers. Yet television won sustained investment all the same as a designated staple in the modern Soviet way of life. By the early 1970s, Soviet broadcasting signals reached upwards of 70 percent of the population, and there were an estimated 35 million television sets in the USSR. By 1985, these figures were 93 percent of the population (for access to Central TV's first channel) and 90 million sets.[130] Like radio, television technology had formidable momentum in the postwar media age. And as it grew in size and scope, television also came under increasingly effective—and from the perspective of many TV workers, oppressive—centralization and control.

It is common to describe Sergei Lapin's arrival as Gosteleradio chairman in 1970 as a turning point, marking the end of the "golden years of national television" (1957–170) and the beginning of its final phase of "development and stagnation" (1970–85), to quote the first full-length history of Soviet TV to emerge from post-Soviet Russia.[131] But Lapin, although an unusually powerful administrator, is, like Filipp Yermash in Soviet cinema, better understood as a symptom than as a cause. Expansion, centralization, and control were the very pith of Soviet media policy across the decades. What changed for Soviet television over time was capacity—both technological and institutional—along with top-level political focus. Capacity and focus fed into each other and were, in the main, "golden years" developments.

On the first point, technological and institutional capacity, the linchpin for Soviet broadcasting was the completion of the Ostankino center in 1967 and the formation of an all-Union network. Thus did the work of Moscow's broadcasters become *Soviet* TV: it was the network that "solved" the problem of regional broadcasting by effectively provincializing and marginalizing it. With a centralized network, controlling all output grew far more straightforward. And as Soviet TV made the switch from live to prerecorded broadcasts, another late-sixties phenomenon (by 1970, about 90 percent of Central TV's output was prerecorded), the center's capacity for control and standardization was strengthened even further.[132]

The second factor, top-level political attention to television, was also a gradual development, and here we must consider the role of personal experience in changing attitudes over time. It was in these years, after all, that TV watching first entered the family lives of the Soviet elite. When programmers moved the children's show *Good Night, Little Ones!* (*Spokoinoi nochi, malyshi!*, 1964–) to a later time slot, it was insistent (possibly desperate?) phone calls from highly placed parents that got it reinstated at its regular time: their children were refusing to

130. T. N. Matiushchenko et al., *Gazeta 'Pravda' o sovetskom televidenii i radioveshchanii: Sbornik* (Moscow, 1972), 27. *Ocherki po istorii rossiiskogo televideniia*, 157.

131. The periodization is from *Ocherki po istoriia rossiiskogo televideniia*, chaps. 2 and 3.

132. Iurovskii, *Televidenie*, 142.

go to bed without it.[133] For those parents—and for others who developed their own first programming addictions in the sixties—the power of television registered loud and clear. We might also think about the personal impact of the USSR's first big television events—Iurii Gagarin's triumphant return to Moscow in 1961, for example, or the state funeral for John F. Kennedy two years later, both broadcast live in the USSR.

Accident-prone as it was, early Soviet television advertised its power to the authorities in a negative sense as well: the need to monitor and control the medium impressed itself scandal by scandal. If, however, we are looking to identify the single most eye-popping experience for the Soviet authorities when it came to TV's negative potential, the best candidate by far would be Prague Spring 1968. Mass media heresy was at the heart of the Czechoslovak crisis in the eyes of the Soviet authorities. Brezhnev hammered away at the point in an August 13 telephone conversation with Aleksandr Dubček. The problem, he said, was "not some isolated instances but an organized campaign; in all the outlets of the mass media and information organs the rightists are firmly implanted." The situation would not be remedied until Dubček took "decisive measures" to resolve the "personnel problem." The first essential step, repeated Brezhnev, was sacking the head of Czechoslovak TV.[134]

When Soviet television was struck by one of its periodic scandals in 1968, the international context amplified the alarm bells to a full-scale alert and hastened change. Like all Soviet media, television was then in the midst of a massive campaign commemorating the hundredth anniversary of Lenin's birth in 1970. In February 1968, a program for amateur filmmakers ran footage showing an actor costumed as the young Lenin but interacting out of character with director Mark Donskoi. The atmosphere was jovial, and as Donskoi gave the younger man directions, he addressed him informally and slapped his shoulder. The show's *redaktor* (editor-producer) later explained the decision to show the clip by saying it demonstrated the "painstaking" work that went into creating Lenin's image.[135] Another TV professional recalled in post-Soviet memoirs that his "heart skipped a beat" when he saw the show, knowing there would be an uproar.[136] This was a minor program, broadcast once, at around 11 o'clock in the evening, on a new educational channel (the fourth) limited to the Moscow region.[137] Very few people

133. Interview with Kseniia Marinina, 2002 (Gosteleradiofond Oral History Project). On the program as a fixture in family life, see Catriona Kelly, "'Good Night, Little Ones:' Childhood in the Last Soviet Generation," in *Generations in Twentieth-Century Europe,* ed. Stephen Lovell (London, 2007), 165–189.

134. J. Navrátil, ed., *The Prague Spring '68,* vol. 2 (Budapest, 1998), 172–181.

135. GARF, f. 6903, op. 1, d. 962, l. 36.

136. V. N. Kozlovskii, *Televidenie. Vzgliad iz vnutri* (Moscow, 2002).

137. Interview with N. N. Mesiatsev, December 2001 (Gosteleradiofond Oral History Project); L. A. Dmitriev, *Ballada o chetvertoi programme TsT* (Moscow, 2000).

would have seen it, in other words, but that was not the point. What the Central Committee demanded to know—and its investigators stepped in straightaway—was how such "extreme tactlessness and disrespect for Lenin's image" had reached the airwaves.[138] Their conclusion (mooted in an April 1968 report) was that far from an isolated incident, the Lenin-actor scandal was symptomatic of widespread laxity within Gosteleradio that stemmed, at least in part, from a lack of managerial focus from without. The solution: a major administrative overhaul of broadcasting that would strengthen control by enhancing the power of the centralized network (and decreasing, or in many cases eliminating, regional programming) and by giving television more clout in the media system overall. The USSR should have a full-fledged Ministry of Television and Radio, the CC's men concluded, with a secure and robust funding stream, full command of broadcasting's technical resources Union-wide, and a related Institute of Television and Radio for professional training. It was time to take television seriously.[139]

In the wake of the Lenin-actor scandal, and in light of Czechoslovak media's "personnel problem," Gosteleradio underwent a sweeping campaign to batten down the ideological hatches. Staff members spent much of 1968–70 in meetings to discuss their responsibility for "ensuring control" over the airwaves and the need to "strengthen educational work" in their ranks.[140] Television's story here fit in with broader trends. In 1969, the CC sekretariat issued a decree designed to shore up ideological control in all Soviet cultural outlets.[141] The main thrust of the new order was to make people in leadership positions personally responsible for ensuring ideological rectitude and, most important, to expand the definition of leadership: in television, for example, organized into editorial groups (*redaktsii*), it was the ordinary redaktor whose job and party card were now on the line. To an extent, this had always been the case: a redaktor worked in concert with writers, directors, and technical staff on the overall organization and production of a show but was alone responsible for signing off on its broadcast. (And the "signing off" was literal: the redaktor signed a more or less detailed outline of the projected live or prerecorded broadcast, known as a "microphone file," *mikrofonnaia papka*).[142] But the 1969 decree, referring to the "conditions of the most intensified ideological battle between socialism and capitalism,"

138. RGANI f. 5, op. 60, d. 28, l. 23.

139. Ibid., ll. 25–26.

140. For example, GARF, f. 6903, op. 1, d. 1046.

141. See T. Goriaeva, ed. *Istoriia sovetskoi politicheskoi tsenzury; dokumenty i kommentarii* (Moscow, 1997), 188–191; T. Goriaeva, "Glavlit i literatura v period 'literaturno-politicheskogo brozheniia v Sovetskom Soiuze,'" *Voprosy literatury*, no. 5 (1998): 276–320.

142. *Mikrofonnaia papka* was one of many terms adopted from radio. On the redaktor profession, see *Televizionnyi redaktor: sbornik statei* (Moscow, 1966); Lilita Dzirkals, Thane Gustafson, and A. Ross Johnson, *The Media and Intra-Elite Communication in the USSR* (Santa Monica, CA, 1982), 43–61.

Figure 4.7. A broadcasting boss and his books: Sergei Lapin. V. Mastiukov and V. Savost'ianov/ITAR-TASS. Used with permission.

along with the obvious, albeit unmentioned connection to recent Czechoslovak events, made it clear that now the stakes for a redaktor—and the penalties—would be far higher. Late in the year, an unusual joint conference of the creative unions called for a stiffer line against bourgeois cultural influence and heightened discipline and party-mindedness among Soviet artists. (The year 1969 also saw Aleksandr Solzhenitsyn's expulsion from the Writers' Union.) The following year, 1970, brought wholesale changes at the top of the CC's ideological apparat, the most important "thick" journals, and Soviet broadcasting.[143] Exit Nikolai Mesiatsev, enter Sergei Lapin.[144]

Gosteleradio chairman from 1970 until the perestroika period, Sergei Lapin is a legendary figure in Soviet broadcasting. Former TV professionals speak of him with loathing, respect, even awe, but never indifference. A 2008 Russian television documentary devoted to Lapin used moody background music and a "masked man" motif to present his story in the manner of a spy drama. (And, of course, the very fact of a documentary about a figure so seemingly lacking in glamour as a broadcasting bureaucrat says a great deal about his ongoing mystique in media circles.)[145] For the people who worked in television, Lapin came to symbolize party-state power in all its contradictory guises: productive and destructive, cultured and abusive, ideologically steadfast and cynical. There is an extraordinary consistency to the tales of Lapin's cultural level (*kul'turnost'*) typified, in true Soviet fashion, by his love of literature. The references to his personal library, said to hold an extensive collection of émigré publications unavailable in the USSR, reach the level of fetish among his former staff. Lapin also gets high marks for boosting TV's finances and prestige. Yet at the same time, many people recall him as a strangling hand on creativity, a toady to his patrons in the Kremlin, and a ruthless boss.[146]

Within days of his arrival in April 1970, roughly 1,500 people at Gosteleradio in Moscow lost their jobs, including, at Central Television, eight of the twelve heads of editorial groups (*glavnye redaktory*).[147] The 1969 decree on strengthening ideological control brought an ax down on Gosteleradio too, but these new measures registered on a different scale: 1,500 employees amounted to roughly 10 percent of the total.[148] At a meeting with comrades from the CC in 1971, Lapin

143. Krechmar, *Politika i kul'tura,* 34–37, 232.

144. Mesiatsev claimed he was fired because Brezhnev feared he was part of a faction (associated with A. N. Shelepin) plotting against him. Mesiatsev, *Davnoe perezhitoe,* 93–94.

145. *Za zheleznoi maskoi. Sergei Lapin,* RTR-Planeta (2008).

146. "Zapreshchaetsia zaplyvat' dal'she vsekh!" 28; "Sergei Lapin, rukovoditel' Gosteleradio," *Nashe vse,* Ekho Moskvy Radio, 2 March 2008; Interview with L. Zolotarevskii, January 2002 (Gosteleradiofond Oral History Project); Interview with M. Krasn'ianskaia, January 2002 (Gosteleradiofond Oral History Project); Interview with G. V. Kuznetsov, 2002 (Gosteleradiofond Oral History Project).

147. Kozlovskii interview, February 2002; *Ocherki po istorii rossiiskogo televideniia,* 163. Some former TV professionals claim that the 1970 cuts targeted Jews disproportionately and that Lapin was an anti-Semite. Though there is no question that Lapin administered a massive purge of Jewish radio employees in the late forties, his personal prejudices are difficult to assess, and the evidence for 1970 is inconclusive. An interesting discussion can be found at "Sergei Lapin, rukovoditel' Gosteleradio." Cf. Nikolai Mitrokhin, *Russkaia partiia: Dvizhenie russkikh natsionalistov v SSSR, 1953–1985* (Moscow, 2003), 93–94.

148. In March 1968, Mesiatsev cited figures of 41,633 employees Union-wide and 16,831 in Moscow. GARF, f. 6903, op. 28, d. 40, ll. 217–218.

mentioned the move as an example of fiscal probity, saying it had saved 1.8 million rubles.[149] But in the eyes of many at Gosteleradio, it looked like a purge and set the tone for the new chairman's tenure. Second only to the festishizing of Lapin's library are tales of his sacking staff on the spot for such sins as wearing miniskirts and beards.

Locating Lapin the man amid the mists of his legend is probably a lost cause. Although we have many anecdotal reflections, the archival record for broadcasting grows ever more wooden and formulaic over time (and this is already evident in the sixties); the most important business in broadcasting, as in other cultural fields, was clearly conducted on the telephone and in person.[150] We know that Lapin was considered a "Brezhnev person"—a favorite of the general secretary, it was said, since his tenure in the late fifties as ambassador to Austria, where the two men first met, and then as ambassador to China in the critical years 1965 to 1967, when he reported directly to Brezhnev about the Cultural Revolution.[151] Lapin also boasted significant experience in Soviet media, having served as deputy chairman of the radio administration in the late Stalinist era and as the head of TASS after his post in China.

In the summer of 1970 came the long-planned administrative overhaul of Soviet broadcasting. The State Committee for Radio and Television *under* the USSR Council of Ministers became the State Committee *of* the USSR Council of Ministers for Television and Radio. Although this was not the full-fledged ministry proposed in 1968, the change in nomenclature did signal a major elevation in status for broadcasting overall and especially for television, which now got first billing. The new structure also succeeded in boosting the power of Moscow's broadcasting bureaucrats over their counterparts at the republic and regional levels, as envisaged earlier. (The 1977 constitution introduced a final name change that dropped all reference to the relationship to the Council of Ministers—broadcasting was now simply the USSR State Committee for Television and Radio—and signaled another boost in status.) Throughout the 1970s, the regime accelerated its investments in broadcasting: the planned budget (radio and television) for 1979 was, at 1,314.4 million rubles, roughly four times the size of that for 1967.[152] Soviet television greatly enlarged its reach, with new radio-relay and cable lines and satellite connections, including new connections to international satellite networks that gave Soviet broadcasts the theoretical possibility of expanding as never before. TV won far greater clout in the Soviet cultural system, as salary levels increased and its leading lights were eligible at last for state awards

149. *General'nyi sekretar' L.I. Brezhnev, 1964–1982* (Moscow, 2006), 100.

150. Krechmar, *Politika i kul'tura*, 17.

151. "Sergei Lapin, rukovoditel' Gosteleradio,"; V. Egorov, *Strannitsy istorii* (Moscow, 2004).

152. For the 1967 plan (353.4 million rubles), GARF, f. 6903, op. 1, d. 920, l. 126. For 1979, *Ocherki po istorii rossiiskogo televideniia*, 155.

("people's artist" honors and so on) analogous to those granted in the arts. TV professionals enjoyed unprecedented perks across the board, including access to new apartment blocks and vacation resorts for ordinary mortals and, for TV's elite, to foreign travel, chauffeurs, restricted shops, and a special restaurant high above Moscow in Ostankino's needle tower, Seventh Heaven.[153]

Soviet TV, we can say, hit the big time at last in the seventies, and Lapin is often credited with masterminding the success. Broadcasting now had a full-fledged member of the CC at its head (Mesiatsev had been a candidate member), and many people cite his personal relationship with Brezhnev as vital. Chairman Lapin evidently made a habit of phoning the general secretary in the presence of staff and quoting from conversations with him at meetings. At least one source close to Lapin claimed he was also personally responsible for designing the 1970 overhaul.[154] Perhaps, but we should recall that plans to restructure broadcasting dated back at least to 1968 and the proposed Ministry of Television and Radio, when, interestingly enough, Lapin's name did not even appear on the list of candidates for minister (Mesiatsev's did).[155] The drive to expand, centralize, and standardize Soviet television long predated Lapin, and arguably, it enjoyed its strongest momentum and most significant gains in the decade before he arrived with the construction of the all-Union network. In sum, many of the things attributed to him—a harder-edged ideological line, Moscow domination, TV's growth and rising status—were in fact broader trends. Lapin inherited and built upon a system; he did not originate or transform one.

And yet, for all the continuities in television's development, we remain on solid footing when we refer to a Lapin era. After roughly twenty years of bureaucratic shuffling and shifts in leadership, as of 1970 Soviet television had one boss in place for a full fifteen years. His tenure provided a stability—or, some say, stasis—hitherto unknown, and for this reason alone, it makes sense to consider it as an era. What is more, the chairman's image and the values it conveyed were critical. The Lapin legend is one of an enigmatic and limitless power fused with *vlast'*, the power of the Soviet party-state. Not a few people have compared his image to Stalin's, but more pertinently, it overlaps with the imagery of Soviet television itself in the 1970s and early '80s. Lapin cultivated his legend, and with the power of his personality and his policies promoted a particular way of thinking about TV.

Soviet television was, like Soviet cinema-art, not only an instrument for ideology; it was itself an ideological construct, a brand identity—Soviet TV. And while Mesiatsev and other broadcasting heads would have agreed in principle

153. For Mesiatsev's efforts in 1968 to secure nomenklatura status and benefits for staff, see GARF, f. 6903, op. 28, d. 40, ll. 93–94, 141, 217–218. On elite perks, see Paasalinna, "Glasnost and Soviet Television," 123.

154. *Ocherki po istorii rossiiskogo televideniia*, 163.

155. RGANI, f. 5, op. 60, d. 28, ll. 55–61, 146–151.

without question, it was Lapin who implemented this mode of thinking in policy most fully and effectively. The unofficial ban on press criticism of television under Lapin was logical because, as he reputedly enjoyed saying, "to criticize Soviet television is to criticize Soviet power." The shutting down of Gosteleradio's research division made sense because its very existence implied an impossible division between the Soviet people, their media, and their leaders. (Just as true love means never having to say you are sorry, true ideological unity means never needing to poll for opinions.) Audience research also smacked of masscult methods. Rudol'f Boretskii, one of Moscow TV's first enthusiasts, whom we will meet in the next chapter, saw his career frozen in the early seventies because Lapin took offense at a book he had written proposing that television introduce regular program schedules targeted to specific viewers and backed up by audience research rather than continue with, in his words, its "disorderly, unsystematic flood of information [that] of course the viewer cannot assimilate."[156] In fact, TV broadcasting, like radio, was moving in this direction; *Vremia,* the flagship news program, would have an ironclad spot at 9:00 p.m. as of 1972. But Lapin flared reading Boretskii's work because of its favorable references to capitalist media practices. "What, so *Pravda* should be taking lessons from the *New York Times* now?!" the chairman harangued Boretskii at a lengthy one-on-one meeting in his office.[157]

Sergei Lapin's broadcasting universe was nothing if not stridently Soviet. Again, the point is not that other media bosses held different views. Soviet television was forever "blazing totally new trails." This was the essence of the Soviet media concept. Yet the implementation of the basic principles under Lapin had a distinctive tone, focus, and outcome. Mesiatsev had not only been willing to consider foreign experience but had traveled abroad himself to investigate what the capitalists were doing and had kept his eyes open for improvements—for example, in the realm of videotape technology, where the USSR lagged behind.[158] Mesiatsev's predecessors demonstrated an openness to learn from foreign practices as well.[159]

Under Lapin, Soviet television's focus was far more inward, its international stance far more defensive. It was in some ways a curious approach for the chairman in light of his background in diplomatic work and at TASS; Soviet broadcasting had no more cosmopolitan head than Sergei Lapin. But Lapin, although a forceful political persona in his own right, took his direction from above, just

156. R. A. Boretskii, *Televizionnaia programma: Ocherk teorii propagandy* (Moscow, 1967), 121.

157. R. A. Boretskii, *V bermudskom treugol'nike TV* (Moscow, 1998), 15.

158. For Mesiatsev's 1966 trip to Western Europe, see RGANI, f. 5, op. 58, d. 25, ll. 2–52.

159. One example: a 1959 Ministry of Culture draft proposal for an educational channel referencing American television as a model. RGANI, f. 5, op. 33, d. 105, ll. 31, 34, 35.

as his predecessors had done. (We might also speculate that he understood better than most what Soviet culture was up against in the international sphere.) And by the time he came to power at Gosteleradio, the Soviet regime had been plagued by the problem of the enemy voices for more than two decades. Memories of the dangerous informational seepage in 1968 were raw, and the specter of a foreign satellite invasion loomed large. While Soviet radio continued its own sizable international effort, there was no TV Moscow to match Radio Moscow. Soviet television reached its greatest potential for international influence in the 1970s but made no serious bid to be the world's service.[160]

Rather, the Soviet regime focused its attentions on using international institutions to argue against the "free flow of information" across borders in the name of national sovereignty. In the Lapin era, the USSR proposed an international convention to block the use of satellites for broadcasts to private homes without prior consent from governments—a position supported at various points by countries in both the developing and developed world fearful of even greater American domination of the global TV market.[161] Nevertheless, by the decade's close, the Soviet regime had essentially lost the argument in international law with UNESCO's 1978 Declaration on the Media. In everyday practice it had lost it long before, as people across the USSR opted for "free flow" with their radio and TV sets.[162] Soviet television under Lapin focused on expanding, controlling, and promoting its internal empire. When, in June 1970, the new Gosteleradio chairman criticized his staff and demanded they be "more up-to-date, more politically mature, more responsive" in their work, he was not talking about taking on foreign competitors in the news race, as had Mesiatsev, or responding to the needs and desires of the audience; he was referring to a recent Lenin Prize ceremony with, he said, "acutely party-minded speeches" that radio and television somehow had failed to cover adequately. "And unfortunately, this is not a single slip—we have lots of slips like this," said Lapin. "We have got to attune ourselves to support the party's line."[163]

One of the participants at a 1988 roundtable of former TV professionals suggested that we consider television in the Lapin era a kind of "court" TV (*pridvornoe TV*) to the Kremlin, with Lapin in the role of chief courtier.[164] Culturally and socially speaking, television was a far more complex phenomenon, to be sure; and if the history of its first two decades, the 1950s and '60s, indicates anything, it is that Soviet political elites were never the only important actors and, at various points, far from the most dynamic ones. Television was and would remain an

---

160. See chapter 5.

161. Kerry Segrave, *American Television Abroad* (Jefferson, NC, 1998), 110.

162. "UNESCO's Mass Media Declaration: A Forum of Three Worlds," *Journal of Communication*, Spring 1979, 186–198.

163. GARF, f. 6903, op. 1, d. 1050, l. 143.

164. "Zapreshchaetsia zaplyvat' dal'she vsekh!" 25.

awkward fit with certain core Soviet values—a round peg in square-holed ways of thinking about the nature of political communication and collective action, education and cultured leisure. Yet television in the USSR did find a home in people's lives, including the lives of Soviet leaders and the life of the Soviet regime. The concept of court TV, while not encompassing the totality of Soviet television in its mature form, is essential in understanding this development.

First, we should recall the fundamental fact that political elites and their families were now consuming television and forming opinions about their experience. Soviet TV, no less than Soviet cinema, was designed and duty-bound to respond to signals from above. A scientific approach to television programming like Boretskii's was nothing in the face of telephone calls to Gosteleradio from highly ranked parents who needed *Good Night, Little Ones!* to get their children to bed. Second is the no less basic fact that, as Soviet broadcasting developed, political elites themselves appeared on-screen with increasing frequency. Soviet leaders never embraced the kind of broadcasting promoted by its first professionals (and by their own pronouncements) in the late fifties and sixties: direct contact with audiences in the form of write-in and call-in shows, roundtables, and interviews. On Lapin-era TV, it was, in the main, an elite crew of specialists who took on this role in programs such as *Pravda's Political Commentator Iu. A. Zhukov Answers TV Viewers' Questions* (*Na voprosy telezriteli otvechaet politicheskii obozrevatel' gazety 'Pravda' Iu. A. Zhukov*). TV's elite served as proxies for run-of-the-mill Soviet leaders, who had little to gain from such appearances. Far better from their point of view were the carefully stage-managed and, thanks to video, edited appearances at official meetings, holiday celebrations, receptions for foreign visitors, and the like. TV professionals had a name for this kind of programming: "parquet floor stories." Documentary filmmaker Marina Goldovskaya, then a camerawoman at Central TV, recalled how she and her colleagues approached a parquet floor assignment:

> All general shots had to be done in the first fifteen to twenty minutes. After that, participants would doze peacefully, which our millions of viewers were not supposed to see.... I had to get all the close-ups in the first few minutes—interesting faces, eyes filled with wisdom and sparkle.... If you didn't get them right away, you had to wait until after the lunch break, when the delegates returned cheerful and ready to stay awake for at least the next quarter of an hour.[165]

Brezhnev, it is said, had specific standards for his own parquet appearances: three times as much screen time as any other leader (the "3:1 rule") and a medium-range shot (head and shoulders filling the frame) at a minimum.[166] When the

---

165. Marina Goldovskaya, *Woman with a Movie Camera,* trans. Antonina W. Bouis (Austin, TX, 2006), 48.
166. Mesiatsev, *Davnoe perezhitoe,* 138–139; Paasilinna, "Glasnost and Soviet Television," 128.

general secretary fumbled presenting Lapin with an Order of Lenin in 1982, dropping the medal before the TV cameras, Lapin reassured him that no viewer would see his shaky hands. "It's nothing, Leonid Ilich. Our guys will take care of it."[167] Soviet television served the Soviet elite, and as such it was television very much at home in and in the service of the Soviet system.

Many people have speculated about Chairman Lapin's personal perspective on his TV empire. The presumption among some former staffers is that a man so "cultured," a man who could quote Anna Akhmatova's poetry at length and discuss the fate of novelist Boris Pasternak with great sensitivity, must have suffered in his role as courtier to the Kremlin gerontocracy. Others prefer to see him as the ultimate Soviet cynic, laughing alone in his office with his rare books and many telephones, secure in his sense of superiority to his bosses and underlings alike. The multifaceted Lapin legend was, of course, something cultivated by the chairman himself, a management tool, then taken up and elaborated by people who worked in broadcasting. It offers more solid information about their values than his, the suffering sage and cynic being two poles of their collective identity. Lapin the man may well have fit either, or neither, extreme.

And so we are left with Soviet television in the Lapin era, symbol of technological and organizational prowess, national unity, and a modern lifestyle: the Soviet flag planted foursquare on the terrain of the postwar media age. The awkwardness of television in the Soviet context that was so evident in the early years did not vanish. That TV watching developed into the most popular leisure-time activity for most of the Soviet population in the 1970s could never rank as a source of uncomplicated pride. (Even the master of Soviet TV at its zenith was legendary for his reading habits.) Yet with time, the imagery and the pleasures of power wore away at television's awkward edges. Soviet leaders did not brag that the nation was sacked out on the sofa every evening in front of the set. They boasted that Soviet television provided viewers with the best cultural and political education in the world and that it was the largest network in the world with the tallest TV tower, the most languages spoken, and the greatest expanse of broadcast might, and that it was Soviet. They appreciated the flattery of the coverage and enjoyed the hockey matches or maybe the opera programming, the nightly ritual of *Vremia,* the game shows, or the popular science programs. Soviet television, perhaps the most important challenge to traditional Soviet cultural ideals, was also in many ways the most successful of all Soviet mass cultural forms.

167. The original tape, with both the fumble and Lapin's comments on the soundtrack, somehow survived. *Za zheleznoi maskoi. Sergei Lapin.*

TELEVISION AND AUTHORITY IN SOVIET CULTURE

May 7, Radio and Television Day in the USSR, was a time for media professionals to pat themselves on the back, and it was in this spirit that the host of the popular TV show *Little Blue Flame* (*Goluboi Ogonek*) told viewers about a little girl she knew who had declared there was no God "because if there were, they would have already shown him on television."[1] This was in 1967, the year the Soviets opened the hub of their all-Union network, Ostankino, with great fanfare. But for many people then working in television, the wellspring of excitement ran far deeper, as suggested in a humorous way by *Little Blue Flame*'s host. The generation that pioneered TV broadcasting in the USSR—the enthusiasts of the 1950s and '60s—saw a medium with intrinsic, extraordinary powers: television by its very nature revealed what they called truth, reality, and the contemporary *lichnost'* (individual or personality). The father of the little girl who asked about God, Iurii Beliaev, was himself a pioneering director of TV documentaries who spoke of "penetrating into the little secrets of the soul" in films with titles such as *A Sakhalin Character* (*Sakhalinskii kharakter*) and *Journey into the Everyday* (*Puteshestvie v budni*).[2] Beliaev and his colleagues had no doubt that the exploration of the individual and the everyday was what viewers wanted and, more to the point, what they needed in the wake of Stalinism. TV enthusiasts saw television truth supplanting Stalinist fakery and bombast; they envisioned the *kul't lichnosti* (cult of personality) purged from people's minds definitively by a culture that celebrated many *lichnosti*—worthy individuals who would serve as models for personal growth and civic activism. In this way, Soviet TV enthusiasm imagined the medium as a revolutionary mechanism for building a new Soviet community; TV watching in the USSR would be productive leisure for a better, truer world.

Most Russian-language studies of Soviet television[3] are written from the perspective of its early enthusiasts; in fact, the most prominent scholars in the field

1. *Goluboi ogonek* (*Little Blue Flame*), 1967 (Gosteleradiofond). The story has an apocryphal whiff, but it does also appear in a book written by a friend of the girl's father. G. Fere, *Tovarishch TV* (Moscow, 1974), 29.

2. Fere, *Tovarishch TV,* 23.

3. "Soviet television" for the purposes of this chapter refers primarily to the work of Central TV, which not only employed the majority of TV workers but also set the standard

are all former TV professionals themselves. Unsurprisingly, they tend to affirm Soviet television's self-proclaimed humanism and consider the fifties and sixties its golden years.[4] The enthusiasts' focus on reality, everyday life, and lichnost' is understood as an inherently progressive phenomenon with long-term positive effects. Much like film, literature, and journals in this period, television wins praise for having nurtured respect for the individual and a hunger for openness and sincerity in political and social life; these values are said to have contributed to society's ideological demobilization—the tacit withdrawal of support from official Soviet values—and to a growing orientation toward private life and values. In the 1970s, the story goes, these progressive trends were largely forced off the home screen as increased political control stifled the innovative spirit of early TV and ushered in a period of cultural stagnation. The explosion of civic-oriented television in the Gorbachev era is then represented as a kind of resurrection; Soviet TV in the fifties and sixties as a protoglasnost smothered in the cradle.

This is, of course, the familiar narrative of the thaw, and in this chapter I want to reexamine it by exploring how Soviet TV enthusiasm worked in practice—in particular, how key enthusiast categories like lichnost' and reality functioned to structure the era's most famous programs. Which individuals and whose reality belonged on the home screen were far from neutral questions for TV's enthusiastic pioneers, as the screen itself was far from a neutral space in their eyes. Early Soviet TV professionals saw all culture as a mechanism for moral (usually marked "spiritual") education as well as for political mobilization. The drive to define and deploy concepts like reality and lichnost' did pitch TV's new professionals into conflict with the political authorities on numerous occasions. But in most important respects, TV enthusiasm was in concert with the values of the regime, especially when it came to attitudes toward audiences, who were understood to be culture's patients rather than its patrons. Although reformist, TV enthusiasm was far from nonideological, and even the most controversial

---

for studios throughout the USSR. Though some regional studios did generate innovative programming, the twin processes of centralization and provincialization described in chapter 4 guaranteed that the vector of influence usually ran from Moscow outward. Moreover, there is little to suggest that the staff of regional studios differed significantly in social background from their Muscovite counterparts or developed an understanding of the medium inconsistent with theirs.

4. For "golden years," see *Ocherki po istorii rossiiskogo televideniia* (Moscow, 1999), a joint project of many important Soviet-era scholars and professionals. S. A. Muratov, A. Ia. Iurovskii, V. V. Egorov, G. V. Kuznetsov, and R. A. Boretskii are perhaps the most prominent of those who worked at Central TV in the fifties and sixties. B. M. Firsov, the most important sociologist of Soviet TV, was also for a time the head of the Leningrad studio. Please see the bibliography for their major publications. In English, see the works of Ellen Mickiewicz and also Mark Koenig, "Media and Reform: The Case of Youth Programming on Soviet Television (1955–1990)" (PhD diss., Columbia University, 1995). Koenig, a political scientist, follows the Soviet enthusiasts' interpretation very closely.

programming never saw itself as anti-Soviet. And at the same time, TV enthusiasm in the USSR showed kinship ties to contemporary notions of public service broadcasting in Europe and the United States, despite widely varying political contexts.

What marked the enthusiasts in their own, Soviet context was less their values (moral or political) per se than the way they saw themselves as a group and the way they conceptualized television itself—two stances rooted in the tradition of the Soviet cinematic avant-garde and, more broadly, of the Russian-Soviet intelligentsia.[5] TV enthusiasts believed it was *they* who should decide which slice of reality was to be broadcast and who counted as a lichnost' appropriate for the home screen; it was they, after all, who were inventing a new space in television for the regeneration of Soviet individuals and community. For this reason, I argue, the baseline conflict in early television was one mostly obscured by enthusiast narratives of "liberal" experimentation and "conservative" regime control: the struggle for authority over Soviet audiences. The story of TV's creative development in its first two decades is one of a cohort's and a medium's search for authority inside the framework of Soviet culture.[6] It is, moreover, the story of an ambiguous success. Though TV enthusiasm failed on its own terms to create a new culture of socialist humanism and a new Soviet community, TV broadcasts won ever-larger audiences. Television in the 1970s provided the leisure-time activity of choice for the majority of the Soviet population. Yet overwhelmingly these were viewers who enjoyed—and even preferred—the very forms of programming that the enthusiasts had rejected as reactionary. For TV enthusiasm, the ideal viewer was an active, creative, civic-minded lichnost'. What it helped to create, by its lights, was the other side of the looking glass: the TV viewer as a passive consumer of entertainment.

EARLY SOVIET TELEVISION AND THE ENTHUSIASTS

The men and women who pioneered Soviet television programming called themselves enthusiasts, but they also used terms like "dilettante" and even "loser."[7] Few people came to TV with a passion for the new medium, and none brought expertise; many had never seen a broadcast. Rather, early TV workers were often people who had failed at or saw no future in the professions for which

---

5. On lichnost' in Russian cultural history, see Catriona Kelly and David Shepherd, eds. *Constructing Russian Culture in the Age of Revolution, 1881–1940* (London, 1998), 13–26. On lichnost' and socialist activism in 1960s print media, see Thomas Wolfe, *Governing Soviet Journalism: The Press and the Socialist Person after Stalin* (Bloomington, IN, 2005), esp. 33–70.

6. Cf. Sheila Fitzpatrick, *The Cultural Front: Power and Authority in Revolutionary Russia* (Ithaca, NY, 1992), esp. 1–15.

7. R. Boretskii, "Otkroveniia dilettantov," in *Shabolovka, 53: Stranitsy istorii televideniia,* ed. A. Iu. Rozov (Moscow, 1988), 148–158.

they had been trained. They were typically well educated—often in film, theater, or journalism—and overwhelmingly young. In the 1950s, it was possible for an educated young person literally to walk in off the street and get a job in TV. Leonid Dmitriev did just that in 1956. When he and a friend, both graduates from the prestigious Institute of International Relations, heard that the Moscow studio was looking for staff, they took a tram there and told the guard it was their dream to work in TV. (In reality, Dmitriev at least dreamed of a career in cinema but had been rejected by the film institute, VGIK.) Ten minutes later, they met the director of the studio, known as Shabolovka, and in another ten minutes, they were employees of Soviet television.[8]

In their memoirs and recollections, Dmitriev and his former colleagues are unanimous in describing the atmosphere of early TV as uniquely vibrant and egalitarian. L. Zolotareva recalled a workplace suffused with a "youthful, creative spirit" that "inspired hope." "You could sense a kind of freedom and a chance for creativity and self-expression," she commented in a 2002 interview.[9] A. Grigorian remembered the fifties as a time when "there were new faces in the hallway practically every day" and the use of *ty* (informal "you") predominated, even among people of different rank. "[A]t that time, we were all equal before television's unexplored potential," he explained. "We were young, and that linked us [to television]. We happily hoisted a significant load of responsibility on our shoulders, and we carried it not because of fear but because of conscience."[10]

A spirit of freedom, hope, and community is something many people associate with the Khrushchev era, especially those who were young at the time. Yet television was a special case all the same, thanks to both the newness of the medium and the composition of its staff. The remarkable fact is that in the fifties (and well into the sixties), faute de mieux, young, enthusiastic dilettantes did dominate Soviet studios, delivering programs that reached millions of TV sets all over the Union. The enthusiasts saw themselves as engaged in a process of pure invention. "No one knew what television was. No one had any idea how to make it," Dmitriev told an interviewer. "It was a time of constant discoveries."[11] And as enthusiasts like Dmitriev went about inventing TV, as they saw it, they were also inventing themselves as creative professionals in a new sphere. What Soviet TV's pioneers experienced was an unusually personal and intense identification with television—indeed, a happy confusion between self (or cohort) and the medium. The experience of working in early television was a dynamic

8. L. Dmitriev, "Televizionnaia spiral'" in Rozov, *Shabolovka,* 96–97; interview with L. Dmitriev, 2002 (Gosteleradiofond Oral History Project).

9. Interview with L. S. Zolotareva, 2002 (Gosteleradiofond Oral History Project).

10. A. Grigorian, "Rabotaem!" in Rozov, *Shabolovka,* 125.

11. Dmitriev interview, 2002.

process of self-discovery; successful TV broadcasting became for them a form of self-actualization.

The fact that television was seen by many as terra incognita lent an air of adventure to the work, and it meant that enthusiasts in the early days enjoyed a certain latitude as well. The first television broadcast of a major news event—the arrival of Ho Chi Minh in Moscow in 1954—was the brainchild of Aleksandr Iurovskii, a former reporter for the illustrated magazine *Ogonek*. Iurovskii had already run one newscast, Soviet TV's first (sports reporting aside), from a Moscow chocolate factory, and when he read in the paper one morning that Ho's delegation was to arrive in Moscow that day, he decided "to take a chance" and cover the event live on television. The broadcast was successful, but in retrospect, what is most notable about it is that the impetus came from a rank-and-file redaktor at Shabolovka. Although Iurovskii did use the *vertushka* (special phone line) at the offices of the radio and television administration to secure approval "upstairs," as he put it, upstairs was apparently not at that point communicating its own ideas or demands to him. Iurovskii played a complicated game. First he told the people upstairs that he had orders to cover the event without specifying from whom—and without clearing the idea with the Glavradio, the head of radio and TV, who was out of the office. Once the people upstairs had approved the plan, he reported to the Glavradio that he had orders from them.[12]

Iurovskii's account, though painting him in the best possible light, rings true in the overall context for TV circa 1954. The fact that Soviet political elites mostly dismissed (or ignored) the medium in its early years not only gave technology buffs a window of opportunity to develop local stations; it also allowed enthusiasts like Iurovskii to take the initiative in programming. The creation of a more streamlined central administrative structure, Gosteleradio,[13] the stepped-up involvement of the Central Committee apparat with its new working group for television (both in 1957), and particularly its 1960 decree on television all worked against the decentralized, ad hoc nature of early TV. And these changes also brought increasing control on the creative side, as an ever-increasing number of administrative eyes were trained more attentively on television at all points in the production process. It is hard to imagine Iurovskii's 1954 stunt ten or even five years later.

In reality, television broadcasting was not genuine terra incognita, and thus the mythic sense of the new shared by so many of its enthusiasts is all the more interesting. Radio had set a clear precedent for broadcasts such as the Ho reportage (as Iurovskii acknowledged), and Soviet TV and radio had very strong links technically and organizationally. TV production was managed by redaktsii

---

12. Rozov, *Shabolovka*, 94–95.

13. As in chapter 4, for simplicity's sake, I use "Gosteleradio" throughout to refer to the central radio and television administration in Moscow.

in the same manner as radio (which itself mimicked print), and both were administered by the same governmental and party structures. But just as there was nothing preordained about broadcasting's location in the home, so too was the development of original programming—its philosophy, forms, and ends—less an inevitable progression from radio than a series of specific choices.

Let us take a look at the schedule for the Moscow studio (already known as Central Television) on Wednesday, 10 October 1956.[14]

FIRST CHANNEL

7:00 p.m. *Million v meshke (A Million in a Sack)*—new cartoon film

7:30   *Program on the Seventh Anniversary of the GDR*

8:00   *U nashikh druzhei (At Our Friends' Place)*—TV program

8:10   *Trista let tomu nazad (Three Hundred Years Ago)*—1956 feature film from Kiev Film Studio

9:50   *Pyshka*—1934 feature film from Mosfil'm

SECOND CHANNEL

6:55   Torpedo-Zenit—soccer match

What jumps to our attention is the tiny proportion of airtime given to original programming. Only the ten-minute *At Our Friends' Place* and the thirty-minute GDR anniversary show were possibly live broadcasts (the anniversary show was more likely a newsreel), leaving about four hours of airtime for cinema and two or more hours for soccer that evening. Even Shabolovka, Central TV, the largest and best-funded operation in the Union, had few resources for producing original studio programming circa 1956. The main studio measured only three hundred square meters. There were no facilities for developing film, no costume or prop department, not even rehearsal space at the time.[15] One Shabolovka veteran, Boris Livertovskii, described to me in detail the method he devised for a presenter to show still photographs without having her fingers slip into the frame: viewers had been complaining about the fingers, the press had even run letters about them, and he had solved the problem.[16] And if this was Soviet Central TV, imagine the working conditions at Kazan TV (est. 1955) or in Kazakhstan's Ust-Kamenogorsk studio (est. 1958). A 1957 article sympathetic to the trials of local broadcasters described "anxious young men"—workers from the Vladivostok studio—making the rounds of city shops in search of chemicals to develop their film.[17]

Everywhere across the Union radio was on a far more solid footing than TV. Not only was it better equipped, but it had an experienced professional staff,

14. Fedor Razzakov, *Zvezdy televideniia* (Moscow, 2000), 10.

15. GARF, f. 6903, op. 1, d. 543, l. 69.

16. Interview with B. M. Livertovskii, Moscow, July 2002.

17. G. Khaliletskii, "Goresti mestnogo televideniia," *Literaturnaia gazeta,* 27 August 1957.

including correspondents throughout the USSR and in foreign locations as well. Radio produced the kind of original programming—dramas, musical revues, educational and informational shows for different groups, and so on—that early television could only dream of. Radio production was comparatively cheap too, and throughout the fifties and sixties radio broadcasts had far greater reach in most of the Soviet Union than did TV.

Given these disparities, why not promote a division of labor in broadcasting, assigning radio and television different functions? Gosteleradio head Mikhail Kharlamov told his staff in the early sixties that their work boiled down to three tasks. The first, "most important thing," he said, was "to mobilize the people to solve current problems—economic, political, aesthetic, and so on." The second goal was "to give the people educational material, develop culture, and raise the level of the people." And broadcast media's third task, which Kharlamov described as "no less important," was "entertainment."[18] With this framework in mind, we can imagine a functionally divided system that assigned mobilization and education in broad terms to radio, leaving high culture and entertainment largely to television. That is, radio might continue with daily news coverage and some educational and artistic programming; television in its turn would be free to fulfill the long-standing goal of making high culture a part of every Soviet's daily life while also delivering appropriate light entertainment to the many millions who lacked access to organized recreation. Newsreels, a well-developed sector of the film industry, might continue to provide imagery of important national and international events.

Soviet broadcasting eschewed this functional route, choosing instead to develop television intensively across all sectors as a universal medium. One factor was the perceived threat of foreign radio broadcasting on Soviet territory and the desire to develop a compelling (and presumably "safe") alternative medium. The enthusiasm of ordinary Soviets was important too, meaning not only the local technology buffs who, in many areas, beat the central authorities to the punch in developing the technology but also people across the USSR who decided they wanted to be TV viewers and demanded a breadth of programming. And last, we should not underestimate the influence of TV's newly minted professionals, the Iurovskiis and Livertovskiis, who pushed hard for the medium's creative development from the inside.

Television's enthusiasts brought to their work a special kind of messianic zeal. In the early years, when studios were the size of closets (and might have well been closets a month before), they had little choice but to rely on other cultural forms, particularly film and theater, to feed the hungry air. But the goal they set for themselves was not just to televise culture, but "television-ize" it. If TV were to broadcast theater, for example, then it should be TV theater (*televizionnyi*

18. GARF, f. 6903, op. 1, d. 777, ll. 48–49.

teatr), designed for the specificities of the medium. The distinction between theater on TV and TV theater may appear insignificant at first glance, but it was crucial for the enthusiasts. "We thought of television as an art—as something which was not yet an art, but which was becoming one, and we were participating in that," recalled R. Kopylova in 2002.[19] Her contemporary, Iurovskii, was not so hesitant when he published his battle cry for TV in 1960—and in the leading Soviet film journal to boot: "Television now is already a big and bright window on the world. Already now, today, television is a remarkable means of artistic expression, a new, attractive, and important art for the people."[20] It was a controversial—and to some in the established arts—even laughable position. When a trio of enthusiasts, L. Dmitriev, A. Grigorian, and R. Boretskii presented their own battle cry, "Television Is Art" for publication to the leading cultural weekly *Soviet Culture* (*Sovetskaia kul'tura*) in 1957, they had to fight against the insertion of a question mark.

LIVE BROADCASTING: LIMITATION AND PERSPIRATION

If TV was indeed a new art, the task was to discover its distinctive aesthetic principles and modes of address, thus unlocking its true might. And on this question, the enthusiasts were unanimous: the essence of the art was live broadcasting (*zhivoi* or *priamoi efir*). People who worked in television and people who wrote about it for Soviet print media—and there was, significantly, a large overlap between these two groups—shared this conviction.

Live broadcasting was the mainstay of Soviet TV broadcasting throughout the 1950s and most of the '60s. The only other option in these years before videotape technology took hold in the USSR was filming for broadcast, and as this was comparatively pricey, the Soviets tended to reserve it for events they considered of cultural and political import: anniversary days of the October Revolution, a performance by Maia Plisetskaiia, Konstantin Fedin reading his work in his office, Iurii Gagarin reporting back to Khrushchev after his historic space flight—these were the sorts of things most often filmed for television. Throughout the early period, Soviet TV lacked adequate equipment and production facilities to work with film: the fact that news programs in the 1950s actively solicited material from amateur filmmakers is one sign of their own limitations.[21] Soviet movie studios in turn lacked incentives to turn over their production facilities to TV, which many cineastes regarded with a mix of condescension and

19. Interview with R. D. Kopylova, St. Petersburg, June 2002.

20. A. Iurovskii, "Pogliadim na ekran," *Iskusstvo kino* [hereafter *IK*], no. 4 (1960): 125. Iurovskii was responding to an earlier article by film director M. Romm, "Pogliadim na dorogu," *IK*, no. 11 (1959).

21. Interview with V. N. Kozlovskii, February 2002 (Gosteleradiofond Oral History Project); Livertovskii interview, July 2002.

apprehension. One solution to the problem of competition was to take the bull by the horns, as director Sergei Gerasimov proposed in 1963. "We need to fight with TV very harshly," he told his cineaste colleagues. "I think it's within our capacity to come to an agreement with TV once and for all that we will make films for their use and in the future to separate TV and cinema utterly."[22] Although Gerasimov's vision did not materialize—Soviet television continued to screen mainstream studio productions in great quantities—the film world did assume a growing role in TV as the new medium expanded and professionalized. The Soviets' first made-for-TV movie was a four-part World War II drama, *We Draw Fire on Ourselves* (*Vyzyvaem ogon' na sebe*), produced by the Mosfil'm studio for Gosteleradio in 1964–65. The 1970s saw a heyday of Soviet TV movies and serials, with some produced by TV's own film unit, Ekran (founded in 1968), some commissioned from studios, and many featuring mainstream cinema stars. The overlap between Soviet cinema-art and the upstart Soviet TV was far greater in the end than many a snobbish cineaste circa 1960 could have imagined.

Still, the USSR relied on live television broadcasting for many years—longer than most other developed countries and far longer than its self-declared main rival, the United States, where as early as 1961 it accounted for only 27 percent of total airtime (and was failing fast).[23] The implications of the Soviet lag were tremendous, but they went mostly unrecognized at the time. American producers and advertisers discovered quite early that audiences were more than willing to watch repeat broadcasts of filmed shows[24] and that although the initial outlay for film was higher than for live broadcasting, the profits from syndication were potentially enormous—and not only inside the United States. The shift from live to filmed programs facilitated the American TV industry's penetration into foreign markets, which was already well advanced by the late fifties. As early as 1962, the syndication revenues from U.S. programs marketed abroad equaled those for the domestic market.[25] The Soviets, for their part, did put some of their TV shows on foreign screens via Intervidenie, an organization for socialist bloc exchanges begun in 1960, and Intervidenie also arranged exchanges with Eurovision, the Western European group that served as its model. These were, however, very limited in scope: the most the Soviets originated for Eurovision in the 1960s in any given year was about twenty programs, or forty hours of airtime

22. RGALI, f. 2944, op. 1, d. 19, l. 47.

23. Jeff Kisseloff, *The Box: An Oral History of Television, 1920–1961* (New York, 1995), 272.

24. See William Boddy, *Fifties Television: The Industry and Its Critics* (Urbana, IL, 1990), 141–143; Wilson Dizard, *Television: A World View* (Syracuse, NY, 1966), 157–158.

25. Michael Curtin, "Beyond the Vast Wasteland: The Policy Discourse of Global Television and the Politics of American Empire," *Journal of Broadcasting and Electronic Media,* Spring 1993, 133.

(in 1965).[26] The exchange program was plagued by technical problems on the Soviet side—an estimated 50 percent of initiated exchanges failed as a result of faulty cable transmissions and other glitches. The Soviets consistently got more from Eurovision than they gave, and the same was true of Intervidenie, where in 1968, for example, the Soviet intake in hours was roughly double its output (281 to 144).[27]

These are all, let it be said, piddling figures for Soviet television—a droplet in the international torrent of programming that flooded the media age. By limiting their use of film in original television programming, botching the technology of exchanges, and dragging their heels on video as well, the Soviets closed off the possibility of promoting their TV culture internationally at a critical moment in the medium's development. By the 1970s, when the USSR had developed not only a potential supply (a stockpile of product) but also a vast and sophisticated satellite network for distribution, U.S. hegemony in the international market was well established.[28]

Of course, successfully marketing Soviet TV abroad would also have meant selling to governmental services and commercial firms, and it is an open question whether they would have been interested in Soviet fare. Some contemporaries thought yes. In 1963 officials in charge of cultural exchange told the CC that U.S. and Canadian companies had been "insistently requesting" multipart television films; Soviet TV's inability to deliver them "deprives us of a wide channel for propaganda as well as additional opportunities for earning hard currency," they argued.[29] Yet considering the lackluster box-office performance of many Soviet movies abroad and the difficulties Sovexportfil'm faced in finding distributors, we should question how well Soviet TV productions would have fared, at least commercially. In 1970, the Intervidenie Teleforum, an annual event for marketing socialist TV productions to the capitalist world, attracted ninety-three representatives from Western Europe, North America, Japan, and Pakistan but yielded only 80,000 (convertible) rubles in sales for the USSR.[30] (By way of comparison, Gosteleradio's annual budget for buying TV programs from capitalist-country producers was about US$500,000 in the seventies, according to a former staffer.)[31] The Soviets always did better with exchanges than

26. Burton Paulu, *Radio and Television Broadcasting in Eastern Europe* (Minneapolis, 1974), 62–63.

27. GARF, f. 6903, op. 3, d. 491, l. 9, 20. A whopping 112 of these 144 hours went to the GDR.

28. See John Downing, "The Intersputnik System and Soviet Television," *Soviet Studies* 27, no. 4 (October 1985): 465–483.

29. RGANI, f. 5, op. 55, d. 51, l. 66.

30. GARF, f. 6903, op. 1, d. 1051, l. 57.

31. Zolotareva interview, 2002.

sales, it is true, but even among "brother" socialists, it took a certain amount of arm-twisting to place Soviet programming.[32]

The USSR's relative backwardness in film and video technology only worsened an already difficult situation on the international market, and it also had important consequences for TV development at home. As long as Soviet TV relied on live broadcasting, Soviet Central TV and the regional studios had relatively little to offer one another in terms of programming. Some contemporaries recognized the reliance on live shows as a liability, but there was significant skepticism among professionals in the sixties about the viability of repeat broadcasts and multipart films on TV. The suspicion that audiences would not watch them persisted for a number of years even after the success of 1965's *We Draw Fire*. And though Soviet TV did turn to multipart films in the 1970s, it never embraced the spectrum of serial fictional programming familiar to viewers in the United States and other Western countries. Ultimately, the problem of feeding the domestic market was resolved by the effective use of satellite transmissions and especially by videotape, which Gosteleradio head Nikolai Mesiatsev ranked as a top priority for development in the USSR after his 1966 trip to assess television facilities in Western Europe. Throughout most of the sixties, though, all of Soviet TV, central and regional, limited its scope to a drastic extent by producing mostly one-off, live shows.

By and large, these longer-term and strategic implications of live broadcasting did not figure prominently in Soviet discussions at the time. Everyday control was considered the more pressing problem. Live television broadcasting was a dicey and nerve-racking affair the world over in the 1950s and '60s. The annals of TV history are filled with live gaffes, such as the story of the jittery American anchorman who, when required by contract to enjoy the sponsor's product on air, lit cigarette after cigarette from the filter end. But whereas the American anchor kept his job in this case, his Soviet counterpart would not have been so lucky. Gaffes and particularly verbal slipups were matters of the utmost gravity on Soviet TV and commanded a tremendous amount of attention. In one notorious case from the mid-fifties, an announcer was fired on the spot for an accidental slip of the tongue. Instead of "a generation of Leninists" (*pokolenie lenintsev*), he said "a generation of lazybones" (*pokolenie lenivtsev*). A filmed version, much like a taped radio program or the page proofs for an article, could easily have been edited. Nikolai Kartsov of Central TV recalled editing a segment of film shot during Khrushchev's trip to Denmark in the late fifties so that the Soviet leader's comments would be momentarily inaudible. (Kartsov and his colleagues agreed they would be embarrassing to air.)[33] In similar fashion, Soviet TV regularly edited international figure skating competitions to replace Western pop music

32. GARF, f. 6903, op. 3, d. 491, l. 20.
33. N. P. Kartsov, *Ia ne rasstaval'sia s televideniem* (Moscow, 2000), 12–14.

with more acceptable classical or Soviet tracks.[34] Though some manipulation was possible with live television, the control and security of true editing could come only with filmed (or taped) programs.

Mistakes and accidents could have wide-ranging consequences for TV staff. As director Kseniia Marinina recalled, "If a host blurted something out, we all had to pay for it. Our backs were wet [with perspiration] all the time."[35] In the case of the "lazybones-Leninist" slip, not only was the hapless announcer barred from TV for life, but the incident cost the head of the Moscow studio her job as well.[36] TV personnel also paid the price if invited guests said something untoward in a live broadcast. It was standard practice for TV staff to rehearse with guests prior to the show what they would be saying. This information was logged in the "microphone file" (*mikrofonnaia papka*) signed by the redaktor. Glavlit censors did work at Gosteleradio, as they did in all publishing houses and newspapers, but there were very few of them. In 1960, a representative from Glavlit appealed to members of Gosteleradio's party cell to show more cooperation; there were only four censors at Shabolovka at the time for both radio and television.[37] Clearly this level of staffing was inadequate to the task of censoring hours and hours of daily programming, and besides, the predominance of live broadcasting at the time posed technical problems for censorship. The onus fell largely on TV workers themselves to practice mutual and self-censorship.[38]

Microphone files and preshow preparation varied in their level of detail. In many cases, interviewees would memorize a script written with or by the show's staff ahead of time and rehearse their parts extensively. This was the most common scenario for live man-on-the-street—or, more likely, worker-at-the-factory or engineer-in-the-studio—interviews. The arrangements with "expert" figures such as artists and intellectuals were often more open-ended and, from the perspective of TV staff, more problematic. For an expert guest to veer from the themes set down in the file was considered a more serious violation than for an ordinary person to do so.

Writer Lev Kassil"s participation in a 1959 program, *Encounters in America* (*Vstrechi v Amerike*), was one case in point. Recently returned from a trip to the

34. Ibid., 15.

35. *My nachinaem KVN* (Moscow, 1996), 7.

36. Dmitriev interview, 2002. The head of the Moscow studio (its first) was E. Sharoeva. The fact that Sharoeva had a background in theater rather than radio or print media and that she was a woman are telling indications of the low status of television in its earliest period. Her successors were all male.

37. TsAOPIM, f. 2930, op. 1, d. 16, ll. 7–10.

38. Émigré media professionals interviewed in the seventies ranked self-censorship as more important than either Glavlit or redaktor-level interventions. See Lilita Dzirkals, Thane Gustafson, and A. Ross Johnson, *The Media and Intra-Elite Communication in the USSR* (Santa Monica, CA, 1982), 37–40.

United States, Kassil' used his appearance on television to, in his words, "talk simply about Americans," whom he described as "a great people" who "really know how to behave with an independent spirit" and "are free of the slightest primness and hypocrisy." The writer waxed rhapsodic about jazz dancing he had seen on a riverboat cruise along the Hudson and was also voluble on the subjects of air-conditioning and skyscrapers.[39] Gosteleradio responded immediately with a report to the CC explaining that Kassil' had "deviated" from the themes they had agreed on.[40] This was 1959, not 1954, the year Iurovskii maneuvered to broadcast Ho Chi Minh; the CC apparat was now far more alert and involved, and it ordered the trade journal *Soviet Radio and Television* (*Sovetskoe radio i televidenie*) to publish criticisms of both Kassil' and the central studio ("for giving the writer the possibility of improvising on a political theme before the TV camera").[41] TV staff in charge of the show got away with official reprimands—a comparatively light punishment but significant nonetheless, as V.N. Kozlovskii explained in a 2002 interview:

> Were we afraid of reprimands then? [Laughs] I don't know. It seems somehow funny now, but we were afraid then. And not only because, well, they took away your bonuses. These things were posted, and everyone came up to you: "So, what was it for? How did it happen?"...You had to explain to all of your acquaintances dozens of times a day why you got a reprimand. It was an unpleasant thing.[42]

The very public nature of the official reprimand served as a ringing reminder of the mutual dependency at the core of Soviet broadcasting culture. TV professionals had no choice but to rely on each other and on the people they invited as guests to show good judgment—to avoid deviations and play by the rules.

Given these difficulties, how can we explain early TV enthusiasts' ecstatic embrace of live broadcasting? Professional bravura? Certainly, the risky nature of live broadcasting added to the excitement and sense of camaraderie. No sooner had Kseniia Marinina recalled the sweat that rolled down her and her colleagues' backs during live shows than she declared, "But we were uncommonly enthusiastic about our work." Fear and enthusiasm, nerves and inspiration were two sides of one coin for early TV. Moreover, for people passionate about creating

39. RGANI, f. 5, op. 33, d. 105, ll. 53–56.

40. Ibid., l. 50. For excerpts from the Gosteleradio and CC reports as well as Kassil's speech, see N.S. Khrushchev, *Vospominaniia: Kniga vtoraia* (Moscow, 1999), 810–813.

41. "Telezriteli vozmushchaiutsia spravedlivo," *Sovetskoe radio i televidenie,* no. 6 (1959): 26. Kassil's comments may have been considered particularly noxious because he was best known as a writer for youth. Ann Livschiz, "De-Stalinizing Soviet Childhood," in *The Dilemmas of De-Stalinization: Negotiating Cultural and Social Change in the Khrushchev Era,* ed. Polly Jones (London, 2006), 129–130.

42. Kozlovskii interview, 2002.

television art, live broadcasting was the tool at hand in the 1950s and '60s. It is true that once videotape became more widely available, many people in TV welcomed the technology as a professional step up. But the fact that many others did not indicates that there was far more to the romance with live broadcasts than simple professional pride or a dearth of options. For many of TV's early enthusiasts, live broadcasting was the essence of television and a powerful social and moral force.

TELEVISION ART AND THE ENCHANTMENT OF "LIVING REALITY"

The most compelling elaboration of this vision of live television came not from an insider, interestingly enough, but from a theater critic named Vladimir Sappak, whose 1962 book, *Television and Us* (*Televidenie i my*), became the enthusiasts' bible.[43] To this day, it is rare to meet an enthusiast who fails to mention its genius. There are many reasons for this, not the least of which was its sheer novelty. Soviet newspapers and journals ran very little television criticism at the time, and book-length treatments were scarcer still. (We can recall that the party's first major statement on TV in 1960 directed print media to devote more attention to the medium.) But more important than the uniqueness of a book called *Television and Us* appearing on Soviet shelves was the uniqueness of the author's voice. From the very first page, Sappak presented the hallmark of his approach: an intensely personal and at times almost mystical reading of television's power.

Although Sappak was not among those ready to declare television already an art, he did see art in the making, and one of the tasks of his book was to help define the medium's formal qualities and promote its development. The essence of TV, he maintained, was the *effekt prisutstviia* ("presence effect"), or the ability of television broadcasting to transport its viewers psychologically, creating the sensation that they were present at the scene of the on-screen action. This quality was the purview of live broadcasting alone; for Sappak, film on television was not true television. What he wanted from TV—and what he thought only live TV could offer—was not fiction but truth.

> Yes, I can think of nothing more interesting than if the eyes of TV cameras managed to follow retirees on the boulevard or children playing on the street or—let's assume the impossible—the changing passengers of one taxi driver over the course of half an hour. We cannot even imagine which secrets would be revealed to us by life caught unawares [*zhizn', zastignutaia v rasplokh*].[44]

This statement, with its direct reference to the theoretical work of filmmaker Dziga Vertov, who first spoke of "catching life unawares" in the 1920s, is one of

43. G. V. Kuznetsov, *Sem' professional'nykh granei zhurnalista TV* (Moscow, 2001), 53.
44. V. Sappak, *Televidenie i my* (Moscow, 1962), 66.

the most frequently quoted passages from *Television and Us* and also, on the face of it, one of the most mysterious. Why, when there are children on the street and taxis on the corner, would we want to watch them on a screen? Why do we need a camera to see our neighbors?

The man who wrote *Television and Us,* it seems, had a simple and poignant answer. Chronically ill since childhood, Sappak was forced to spend much of his short life indoors (he would die before his book was published); we can well imagine TV broadcasting's particular vitality in his everyday world. But Sappak himself maintained that the experience of watching the world live on television had the power to transform everyday life for everyone and not only those who lacked social or cultural outlets. As he understood it, to watch life caught unawares by the TV camera was a qualitatively different experience than witnessing life physically before your eyes (or life represented in art). Sappak thought that live television had "perfect pitch for truth";[45] *podlinnost'* (authenticity) was in its very nature, and for this reason any false note or inconsistency was immediately apparent on the screen. *Television and Us* contains numerous examples of TV programs Sappak felt had been unmasked by the truth-telling capacity of the camera, often because they violated another of TV's natural qualities, *improvizatsionnost'* (spontaneity, or the quality of improvisation). These were not cases of gross deception but rather of small fakeries and insincerities—what Sappak called the "little lie." A journalist has a traffic cop stop a driver "at random" for an interview, but it is clear from each person's delivery that the entire episode has been carefully rehearsed.[46] Two doctors, a married couple, discuss their personal experiences working in Iraq, but their stories are unconvincing and the program boring because the doctors never even look at each other.[47] An actress in elegant evening wear discusses how hard she worked "to create the image of a modest laborer."[48] Voters interviewed at a polling station rattle off canned answers: "'Is this your first time voting? Is it a big event in your life? Is that so?'—'Yes, it is Election Day for the local Soviets. It's a big event in my life.'" Meanwhile, the reporter conducting the interview "has a constantly distracted look, doesn't listen to the answers, and shifts his weight from one leg to the other."[49]

In each of these cases, live television enabled viewers to see what would have been obvious had they been physically beside the camera: the staged quality of the action or emotion. This was part of the magic of TV's presence effect. But Sappak took the point even further by arguing that the experience of watching live television actually "sharpens our sense of truth"[50] and improves our

45. Ibid., 98.
46. Ibid., 58
47. Ibid., 117–122.
48. Ibid., 60.
49. Ibid., 123.
50. Ibid., 61.

ability to see the world around us. Because the television camera is "more sharp-sighted"[51] than the human eye, it can open up unknown vistas in everyday life, including the emotional and spiritual world of individuals. Only television, Sappak argued, was up to the task of reporting on Iurii Gagarin's historic space flight because only television was able to fulfill people's needs "to understand this person... to break through to something internal, confidential, and intimate."[52] For Sappak, *intimnost'* (intimacy) was, along with authenticity and spontaneity, one of live television's intrinsic qualities. He considered the special intimacy of TV important in relation not only to figures like Gagarin but also to the retirees on the boulevard, the married doctors just returned from Iraq, and the people at the polling station. Viewers needed to see and understand ordinary people from everyday life as much as, if not more than, they required knowledge of historic events and great figures; television, the "X-ray of character," would help them. In this sense, Sappak's vision of TV worked to resolve the paradox of the viewing experience—the private consumption of public culture—by socializing the medium. The intimacy engendered by the physical location of TV in the home was, for Sappak, a vital social link; thanks to the power of television broadcasting, solitary viewers gained new knowledge of one another and a new sense of community; viewership became participation, a civic act. Hence the title of his book: not *Television and Me* but *Television and Us*.

Though Sappak's was by far the most eloquent of voices in the contemporary discussion of television, many of the ideas discussed in *Television and Us* were then common currency. The defense of television as an art form (or a potential art form) typically began with praise for live broadcasting as "realistic and convincing by its very nature."[53] There was general agreement that TV, if true to itself, was natural, spontaneous, and sincere. Even the Glavradio, A. Puzin, complained at a 1956 meeting that people who appeared on television were "painfully constrained" and needlessly attempted to hide their prepared texts. "If someone cannot speak without a text, then sit him down at a table and let him use the text without hiding it from the viewer.... People [on television] need to behave more simply and more freely," he instructed.[54]

Sappak's sense that television's calling was to broadcast not fiction but life was also widely shared in this period, and as is so often the case with postwar Soviet cultural history, many people cite the International Youth Festival in 1957 as a major turning point in promoting change. Enthusiasts who chafed at TV's status as cultural go-between seized upon the festival as an opportunity to prove

51. Ibid., 57.

52. Ibid., 45.

53. Iurovskii, "Pogliadim na ekran," 126. More than forty years later, Iurovskii still proclaimed "live shows are what television was invented for." Interview with A. Iurovskii, December 2001 (Gosteleradiofond Oral History Project).

54. GARF, f. 6903, op. 1, d. 500, l. 9.

the medium's mettle: "to proclaim the power and capabilities of television far and wide," as one young TV worker put it.[55] To that end, Central TV undertook a serious lobbying campaign to improve its production capacity: the staff at Shabolovka (Boretskii again, plus Leonid Zolotarevskii and Sergei Muratov) drafted a letter, circulated it to various actors, writers, academicians, and other public figures for their signatures of support, and presented it directly to Khrushchev. It worked, and Central TV got an entire new studio built by military construction brigades, six new mobile cameras, and other equipment as well.[56] The boost to Central TV's production capacity made possible its extensive live coverage of the festival—221.5 hours over a period of roughly two weeks. For the first time in Soviet history, television cameras roamed Soviet public spaces, putting literally thousands of ordinary people on the screen, individually and in mass groups.[57] Thanks to its new studio space, Central TV was also able to offer countless interviews with foreign and Soviet delegates and to broadcast live performances. It was a crash course for Shabolovka's enthusiasts and, they thought, a resounding success. As they saw it, coverage of the festival demonstrated television's unique capacity to engage viewers as participants in civic life. "No, television did not talk about the festival," wrote Muratov and Georgii Fere. "It expressed the festival itself. [*Ono govorilo samim festival'em.*] For those days, we were not just viewers; we felt we were eyewitnesses.... No one doubted that this was truth of the highest order."[58]

Many enthusiasts, like Sappak, imagined that the most remarkable and unpredictable discoveries in life caught unawares by the TV camera would be in the workaday world of ordinary people. Val'do Pant, a director from Estonia, said that though there was "nothing simpler" than broadcasting an event like the festival—or, to give his example, an awards ceremony for a model milkmaid—there would be little to distinguish the report from ten others of the same type. "But visit her on an ordinary day and have her talk about her children, the apple trees, and the sick calf on the kolkhoz... this will be the most interesting event of the day."[59] Thanks to the TV camera's incomparable ability to penetrate into its subjects, viewers would gain a new, intimate, and most meaningful form of knowledge: an understanding of an individual personality.

The flip side of TV's inherent intimacy, its special connection to viewers at home, was another of Sappak's points with broad contemporary resonance. Iraklii Andronikov, a well-known literary scholar who was also an early enthusiast for TV, argued that the television broadcast was a fundamentally new

55. E. V. Gal'perina et al., eds., *KVN? KVN...KVN!* (Moscow, 1966), 9.

56. Interview with R. Boretskii, 2002 (Gosteleradiofond Oral History Project).

57. Local TV studios reported on preparations for the festival. RGASPI-m, f. 3, op. 15, d. 257, ll. 49–70.

58. S. Muratov and G. Fere, *Liudi, kotorye vkhodiat bez stuka* (Moscow, 1971), 3.

59. Fere, *Tovarishch TV*, 31.

form of cultural communication. "By addressing itself directly to the viewer, television breaks down the 'fourth wall' that separates the viewer from film and theater." The nature of speech on television, he maintained, was conversational and participatory in a way that distinguished it from other artistic media.[60] Film director Mikhail Romm, like Andronikov, was among a handful of intelligentsia figures in the fifties and sixties to write seriously about television's relationship to the established arts and to attempt an analysis of what made the new medium tick. Romm also stressed TV's intimacy, which he traced to the difference in filming techniques for the large and small screen. Whereas in cinema the cardinal rule was never to look directly into the camera, in television the opposite was true; the expectation was that the screen subject would meet the eyes of the viewer. For this reason, Romm reasoned, "when an announcer or a public figure invited to the studio speaks to the viewer, the viewer feels he is associating directly with him."[61] Television created a new kind of sociocultural experience.

Andronikov, Romm, and many others associated television's intimacy not only with its forms of address but also with its physical location in the home and its place in family life. An enthusiast from Ulianovsk TV drew a direct connection between domesticity and the style of broadcasting his studio pursued in 1961. "Thousands of people watch every program, but they watch in a domestic setting. And for this reason, we television workers aim for our shows to be natural [and] for there to be sincere [*zadushevnyi*] conversation and unconstrained talk on television."[62] In this connection, the figure of the television *diktor* (announcer; plural, *diktory*—a term adopted from radio) was considered by many people to be particularly important.

Soviet TV's first diktory were young and mostly female, and their function was to announce the following day's program schedule and to introduce and host individual shows. Their work also veered into the journalistic—they might conduct interviews, for example—although they were not responsible for writing their own material.[63] They were, by all accounts, the subject of intense viewer interest and sympathy.[64] Glavradio Puzin told his staff approvingly that viewers felt themselves to be on intimate terms with diktory, and that this was to be ex-

60. Iraklii Andronikov and Manna Andronikova, "Zametki o televidenii," *IK*, no. 2 (1963): 98.

61. M. Romm, "Pogliadim na dorogu," *IK*, no. 11 (1959): 128.

62. "Svetiat golubye ekrany," *Ulianovskaia pravda,* 14 December 1961, in GARF, f. 6903, op. 3, d. 175, l. 36.

63. The diktor was especially important prior to 1959, when print media first began publishing TV schedules. Female announcers were also common in early television in Europe and North America.

64. For a cinematic portrayal of the viewer-diktor relationship, see Nikita Mikhailkov's 1978 film *Five Evenings (Piat' vecherov)*.

Figure 5.1. Diktor Svetlana Zhil'tsova, 1965. V. Gende-Rote/ITAR-TASS. Used with permission.

pected: "We really are entering into people's apartments, you see." When Nina Kondrat'eva was injured on the job, he reported, people telephoned the studio asking after her. "You know, she's like a member of the family at our place," they explained. "When she wasn't there anymore, it was as if a relative were missing."[65] Viewers called Kondrat'eva and her colleagues at Central TV by their first names and diminutives (e.g., Nina, Valechka), and viewers of local television also developed relationships with their own diktory; in 1961 one regional newspaper objected strongly to the fact that diktory remained anonymous on

65. GARF, f. 6903, op. 1, d. 500, ll. 9–10.

the local station when every viewer felt a natural desire to know their names.[66] Many Soviets avidly followed their clothing and hairstyle changes from evening to evening and inundated them with letters, often of a personal nature.[67] Mikhail Romm noted that children had a tendency to talk back to the image of the diktor, and more interesting still, he reported that he did, too. "I myself feel the need to say goodbye to the diktor when she says good-bye to me. And if I am watching television alone, I do."[68]

Contemporary television enthusiasts admired diktory for their relationship with viewers, which they saw as a talented exploitation of the medium's nature. In another famous phrase from *Television and Us*, Sappak declared diktor Valentina Leont'eva "the most interesting thing on the TV screen."[69] Sappak appreciated Leont'eva for her genuineness and her ability to communicate directly to her viewers; what made her interesting, he thought, was that she was able to remain herself during broadcasts, "an 'ordinary person' and even in some sense our representative on the other side of the screen."[70] Several years later, an article on Leont'eva in the illustrated magazine *Ogonek* (with the tellingly cozy title "Diktor Valia") sounded the same note. "In everything he [sic] does, the diktor achieves truthfulness and natural improvisation. That's the only way the feeling of closeness between those who are in the frame and those who watch the TV screen can arise."[71]

For much of the 1950s, when Soviet consumers had few places to turn for images of their contemporaries, aside from political leaders and model workers, and little information on things like fashion and hairstyles, television could be an important resource. Print media did begin to provide more visually engaging formats and more coverage of individuals in the latter part of the decade. *Soviet Screen,* the movie magazine revived in 1957, was part of the new wave, and we know readers were fascinated by its star imagery and put it to good use in their daily lives. But even if viewers copied diktor Ninochka's hairstyle just as often as Liudmila Gurchenko's or Audrey Hepburn's, we can sense that the relationship enacted was quite different by nature. Viewers typically did not refer to their favorite film stars by diminutive forms as they did with their favorite announcers.[72] Diktory were everyday and domestic figures in a literal sense (they visited viewers daily in their homes), whereas film actors, though domesticated

66. "Ob izcheznuvshei oblozhke iz anonimnykh diktorakh," *Sovetskaia Tatariia*, 23 December 1961 in GARF, f. 6903, op. 3, d. 175, l. 42.

67. Diktor Valentina Leont'eva described her correspondence in *Ob"iasnenie v liubvi* (Moscow, 1980).

68. Romm,"Pogliadim na dorogu," 128.

69. Sappak, *Televidenie i my,* 50.

70. Ibid., 53.

71. E. Kabalkina, "Diktor Valia," *Ogonek*, no. 8 (1966): 13.

72. Razzakov, *Zvezdy televideniia*, 15.

in the form of postcards and mass media imagery, were understood to be figures from a different world. (Hence the frisson of domestication.) Moreover, Soviet announcers themselves cultivated a different kind of relationship with their viewers. A 1958 training seminar for diktory from all over the USSR had them focus on connecting with viewers through a positive frame of mind.

> I am sitting or standing in the studio... in just a few more seconds, the signal light will go on, and I will appear on the screens of thousands and tens of thousands of TV viewers. My mood? It should be wonderful, and everything negative left at the doorway of the studio. I want viewers to be in a good mood too. I want to report to them what I need to report to them but [convey that] everything is very interesting, of course, and that I myself am extremely interested and cannot help but share it all with everyone.[73]

The model diktor reached out to viewers as trusted confidants and was responsible for their psychological well-being. The fact that the diktor's slot in the fifties and early sixties was filled overwhelmingly by women was critical to the image. TV critic Anri Vartanov argued that announcers embraced their role as "custodians of the TV hearth [and] priestesses of the cathedral of television" and were embraced by viewers as representatives of ideal womanhood.[74]

For contemporary enthusiasts, the diktor phenomenon—viewers' evident attachment to Valia, Ninochka, and their colleagues—served to confirm their conceptions about the nature of television broadcasting. The popularity of the girl-next-door diktor demonstrated that TV was intrinsically a medium for ordinary people and everyday life and that its natural mode was one of intimate conversation and documentary realism. "We live in an amazing world, where the interconnection between individual people—even between neighbors on the same floor—is sometimes imperceptible," mused Muratov and Fere in a book of interviews with TV show hosts, including Leont'eva. "And on the other hand, mysterious contacts have sprung up with people who are located practically on the other side of the country. No one today thinks it strange that a certain woman from Siberia would write a letter to a woman she didn't know, a popular diktor from Central TV, and share the kinds of thoughts that one usually shares only with the closest of friends."[75] For TV's enthusiasts, television was consumed *by* isolated individuals, but it was essentially a community space *of* individuals: the milkmaid, the diktor, the guest writer, Gagarin and Khrushchev, and viewers themselves. Television's innate authenticity, spontaneity, and intimacy forced people to experience each other and their world as never before.

73. N. Zimchenko, "Diktor televideniia," *Sovetskoe radio i televidenie,* no. 1 (1959): 26–27.

74. Anri Vartanov, "Bednaia Valia, a takzhe Tania, Anelia i, konechno, Bella," *IK,* no. 6 (1991): 27.

75. Muratov and Fere, *Liudi, kotorye vkhodiat,* 1.

The enchantment with live broadcasting and putting ordinary people on screen was an international phenomenon in television's early years. But in the Soviet context, it had a distinctive resonance in both contemporary and historical terms. TV enthusiasm tapped into a powerful Soviet cultural tradition and, in particular, into Dziga Vertov's aesthetics. Vertov famously anathematized fictional films in the 1920s as "leprous" and "mortally dangerous" and declared *kinopravda*—the filmed exploration of real life—the only true cinema of the revolutionary working class and of communism.[76] It was Vertov, too, who first hailed the camera, or *kinoglaz* (film-eye), as superior to human sight, able to penetrate the essence of all phenomena, including the human character. And it was Vertov who first proclaimed that the consumption of "living reality" would improve viewers by perfecting their understanding of the world and each other; with *kinopravda,* one could "unite all workers scattered over the earth through a single consciousness, a single bond, a single collective will in the battle for communism."[77]

Although most enthusiasts did not cite Vertov directly (Sappak did), his vision—and in a more general sense, the vision of the Soviet cinematic avant-garde—was latent in their understanding of the medium and themselves as TV workers. By embracing the ideal of "living reality" and "truth" on the screen as a progressive social force, TV enthusiasts created a bridge across the Stalinist past to an earlier and, to their eyes, purer era of revolutionary culture.[78] At a meeting of TV staff to discuss the recent Twentieth Party Congress in 1956, many people laid the blame for the poor quality of their broadcasts squarely at the feet of the "cult of personality." The culture of the cult—pompous, dogmatic, and artificial—had been a violation of television's nature. Now people would have to relearn how "to think and lay out their own thoughts" and how to listen to and trust one another.[79]

Television's enthusiasts could make common cause with many contemporary intellectuals in the project of overcoming the Stalinist legacy, but they also stood out in their belief that they alone had enlisted modernity, the incomparable presence effect of live broadcasting, on their side. The TV camera was not only

76. See D. Vertov, "We: Variant of a Manifesto," in *Kino-Eye: The Writings of Dziga Vertov,* ed. Annette Michelson (Berkeley, 1984), 5–9.

77. In the fifties and sixties, the Vertovian term "living reality" (*zhivaia realnost*) was more common than "life caught unawares" (*zhizn', zastignutaia v rasplokh*), although both were in use. Vertov also saluted Soviet experiments with television, which he called "radio-cinema." Michelson, *Kino-Eye,* 49, 56.

78. This leapfrog maneuver was a key mechanism of thaw culture. See Katerina Clark, "Changing Historical Paradigms in Soviet Culture," in *Late Soviet Culture: From Perestroika to Novostroika,* ed. Thomas Lahusen and Gene Kuperman (Durham, NC, 1993), 298; Stephen V. Bittner, *The Many Lives of Khrushchev's Thaw: Experience and Memory in Moscow's Arbat* (Ithaca, NY, 2008).

79. GARF, f. 6903, op. 1, d. 502, ll. 1–26.

truthful for them; it had "perfect pitch for truth," and the simple act of watching actually improved the viewer. Moreover, television for them had a populist sensibility (*demokratizm,* said Sappak) that no other medium could match. With its presumed natural connection to everyday life and ordinary people, television could not help but shift the focus of Soviet society from the leader to the community, from the cult of personality to the development and interaction of many personalities.

Yet this project, for all its language of *demokratizm,* assigned the pivotal role to TV professionals, and here again, the tradition of the Soviet avant-garde was very important. While Vertov rhapsodized about the virtues of the camera as a machine with sensory powers superior to those of contemporary humans, he also stressed the role of the camera operator (or director) in what he called the "organization" or the "choice of facts" (to wit, the title of his most influential film: *Chelovek s kinoapparatom,* usually translated as *Man with a Movie Camera*). The choice of facts was critical, he argued, because "it will *suggest the necessary decision* to the worker or peasant."[80] In this scenario, to apprehend *kinopravda,* viewers needed the people behind the camera as much as the camera itself.

For TV enthusiasts, the promotion of living reality was a bridge over troubled Stalinist waters (a means to transport viewers in spirit to better, purer revolutionary days), but it was also a connection to the heroic era of Soviet cinema in the twenties, enabling TV enthusiasts to imagine their work as its modern-day counterpart. When Leonid Dmitriev and his colleagues spoke of early Soviet TV as terra incognita, they echoed Sergei Eisenstein, to choose one example, who once described Soviet cinema in the 1920s as having no antecedents ("something not yet existent" was his phrase).[81] Neither cinema in the twenties nor TV in the fifties was wholly new. Ian Christie has argued that the denial of the prerevolutionary cinematic tradition was the keystone of a "creation myth" that established Soviet cinema as a "quintessentially 'Soviet'" art form.[82] Although the TV enthusiasts did not deny their creative debts in such a radical manner, they did position themselves in the same tradition as pioneering Soviet artists, discovering a new art for a new age. By making the bridge to the twenties, the enthusiasts gained a vision of themselves as critical cultural authorities—a vision that stressed not only Soviet society's need for television's truth in the aftermath of Stalinism but also Soviet viewers' need for *them* to organize and present it.

---

80. D. Vertov in Michaleson, *Kino-Eye,* 49 (my italics). Consider also some of the film's imagery: the giant striding legs of the man with the movie camera towering over ordinary folk.

81. Eisenstein quoted in Ian Christie, "Canons and Careers: The Director in Soviet Cinema," in *Stalinism and Soviet Cinema,* ed. Richard Taylor and D. W. Spring (London, 1993), 146.

82. Ibid., 146.

Soviet television's young enthusiasts had little opportunity to put their ideas into action as studios struggled with inadequate resources. Their first major break came only in 1957 in conjunction with Moscow's International Youth Festival. As part of the run-up activities to the festival, a group of enthusiasts at Shabolovka designed a show they called *Evening of Merry Questions* (*Vecher veselykh voprosov*), best known by its initials, *VVV*.[83] In theory, the show was to be an engaging forum to educate young people about festival themes, and it took inspiration from two sources: the most popular program on Czechoslovak TV at the time, a quiz show called *GGG*, and the comedy-theater groups, or *kapustniki*, that had blossomed in student circles after Stalin's death.[84] Years later, people remembered *VVV* as a rallying cry for everyone who thought TV's festival programming should "proclaim the power and the capacity of television far and wide."[85]

How did this enthusiasm translate on the screen? *VVV* was live, interactive, person-centered TV and, unlike its distant American cousins, it was wide open; *VVV* did not preselect its contestants but rather invited members of the studio audience to play at random—for example, by choosing seat numbers from a drum filled with ticket stubs. (Granted, the audience itself was not a truly random cross-section of society, as the studio distributed many tickets through Komsomol and university channels.) One show invited newlywed couples on stage and quizzed them separately about their wedding day (e.g., "What was the weather like?"). The winning couple was the one with the most matching answers. An-

---

83. The initial idea for *VVV* is credited to Muratov, who worked in Shabolovka's "Festival'naia" redaktsiia and had met the director of the Czech show in Moscow. (*GGG*, or *Gadai, gadai, gadal'shchik—Guess, Guess, You Guessers*—is the Russian translation of that Czech show). Muratov wrote a first draft of a script for *VVV* with Andrei Donatov and Mikhail Iakovlev; two well-known *kapustnik* performers, Al'bert Aksel'rod and Mark Rozovskii, were soon brought on to the project. Interview with Sergei Muratov, Moscow, June 2002; "KVN: Vzgliad cherez chetvert' veka," in *Televidenie—Vchera, segodnia, zavtra,* vyp. 7th ed. (Moscow, 1987), 84–85; Masha Topaz, "VVV, ili bochka s porokhom," *Sem' dnei,* no. 29 (1995): 38.

84. *Kapustniki* refer to improvisational comedic (often satiric) performances. Historically, they are associated with turn-of-the-century Russian actors, who performed for one another after hours and, too poor to buy meat, shared cabbage *pirozhki* (hence, the name *kapustnik,* from the word for cabbage). Kapustniki are also associated with prerevolutionary university culture, and many thaw-era student groups saw themselves in the kapustnik tradition. Although kapustniki sometimes skirted the edge of political propriety, they were also encouraged by the regime, along with other forms of amateur performance (*samodeiatel'nost'*), as one solution to the youth recreation problem. See L. P. Solntseva and M. V. Iunisov, eds., *Samodeiatel'noe khodozhestvennoe tvorchestvo v SSSR: Ocherki istorii* (St. Petersburg, 1999), especially M. V. Iunisov, "Studencheskii teatr estradnykh miniatur," 281–306. See also Iunisov's interesting monograph, *Mifopoetika studencheskogo smekha (STEM i KVN)* (Moscow, 1999).

85. Gal'perina et al., *KVN?,* 9.

other show asked contestants to specify how a cat climbs down from a tree: head first or tail first? *VVV* also included home viewers in the game, inviting them to the studio during the broadcast. On one show, the challenge was to bring a ficus plant, a samovar, and the third volume of Jack London's collected works to the studio; another called for babies with the initials V.V.V. who had been born on the day of the program's premiere.[86] Viewers who met the challenge were given a small prize (a frying pan, in one case) and interviewed right on the air.

With its open-door policy and open-ended format, *VVV* was a radical departure from Soviet broadcasting norms. But equally radical, perhaps, were its theme and tone. Let us consider for a moment the company *VVV* was keeping on the First Channel on the days of its first and second broadcasts.[87]

MAY 2, 1957

1:00 p.m.	Test frame
1:43	Concert of song and dance by the Central Children's House of Railway Workers—TV program, in studio
2:04	*Starye znakomye (Old Acquaintances)*—cartoon film
2:40	Continuation of Central Children's House concert
2:51	*Korablik (Little Ship)*—cartoon film
2:58	*Kosmetika (Cosmetics)*—film
3:48	Opening of the summer sports season—sports reportage
4:00	*Borzhomskoe ushchel'e (Borhzomi Gorge)*—documentary film sketch
4:55	Soccer: first half—sports reportage
5:05	*Sovetskii sport (Soviet Sport)*—newsreel
5:56	Soccer: second half—sports reportage
7:30	Test frame
8:05	*Festival'naia No. 4*—TV journal on the International Youth Festival
8:39	*Songs of the Native Country*—TV program, in studio, literary theme
8:48	*Vesennie melodii (Spring melodies)*—documentary film
10:42	*VVV*
11:01	*Litovskii kontsert, Na lesnoi poliane (Lithuanian Concert, In a Forest Clearing)*—documentary films
12:46 a.m.	Continuation of *VVV*

JUNE 9, 1957

1:45 p.m.	Test frame
1:58	*Etikh dnei ne smolkaet slava (The Glory of Those Days Is Never-Ending)*—TV program, in studio, for children

86. Each of the people involved remembers the details a bit differently. (One says it was the seventh volume of Jack London, another, the third; someone recalls a primus stove instead of a samovar; and so on.) But there is general agreement on the main features of the program's format.

87. Personal archive of Sergei Muratov, Moscow.

2:05	*Bronenosets Potemkina (Battleship Potemkin)*—1925 film
3:10	*V masterskikh MTS (In the Workshops of Machine Tractor Stations)*—documentary film
7:15	TV schedule for the coming week
7:28	*Verses of Italian, German, and Spanish Poets*—TV program, in studio
8:00	*VVV*
9:38	*Kino-zagadka (Cinema Riddle)*—TV program
10:09	Continuation of *VVV*

In comparison with what Central TV had to offer in October 1956, these two schedules show a good deal more original television programming (studio programs with song, dance, and poetry, reportage, etc.). Note, too, that there is no news programming on either day; the only show with a clear and timely connection to public affairs is *Festival'nyi*—a mix of in-studio interviews and performances, journalistic reports, and newsreel footage with commentary. This "TV journal" format was then spreading rapidly on Soviet TV and would become a mainstay of programming for years to come.

The overall impression conveyed by the May and June 1957 schedules is of a serious, educational approach to programming; the only shows evidently geared toward entertainment were the sports programs (and possibly the concert of song and dance). Yet sports, however entertaining for the viewer, still held out the opportunity for educational and ideological work in a Soviet context. Sports programming presented athletes as ideal Soviet types on and off the field and as models for youth, especially young men.[88] Whether or how this complex of ideas about Sovietness and masculinity contributed to the viewing experience is another question. The point here is that sports on Soviet TV had no less a place as educational programming than did *Verses of Italian, German, and Spanish Poets*.

VVV, on the other hand, was a fish out of water in the context of Soviet TV circa 1957. Although the show had a nominal connection to the International Youth Festival and incorporated some questions with a festival theme, the emphasis in this evening of merry questions was very much on the merry. The contestants were not presented as models; they were random people answering random questions with no discernible goal. (The show's creators, after flirting with the idea of offering more substantial prizes, decided that this would run counter to the spirit of the show and settled on funny, token ones.) This was an entertainment, it would seem, for entertainment's sake.

VVV was, by all accounts, very popular among viewers, but scandal brought it to an early end just a few months after its debut. For its third broadcast on September 29, 1957, the show's writers designed a contest around the Russian

---

88. On sports, Soviet culture, and Soviet gender ideals, see Robert Edelman, *Serious Fun: A History of Spectator Sports in the USSR* (New York, 1993), and *Spartak Moscow: A History of the People's Team in the Workers' State* (Ithaca, 2009).

proverb *gotov sani letom, a telegu zimoi* ("Get your sled ready in the summer, and your cart ready in the winter"); the challenge was to show up during the broadcast wearing a sheepskin coat, felt boots, and a hat and carrying a samovar. Earlier *VVV* competitions had attracted at most a few dozen contestants; this challenge brought six to seven hundred to the theater in the MGU complex where they were broadcasting. It was a hot day, and according to eyewitnesses, cars and buses packed with overdressed, sweaty people hauling samovars caused giant traffic jams along local roads. One of the ushers at the theater that night later said the people who came to the studio were agitated because the prize was a comparatively luxurious one: a new bicycle.[89] Here is how the head of the Moscow studio described the scene: "The audience that showed up was frightening to watch; drunk, wearing tattered, ripped sheepskin coats, they forced their way through the gates of MGU and broke down the door to the auditorium."[90] Someone brought a live chicken. With the cameras still rolling, the crowd rushed the stage, shouting and cursing, and the curtain was torn down.[91] The show's host, the popular composer Nikita Bogoslovskii, stood by in shock and was soon toppled off the stage in the melée. (Ultimately he would flee the scene altogether.)[92] Meanwhile, the head of the MGU Komsomol organization stood up from his seat in the audience and shouted, "Komsomol members, gather around me!" A group of students then took control of the situation by forming a human barrier to the stage. After some delay, *VVV*'s director decided to cut the transmission, leaving viewers with a silent screen that announced a station break "for technical reasons." Only later did the police arrive, approximately forty-five minutes after they had been summoned by Shabolovka's director.

The response of the Soviet authorities to the scandal was swift and harsh. Within a day, Gosteleradio called a postmortem, and punitive decrees from its offices and those of the CC soon followed. The story that emerged from the official investigations was one of miscalculations and mishaps. As it turned out, the host, Bogoslovskii, had neglected to mention a key element in the contest (a copy of a newspaper from December 31, 1956) that would have made it far more difficult and presumably lowered the number of would-be contestants.[93]

89. *Kak eto bylo* (*The Way It Was*). ORT (Obshchestvennoe Rossisskoe Televidenie, the post-Soviet Russian successor [as of 1995] to Soviet TV's Channel One), 1998.

90. GARF, f. 6903, op. 1, d. 532, l. 5. Boretskii, who was in the fourth row, recalled a "huge crowd" of "construction workers... some sort of *zeks* [ex-cons] who, given that it was a Saturday, were three sheets to the wind." Boretskii interview, 2002.

91. Masha Topaz, "VVV," 38.

92. Accounts of what happened to Bogoslovskii vary. One report has it that he hid in a wardrobe. *My nachinaem KVN*, 9. He remembers fleeing in a car with his cohost. N. Bogoslovskii, *Chto bylo i chego ne bylo i koe-chto eshche* (Moscow, 1999), 277.

93. *My nachinaem KVN*, 11. Muratov recalled rejecting the contest idea as too simple, remembering a warning from the director of *GGG* about easy contests. He was on a business trip when the show aired; Aksel'rod and Iakovlev approved the contest at the last minute,

The size of the crowd had been unexpectedly swollen by the large numbers of construction workers who were then building the new housing sites nearby (the projects at Novye Cheremushki) and lived in dormitories, where people kept all their winter gear at hand. Even once the crowd had grown, the director of the program, Kseniia Marinina, had hesitated to cut the transmission because she had nothing on hand to replace it. Though it was standard practice to have a feature film available in case of technical problems, in this case, the reserve film was locked in a safe, and the young man who held the keys had left work early to go on a date.[94] Besides, as Marinina reported to the postmortem meeting, the studio was getting phone calls from viewers pleading with them *not* to cut the transmission—itself an interesting comment on at least some viewers' taste.[95] And who could blame them? *VVV* under siege must have made for a gripping spectacle, particularly in its context. Television broadcasting itself was still an exotic and exciting phenomenon in these early years, and what happened on 29 September 1957 was something more than just television; it was an eruption of everyday Moscow life and Muscovites, messy and unpredictable, inside Soviet media space.

In the official discussions and decrees that followed the broadcast, television and party authorities repeatedly returned to the question of who had been allowed on the Soviet screen and how they had looked. Gosteleradio chief D. I. Chesnokov exclaimed, "You let ragged and drunk people on television—it's a kind of sacrilege [*profanatsiia*]."[96] "Just the fact that the program was cut off midway, even if it had been a good one in all respects, is already a scandal. But it is not only that. Everything here has marks of a political nature. We saw a crowd, dirty people, people dressed for the dirtiest jobs. This borders on provocation."[97] The CC went so far as to suggest that poorly dressed people had been "clearly seeking to underscore their poverty and slovenliness" on Soviet television.[98] But whatever the motives of either TV professionals or would-be contestants, the end result, from the perspective of the authorities, was the same: Soviet TV had broadcast "a large group of unorganized and random [*sluchainye*] television viewers who *cannot be shown on television.*"[99] The scandal at *VVV* cost the director of the central studio his job, along with those of the studio's top redaktor and a handful of lower-rank-

---

adding the newspaper element to make it more difficult. Bogoslovskii forgot to mention this last element. "KVN: Vzgliad cherez chetvert' veka," 86.

94. *My nachinaem KVN,* 9.

95. GARF, f. 6903, op. 1, d. 532, l. 15.

96. Ibid., l. 8.

97. Ibid., l. 26.

98. "'Veselye voprosy' s pechal'nym otvetom," published in *Sem' dnei* in 1995. From personal archive of Sergei Muratov.

99. GARF, f. 6903, op. 1, d. 532, l. 2 (my italics).

ing personnel.[100] The festival *redaktsiia* responsible for the show (which was de facto the "youth" *redaktsiia*, as the studio had no other) was liquidated.

VVV was already challenging convention by inviting ordinary people to participate in the shows as themselves—not as scripted props or social categories brought to life (the leading worker, the prize-winning athlete, the model plant manager, and so on) but as game show contestants, Muscovites, ordinary people. What the *VVV* scandal exposed was the very uneasy status of the real and the ordinary inside Soviet media space. As Chesnokov had pointed out, there were some people who simply could not be shown. Soviet television was no place for the workaday world with its dirty clothes, unruliness, and drunkenness.[101] For Chesnokov, who had joined the party in 1939 and made a career in the Stalinist era, the image of dirty and drunken people on *VVV* was nothing short of sacrilege; Soviet media space was sacred. But even outside the quasi-religious idiom of Stalinism, all Soviet media had an "otherworldly" quality because they were fundamentally aspirational and instructional. When drunken, unruly people appeared in a Soviet newspaper or on TV, they were clearly marked; they were hooligans or some other identifiable category, and whether in a satiric or a serious context, they were there to make a point. But the people who erupted on screen during *VVV* and even the show's usual contestants were not at all defined; they were random characters and so bereft of obvious purpose. In the language of the day, these people were parasites in Soviet media space; they had no *work* to do there. Worse still, their very presence ran the risk of degrading ideals altogether. While the discussion at Gosteleradio (and its subsequent decree) focused largely on the issues of control—how the contest had been approved, why TV staff did not respond sooner, etc.—officials at the Central Committee damned *VVV* altogether for its vulgarity (*poshlost'*) and lack of ideological principle (*bezydeinost'*). Citing the "which way does a cat climb" question and others, they concluded that the show's content was "calculated to make fools of and degrade the dignity of the Soviet people." In the eyes of the Central Committee, the problem with *VVV* had begun long before the scandal; by design, the show was a "mockery" of the Soviet citizenry inspired by "the worst methods and morals of bourgeois television."[102]

100. Muratov was asked to resign and complied. He continued to work for Soviet TV on a freelance basis, but the focus of his activities shifted to TV criticism and scholarship.

101. According to contemporary codes of conduct, wearing work clothes anywhere outside work was *nekul'turno* (uncultured). See Olga Vainshtein, "Female Fashion, Soviet Style: Bodies of Ideology," in *Russia—Women—Culture,* ed. H. Goscilo and B. Holmgren (Bloomington, IN, 1996), 66–67. Broadcasting a violation of this work/nonwork boundary made it even more transgressive given the nature of Soviet media culture (its modeling role).

102. "'Veselye voprosy' s pechal'nym otvetom." The CC's comments may have been partly motivated by the fact that there were foreign correspondents in the audience. Muratov

In recent times, *VVV* has been presented as a symbol of the thaw and the dreams of the *shestidesiatniki* (people of the sixties). A 1995 article (written, not coincidentally, by Muratov's wife, Masha Topaz) set the stage for its account of the scandal by invoking the "sun of freedom" that "rose over the country" in 1956. "The youthful minds of the 'children of the Twentieth Party Congress'... were filled with joyful hopes, creative projects, and brilliant ideas," one of which, we are given to understand, was *VVV*.[103] A 1998 TV program on the scandal from the series *The Way It Was* (*Kak eto bylo*) struck a similar bittersweet tone, as Muratov, Bogoslovskii, Marinina, and other people involved in the show reminisced on stage about their youthful passion for television, and the program's host played for laughs by reading from the CC's report with mock gravitas. Enthusiast historians have also presented the scandal as a deliberate move by the authorities to put young TV workers "in their place" lest the success of their festival programming go to their heads and, in a broader sense, as part of Khrushchev's crackdown on the intelligentsia in the latter part of 1957.[104]

Though the timing of the scandal does place it in the midst of one of Khrushchev's periodic cultural sweeps,[105] the fact is that the authorities were undoubtedly right, on their own terms, about the inappropriateness of a show like *VVV* for Soviet television. *VVV was* meaningless entertainment, in context, and this was a problem in itself. But even if it had provided an evening of serious rather than merry questions, its wide-open format would still have made it incompatible with Soviet media practices. The brainchild of young TV workers experimenting with the medium, *VVV* shows many elements of the TV enthusiasm I have described: the romance with live television and its ability to break the screen barrier between subject and viewer, the ideal of audience participation, the interest in ordinary people and everyday life, and the open, unpredictable quality implicit in the idea of life caught unawares. By design, *VVV* extended an open-door invitation to anyone, and thus to anyone's problems (alcoholism, poverty), without incorporating them into a broader ideological framework. What the *VVV* episode demonstrated, then, was not so much the impossibility of the real and the ordinary on Soviet television as the necessity for framing and

---

and his colleagues are convinced to this day that the *VVV* scandal was reported in the *New York Times* and other Western media outlets. Muratov interview, June 2002. I have not found any reports in the New York press. NBC's Moscow correspondent did later recount the scandal in a book, but it is not clear whether he was in attendance at the broadcast. Irving R. Levine, *Main Street, USSR: Selections from the Original Edition* (New York, 1960), 68.

103. Topaz, "VVV."

104. *Ocherki po istorii rossiiskogo televideniia,* 78–80.

105. State Department Intelligence Report, "The Soviet Union in 1957: A Review of Internal Developments," February 1958, 14.

packaging them; life caught unawares demanded an interpretation on Soviet television.[106]

There would be no more live, open-access shows like *VVV* on Soviet TV until the days of perestroika, and in this sense, the events of September 1957 demonstrate the defeat of a certain idealized vision of television. Yet at the same time, the subsequent evolution of Soviet TV programming shows that the same enthusiasts who had devised *VVV* also supported and developed the idea of packaging the real and the ordinary for viewers. And in this light, the *VVV* episode looks less like a defeat than a learning experience. TV enthusiasts stepped up to the plate to fulfill the interpretive demand on Soviet television—to replace the random with the marked, give purpose to the purposeless, provide models for lichnost' and social activity. And for the most prominent example of this, we need look no further than the successor to *VVV,* the famous *KVN.*

KVN AND THE MODEL INDIVIDUAL

Soviet TV turned its back on the game show format for four long years after *VVV.* Around Shabolovka, the show was a "symbol of calamity," remembered Elena Gal'perina, who joined the staff after its demise. Although Gal'perina heard the warnings of her colleagues, she admired *VVV* as "the kind of real television for which so many of us—print journalists, theater critics, actors—...had switched our vocations."[107] In 1961, as head of a new youth redaktsiia, Gal'perina enlisted *VVV* veterans and other enthusiasts to work on a new game show.

The result was a live contest of wits they called *KVN,* for *Club of the Merry and Quick-Witted* (*Klub veselykh i nakhodchivykh*)—a clever name, not only because the concept of clubs as a way to organize youth recreation was then current but because the initials K.V.N. were well known from the KVN-49, one of the first Soviet TV sets.[108] *KVN* debuted in November 1961 as a monthly (more or less) broadcast and went on to become one of the most popular Soviet television shows of all time and an important social phenomenon as well. *KVN* competitions ran on regional TV too, and there were local *KVN* teams in schools and factories, on kolkhozy and in the armed forces, among taxi drivers and shop clerks. *KVN-shchiki* (*KVN* players and fans) today claim that the popularity of the game was so great that even Soviet prisoners set up teams. *KVN,* they say, was and remains a "way of life."[109] Some contestants on the televised show went on to become

---

106. I am not arguing that the drive for interpretation was unique to Soviet TV. The field of television studies has produced an extensive literature on how the process of framing and packaging works on TV and to what ends, primarily in the English-speaking world.

107. Rozov, *Shabolovka,* 206.

108. The KVN-49 set was named for its three designers (V. K. Kenigson, N. M. Varshavskii, and I. A. Nikolaevskii) and the year it went on the market. For the history of TV technology in the USSR, see V. A. Urvalov, *Ocherki istorii televideniia* (Moscow, 1990).

109. *My nachinaem KVN,* 15.

Figure 5.2. Enthusiasts: KVN's founders (from left to right), M. Iakovlev, E. Gal'perina, A. Aksel'rod, S. Muratov. Courtesy of the personal archive of Sergei Muratov.

well-known performing artists; many *KVN* team members, especially captains, enjoyed popularity rivaling that of contemporary movie stars. The show itself was resurrected in the glasnost era and still runs on Russian TV today.[110]

KVN's origins in Soviet TV's flirtation with merry questions are not difficult to detect. Like *VVV, KVN* was broadcast live before a studio audience, and it was meant to be funny, zany, and somewhat irreverent. But it was also different in important and telling ways. First, *KVN* took care of the social-category

110. Among the most famous *KVN-shchiki* who went on to stage careers were Gennadyi Khazanov, Leonid Iakubovich, and Mikhail Zhvanetskii. On the work of Khazanov and Zhvanetskii, see Richard Stites, *Russian Popular Culture* (New York, 1992), 184; 167–168. On the popularity of *KVN* teams, see Petr Vail' and Aleksandr Genis, *60-e: Mir sovetskogo cheloveka* (Moscow, 1996), 151; interview with Iurii Makarov (former captain of the Odessa team), New York, May 2002. *KVN* has become an international phenomenon, with clubs and competitions in many former Soviet republics as well as the United States, Israel, Germany, and other countries. For information on today's International Union of KVN, see the official site at http://www.amik.ru.

problem—the troublesome randomness of *VVV*—by limiting contestants to one group: students, overwhelmingly male, who competed in teams to defend the honor of their institutes. (This was the initial design; only under pressure did the show expand its base in later years to include teams from factories and, ultimately, cities and republics.) Moreover, *KVN* had none of the uncomfortable domesticity, no intrusion of personal objects and problems, that was evident in *VVV*; the contestants were on air in a semiprofessional capacity as students (or, later, workers, Kiev-ers, etc.), and they had a job to do: to win for the honor of their group. Second, all the young people who appeared on *KVN* were well screened and well scrubbed; they were models of youthful energy, camaraderie, and wit. And although the program was broadcast live, television workers did their best to rule out unpredictability by standardizing the competitions.[111] *KVN* teams were required to think on their feet—one contest presented them with a briefcase full of odd items and had them devise a story on the spot about its owner and how he had lost it—but they were also allowed to prepare some material (skits, songs, verse, etc.) ahead of time that was thoroughly vetted by the show's editors. For example, there was a standard contest called BRIZ for Biuro po Ratsionalizatsii i Izobretatel'stvu (Office for Rationalization and Inventiveness) that had competitors present their ideas for, say, a university on the moon.[112] Finally, *KVN*, unlike *VVV*, worked to censor shows in progress; in theory, as soon as contestants began to tell a joke that had not been cleared or was considered too controversial, the sound would be cut off and the camera would cut to a shot of one of the show's young assistants sitting in the audience.[113] As of 1968, the show was also videotaped and edited.

KVN earned a reputation for daring, and it is true that there were instances when contestants pushed their satire further than the authorities felt acceptable, with predictable consequences for the show's staff.[114] But in comparison with *VVV*, *KVN* was controlled entertainment, and, perhaps more important, it could be said to have a clear purpose. It was, after all, not just an *evening* (*vecher*), a passing fancy, but a club, a collective and useful activity. And while the emphasis was always on wit and humor, with its contests on themes like improving

111. Interview with M. E. Krasn'ianskaia (former *KVN* redaktor), Moscow, July 2002.

112. For descriptions of contests, see V. Grigor'ev, "Televizionnaia mechtaniia," *Teatr*, no. 5 (1963): 121–128; "KVN: Vkhod tol'ko telezriteliam," *Sovetskoe radio i televidenie*, no. 2 (1968): 15–17; "KVN. Vozvrasheniia k skazke" in *TV-publitsist: Sbornik tsenariev*, ed. E. V. Gal'perina (Moscow, 1971), 110–163; "KVN: Vzgliad cherez chetvert' veka;" *Ocherki po istorii rossiiskogo televideniia*, 106–109.

113. Soviet television's technical capacity to perform this function consistently is doubtful at best. See "Igroki-starozhily ne liubiat segodniashnii *KVN*," *Komsomol'skaia pravda*, 11 October 1999.

114. Krasn'ianskaia interview, July 2002. *KVN* was on TV's Second Channel for almost a year because it was perceived as too prone to problems.

Figure 5.3. KVN: the Baku team, 1970. RIA Novosti. Used with permission.

the educational system and satire on societal "shortcomings" (*nedostatki*), *KVN* also had an obvious civic element that *VVV* had lacked. Even its audience was brought into the orbit of purposefulness. The studio audience was made up of students from the competing institutes who engaged in a "fans' contest"—usually some physical task, such as rapidly passing an object from person to person—for points to be added to their team's overall score. For the home audience, *KVN* offered itself as one solution to the problem of youth recreation; in the words of its creators, *KVN* was the answer to "the very topical question: 'what to do when there's nothing to do.'"[115] The TV program encouraged thousands of offshoots. Muratov and his colleagues published how-to books for local clubs complete with sample competitions and scripts for would-be hosts.[116]

KVN was also purposeful and meaningful in a way *VVV* was not because it was said to present positive role models for Soviet youth. Gosteleradio chief Kharlamov certainly thought so; he even objected to broadcasting a contestant who wore a beard to cover a facial defect because it projected the wrong

115. A. Aksel'rod, S. Muratov, and M. Iakovlev, *Klub veselykh i nakhodchivykh* (Moscow, 1965), 3.

116. Ibid. See also E. V. Gal'perina and B. I. Sergeeva, eds., *KVN otvechaet na pis'ma* (Moscow, 1967).

image: "They're also abstractionists [a reference to Western artists]," he told staff. "They need to be removed from society. Long-hairs, bearded ones, and so on. These are all phenomena of the same type. Peter [the Great] shaved off beards forcibly, and we have to do the same."[117] Soviet press coverage, though less categorical, also took *KVN*'s modeling role seriously. In the mid-sixties a reviewer who had previously criticized the show for focusing on students and failing to relate to the "mass TV viewer" praised its presentation of "new heroes"—military academy students and workers from a watch factory: "Perhaps this contest did not shine with sharp wit, but it was merry and unconstrained, and young TV viewers could at least see the manners of a Soviet warrior, the masculine grace with which he offered his hand to a girl to help her... off the stage, how he escorted her back to her seat, and the maidenly modesty and dignity with which she thanked her opponents."[118] Another reviewer was impressed by a competition between students in physics and medicine in which the med students produced two posters on the spot: "Hippocrates was a hundred times smarter than Archimedes!" (a clever rhyme in Russian) and "Physics is the medicine of the future!" Reflecting on the second poster, the reviewer decided it was more than "simply a gentleman's gesture toward his opponent" (although it did win an extra point from the jury for sportsmanship), but "far deeper in meaning" because it made people think about the "evolution of science... and the atmosphere of science... in which today's youth naturally lives." In their "sincerity and determination," he saw *KVN* contestants as "expressing their generation."[119]

The search for "young heroes" was a leitmotif of Soviet culture, and so the fact that Soviet print media looked to *KVN* contestants to fill these shoes is certainly no surprise. The important thing from the perspective of the evolution of TV programming, however, is that the people who worked on *KVN* also considered its contestants role models; the modeling idea was central to the show's design. Muratov and his colleagues created *KVN* as a form of "intellectual soccer." Each team had a captain plus ten main contestants and two on reserve, and they had "positions" in the sense that people tended to specialize in different sorts of tasks (musical, verbal, and so on). Although under pressure from the authorities, the program did open its doors to other groups within a few years, the initial concept was entirely oriented toward students and was, in a broader sense, a celebration of the young, male intelligentsia. Gal'perina emphasized this at a 1964 meeting at the Filmmakers' Union. *KVN,* she told her audience, was "100 percent propaganda" and not entertainment, as some

117. GARF, f. 6903, op. 1, d. 777, ll. 56–57. The image of the hosts was equally important: *KVN* was ordered to drop its first female host after she took the role of a prostitute in a play. *My nachinaem KVN,* 15.

118. V. Nemtsov, "Neskol'ko vecherov u televizora," *Sovetskaia kul'tura,* 18 August 1965, 2.

119. Grigor'ev, "Televizionnaia mechtaniia," 123.

people thought. "What do we propagandize?" she asked rhetorically. "We propagandize the intellect of student youth. We propagandize their positive frame of mind...their optimism...their sense of humor, [and] their ability to laugh at themselves."[120]

VVV and *KVN* had much in common, and their creators have always spoken of them as older and younger siblings. Like *VVV, KVN* was live and largely improvisational TV (at least in its initial design), and though the authorities repeatedly pressured staffers to film the program, they resisted because for them, live broadcasting remained "the ne plus ultra of television art."[121] *KVN* also put a premium on audience participation and made the creation of community—the community of teams and fans and also the wider community of *KVN* lovers, united by television—a central feature of its design.[122] Finally, *KVN* was a show that put ordinary people at the center of viewers' attention and banked on the presumed intimacy of television as a medium. The show's contests were designed to "reveal the character" of its young contestants.[123] As Gal'perina detailed in a 1967 article, the tactic was "to find interesting people, create a natural and uninhibited atmosphere and, finally, figure out a situation which, like a magic 'Open, sesame!' exposes people in front of us." When the show succeeded in this, Gal'perina thought, it was nothing less than television art.[124]

Like its commitment to live broadcasting, *KVN*'s drive to "expose" or "open up" the person (*raskryt' cheloveka*) on-screen was of a piece with the ideals of TV enthusiasm. But it is worth lingering for a moment on Gal'perina's formula for success: the first requirement for TV art was finding not just any subject but "interesting people." As she explained, *KVN*'s staff found that many people were unable to overcome their inhibitions in front of the camera and, more important, most seemed incapable of thinking on their feet. Students, the staffers discovered, were their perfect participants—less reserved, as young people generally were, but also more interesting and worthwhile subjects than the average person. Much the same might be said about the show's attitude to female contestants, who were comparatively rare; the general assumption appears to have been that men made better players at intellectual soccer because they were naturally bolder and wittier.[125] This, then, was no *VVV*, with its wide-open doors, its

120. RGALI, f. 2936, op. 3, d. 106, l. 7.

121. E. Gal'perina, "Ispoved' redaktora," in Rozov, *Shabolovka,* 218.

122. Teams who showed extraordinary "civic wit" (*grazhdanskaia ostrota*), demonstrating that they saw *KVN* "not only as a game, but also as a means of struggle," could win extra points from the jury. "*KVN:* Vzgliad cherez chetvert' veka," 90.

123. Rozov, *Shabolovka,* 218.

124. E. V. Gal'perina, "V gramm dobycha, v god trudy," in *Iskusstvo golubogo ekrana,* ed. G. Mikhailova (Moscow, 1967), 109.

125. M. E. Krasn'ianskaia made precisely this point in my interview with her in July 2002.

sloppy populism, its lack of purpose. *KVN* delivered a neat and useful package by design: "the thinking person on the screen" (a male figure marked universal) as a model for Soviet viewers.[126]

In contrasting the two shows, it is possible to read *KVN* as a sort of middle ground between a more radical, open-ended vision of television represented by *VVV* and its polar opposite: seamless, scripted, and, preferably, filmed and edited TV. It was, after all, toward the latter vision of broadcasting that Soviet TV was organizationally and ideologically inclined. Even as enthusiasts rallied for live, spontaneous TV, the organization of Soviet broadcasting, with its microphone files and ex post facto punishments, was evidently pulling in the other direction. As we know, 1957, the year *VVV* went down, taking leading figures in Soviet TV with it, was also the year when the regime began to train its eyes more sharply on television overall. Perhaps *KVN*'s format was a shrewd compromise brokered by idealists—the best that TV enthusiasts could do under the circumstances?

In their recollections of *KVN*, Gal'perina and her colleagues have often described the pressure they felt from political authorities, and the show has entered Soviet historical memory as one of the archetypal signs of youthful guts and verve in the sixties.[127] Far more than *VVV*, which is, of course, far less well known, *KVN* has become a symbol of lost *shestidesiatnik* dreams.[128] Its reputation for daring was formed at the time by its sometimes edgy satire, but it was sealed by the program's cancellation in 1972.[129] In the absence of any official explanation, many viewers concluded that the authorities had found the program too politically threatening; there were widespread rumors that the host was under arrest.[130]

We know that the regime did take measures in the late sixties to combat what it saw as a dangerous lack of discipline in Soviet cultural outlets across the board. But arguably, when it came to television, the most effective tool at

126. "*KVN:* Vzgliad cherez chetvert' veka," 89.

127. See M. V. Iunisov, *Mifopoetika; L. Brusilov'skaia, Kul'tura povsednevnosti v epokhu 'ottepeli': Metamorfozy stiliia* (Moscow, 2001), 141–146; Vail' and Genis, *60-e,* 151.

128. This reputation is beatified in a way by the fact that, as Muratov and others often mention, Vladimir Vysotskii was present when they were hashing out the show's initial design. (He was a neighbor in Iakovlev's *kommunalka* and liked to listen in.) Although Vysotskii is more of a seventies than a sixties figure and was not a dissident, he is associated with many of the thaw tropes—truth telling, authenticity, youthful daring, etc.

129. According to researcher Bella Ostromoukhova, who has interviewed several former *KVN* players, the main thrust of the program shifted from wit to politically charged satire around the mid-sixties. Ostromoukhova argues that players were picking up on the desire of a certain segment of the audience to see criticism of the regime; "humor on 'dangerous' themes even became fashionable" among participants. Bella Ostromoukhova, "KVN-molodezhnaia kul'tura shestidesiatykh?" *Neprikosknovennyi zapas,* no. 36 (2004): 34–39.

130. See an interview with one of *KVN*'s hosts, Aleksandr Masliakov, http://www.facts.kiev.ua/Jun2001/0806/09.htm.

its disposal was technological rather than political: video. Once content could be prerecorded and edited, management and discipline in television were on a whole new footing. *KVN* made the switch from live TV to video as early as 1968. It seems unlikely that the decision to cancel four years later reflected fears of its uncontrollability.

In fact, *KVN* was moving in the direction of increased control, albeit of a different type altogether: professionalization. (And there were signs of this tendency even before the show shifted to videotape.) Over the years, the improvisational, amateur quality of *KVN* diminished, and the number of prepared skits increased dramatically; some teams even hired theatrical coaches and writers to boost their competitive edge.[131] Once *KVN* teams began representing not just institutes but also cities and even republics, the stakes of the game ran far higher. Party and Komsomol organizations were likely to get involved as sponsors and managers. One Baku newspaper reported that more than sixty people flew to Moscow weeks ahead of the all-Union competition in 1968 to help the city's team get ready. Newspapers, magazines, and letters from Baku were also jetted in on a daily basis to keep team members up to date for the competition, although one wonders when they had time to read: according to the paper, the *KVN-shchiki* were in rehearsals eight to ten hours a day. On the eve of the contest, the Baku Komsomol flew eighty fans, handpicked from more than a thousand applicants, to take part in the show. And when Baku's team came home victorious, the heads of the city and the republic Komsomol organizations joined local media at the airport to greet them.[132]

KVN, in short, was looking rather less like amateur night and rather more like show business. The transformation was criticized in the central press, where there were also more or less open allusions to the backstage element as a corrosive influence on the game.[133] One possible reason for the show's cancellation in 1972 is that TV's overseers in Moscow agreed, seeing a professional *KVN* as needlessly divisive and a waste of resources. It is also likely, as many people around *KVN* have argued, that personal passions were instrumental. Gosteleradio chairman Sergei Lapin reportedly despised the show, according to some, because it had a large number of Jewish players.[134]

---

131. "*KVN:* Vzgliad cherez chetvert' veka," 90–97; *My nachinaem KVN*, 15–20; Makarov interview, May 2002. Makarov reported that he and fellow Odessa team members coached teams from Riga, Minsk, and Baku in the late sixties and that although they were paid, their motivation was not financial: they wanted to help provincial teams win in the face of the jury's perceived Moscow bias.

132. F. Kasilov, "KVN: Sem' funtov pod kilem," *Molodezh' Azerbaidzhana*, 18 June 1968.

133. See, for example, G. Kuznetsov, "Kogda Otgremeli Batalii," *Sovetskaia kul'tura*, 9 July 1966, 3; A. Akel'rod, "Klub? Veselykh? Nakhodchivykh?" *Literaturnaia gazeta*, 25 February 1970. The *New York Times* reported on viewer disappointment in the 1970–71 season. "'Quick-Witted' Variety Show Returns to Soviet TV," *New York Times*, 29 October 1970.

134. Makarov interview, May 2002; *My nachinaem KVN; "KVN:* vzgliad cherez chetvert' veka." Former host Svetlana Zhil'tsova said the formal reason for the cancellation was the

Yet though *KVN* ended its first phase on Soviet TV cloaked in controversy, this should not cloud our understanding of its origins. *KVN* was not an oppositional program by design, nor did it represent artistic compromise in the eyes of its creators. *KVN,* they thought, was a step ahead for Soviet TV—a move toward packaging and promoting a particular image of real life and individuals and a certain kind of community consciousness. It was still person-centered, interactive TV, very much in the enthusiast idiom of *VVV.* But *KVN* went further: it offered model people and model forms of interaction, both of which were, in large measure, reflections of the show's creative milieu. All the attributes of *KVN*—youth, intellect, optimism, daring, team spirit, civic consciousness—were also the attributes of Shabolovka, at least in the eyes of those who worked there. *KVN* was a projection of its creators' sense of self into Soviet media space, an emanation of their cultural authority.

PROGRAMMING CULTURAL AUTHORITY

How did *KVN* compare with the rest of Soviet television in the sixties? Here we have Central TV's programming schedule for one November day in 1961, the year of *KVN*'s launch.

FIRST CHANNEL

12:00 p.m.	*Drevnye sobory Kremlia* (*Ancient Cathedrals of the Kremlin*)—new documentary film
12:20	*Posle smeny* and *Liudiam bol'shogo serdsta* (*After the Shift* and *For Big-Hearted People*)—amateur films
12:40	TV news

[Note: As the news typically lasted fifteen minutes, there would have been a long break in broadcasting here.]

5:25	*Pionery geroi* and *Pavlik Morozov* (*Pioneer Heroes* and *Pavlik Morozov*)—films for children
6:15	TV news
6:30	Concert of romances and songs by A. Varlamov—most likely studio TV program
7:05	*Problemy sovremennosti i vsevidiashchie luchi Rentgena* (*Contemporary Problems and the All-Seeing X-Rays*)—film
7:30	*Klub kinoputeshchestvii* (*Club of Film Travel*)—TV program, in studio
8:50	*Muzykal'nyi slovar'—Ballada* (*Musical Dictionary—The Ballad*)—TV program, in studio
9:25	*Pis'ma s fronta* (*Letters from the Front*)—Chinese feature film

---

Odessa team's defiance of a ban on long hair and beards; the real reason was that the show was "too controversial and too free." Aleksandr Mel'man, "Geroi vcherashnikh dnei. Svetlana Zhilt'sova: Ia ne o chem ne zhaleiu," *Moskovskii komsomolets,* 13 September 1999.

10:30	*Vystuplenie kommentatora po vneshnepoliticheskim voprosam* (*Commentary on International Questions*)—TV program, in studio
10:45	TV news

SECOND CHANNEL

6:40 p.m.	Moscow news
7:00	*Vystavka Buratino* (*The Buratino Exhibition*)—children's TV program
7:30	*The Marriage of Figaro*—performance by the theatrical collective of the V.I. Lenin Pedagogical Institute. During the intermission, *Luchshii otdykh v vykhodnoi den'* (*The Best Recreation on Your Day Off*)[135]

Aside from its lack of sports programming, an anomaly on this day, this lineup is broadly representative of what Soviet Central TV was offering in the sixties. Television was still very much a cultural go-between, and though schedules from the end of the decade would show a definite increase in the amount of airtime overall and in original TV programming (perhaps including a live feed from a regional studio or Intervidenie), the arts, including cinema, would retain their stronghold.[136] In terms of original TV programming, news was the most notable addition here, and news would rise in prominence on Central and regional broadcasts throughout the 1960s. Still, Soviet Central TV had no regularly scheduled, in-depth nightly news broadcast until the inauguration in January 1968 of *Vremia,* a thirty-minute program; *Vremia* did not settle into its ironclad 9:00 p.m. time slot until 1972.[137] Throughout the 1960s, Soviet programmers would continue to place greater overall emphasis on arts and education than on either public affairs or light entertainment.

Soviet television remained mostly sober in tenor. Viewers often complained that it was dull. M. Semenov, a journalist for *Krokodil* magazine, expressed the frustrations of many in 1961. "Have you ever fallen into the hands of an ignorant dentist?" he asked. "Listened to a lecture about sleep and dreams? . . . No? Then it's unlikely you'll understand the suffering of someone who keeps watch by the TV screen." Semenov went on to describe an evening of flipping channels in a fruitless quest for something interesting to watch. "Yes, there are mysterious people sitting in those redaktsii," he mused. "Why do they think that I might be interested in watching a third-rate water polo match that didn't even draw forty spectators? Why do they have to show an amateur production two and three times to millions of TV viewers when its premiere ran to a half-empty hall in the House of Culture?"[138] Semenov's piece elicited a lively response from

135. *Pravda,* 24 November 1961.

136. Richard Tuber, "A Survey of Programming on the Central Studios of Television, USSR: January–June 1960," *Journal of Broadcasting* 4, no. 4 (Fall 1960): 315–326.

137. On the importance of *Vremia*'s fixed time slot for its image as a voice of the regime, see Iurovskii, *Televidenie: Poiski i resheniia,* 117–118; Stites, *Russian Popular Culture,* 168.

138. M. Semenov, "Vakhta u ekrana," *Krokodil,* 20 April 1961, 8.

Figure 5.4. The USSR's best bricklayer shows off his talents on TV, ca. 1960. Copyright Dmitrii Baltermants/Corbis.

Krokodil readers, but many wrote in to say they had no hopes for improvement. "It's not the first time that people have written about TV, but clearly, the guys who make the programming have strong nerves," wrote one. Another woman suggested that TV workers did not concern themselves about the content of their shows because they did not own sets and did not have to watch them. (Note the demanding presence—watch me!—of television in the home.)[139]

If this November 1961 schedule looks quite a lot like what we would have found in, say, November 1967, and also resembles what we saw on offer a decade before, then why are the sixties so often lionized as Soviet TV's golden years? The answer is *KVN* and, broadly speaking, the generation of sixties shows seen to embody "enthusiast" values like authenticity, lichnost', and community.

139. "Otkliki i repliki," *Krokodil*, 10 July 1961, 10.

Figure 5.5. Composer Jan Frenkel' performs on *Little Blue Flame,* 1960s. RIA Novosti. Used with permission.

Sergei Muratov hailed this as the moment when "the hero of the screen became a partner in a conversation," rather than a mere "performer" or a "talking–head...delivering his monologue to the camera."[140] *Little Blue Flame* and *Kinopanorama,* the two programs we met in chapter 2, are typically cited as among the new breed, along with *Club of Film Travel* (*Klub kinoputeshestvii,* on geography and travel), *Musical Kiosk* (*Muzykal'nyi kiosk*), *News Relay* (*Estafeta novostei,* a weekly newsmagazine), and *Stories of Heroism* (*Rasskazy o geroizme,* a program about and for veterans of World War II), to name a few.[141] All these shows were live and conversational, and they prided themselves on introducing viewers to interesting individuals in an intimate setting, one-on-one; they were televisual spaces for *obshchenie* (social interaction) both on the screen and across the screen barrier. But like *KVN,* all these programs made choices about their subjects that demonstrated a hierarchy in the idea of lichnost': some people were more interesting and more useful for television than others. On most of the new shows, an authoritative host (*vedushchii*) took center stage. Where *KVN* highlighted the young, usually male, intelligentsia as a group, programs like *Kinopanorama* and *Stories of Heroism* put well-spoken, usually male, individuals at the center of viewers' attention.[142]

For *News Relay,* the first Soviet weekly newsmagazine, the focus on a personality was one of several "founding principles," and so the show refused to use voice-overs (a host had to be on-screen at all times). *News Relay* also conceived of itself as a club, in the style of the day, and invited its guests to speak openly and without scripts. It was a rather exclusive club, though, at least by design: another of the show's founding principles was that it would bring together only "very interesting, very brilliant, and very unusual people."[143] What *News Relay*'s creators hoped was that the dynamism of its hosts and guests and their open form of address would engage viewers in public affairs in a new and vital manner. In this sense, it was a program speaking in the enthusiast idiom: the authenticity and immediacy of live broadcasting, the importance of intimacy on the screen and across the screen, and the value of community—all these core enthusiast concepts are evident in *News Relay*'s design. And at the same time, the centrality of the host and the exemplary quality of the guests indicated its kinship with a show like *KVN* and its projection of intellectual and cultural hierarchy.

Consider, for example, how Iurii Fokin, *News Relay*'s most well-known host and one of the most famous TV figures of his day, described his work on the program during the Cuban Missile Crisis of 1962. Fokin recalled telling viewers

---

140. *Ocherki po istorii rossiiskogo televideniia,* 101.
141. Most of these programs quickly spawned imitators on regional television stations.
142. *Estafeta novostei, Kinopanorama, Rasskazy o geroizme,* and *Klub kinoputeshestvii* all had male hosts. *Goluboi ogonek* was an exception in that it typically used TV diktory or actors as hosts. *Muzyka'lnyi kiosk* was hosted by a woman.
143. Leonid Zolotarevskii, *Tsitaty iz zhizni,* (Moscow, 1971), 7.

about his conversation earlier that day with a woman he had seen in his court-yard carrying a shopping bag full of matches, soap, and salt. He had argued with his neighbor, telling her soap and matches were useless when "one match can set the whole world aflame," but had failed to convince her. Fokin recalled using the story on *News Relay* to open up the general theme of the crisis, and he de-scribed his speech to viewers as being "like an icebreaker on a river." "It wasn't important if I was convincing or not," he said. "The important thing was . . . that every viewer understood that nothing was being hidden from him and nothing was being hushed up."[144]

Although Fokin himself characterized his approach to viewers that night in a language of intimacy and peer relations ("I spoke to everyone as if I were speak-ing to a friend," he said), his own description of his speech indicates a somewhat different relationship. As host of *News Relay,* Fokin spoke to his audience rather as he had spoken to the woman in the courtyard—from a position of superior knowledge—and also as a comforting authority figure, assuring them that noth-ing was hidden. Though *News Relay*'s host may have imagined his viewers as in-timates, his relationship with them was not one of equals. The ordinary woman in the courtyard and the abstracted ordinary viewers may have been part of the show (confirming its connection to reality and everyday life), but they were never in the club. Knowledge and insight were clearly Fokin's to share. *News Relay* was his show.

In the same way, *Stories of Heroism* was Sergei Smirnov's show and *Club of Film Travel* was Vladimir Shneiderov's. Smirnov, a well-known writer and war correspondent, began *Stories of Heroism* as a program to tell the stories of Soviet soldiers who had been taken prisoner by the Germans during World War II and to rehabilitate them from charges of treason and cowardice. The program soon grew beyond this theme to include the stories of Soviet veterans more gener-ally, and it became a kind of mass veterans' forum and public assistance bureau. Over the years, hundreds of thousands of viewers contacted *Stories of Heroism* to share their stories, but especially to ask for help in locating lost friends and rela-tives and in establishing their claims to pensions and other benefits. Although *Stories* did champion a controversial group of Soviets as heroes, its genre was in many ways a familiar one for Soviet culture (the ordinary person found to be extraordinary and exemplary). Moreover, Smirnov, the writer, was its host and center and the hero of the program in an important way, as the masses of people who wrote—sometimes to "Minister Smirnov," or "Deputy of the Supreme So-viet Smirnov" or simply, "The Author Who Talks about the Lost"—understood when they asked for his assistance.[145]

---

144. Muratov and Fere, *Liudi, kotorye vkhodiat,* 54.

145. The show started out on radio and moved to TV. Smirnov claimed he received over a million letters related to the show; in the summer of 1965, the Moscow post office was handling up to two thousand per day. Ibid., 62. Many people included personal documents

Like *KVN* and *News Relay,* the travel show *Club of Film Travel* was a club and so in the enthusiast language of the day another media space for conversations among equals. But just as Smirnov and his veteran guests and correspondents were not on equal terms, so *Club of Film Travel* positioned host and viewers in an evident hierarchy. The program's host, Vladimir Shneiderov, a film director and explorer, was the club's *only* traveler, after all. He presented in-depth reports on foreign locales that few ordinary viewers might ever hope to see; he was in effect the surrogate traveler for the Soviet people, who were functionally dependent upon his extraordinary mobility and expertise. The centrality of the authoritative host to the Soviet viewing experience could not have been clearer.

As shows like *Stories of Heroism* and *Club of Film Travel* sprang to life on Soviet television in the early sixties, TV's enthusiasts saw in them the marks of television's growing maturity. Muratov called thirty minutes with Sergei Smirnov a "civic event," and he emphasized that it was time with hosts like Smirnov that mattered most for viewers: "[S]ocial interaction with these people may be no less aesthetically valuable than the subject of the conversation itself."[146] Though announcers also engaged with viewers, hosts and commentators were considered a qualitative advance because the source of their connection was reputedly less emotional than intellectual. Not only were hosts personable, but their personalities were backed up by knowledge and creativity. In other words, a host was a lichnost' in the way a diktor, who did not write her own texts, could never be. Where the diktor was ordinary, a representative of the viewer on the screen, a host represented the television studio, his (less often, her) field of expertise, and Soviet culture in the broadest and best sense.

Although TV's enthusiasts did not speak in these terms, the gendered nature of their distinction between diktory and vedushchye is very apparent, and it translated into practice as well. Most hosts and commentators were male, and though the ranks of diktory were filled with both men and women in the sixties (the period when nearly all diktory were female having lasted a few short years), the profession stayed gendered in a fundamental way. A critic writing in 1966 for *Soviet Radio and Television* expressed the expectations for the role concisely: "[A] diktor on television should read the news more or less the way, say, your wife would, if she picked up the paper, saw something interesting, and read it to you out loud."[147] Critic Anri Vartanov described this period as one when "the hostess of the TV house was turned into a servant."[148] In theory, the (female)

(workbooks, military ID and pension cards) hoping to substantiate their claims. Gosteleradio established a special seven-person unit to process the mail in 1966. GARF, f. 6903, op. 1, d. 967, l. 95.

146. Sergei Muratov, "Kofe i liudi," *Sovetskaia kul'tura,* 21 January 1965, in *Televidenie v poiskakh televideniia,* 43–46.

147. Quoted in E. Bagirov and I. Katsev, *Televidenie XX vek* (Moscow, 1968), 125.

148. Vartanov, "Bednaia Valia," 27.

diktor remained a figure on the air to present the real discovery of Soviet television in its so-called golden years: male cultural authority.

CULTURAL AUTHORITY AND THE SOVIET AUDIENCE

The enthusiasts who pioneered Soviet television were convinced that they were performing a valuable service, and despite the perennial complaints about programming, they saw their audiences expand exponentially year after year. But what was known at the time about the people on the other side of the screen—who they were, what they watched, why they watched—and what were the uses of this knowledge? Soviet broadcasting in the sixties was swept up in the vogue for sociology as TV watching and its effects on other activities became a topic of interest to researchers studying leisure. There were also a few media-specific research projects, such as Boris Firsov's study of Leningrad viewers, and in 1957 Gosteleradio founded its own division for studying the audience, the NMO (Nauchno-metodicheskii otdel—scientific-methodological department). Although initially responsible only for cataloging and coordinating responses to viewer mail, the new division soon set its sights on sociological research. Its first survey dated to 1962, and over the course of the decade, the NMO managed to conduct about fifty more studies, often with the cooperation of regional studios, with samples ranging from a few hundred respondents to over five thousand.[149] It also published a series of reports about radio and TV audiences for broadcasting administration use.

Even by the standards of early Soviet TV, with its self-described dilettantes feeling their way in the dark and often tripping, the NMO was a slapdash affair. In the mid-sixties, it had a staff of twenty-two housed in a rundown building where temperatures in the winter dropped to ten degrees Celsius.[150] It goes without saying that the work of the NMO was not mechanized (pen and paper reigned), but more than that, the department lacked professional expertise in survey design and analysis. And given the state of Soviet sociology at the time, it had very few models to work with. NMO researchers improvised. Most of their surveys were conducted face-to-face, in housing complexes and workplaces, without anonymity, and typically by volunteers. Outside Moscow they would have been a volunteer force rounded up by local TV committees and party organizations. For surveys of young viewers, the NMO sometimes relied on teachers to distribute their questionnaires as a classroom assignment.

What did it mean to people to have their opinions canvassed in this way, and how did they parse the implications of shutting the door on a volunteer researcher or inviting her in? We have very little information on this all-important social dimension to sociological research, although the NMO itself reported that

---

149. A. V. Grigor'eva and V. E. Zhivoderov, eds., *Izuchaem nashu auditoriiu*, (Moscow, 1971), app.
150. Koenig, "Media and Reform," 112.

compliance was often a problem. One survey sent out in two hundred copies to the Novosibirsk broadcasting committee yielded a mere fifteen responses.[151] Researchers studying a program called *The Screen of Big Chemistry* found people refused to participate because they said they disliked it so much.[152]

NMO surveys themselves were characterized by their leading questions (and I suspect that many interviewers contributed "guidance" on the spot as well). Consider this excerpt from an interview with a fourteen-year-old Muscovite for a 1962 study "on the role of radio and television in the cultural and aesthetic education of the population":

> How has the appearance of television in your family affected your relationship to newspapers, magazines, and books? Do you read more or less? Does television affect your choice of books?
> *We choose books ourselves.*
> Which kind of TV programs do you watch regularly?
> *Sports, Little Blue Flame.*
> How does television contribute to widening your worldview, to relaxation, to fulfilling your aesthetic requirements?
> *It contributes a lot to relaxation.*
> What do you think should be the content of TV programming?
> *I would like to watch more good films on TV.*[153]

Another NMO survey determined that young viewers had a taste for "educational" programming—not such a surprise, when they had been asked to select from a list of possible reasons for enjoying a show loaded with such answers as "has an instructional character," "poses current problems about science and technology," and "provides food for thought"; the answer "is entertaining in form" was a possibility, but it was in an ideologically crowded room.[154]

Soviet audiences were nothing if not schooled in the official goals of Soviet culture, and NMO survey results often demonstrated their agreement with TV's educational and mobilizational mission. So, too, did many letters published in the press. Yet when it came to the question not of what people thought they should watch but rather of what they *did* watch and what they would like to watch ideally, the portrait of the audience that emerges from contemporary research is rather different.

Soviet viewers reported watching feature films on television more often than any other form of programming.[155] The young Muscovite who said he wanted

---

151. GARF, f. 6903, op. 3, d. 320, l. 60.
152. Grigor'eva and Zhivoderov, *Izuchaem nashu auditoriiu*, 54.
153. GARF, f. 6903, op. 3, d. 208, ll. 36–38.
154. Cited in Koenig, "Media and Reform," 116–117.
155. Grigor'eva and Zhivoderov, *Izuchaem nashu auditoriiu*, 78; GARF, f. 6903, op. 3, d. 320, l. 105.

to see more cinema on TV was not just some movie-mad teenager; viewers commonly complained to the press that television did not broadcast enough films or repeated the same films too often. (They also rated the few TV movies in the sixties highly.) At the next level of popularity were programs with performers (variety or café shows like *Little Blue Flame*) and especially *KVN.* In one 1966 NMO study, 74 percent of viewers aged fourteen to thirty reported that they "always" tuned in for *KVN;* for the fourteen-to-eighteen age group, that number approached 90 percent.[156] Boris Firsov's research on the Leningrad audience echoed NMO findings: cinema was most popular with viewers, followed by *KVN* (popular with all ages).[157] Viewers also reported regularly watching theatrical performances, concerts, and documentary films. News and public affairs programming—indeed, almost all *original* television programming, the stuff of enthusiast dreams—appeared lower down the list of ratings.

We might imagine that this information would have given TV's enthusiasts pause. It did not. For one, they could point to some genuine successes in their preferred idiom, shows like *Little Blue Flame* and *KVN,* and also to the obvious popularity of television watching overall. For another, they could often hoist heavy mailbags in their defense: although far fewer people reported watching *Stories of Heroism* or *Musical Kiosk* than feature films, television as an institution received masses of viewer letters. And letters registered in Soviet bureaucracy in a way that questionnaires and studies never did.

Let us be clear: TV's mailbag was not representative of its audience (and this was true of other media mail as well). Retirees and the disabled wrote a large proportion of the letters, and most comments were from people who held either extremely negative or extremely positive points of view.[158] But more to the point, the overwhelming majority of people who wrote to Soviet media did so with requests for information and assistance; they needed help with a housing application or wanted to know where to find parts for their refrigerator. Most letters did not offer any sort of commentary on media content at all.

Television's own research division stressed the unreliability of the mailbag in its pitch to begin proper sociological research in 1962.[159] But the mail fetish in Soviet broadcasting endured and, indeed, outlived the sociological approach. Even as the NMO struggled to run a scientific research program in the sixties, its staff tallied letters by program and redaktsii and published the results regularly in booklet form. TV staffers suffered routine slaps on the wrist for failing to respond in a timely manner. But they could also turn to letters for proof

---

156. GARF, f. 6903, op. 3, d. 329, ll. 11–13. This was a large survey (2,245 respondents) run in January—February 1966 using a random sample in twenty-five cities throughout the USSR.

157. B. M. Firsov, *Televidenie glazami sotsiologa* (Moscow, 1971), 126–130.

158. Boretskii, *Televizionnaia programma,* 82–83.

159. GARF, f. 6903, op. 3, d. 185.

of their connection to audiences if they wished. Viewer mail, like attendance figures for lectures, lent itself beautifully to a bean-counting approach; the method was straightforward, and the numbers were pleasingly large and always growing. Central TV received over 215,000 letters in 1966 (up from only 42,000 for 1960). In 1971 Gosteleradio logged almost 2 million.[160] Sociological studies were abstract in comparison (no "sample" has the ring of a "million") and often unflattering.

The NMO was a marginalized division at Gosteleradio because its research was superfluous from the perspective of the people who developed programming, much like box-office statistics for Soviet filmmakers. In their memoirs and recollections, Soviet TV professionals never mention the work of the NMO, seldom recall viewer letters, and, in truth, spend precious little time reflecting on their audiences at all. They are far more likely to speak of their responsibility to television as a new art and to the constant pressure to feed the air and to satisfy audiences upstairs. When viewers do enter the picture, it is typically in the most sweeping terms ("the streets emptied when X program was on the air" is a commonplace) and with reference to their duty to help them, usually in terms of cultural uplift. The host of *Musical Kiosk* remembered sobbing when she realized that she had, in speaking of Tchaikovskii's music, used the familiar term *muzychka* (a diminutive of "music") on a live broadcast and in this way, she thought, undermined the show's pedagogical mission. She also recalled that *Musical Kiosk* received a lot of letters from viewers who did not like ballet or, as she revealingly put it, did not understand it and complained about the show.[161]

Soviet TV professionals did not see themselves as catering to public taste but rather educating and directing it. The ideals of TV enthusiasm related less to what people wanted than to perceptions of what they needed—of what Soviet culture could do to improve Soviet people and society when endowed with the extraordinary powers of a new medium. And in this regard, TV enthusiasts and the regime were very much on the same page.

Let us recall Kharlamov's tripartite definition of broadcast media's goals: mobilization (to solve current "political, economic, and aesthetic problems"), education or uplift ("to develop culture" and "raise the level of the people"), and entertainment. TV enthusiasts saw their work in roughly the same terms and with the same order of priority. When conflicts arose, they were often over interpretations of current political and cultural questions, and they pitted the authority of TV's overseers against the counterclaims of the enthusiasts. The staff of *Stories of Heroism,* for instance, was called on the carpet in 1964 after the KGB lodged a complaint with the CC's ideological department: Smirnov, the program's host, was said to be lauding people for heroism who did not deserve it

---

160. GARF f. 6903, op. 3, d. 306, l. 6; V. V. Egorov, *Televidenie i zritel'* (Moscow, 1977), 59.
161. Interview with E. V. Beliaeva, 2000 (Gosteleradiofond Oral History Project).

and denying the guilt of others who had been correctly punished.[162] In another example of a dispute that had more serious consequences, Boris Firsov, then head of the Leningrad TV studio, was fired in 1966 along with several others after a group of writers deviated from their prepared comments to extol the virtues of Solzhenitsyn and Pasternak on a live literary program, *Literary Tuesday* (*Literaturnyi vtornik*).[163] This scandal in Leningrad, with echoes of the earlier Lev Kassil' incident on Central TV, was replicated many times in cases of greater or lesser ideological freight. As long as television was dependent on live broadcasts, there would be incidents when invited guests acted or spoke in unpredictable ways. In nearly all cases, TV's new professionals did not encourage these incidents (Firsov did not plan the controversial program in 1966), nor did they necessarily approve. They did, however, tend to take a less dire view of them than the political authorities did. From their perspective, they were responsible Soviet professionals who deserved to be entrusted with authority over Soviet airwaves and viewers. They did not have that authority. As Kseniia Marinina said, in the days of live broadcasting, TV workers had backs wet with perspiration at all times.

I would not wish to minimize the seriousness of these conflicts for people's careers or their impact on TV production overall. As Soviet enthusiast historians emphasize, the constant pressure to avoid slip-ups and to keep upwind of ideological scandal discouraged risk taking and helped produce a great deal of dull programming, even in television's so-called golden years. But the conflict between TV's overseers and creators was less fundamental than the trail of reprimands and firings would imply. TV enthusiasts saw television as a means to educate and mobilize the masses in an anti-Stalinist yet distinctly Soviet framework. (Even the word "enthusiast," after all, is straight from the Soviet lexicon.) G. Kuznetsov described his and his colleagues' work on *News Relay* as "a little island of freethinking on the airwaves" in a post-Soviet publication. "But not," he hastened to add, "in the sense that we cast the virtues of our native party and Soviet power into doubt. On the contrary, we tried to portray them in as human a manner as possible [*kak mozhno chelovechnee*]." Kuznetsov went on to say that their work "anticipated the notion of 'socialism with a human face' that appeared in Prague a year later."[164]

For Soviet television, the critical question was whose face would represent socialism on the screen, and for Soviet TV workers and their overseers, who

162. Smirnov was called in to the CC to discuss the program along with representatives from Gosteleradio, the army, the Council of Ministers Committee on publishing, the Writers' Union, and *Pravda*. RGANI, f. 5, op. 55, d. 78, ll. 79–84.

163. GARF, f. 6903, op. 1, d. 886, ll. 5–34; RGANI, f. 5, op. 33, d. 239, ll. 13–70; interviews with B. M. Firsov and R. D. Kopylova, St. Petersburg, June 2002.

164. G. V. Kuznetsov, "Zapiski lishnego cheloveka," in *Televizionnaia mozaika*, ed. Ia. N. Zasurskii (Moscow, 1997), 38.

would be responsible for selecting and controlling that face. Soviet TV enthusiasts sought to replace the Stalinist kul't lichnosti with lichnosti—a concept that, though pluralistic, did not include all comers. A lichnost' was someone worth emulating, a person with something to teach, a cultural authority. And given their educational and moral goals and their sense of superiority over their audiences, lichnosti were a natural choice for TV enthusiasts to foreground in their programming; they were an extension of themselves as they understood or wished themselves to be. Soviet television was a means for an entire new group to write themselves into the ranks of the intelligentsia as the people's conscience and teachers. Gosteleradio chairman Mesiatsev, too, wrote proudly in his memoirs that he thought he had the right to be considered a lichnost', underscoring how much he had promoted culture and valued his relationships with artists. When conflicts arose between the chairman (or his superiors) and TV staff, they were sometimes ideological in an obvious way: e.g., was poet Evgenii Evtushenko an appropriate lichnost' for Soviet TV? But the more basic problem was one of authority: who would determine the appropriateness of any lichnost'? What was not in question at any time was the position of Soviet viewers, who were seen by all parties as needing an authority to direct their desires. Television, the media-age darling, created new Soviet producers and consumers: the producer-consumer relationship as structured in Soviet culture remained very much the same.

TV CULTURE AS SOVIET CULTURE: THE LAPIN ERA

But what about the television experience, we might ask: Did watching Soviet TV embody a new-model Soviet culture, a path to a better future? It is this question that cuts to the heart of the enthusiasts' story. For even as they struggled to realize their ideals in broadcasting—battling technological constraints and their own ignorance, snobbish cultural brokers and officious political ones—their viewers demonstrated a clear and constant preference for filmed fictions, the very opposite of those ideals. Putting aside a few programs, such as *KVN* and sports broadcasts, living reality fell flat with Soviet audiences. And Soviet television in the Lapin era, 1970–85, mostly abandoned that reality as prerecorded broadcasting finally gained the upper hand. Let us take a look at what viewers of the First Channel would have found on 13 October 1975.[165]

9:10 a.m.	Gimnastika (daily calisthenics)
9:30	Concert—unspecified
9:55	Opening Ceremonies for the World Meeting of Girls. Broadcast from the Hall of the Columns, House of the Soviets
11:00	*Klub kinoputeshestvii (Club of Film Travel)*

165. *Pravda,* 5 July 1975.

2:10 p.m.	*Dorogami soglasiia, dorogami sodruzhestva.* Dok. telefil'm (*Roads of Agreement, Roads of Cooperation.* Documentary TV film)
3:10	*My znakomimsia s prirodoi* (*We're Getting to Know Nature*)—TV program
3:35	*Mamina shkola* (*Mom's School*)(children's TV program)
4:05	*Pesnia o Kol'tsove* (*Song about Kol'tsov*—feature film, 1959. Date not cited in schedule.)
5:30	*Molodezh' planety* (*Youth of the Planet*)—TV program
6:15	*Aleshiny skazki.* Mul'tfil'm (*Alesha's Fairy Tales*—cartoon)
6:25	Ahead of 25th Congress of the CPSU. Workers of Iaroslav oblast compete. The first secretary of the Iaroslavl' Regional Party Committee, F. Loshchenkov, will take part in the program.
7:10	Concert of works by M. Glinka
7:40	E. Radzinskii. *Ol'ga Sergeevna.* Telepovest' Glava 1-i. (E. Radzinskii's TV tale "Ol'ga Sergeevna," chapter 1)
9:00	*Vremia*
9:30	Film of the ballet *Giselle*
10:50	*Sportivnyi dnevnik* (*Sports Daily*)—TV program

Although continuities with sixties programming here are obvious—in individual shows like *Club of Film Travel* and in the generally sober and educational tenor of the broadcast day—there is a marked difference in the proportion of prerecorded material. With the exception of the morning broadcast from the House of Soviets, the evening broadcast from Iaroslavl', and *Vremia* (and possibly the concerts), these would have been taped and edited shows or films. The TV day was now long: viewers could spend nearly the whole day watching if they wished. (Their TVs would sound an unpleasant noise during broadcast breaks to remind them to turn them off.) And for those who had up-to-date sets in 1975, the screen would have flickered in color for many programs.

In many areas, viewers would also have had access to Central TV's Second or Third Channels in the evening and to one or two regional channels as well. On 13 October 1975, those not interested in the Glinka concert at 7:10 might have tuned in for a Riga-Moscow hockey match on Channel 2. The First Channel had hockey in the evening on 14 and 17 October as well. Sports programming did take on a larger role in the Lapin era: official figures indicate an increase from 1.8 percent of total broadcast time in 1966 to 5.8 percent in 1975 but still fail to do justice to its prominence, since much of sports programming aired at times of peak viewership (weekends and evenings).[166] A good proportion of sports came via Intervidenie exchanges, and they expanded from a few hundred hours annually in the sixties to about five thousand hours by 1982.[167]

---

166. Egorov, *Televidenie i zritel'*, 60.
167. Iurovskii, *Televidenie: Poiski i reshenie*, 48.

Soviet viewers now also watched the occasional capitalist TV production, of which the first miniseries, the BBC's *Forsyte Saga* in 1970, was the most celebrated. In addition to the ubiquitous parquet stories devoted to the aging political elite, Soviet TV in the Lapin era ran a large number of documentaries chronicling the lives of factories and working-class families (often dubbed "dynasties") and continued with a political education in the form of programs like *Ahead of the 25th Congress of the CPSU* and the series *Leninist University of the Millions* (*Leninskii universitet millionov*), always announced a month in advance and marked in bold in TV listings. (In the week of 13 October 1975, the lecture was on the "historic meaning of the Commission for Security and Cooperation in Europe.") Counterpropaganda took on a more prominent role as well in documentary programs hosted by TV's elite commentators exposing the ills of capitalist society. But so, too, did popular music programs and game shows, such as *Let's Go, Girls!* (*A nu-ka devushki!*), which pitted teams of young women against each other in gendered, skills-related contests (baking, for example), and *What? Where? When?* (*Chto? Gde? Kogda?*), a quiz show that used questions mailed in by viewers to challenge panels of invited experts. The most famous of early TV's diktor darlings, Valentina Leont'eva, now a gray-haired matron, hosted a program *From the Bottom of the Heart* (*Ot vsei dushi*) that traveled around the USSR reuniting members of the older generation separated during the country's turbulent past. Children's programming—game shows and clubs, cartoons, movies, and school tie-in programs—blossomed in the Lapin era. Arts remained essential to the program, as did feature films: in the mid-seventies Central TV was showing up to seven feature films a week and scores of documentaries, while at the regional studios, film accounted for a weighty 40–50 percent of total airtime.[168] Finally, the 1970s were also the era when Soviet made-for-TV movies came into their own, many in the spy and detective story genres. Some, such as the 1973 *Seventeen Moments of Spring* (*Semnadstat' mgnovenii vesny*), enjoyed blockbuster popularity to rival that of any feature film, Soviet or foreign.[169]

Soviet television had grown up: not only was the broadcast day far longer than ever before, but it was also far more diverse and sophisticated in terms of programming. Technologically and organizationally, TV had been transformed from the days when Boris Livertovskii had experimented with ways to keep errant fingers out of the frame. To broadcast a counterpropaganda documentary on unemployment in the United States, an edition of *From the Bottom of the Heart* reuniting a factory worker in Cheliabinsk with her wartime medic buddies now living in Brest, not to mention an epic TV film like *Seventeen Moments,* was a complex endeavor requiring expertise, funding, and time. With tape technology

168. E. Ia. Dugin, "Tipologiia programm mestnogo televideniia" (avtoreferat, Moscow State University, 1977).

169. On the 1970s TV movie boom, see Elena Prokhorova, "Fragmented Mythologies: Soviet TV Mini-Series of the 1970s" (PhD diss., University of Pittsburgh, 2003).

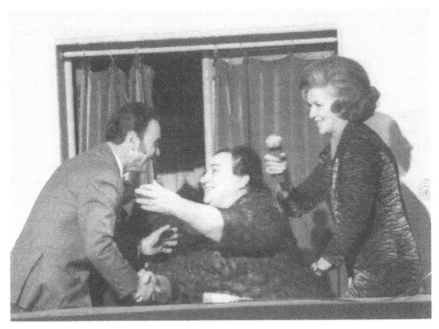

Figure 5.6. Valentina Leont'eva and decorated pilot Valentina Grizodubova (center) on *From the Bottom of the Heart*. O. Makarov, RIA Novosti. Used with permission.

came an end to most of the glitches that had plagued early broadcasts, including perceived ideological ones; there were far fewer scandals in the Lapin era than in previous decades.

Yet if Soviet TV production was no longer a world of dilettantes living on the razor's edge and accordionists in overheated studios, what did that mean for TV as Soviet culture, Soviet art? For enthusiasts who believed that the essence of the medium was live broadcasting with real people, the technological and organizational developments of the sixties and seventies were at best a mixed blessing. What TV gained in professionalism, it lost in authenticity, artistry, and social relevance.[170] Standard post-Soviet accounts of the Lapin era emphasize not the sixties shows that endured, like *Club of Film Travel* (and there were many) but those that did not. *News Relay*, *KVN*, and *Stories of Heroism* were all canceled early in the Lapin era; *Kinopanorama* endured but without its dynamic host, Aleksei Kapler, who left in the early seventies. The picture is one of Soviet television's

170. *Ocherki po istorii rossiiskogo televideniia*, 154–170; Sergei Muratov, "The Structure of Broadcasting Authority," *Journal of Communication* 41, no. 2 (Spring 1991): 172–184; B. Firsov, "Televidenie i my: K istorii nashikh otnoshenii," in *Televidenie—Vchera, segodnia, zavtra*, vol. 9 (Moscow, 1989).

promising youth crushed by the forces of conservatism: *KVN*'s fresh and witty sparring replaced by the vapid contests of *Let's Go, Girls!; Stories of Heroism* giving way to stories of sentimentality in the tear-jerking *From the Bottom of the Heart;* the live give-and-take of genuine *lichnosti* on *News Relay* thrown over for the slick reportage of a counterpropaganda documentary. The regime, the argument goes, had finally woken up to the power of television and, fearing the innovations of the enthusiasts, had implemented a bread-and-circuses approach instead. Careerists rushed in to replace enthusiasts once television had grown prestigious and lucrative.[171] Sergei Lapin served as expert ringmaster of the new show.

As we have seen with the story of *KVN,* though, black-and-white versions of television's colorful history are atmospheric but unsatisfying. How *should* we allocate responsibility for the show's rising glitz and ultimate demise? Was it censorship (from TV workers or their party minders), video technology (imposed or embraced), or competition and the pressures to defend local pride? Aleksei Kapler may have been renowned for speaking off the cuff, but TV's new capacity for prerecording and editing could easily have taken care of any "mistakes" he made, and this was true of Iurii Fokin too. In post-Soviet recollections, Fokin claimed that he was run out of Ostankino for ideological reasons. "We're closing you down," Fokin recalled Lapin's telling him. "We are not interested in your point of view or anyone else's. We have one point of view—the Central Committee's. I hope that is clear?"[172] But the head of TV's propaganda *redaktsiia* at the time insisted that Fokin was fired because he suffered from "star mania" (*zvezdnaia bolezn'*) and got on Lapin's and many other people's nerves.[173] *Kinopanorama*'s *redaktor,* Kseniia Marinina, recalled that Kapler quit the show over a conflict with her, not with those upstairs, on a programming question (although she added that she was aware that the chairman did not like him.)[174]

The question is not whether ideology came into play in the development of Soviet TV culture in the Lapin era. It is entirely plausible that Lapin browbeat Fokin just as he remembered. But it is also clear that a host of other factors were working in tandem with ideology in TV's evolution. First, the switch from live to prerecorded broadcasting was not only a bid for greater control; it was a means to improve quality by eliminating gaffes and allowing for more complex, sophisticated broadcasts. Far from uniquely authoritarian or Soviet in nature, prerecorded broadcasting was, by the time the USSR managed it, standard practice for television in most Western democracies. And many Soviet TV workers accepted it in the name of professionalism and—no small thing—as a way to

171. Firsov, "Televidenie i my," 11.

172. "Legenda teleradiozhurnalistiki, laureate TEFI Iurii Fokin: 'Mne peredali pros'bu glavy pravitel'stva "uspokoit" narod,'" *Vek,* 31 August 2001.

173. *Ocherki po istorii rossiiskogo televideniia,* 72.

174. "Mnogie khoteli skorrektirovat'," *Nezavismaia gazeta,* 15 October 2004.

protect their jobs.[175] Second, and not unexpectedly, personalities and personal prejudices were important in the world of Soviet television. Fokin may well have been fired because Lapin disliked him and saw him as treading on ideologically shaky ground. The two judgments are not mutually exclusive; on the contrary, they might be mutually reinforcing. Like the demise of live broadcasting, what Fokin's (Kapler's, etc.) fate demonstrates is less a master plan to rid Soviet TV of its enthusiasts and their ideals than a convergence of political, technological, and social factors.

Similarly, understanding the *kind* of broadcasting culture that came to the fore in the 1970s and early '80s means considering multiple inputs. Soviet television reached its zenith of popularity in the Lapin era; that is, from the enthusiasts' point of view, the worse television got, the more people watched. It was a bittersweet irony, and it demanded an explanation. For many enthusiasts, there was simply no comparison between a show like *KVN* and *Let's Go, Girls*! Although both were youth-oriented and team-based game shows and even shared the same host, one was intellectual soccer with genuine civic purpose, the other frivolous entertainment.[176] Their conclusion was that TV's political minders had explicitly fostered escapism to pander to the mass audience or to distract it from contemporary problems or both. In explaining this strategy, the Lapin legend proved very helpful because it would, of course, take a clever, cultured man like Lapin to identify the genuine potential of television and orchestrate its subversion with the ersatz TV culture of the 1970s and early '80s. Note, too, the strong similarities between this vision of TV and contemporary critiques of capitalist masscult—Soviet and Western—including the typical association of "real" culture with the male and masscult with the female.

In fact, Soviet TV was always willing and able to bore its audiences to tears (judging by audience reactions). The bread was chewy and copious; the circuses never trumped political education and cultural uplift, even in the Lapin era. We might consider this a question of incompetence—contemporary foreign observers often did—but it was matter of values, of worldview. Who was the audience for Soviet television as conceived by Lapin and his colleagues, the people in charge of TV's direction? Yes, there were the tens of millions of ordinary viewers in their homes, but there were also Soviet political elites in *their* homes to consider, as well as, in an abstract sense, the audience of history: this was, after all, *Soviet* TV, forever blazing new trails for the world to follow. And while we will never know the true cast of Lapin's heart—cynic or true believer—we can be certain that the idea of Soviet TV he inherited had a significant impact on not only its institutional but also its cultural profile.

---

175. See, for example, T. Elmanovich, *Obraz fakta: Ot publististiki k fil'mu na Estonskom televidenii* (Moscow, 1975).

176. The point was made to me by several people, including one man with a key role on both shows. Interview with M. Kh. Giul'bekan, Moscow, July 2002.

As was the case in cinema, the tastes of highly placed viewers carried extraordinary weight in decisions about television programming; Lapin and his staff, no less than Yermash and his, were subject to telephonic assaults from demanding patrons. The anecdotal record is far leaner for TV than for cinema, but a few stories circulate, almost all regarding Brezhnev. The demands for expert parquet-floor coverage form one genre—Lapin reputedly managed Brezhnev's television image in particular, down to the last detail—while other stories concern Brezhnev and family as TV watchers.[177] It was the general secretary's taste for the program *Café of Thirteen Chairs* (*Kabachok trinadtsat' stul'ev*) that kept it on air despite Lapin's personal animosity. The first family's passion for hockey (Brezhnev himself) and figure skating (his wife) is held responsible for the surge in coverage of both in the seventies.

On one level, this kind of relationship speaks to the notion of court TV: television as a bespoke service to the Soviet political elite. But serving the elite was not only about flattering egos and meeting individual desires. It also meant fulfilling a certain idea of Soviet TV that was about Soviet state power and largesse and about the enduring value of culture in the Soviet system: the USSR as a culture-giving *and* leisure-providing state. Audience research was indeed out of the picture under Lapin, but this was not a major adjustment for a system that had always calibrated itself to perceived needs rather than desires. Political elites set the parameters for audience needs: they had the ultimate cultural authority TV's enthusiasts felt they deserved. And they were, by and large, traditionalists; they held tight to the model of Soviet TV as political education and mobilization, cultural uplift, and entertainment, in that order.

The fact that Soviet TV offered more entertainment-oriented programs in the Lapin era relative to earlier decades relates to input from above (Brezhnev as hockey fan, the minister of light industry's grandchildren, say, as pop music mavens) and to perceptions of the world below (as Brezhnev said, "the Soviet person has the right to relax in front of the television after day's work"—that is, Soviet culture had obligations to ordinary people too). And yet the opera singers never stopped singing on Soviet TV, and the lecturers at the *Leninist University of the Millions* soldiered on. Did the Brezhnevs watch? The Lapins? The head of Brezhnev's security detail recalled that the family house had two televisions—one, a Soviet Rubin for the general secretary and his wife, the second a Japanese model with a VCR for the younger generation. His recollections of TV time with the senior Brezhnevs ran to *Vremia* and sports; to imagine the members of the younger generation in the next room using the VCR to catch up on missed lectures strains our credulity (far easier to picture them watching masscult movies)[178]

177. Reino Paasilinna, "Glasnost and Soviet Television" (YLE–Finnish Broadcasting Co., research report May 1995), 128.

178. Fedor Razzakov, *Dos'e na zvezd: Tainy televideniia* (Moscow, 2000), 48; *Ocherki po istorii rossiiskogo televideniia,* 139.

The operas and the *Leninist University* remained on air and relevant nonetheless because cultural and political enlightenment remained the core of Soviet TV culture by design. Even if no one was watching, the show would go on.

As critic Anri Vartanov wrote, "TV in Lapin's time had the luxury of not counting every kopeck...and not calculating the percentage of viewers who watched one show or another."[179] Television was thus in a somewhat different position than cinema. Although in real terms the Soviet film industry was no more dependent on viewer approval to keep its funding flowing than TV, it was more vulnerable to criticism because its audience was more visible and quantifiable. The television audience was a comparative mystery, and maybe even more than its cinematic counterpart, it could take on symbolic functions in Soviet discourse To talk about the Soviet TV audience was to talk about its huge size, its unity, its political and cultural sophistication (to match the programming, so superior to masscult offerings), and its gratitude to the Soviet state for the gift of TV.

In this symbolic package the only feature we can speak of with any certainty is audience size; we know from time-budget studies that the majority of the Soviet population did watch regularly. Lapin's Soviet TV was a domestic empire in two senses: an all-Union broadcasting empire ruled from Moscow and an everyday empire based in tens of millions of homes. TV's pioneering generation, the enthusiasts, had identified this potential long before most of the political and cultural establishment, and their hard work in the fifties and sixties was essential to its realization. Yet the success of the Lapin era was cold comfort to those who had dreamed of a new art and a new community. This Soviet television was not *their* Soviet television—not real television at all, they would say. Their enthusiasm withered; the enthusiasm of the Soviet audience only grew and grew, along with TV's authority. Soviet television proved in the end to be the dominant face of Soviet culture in the media age.

179. Anri Vartanov, "Eto sladkoe slovo 'menedzhment,'" *Trud,* 14 July 2005, 19.

EPILOGUE

━━━

Moscow Does Not Believe in Tears (*Moscow slezam ne verit,* 1979) was not the most popular film of the Soviet era (that honor went to the Mexican tearjerker *Yesenia*), nor was it the most popular *Soviet* production; *Pirates of the Twentieth Century* (*Piraty XX veka,* 1979), beat *Moscow's* 84.5 million viewers by a nose.[1] But more than any other film, it is *Moscow* that has become a byword for Soviet cinema's slide toward masscult forms in the 1970s, at least in part because it won the Oscar for Best Foreign-Language Film in 1980.[2] When this sprawling melodrama directed by a relative unknown, Vladimir Men'shov, beat out the likes of François Truffaut's *Le dernier métro* and Akira Kurosawa's *Kagemusha,* Soviet and American critics agreed: imitation is the sincerest form of flattery, and Hollywood had been pleased to honor a film it recognized as *svoe,* one of its own.[3]

Moscow tells the story of Katia, a wide-eyed and hardworking provincial girl who comes to Moscow in 1958 to seek her fortune. Caught up in the whirlwind of big city life and under the influence of a frivolous and materialistic roommate (Liuda), Katia falls for the seductions of a TV cameraman (Rudol'f) and is left pregnant and alone. Flash-forward to 1978, though, and she has morphed into a successful industrial executive and mother whose only problem in life—and it is an acute one—is the lack of a man. *Moscow* solves this problem by bringing Katia together with an intelligent and sensitive mechanic (Gosha) and, more important still, by securing her submissiveness to Gosha at home. Once she has found her soul mate and her proper role as a woman at last, Katia's remarkable success story is complete.

Although critics dismissed *Moscow* as a modern-day Cinderella story,[4] Men'shov defended his film as depicting a "normal life story" in the Soviet context. "[I]t's as if there's some kind of agreement in our artistic circles," Men'shov complained.

> Life here is bad, there are no opportunities in this social order, you can only get where you want through connections [*po blatu*], and so on. . . . I never used

---

1. *Piraty XX veka* drew 86.7 million viewers.

2. Julian Graffy, "Cinema," in *Russian Cultural Studies,* ed. Catriona Kelly and David Shepherd (Oxford, 1998), 185

3. *Newsweek's* reporter declared, "Hollywood honored what it loved best—its own formulas." Quoted in Anna Lawton, ed., *The Red Screen: Politics, Society, and Art in Soviet Cinema* (New York, 1992), 222.

4. One of the first reviews of the film, published in *Sovetskaia Rossiia,* was critical and ran under the title "Variations on a Cinderella Theme." Neya Zorkaya, *The Illustrated History of Soviet Cinema* (New York, 1989), 299.

blat. [Yet] I rose up from total poverty. How could the people who hewed the coal beside me in mine no. 32 imagine that, after twenty years, I, a hauler on the main tunnel, would receive an Oscar?[5]

Men'shov rejected the term "fairy tale" to describe his work, and he denied its universality: *Moscow,* he said, was a film made with a "clear-cut audience"[6] in mind—the Soviet audience—and it both captured the "Russian national character"[7] and celebrated the "Soviet way of life."[8] The relationship between these two categories, Russian and Soviet, is central in the film, and as a number of scholars have pointed out, *Moscow* properly belongs to the wave of anxious Russian nationalism that swept through Soviet culture, high and low, in the 1970s and '80s.[9] But it betrays equally profound anxieties about the future of the very Soviet way of life it celebrates, related in large measure to the dynamics of the postwar media age. Or, to put it another way, the influence of the West on Soviet-Russian culture is but one factor in the broader question the picture poses about the place of mass-media culture, leisure, and pleasure in modern Soviet life.

Take the character of Liuda, the Soviet gold digger, for example. *Moscow* repeatedly pokes fun at her for her shallow infatuation with masscult as a young woman in the fifties, and it is clear that she imaginatively associates the West with the chic and the modern. However, the West itself is not a sine qua non in her vision of the good life: it is *Soviet* chic that she craves, and though a connection to foreign culture does form one part of that chic, it is only one part. When *Moscow* shows Liuda and Katia crowding the red-carpet entrance to a festival of French cinema in 1958, it is the sight of Soviet, not foreign stars that takes their breath away. "If I could live like she does, I wouldn't be a scientist," Liuda sighs, as a favorite actor, Tat'iana Koniukhova, walks past. The objects of Liuda's

5. Men'shov quoted in George Faraday, *Revolt of the Filmmakers* (University Park, PA, 2000), 108.

6. Men'shov quoted in Richard Stites, *Russian Popular Culture: Entertainment and Society Since 1900* (New York, 1992), 173.

7. Men'shov quoted in Lawton, *The Red Screen,* 240.

8. Men'shov quoted in Faraday, *Revolt of the Filmmakers,* 108.

9. See John Dunlop, "Russian Nationalist Themes in Soviet Film of the 1970s," in Lawton, *The Red Screen,* 231–248. There is also an argument to be made for the Soviet-specific nature of the gender dynamics in *Moscow,* which was one in a spate of films in the seventies about unhappy professional women (*zhen'skie fil'my*—women's films). Katia's troubles finding a "real man," the terrible loneliness and implicit pointlessness of her life without one, and the eventual joy she finds in domestic submission were themes common to *zhen'skie fil'my.* Françoise Navailh argues that the popularity of these films stemmed in part from their resonance with actual problems in Soviet society, marked as it was by high rates of divorce, male alcoholism, and a typically crushing double burden for women at work and home. See Françoise Navailh, "The Image of Women in Contemporary Soviet Cinema," in Lawton, *The Red Screen,* 211–230.

longing are Soviet fame and Soviet luxury. And her wrong-headedness—imagine not wanting to be scientist in the age of Sputnik!—cannot be attributed to Western influences alone.

Similarly, Katia's seduction by a dashing young man with a foreign name, Rudol'f, is not only a metaphor for an innocent Russia taken with—and taken by—the foreign. Let us remember that Rudol'f is a TV cameraman; he is also an enthusiast in the visionary mode we met in chapter 5. As Katia looks on enraptured, Rudol'f declares that television is "the art of tomorrow" and "the future of mankind." Soon, he assures her, cinema, theater, and literature will all wither away as independent art forms; television will provide everything, and everyone will stay at home by their TVs. Katia's delight with Rudol'f and the modern world that he represents is splashed across her face while she attends a broadcast of *Little Blue Flame,* the TV café. As Katia laughs at the comedic duo performing on stage and Rudol'f sends out her image to the USSR's new TV-viewing world, we see a perfect crystallization of a certain idea of mass culture: love and fun, fame, glamour, and technology all come together for Katia, and for a moment she herself is modern Soviet star.

Yet *Moscow Does Not Believe in Tears* wastes little time in bursting this bubble. Just as we, the viewers, know that Liuda's gold digging and infatuation with star culture will come to no good, it is clear that Rudol'f will betray Katia and that television, too, will not sustain its early magic moment. Indeed, it is no exaggeration to say that television figures as a villain in *Moscow.* Katia is abandoned by her shallow TV enthusiast, of course, but there is more to the medium's treachery. The next time our heroine appears on TV, it is in a shop-floor interview filmed by Rudol'f. An imperious and distinctly foreign-looking producer (she wears sunglasses indoors) shoves a script into her hands to memorize, but once the camera begins to roll, Katia is flustered and blurts out her own, contrarian opinions instead. The contrast between honest Katia and the slick and manipulative world of broadcasting could not be clearer.

When *Moscow*'s narrative jumps to the 1970s, Katia again appears on television, and this time she has the firm upper hand. In an interview in her posh office, Katia the industrial executive speaks with cool confidence and no particular interest in the process; a TV appearance is a routine occurrence for her. Once again, Rudol'f (now a Russified "Rodion"—a further sign of his inconstancy) is behind the camera, but this time Katia is unmoved by him. While she has suffered and grown, Rudol'f's character is static and infantalized.[10] *Moscow* leaves no doubt that Katia has moved beyond him and his TV world, beyond movie stars, beyond all of the ephemera that so impressed a provincial girl in Moscow in 1958.

---

10. Katia owns not one but two TV sets, but we never see her watching them. They appear as signs of modern comfort but do not figure prominently in her busy life.

And yet, though Katia is all grown up in the seventies, *Moscow* explicitly raises the question whether the rest of Soviet society can be considered equally mature in its relationship to mass culture. Rudol'f's enraptured soliloquy about how television will soon displace all other art forms plays for laughs in the scene from the fifties; Katia is swept away at the time, but other people listening with her appear skeptical, and we viewers are invited to smirk as well. By 1978, however, these predictions no longer sound so funny. "Where are all the men nowadays?" gripes Katia when a friend suggests she get married. "You go to the theater or a museum, and what do you see? Only women! The men are all at home watching television or drinking with their friends. After forty, they all vegetate." When Katia visits a lonely hearts club and the director lodges the same complaint, we know that *Moscow* is making a broader point about television's atomizing power, its negative influence on Soviet cultural and social life. "You call this urbanization? It's outrageous!" the director cries indignantly. It is an amusing moment (the director is played by a wonderful character actor, and her fulminations against modern, urban life are overdrawn) but also a serious one. Although *Moscow* does solve its central problem of finding Katia a man and delivers a happy ending, it has little hope to offer to contemporary women in her position.

What is more, *Moscow* leaves viewers in doubt about the younger generation and, by extension, about the very future of Soviet society. When Rudol'f meets his and Katia's daughter (Alexandra) for the first time, he once again launches into his soliloquy on the magic of television, and he invites her to visit the studio, just as he invited Katia to *Little Blue Flame* in the fifties. It is unclear whether Alexandra, a teenager, will be taken in by the glamour of television as her mother once was. We have already seen her entranced by Western pop music, which she listens to on large headphones, ignoring Katia's invitations to talk. The music and the technology associated with it thus have an atomizing, antisocial effect (much like television in the eyes of its critics)—not an encouraging sign. But the logic of *Moscow*'s narrative introduces an even more fundamental problem for Alexandra and for the future.

If Katia was able to see beyond the bright lights of her youth in Moscow and grow up, it is because she was forced by circumstance to work hard and, more to the point, to suffer. *Moscow* spells this out by showing her poring over textbooks in the middle of the night, baby at her side, and sobbing herself to sleep. Katia's rags-to-riches story, while particularly spectacular, did match the trajectory of many millions of provincial strivers who made good in the big city. In this sense, Men'shov's insistence that his picture portrayed a normal Soviet life story was true. But if Katia's hard work and suffering were instrumental in the development of her character, what were the prospects for Alexandra, a girl who, as we learn at one point, does not even know how to cook? We know that Alexandra the Muscovite will never face the same challenges that *Moscow* tells us were critical to building Katia's exemplary character. Given the logic of the Soviet normal life story, why should she strive and struggle when everything has already been handed to her? And why, for that matter, should anyone turn off the television set (take off the headphones, choose a textbook over a detective novel, go to a lecture instead of a movie) when Soviet society has reached the kind of comfort and stability portrayed in *Moscow*? And if no one does, what will that mean for the future of the Soviet way of life?

Perhaps not all societies need archetypal life stories in order to function effectively. Perhaps a shared grand narrative of progress—a common road to a better future—is not indispensable to social solidarity. But Soviet society *was* grounded in a grand narrative that linked the personal to the political and connected the Soviet people's hard work and suffering to the progress of humanity. This connection, the work of mass mobilization for building the communist future, was the task of Soviet culture. Moscow did believe in blood, sweat, and tears.

Vladimir Men'shov did, too, as is clear from *Moscow Does Not Believe in Tears*—a love letter to his generation of provincial go-getters. In this sense, the film is an updated version of the stories Soviet culture had spun when he was young about the struggles and sacrifices of his parents; it is his attempt to gather another generation around the hearth of a proud heritage. But at the same time, *Moscow* also lays bare the fundamental problematic of Soviet culture in the media age: if struggles and tears are no longer necessary and Soviet culture becomes not a means to an end but an end itself—a form of leisure and parasocial activity—how does one become a Soviet person? How does the march to the radiant future go on? Men'shov answered these questions himself with a movie aimed to unite the entire Soviet family in a celebration of a Soviet way of life, and he did in fact offer a common viewing experience to more than 80 million people in the film's first year alone—a mass culture triumph if ever there was one. But the irony of this solution—the irony of Soviet culture's success in the media age—is inescapable. Watching *Moscow Does Not Believe in Tears* was, after all, not work, not a creative or political act, not productive of anything in any explicit way. It was passive, static fun. And in the 1980s, many millions of Soviet viewers took to their sofas to watch *Moscow* and many other engaging Soviet-spun stories on their own, over and over again, on Soviet television. What better emblem of the stunning success of the Soviets' Cold War media empire? What better symbol of the Soviet cultural ideal sapped of its vitality and of a Soviet political project, with culture at the core of its world-historic mission, shambling toward an ever-receding radiant future?

SELECTED BIBLIOGRAPHY

Media culture occupies an anomalous position in Soviet studies. Scholars of all stripes use media sources—print and, to a lesser extent, film—and the importance of mass culture in projecting the regime's goals to the Soviet people is universally acknowledged. Yet we have very few studies of media qua media. Newspapers and cinema again form an exception to the rule, but it is a very partial one: for the post–World War II period we could still count the number of studies on one hand. The reasons for this blind spot are multiple and complex. Many Soviet scholars have their own high-culture biases (in their day jobs if not their free time). The dynamics of ideological competition contributed to a collective fixation on both sides of the iron curtain with unofficial and repressed cultural activity and the infiltration of Western culture. Finally, any would-be media historian faces a problem of sources.

The source problem for media history is partly one of sheer volume, and it is not unique to the Soviet field. Soviet television may have been comparatively late to go live, but there is still an ocean of programming awaiting future researchers. Radio has not been well preserved, but Soviet archives do hold scripts and dense institutional records for radio, television, and film. These archival sources are of course a very mixed bag (in general of decreasing richness over the decades for broadcasting and far better for film than for broadcasting overall). For my research in television, I turned to oral history sources very early on to relieve some of the aridity of the archives and entered unexpectedly into a world of Soviet TV enthusiasts. If I did not do this for cinema and radio, it is only because the published and archival resources were comparatively lush (and perhaps because I was busy talking to the enthusiasts, still enthusiastic forty years later). Oral history interviews with Soviet media's many producers and consumers, in other words, are a rich resource awaiting their historians.

The following is a selected list of the resources used in this project that I hope will help to encourage future research.

Archival Materials
MOSCOW, RUSSIA
Gosudarstvennyi arkhiv Rossiiskoi Federatsii (GARF)
    Fond 6903: Gosteleradio SSSR
    Fond 9401: Osobaia papka N. S. Khrushcheva
    Fond 9425: Glavlit
Rossiiskii gosudarstvennyi arkhiv literatury i iskusstva (RGALI)
    Fond 2329: Ministerstvo kul'tury SSSR
    Fond 2387: Tsentral'naia studiia dokumental'nykh fil'mov
    Fond 2453: Mosfil'm
    Fond 2456: Gosudarstvennoe aktsionernoe obshchestvo po proizvodstvu i
        prokatu kinofil'mov RSFSR

Fond 2918: Soveksportfil'm
Fond 2924: Zhurnal *Iunost'*
Fond 2936: Soiuz kinematografistov SSSR
Fond 2944: Goskino SSSR
Rossiiskii gosudarstvennyi arkhiv noveishei istorii (RGANI)
Fond 5: Apparat Tsentral'nogo Komiteta KPSS
Fond 72: Ideologicheskaia komissiia pri TsK KPSS
Fond 89: Kollektsiia rassekrechennykh dokumentov
Rossiiskii gosudarstvennyi arkhiv sotsial'no-politicheskoi istorii (RGASPI)
Fond 17: Apparat Tsentral'nogo Komiteta KPSS
Rossiiskii gosudarstvennyi arkhiv sotsial'no-politicheskoi istorii-m (RGASPI-m)
(formerly Tsentr khraneniia dokumentov molodezhnykh organizatsii)
Fond 1: Apparat Tsentral'nogo Komiteta VLKSM
Fond 3: Apparat Tsentral'nogo Komiteta VLKSM
Tsentral'nyi arkhiv obshchestvenno-politicheskoi istorii Moskvy (TsAOPIM)
(formerly Tsentral'nyi arkhiv obshchestvennykh dvizhenii Moskvy, TsAODM)
Fond 4: Moskovskii gorodskoi komitet KPSS
Fond 635: Moskovskii gorodskoi komitet VLKSM
Fond 2930: Partiinyi komitet Gosteleradio SSSR
Fond 3221: Partiinaia organizatsiia zhurnala *Iunost'*
Gosudarstvennyi fond televizionnykh i radioprogramm (Gosteleradiofond)
Gosteleradiofond Oral History Project

Tsentral'nyi derzhavnyi arkhiv hromads'kykh ob'ednam' Ukrainy (TsDAHOU)
Fond 1: Apparat Tsentral'nogo Komiteta KP UkSSR
Fond 287: Pervichnaia partiinaia organizatsiia Respublikanskoi studii
televideniia
Tsentral'nyi derzhavnyi arkhiv vishchikh organiv vladi ta upravlinnia Ukrainy
(TsDAVO)
Fond 4667: Kiivs'ka studiia televideniia
Fond 4915: Gosteleradio UkSSR

Open Society Archive (OSA)
Fond 300: Records of Radio Free Europe/Radio Liberty Research Institute

Interviews

V. S. Akopov, July 2002
A. I. Gagarkin, July 2002
M. Kh. Giul'bekan, July 2002
M. E. Krasn'ianskaia, July 2002
B. M. Livertovskii, June–July 2002
N. N. Mesiatsev, July 2002
S. A. Muratov, June 2002
A. I. Vystorobets, July 2002

A. V. Zemnova, June 2002
Iu. L. Zerchaninov, July 2002
ST. PETERSBURG, RUSSIA
I. A. Artiushkova, June 2002
B. M. Firsov, June 2002
R. D. Kopylova, June 2002
E. A. Shumakova, June 2002
UNITED STATES
V. A. Ivanov, June 2002 (by telephone)
Sergei Khrushchev, June 2007
Iurii Makarov, May 2002
Miron Reidel', May 2002
Daniel Schorr, June 2006 (by telephone)
M. S. Sulkin, June 2002 (by telephone)

Websites

http://www.nashekino.ru
http://www.radiojamming.info
http://russiancinema.ru
http://www.tvmuseum.ru

Published Works

Afanas'eva, E. S., and V. Iu Afiani, eds. *Apparat TsK KPSS i kul'tura 1953–1957: Dokumenty.* Moscow: Rosspen, 2001.
——, eds. *Ideologicheskie komissii TsK KPSS 1958–1964: Dokumenty.* Moscow: Rosspen, 1998.
Aksyonov, Vassily. *In Search of Melancholy Baby.* Translated by Michael Henry Heim and Antonina W. Bouis. New York: Random House, 1987.
Aktery sovetskogo kino. Moscow: Iskusstvo, 1964.
Aleksandrov, G. V. *Epokha i kino.* Moscow: Izd. Politicheskoi literatury, 1976.
Arkus, L., ed. *Noveishaia istoriia otechestvennogo kino. 1986–2000, Kino i kontekts.* St. Petersburg: Seans, 2004.
Attwood, Lynne, and M. I. Turovskaia. *Red Women on the Silver Screen: Soviet Women and Cinema from the Beginning to the End of the Communist Era.* London: Pandora, 1993.
Aucoin, Amanda Wood. "Deconstructing the American Way of Life: Soviet Responses to Cultural Exchange and American Information Activity during the Khrushchev Era." PhD diss., University of Arkansas, 2001.
Babochkin, Boris, N. Babochkina, and L. Parfenov. *Boris Babochkin—vospominaniia, dnevniki, pis'ma.* Moscow: Materik, 1996.
Bagirov, E. G., and I. G. Katsev. *Televidenie. XX vek. Politika. Iskusstvo. Moral'.* Moscow: Iskusstvo, 1968.
Barker, Adele Marie, ed. *Consuming Russia: Popular Culture, Sex and Society since Gorbachev.* Durham: Duke University Press, 1999.

Beliaev, I. K. *Osobennosti natsional'nogo televideniia*. Moscow: Institut povysheniia kvalifikatsii rabotnikov televideniia i radioveshchaniia, 2000.

Bittner, Stephen. *The Many Lives of Khrushchev's Thaw: Experience and Memory in Moscow's Arbat*. Ithaca: Cornell University Press, 2008.

Bogomolov, Iu. A. *Mezhdu mifom i iskusstvom*. Moscow: Gosudarstvennyi institut iskusstvoznaniia, 1999.

Boretskii, R. A. *Televizionnaia programma*. Moscow, 1967.

Boretskii, R. A., and G. V. Kuznetsov, *Zhurnalist TV: Za kadrom i v kadre*. Moscow, 1990.

Brandenberger, David. *National Bolshevism: Stalinist Mass Culture and the Formation of Modern Russian National Identity, 1931–1956*. Cambridge, MA: Harvard University Press, 2002.

Brooks, Jeffrey. *Thank You, Comrade Stalin! Soviet Public Culture from Revolution to Cold War*. Princeton: Princeton University Press, 2000.

Brudny, Yitzhak M. *Reinventing Russia: Russian Nationalism and the Soviet State, 1953–1991*. Cambridge, MA: Harvard University Press, 1998.

Brusilovskaia, L. V. *Kul'tura povsednevnosti v epokhu 'ottepeli': Metamorforzy stiliia*. Moscow: URAO, 2001.

Buck-Morss, Susan. *Dreamworld and Catastrophe: The Passing of Mass Utopia in East and West*. Cambridge, MA: MIT Press, 2000.

Caute, David. *The Dancer Defects: The Struggle for Cultural Supremacy during the Cold War*. Oxford: Oxford University Press, 2003.

Cherednichenko, Tat'iana. *Mezhdu "Brezhnevym" i "Pugachevoi." Tipologiia sovetskoi massovoi kul'tury*. Moscow: RIK "Kul'tura," 1994.

Cherniakov, A. A. *Problemy televideniia*. Moscow: Iskusstvo, 1976.

Chertok, S. *Tashkentskii festival'*. Taskhent: Izd. Literatury i iskusstva im. G. Guliama, 1975.

Chukhrai, Grigorii Naumovich. *Moe kino*. Moscow: Algoritm, 2002.

Clark, Katerina. *Petersburg: Crucible of Cultural Revolution*. Cambridge, MA: Harvard University Press, 1995.

——. *The Soviet Novel: History as Ritual*. 3rd ed. Bloomington: Indiana University Press, 2000.

Clark, Katerina, and Evgeny Dobrenko, eds. *Soviet Culture and Power: A History in Documents, 1917–1953*. New Haven: Yale University Press, 2007.

Cohen, Louis Harris. *The Cultural-Political Traditions and Developments of the Soviet Cinema, 1917–1972*. New York: Arno Press, 1974.

Condee, Nancy, ed. *Soviet Hieroglyphics: Visual Culture in Late Twentieth-Century Russia*. Bloomington: Indiana University Press, 1995.

Crowley, David, and Susan E. Reid, eds. *Socialist Spaces: Sites of Everyday Life in the Eastern Bloc*. Oxford: Berg, 2002.

Dizard, Wilson P. *Television: A World View*. Syracuse: Syracuse University Press, 1966.

Dmitriev, L. A. *Ballada o chetvertoi programme TsT*. Moscow: Institut povysheniia kvalifikatsii rabotnikov televideniia i radioveshchaniia, 2000.

Dobrenko, Evgeny. *The Making of the State Reader: Social and Aesthetic Contexts of the Reception of Soviet Literature*. Stanford: Stanford University Press, 1997.

———. *The Making of the State Writer: The Social and Aesthetic Origins of Soviet Literary Culture.* Palo Alto: Stanford University Press, 2002.

Dolynina, B. P., ed. *Trudy Vsesoiuznogo nauchno-issledovatel'skogo kinofotoinstituta.* Vol. 66, *Sotsiologicheskie issledovannia kinematografa.* Moscow: Goskino SSSR, 1973.

Dondurei, D. B., ed. *Otechestvennyi kinematograf: Strategiia vyzhivaniia: nauchnyi doklad.* Moscow: NIIK, 1991.

Dugin, Ia. A. *Mestnoe televidenie: Tipologiia, faktory i usloviia formirovaniia programm.* Moscow: Izd. Moskovskogo universiteta, 1986.

Dunham, Vera Sandomirsky. *In Stalin's Time: Middleclass Values in Soviet Fiction.* Enlarged and updated ed. Durham, NC: Duke University Press, 1990.

Dzirkals, Lilita, Thane Gustafson, and A. Ross Johnson. *The Media and Intra-Elite Communication in the USSR:* Santa Monica, CA: Rand, 1982.

Eggeling, Wolfram. *Politika i kul'tura pri Khrushcheve i Brezhneve, 1953–1970 gg.* Moscow: Airo-XX, 1999.

Egorov, V. V. *Televidenie i zritel'.* Moscow: Mysl', 1977.

———. *Televidenie: Teoriia i praktika.* Moscow: MNEPU, 1993.

———. *Teoriia i praktika sovetskogo televideniia.* Moscow: Vysshaia shkola, 1980.

Eisenschitz, Bernard. *Lignes d'ombre: Une autre histoire du cinéma soviétique: 1926–1968.* Milan: Mazzotta, 2000.

Eisenstein, Sergei, and Richard Taylor. *The Eisenstein Reader.* London: British Film Institute, 1998.

Ekran. Moscow: Iskusstvo, 1964–1970.

Elmanovich, T. *Obraz fakta: Ot publististiki k fil'mu na Estonskom televidenii.* Moscow: Iskusstvo, 1975.

Ezhegodnik kino. Moscow: Iskusstvo, 1955–1963.

Faraday, George. *Revolt of the Filmmakers: The Struggle for Artistic Autonomy and the Fall of the Soviet Film Industry.* University Park: Pennsylvania State University Press, 2000.

Feigelson, Kristian. *L'URSS et sa télévision.* Paris: Institut national de l'audiovisuel: Champ Vallon, 1990.

Fere, Georgi I. *Tovarishch TV.* Moscow: Molodaia gvardiia, 1974.

Firsov, B. M. *Istoriia sovetskoi sotsiologii 1950–1980-x godov.* St. Petersburg: Izd. Evrop. univ. v Sankt-Peterburge, 2001.

———. *Massovaia kommunikatsiia v usloviiakh nauchno-tekhnicheskoi revoliutsii.* Leningrad: Nauka, 1981.

———. *Puti razvitiia sredstv massovoi kommunikatsii.* Leningrad: Nauka, 1977.

———. *Sviaz' vremen.* St. Petersburg: Evropeiskii dom, 1997

———. *Televidenie glazami sotsiologa.* Moscow: Iskusstvo, 1971.

Fitzpatrick, Sheila. *The Cultural Front: Power and Culture in Revolutionary Russia.* Ithaca: Cornell University Press, 1992.

Fomin, V. *Kinematograf ottepeli: Dokumenty i svidetel'stva.* Moscow: Materik, 1998.

———. *Kino i vlast': Sovetskoe kino, 1965–1985 gody: Dokumenty, svidetel'stva, razmyshleniia.* Moscow: Materik, 1996.

———. *Kino na voine: Dokumenty i svidetel'stva.* Moscow: Materik, 2005.

———. *Polka: Dokumenty, svidetel'stva, kommentarii.* Moscow: NIIK, 1992.

Freilikh, Semen. *Besedy o sovetskom kino.* Moscow: Proveshchenie, 1985.

Galochkina, G., ed. *Televidenie priglashaet detei.* Moscow, 1976.

Gal'perina, E. V. *TV-publitsist. Sbornik stsenariev.* Moscow: Iskusstvo, 1971.

Gal'perina, E. V., et al., eds. *KVN? KVN...KVN!* Moscow: Gosteleradio NMO, 1966.

Gal'perina, E. V., and B. I. Sergeeva, eds. *KVN otvechaet na pis'ma.* Moscow: Iskusstvo, 1967.

Ganley, Gladys D. *Unglued Empire: The Soviet Experience with Communications Technologies.* Norwood, NJ: Ablex Publishing, 1996.

Garrard, John, and Carol Garrard. *Inside the Soviet Writers' Union.* New York: Free Press, 1990.

Germanova, I. G., and N. B. Kuz'mina, eds. *Moi rezhisser Romm.* Moscow: Iskusstvo, 1993.

Gessen, Masha. *Dead Again: The Russian Intelligentsia after Communism.* London: Verso, 1997.

Gleizer, M. S. *Radio i televidenie v SSSR: 1917–1963: Daty i fakty.* Moscow: Gosteleradio NMO, 1965.

Gleizer M. S., and N. S. Potapov, eds. *Radio v dni voiny: Sbornik statei.* Moscow: Iskusstvo, 1975.

Goldovskaia, M. E. *Chelovek krupnym planom: Zametki telezhurnalista.* Moscow: Iskusstvo, 1980.

Golovskoi, Valerii. *Mezhdu ottepel'iu i glasnosti: Kinematograf 70-x.* Moscow, 2004.

Golovskoy, Valery S., and John Rimberg. *Behind the Soviet Screen: The Motion-Picture Industry in the USSR, 1972–1982.* Ann Arbor: Ardis, 1986.

Goriaeva, T. M. *Politicheskaia tsenzura v SSSR.* Moscow: Rosspen, 2002.

———. *Radio Rossii: Politicheskii kontrol' sovetskogo radioveshchaniia v 1920–1930-kh godakh: Dokumentirovannaia istoriia.* Moscow: Rosspen, 2000.

Goriaeva, T. M., and Z. K. Vodopianova. *Istoriia sovetskoi politicheskoi tsenzury: Dokumenty i kommentarii.* Moscow: Rosspen, 1997.

Gorsuch, Anne E. *Youth in Revolutionary Russia: Enthusiasts, Bohemians, Delinquents.* Bloomington: Indiana University Press, 2000.

Grigor'eva, A. V., and V. E. Zhivoderov, eds. *Izuchaem nashu auditoriiu.* Moscow: Gosteleradio NMO, 1971.

Grushin, Boris Andreevich. *Chetyre zhizni Rossii v zerkale oprosov obshchestvennogo mnenia: Ocherki massovogo soznanii rossiian vremen Khrushcheva, Brezhneva, Gorbacheva, i El'tsina v 4-kh knigakh.* Moscow: Progress-Traditsiia, 2001.

Gurchenko, Liudmila. *Aplodismenty.* Moscow: Tsentrpoligraf, 1994.

Hixson, Walter L. *Parting the Curtain: Propaganda, Culture, and the Cold War, 1945–1961.* New York: St. Martin's, 1997.

Hoberman, J. *The Red Atlantis: Communist Culture in the Absence of Communism.* Philadelphia: Temple University Press, 1998.

Hollander, Gayle Durham. *Soviet Political Indoctrination: Developments in Mass Media and Propaganda since Stalin.* New York: Praeger, 1972.

Hopkins, Mark W. *Mass Media in the Soviet Union.* New York: Pegasus, 1970.

Horton, Andrew, and Michael Brashinsky. *The Zero Hour: Glasnost and Soviet Cinema in Transition.* Princeton: Princeton University Press, 1992.

Iakovlev, A. N. *Omut pamiati*. Moscow: Vagrius, 2000.

Inkeles, Alex. *Public Opinion in Soviet Russia: A Study in Mass Persuasion.* Cambridge, MA: Harvard University Press, 1958.

Inkeles, Alex, and Raymond Augustine Bauer. *The Soviet Citizen: Daily Life in a Totalitarian Society.* Cambridge: Harvard University Press, 1959.

Iukhtin, Gennadii. *Vokrug da okolo kino: Zabavnyi kinoskop.* Moscow: Knizhnyi magazin "Moskva," 1997.

Iunisov, M. V. *Mifopoetika studencheskogo smekha (STEM i KVN).* St. Petersburg: Gosudarstvennyi institut iskusstvoznaniia, 1999.

Iurenev, Rostislav Nikolaevich. *Kratkaia istoriia sovetskogo kino.* Moscow: BPSK, 1979.

Iurovskii, A. *Istoriia sovetskoi televizionnoi zhurnalistiki.* Moscow, 1982.

——. *Televidenie: Poiski i resheniia: Ocherki istorii i teorii sovetskoi telezhurnalistiki.* 2nd ed. Moscow: Iskusstvo, 1983.

Ivanova, V. *V zhizni i v kino: Iz bloknota zhurnalista.* Moscow: Iskusstvo, 1988.

Jelagin, Juri. *The Taming of the Arts.* Translated by Nicholas Wreden. New York: Dutton, 1951.

Johnson, Priscilla. *Khrushchev and the Arts: The Politics of Soviet Culture, 1962–1964.* Cambridge, MA: MIT Press, 1965.

Jones, Polly, ed. *The Dilemmas of De-Stalinization: Negotiating Cultural and Social Change in the Khrushchev Era.* London: Routledge, 2006.

Kalantar, K., and E. Manukian, eds. *Armeniia kinematograficheskaia, 1963–1971.* Yerevan: Ekran, 1971.

Kalistratov, Iu. A. *Ekonomika proizvodstva i obrashcheniia kinofil'mov v SSSR.* Moscow: Iskusstvo, 1958.

Kapralov, G. A., ed. *Mify i real'nost'. Zarubezhnoe kino segodnia.* Moscow: Iskusstvo, 1974.

Kartseva, E. *Sdelano v Gollivude.* Moscow: Iskusstvo, 1964.

Kartsov, N. P. *Ia ne rasstavalsia s televideniem.* Moscow: Institut povysheniia kvalifikatsii rabotnikov televideniia i radioveshchaniia, 2000.

Kazakov, G. A., A. I. Melnikov, and A. I. Vorobev. *Ocherki istorii sovetskogo radioveshchaniia i televideniia.* Moscow: Mysl', 1972.

Kelly, Catriona. *Refining Russia: Advice Literature, Polite Culture, and Gender from Catherine to Yeltsin.* Oxford: Oxford University Press, 2001.

Kelly, Catriona, and David Shepherd, eds. *Russian Cultural Studies: An Introduction.* Oxford: Oxford University Press, 1998.

Kenez, Peter. *The Birth of the Propaganda State: Soviet Methods of Mass Mobilization, 1917–1929.* Cambridge: Cambridge University Press, 1985.

——. *Cinema and Soviet Society, 1917–1953.* Cambridge: Cambridge University Press, 1992.

Kheifits, Iosif. *Poidem v kino!* St. Petersburg: Isskustvo-SPB, 1996.

Kinematograf segodnia: Sbornik statei. Moscow: Iskusstvo, 1971.

Klimanova, L. S., ed. *O partiinoi i sovetskoi pechati, radioveshchanii i televidenii: Sbornik dokumentov i materialov.* Moscow: Mysl', 1972.

Koenig, Mark Charles. "Media and Reform: The Case of Youth Programming on Soviet Television (1955–1990)." PhD diss., Columbia University, 1995.

Kogan, Lev Naumovich. *Kino i zritel'*. Moscow: Iskusstvo, 1968.

Kokarev, I. E. *Rossiiskii kinematograf: Mezhdu proshlym i budushchim*. Moscow: Rossiiskii fond kul'tury, 2001.

Komarovskii, V. S. "Otnoshenie k televizionnym peredacham razlichnykh grupp zritelei (opyt sotsial'nogo issledovaniia)." In *Obshchestvennaia psikhologia i kommunisticheskaia vospitanie*. Moscow: 1967.

Kopylova, R. D. *Otkrytyi ekran: Televizionnaia zrelishche i dialog*. St. Petersburg, 1992.

Korobeinikov, Valerii Semenovich. *Goluboi charodei: Televidenie i sotsial'naia sistema*. Moscow: Molodaia gvardiia, 1975.

Kosinova, M. I. *Istoriia kinoprodiuserstva v Rossii: Uchebnoe posobie*. Moscow: Uzoroch'e, 2004.

Kostiukovskii, Iakov, Moris Slobodskii, and Leonid Gaidai. *Zhit' khorosho. A khorosho zhit'—eshche luchshe*. Moscow: PIK-Soglasie, 1998.

Kozintsev, Grigorii. *"Chernoe, likhoe vremiia . . ."* Moscow: Izd. "Artist. Rezhisser. Teatr," 1994.

Kozlov, Aleksei. *"Kozel na sakse" i tak vsiu zhizn'*. Moscow: Vagrius, 1998.

Kozybaev, S. S. *Auditoriia—ves' Kazakhstan*. Alma-Ata, 1984.

KPSS o sredstvakh massovoi informatsii i propagandy. 2nd ed. Moscow: Izd. Politicheskoi literatury, 1987.

Kudriavtsev, Sergei. *Svoe kino*. Moscow: Dubl'-D, 1998.

Kuliev, El'shad. *S telekameroi i mikrofonom*. Baku: 1986.

Kushnirov, Mark. *Svetlyi put', ili Charli i Spenser*. Moscow: TERRA, 1998.

Kuznetsov, G. V. *Sem' professional'nykh granei zhurnalista TV*. Moscow: Institut povysheniia kvalifikatsii rabotnikov televideniia i radioveshchaniia, 2001.

——. *TV-zhurnalist*. Moscow: Izd. Moskovskogo universiteta, 1980.

Kuznetsov, G. V., V. L. Tsvik, and A. Ia. Iurovskii. *Televizionnaia zhurnalistika*. 2nd rev. and exp. ed. Moscow: Izd. Moskovskogo universiteta, 1998.

Lahusen, Thomas. *How Life Writes the Book: Socialist Realism and Real Socialism in Stalin's Russia*. Ithaca: Cornell University Press, 1997.

Lahusen, Thomas, and E. A. Dobrenko, eds. *Socialist Realism without Shores*. Durham, NC: Duke University Press, 1997.

Lahusen, Thomas, and Gene Kuperman, eds. *Late Soviet Culture: From Perestroika to Novostroika*. Durham, NC: Duke University Press, 1993.

Lawton, Anna, ed. *The Red Screen: Politics, Society, Art in Soviet Cinema*. London: Routledge, 1992.

Lenoe, Matthew. *Closer to the Masses: Stalinist Culture, Social Revolution, and Soviet Newspapers*. Cambridge, MA: Harvard University Press, 2004.

Leonov, Evgenii. *Dnevniki, pis'ma, vospominaniia*. Moscow: Tsentroilgraf, 2000.

Leont'eva, Valentina. *Ob"iasnenie v liubvi*. 2nd ed. Moscow: Molodaia gvardiia, 1989.

Levshina, I. *Liubite li vy kino?* Moscow: Iskusstvo, 1978.

Leyda, Jay. *Kino: A History of the Russian and Soviet Film*. 3rd ed. Princeton: Princeton University Press, 1983.

Lisann, Maury. *Broadcasting to the Soviet Union: International Politics and Radio*. New York: Praeger, 1975.

Lotman, Jurij. *Semiotics of Cinema*. Translated by Mark E. Suino. Ann Arbor: University of Michigan Press, 1976.

Lovell, Stephen. *The Russian Reading Revolution: Print Culture in the Soviet and Post-Soviet Eras*. London: School of Slavonic and East European Studies, 2000.

MacFayden, David. *Red Stars: Personality and the Soviet Popular Song, 1955–1991*. Montreal: McGill-Queen's University Press, 2001.

Makarova, Inna Vladimirovna. *Blagodarenie*. Moscow: Studiia "TRITE": "Rossiiskii arkhiv," 1998.

Marchenko, T. *Radioteatr. Stranitsy istorii*. Moscow: 1970.

Mar'iamov, G. *Kremlevskii tsenzor: Stalin smotrit kino*. Moscow: Konfederatsiia soiuzov kinematografistov "Kinotsentr," 1992.

Mashchenko, Ivan. *Telebachennia Ukraini*. Kyiv: TETRA, 2004.

Matiushchenko, T. N. et al. *Gazeta "Pravda" o sovetskom televidenii i radioveshchanii: Sbornik*. Moscow: Iskusstvo, 1972.

McMichael, Polly. "The Making of the Soviet Rock Star: Leningrad, 1972–1987" (PhD diss., Cambridge University, 2007).

Mesiatsev, N. N. *Davno perezhitoe*. Moscow: Institut povysheniia kvalifikatsii rabotnikov televideniia i radioveshchaniia, 2000.

Miasoedov, B.A. *Strana chitaet, slushaet, smotrit*. Moscow, 1982.

Mickiewicz, Ellen. *Changing Channels: Television and the Struggle for Power in Russia*. Rev. and exp. ed. Durham, NC: Duke University Press, 1999.

——. *Media and the Russian Public*. New York: Praeger, 1981.

——. *Split Signals: Television and Politics in the Soviet Union*. Oxford: Oxford University Press, 1988.

Mikhailova, G., ed. *Iskusstvo golubogo ekrana*. Moscow: Iskusstvo, 1967.

Mikhailovich, V. I. *Zritel' pered teleekranom*. Vol. 4, *Iskusstvo*. Moscow: Znanie, 1983.

Mikhalkov-Konchalovskii, A. S. *Nizkie istiny*. Moscow: Sovershenno sekretno, 1998.

——: *Vozvyshaiushchii obman*. Moscow: Sovershenno sekretno, 1999.

Mitrokhin, Nikolai. *Russkaia partiia: Dvizhenie russkikh natsionalistov v SSSR 1953–1985 gody*. Moscow: NLO, 2003.

Mordiakova, Nonna. *Ne plach', kazachka!* Moscow: Olimp, 1997.

Muratov, S. A. *Nravstevennye printsipy telezhurnalistiki. Opyt eticheskogo kodeksa*. Moscow, 1994.

——. *Pristrastnaia kamera*. Moscow, 1976.

——. *TV: Evoliutsiia neterpimost*. Moscow, 2000.

——. *Televidenie v poiskakh televideniia: Khronika avtorskikh nabliudenii*. Moscow: Izd. Moskovskogo universiteta, 2001.

Muratov, S. A., and G. V. Fere. *Liudi, kotorye vkhodiat bez stuka*. Moscow: Iskusstvo, 1971.

Muzyria, A. *V efire radiostantsiia "Iunost'."* Moscow, 1979.

My nachinaem KVN. Moscow: Izdatel'skii dom "Vostok," 1996.

Nash drug—Televidenie: Mastera sovetskoi kul'tury o TV. Moscow: Iskusstvo, 1978.

Naumov, Oleg V., and Andrei Artizov, eds. *Vlast' i khudozhestvennaia intelligentsiia: Dokumenty TsK RKP(b)-VKP(b), VChK-OGPU-NKVD o kul'turnoi politike, 1917–1953 gg.* Moscow: Mezhdunarodnyi fond "Demokratiia," 1999.

Nelson, Michael. *War of the Black Heavens: The Battles of Western Broadcasting in the Cold War.* London: Brassey's, 1997.

Ocherki po istorii rossiiskogo televideniia. Moscow: Voskresen'e, 1999.

Paasilinna, Reino. "Glasnost and Soviet Television." YLE–Finnish Broadcasting Co. research report, 1995.

Paulu, Burton. *Radio and Television Broadcasting in Eastern Europe.* Minneapolis: University of Minnesota Press, 1974.

Pavlenok, Boris. *Kino: Legendy i byl': Vospominaniia, razmyshleniia.* Moscow: Galeriia, 2004.

Pechat', radioveshchanie i televidenie Tatarii, 1917–1980: Sbornik dokumentov i materialov. Kazan': Tatarskoe knizhnoe izdatel'stvo, 1981.

Petrone, Karen. *Life Has Become More Joyous, Comrades: Celebrations in the Time of Stalin.* Bloomington: Indiana University Press, 2000.

Pilkington, Hilary. *Russia's Youth and Its Culture: A Nation's Constructors and Constructed.* London: Routledge, 1994.

Pimenova, I. V. *Televizionnnaia redaktor: Sbornik statei.* Moscow: Gosteleradio NMO, 1966.

Pochta sovetskogo radio i televideniia: Metodicheskii material o rabote s pis'mami radioslushatelei i telezritelei. Moscow: Gosteleradio NMO, 1969.

Powell, David E. "The Soviet Television Audience: Viewing Patterns and Problems." Washington, DC: Office of Research, U.S. Information Agency, 1975.

Pozner, Vladimir. *Parting with Illusions.* New York: Atlantic Monthly Press, 1990.

Problemy televideniia i radio. Moscow: Iskusstvo, 1971.

Prokhorova, Elena. "Fragmented Mythologies: Soviet TV Mini-Series of the 1970s." PhD diss., University of Pittsburgh, 2003.

Prokhorov, Alexander, ed. *Springtime for Soviet Cinema: Reviewing 1960s.* Pittsburgh: Russian Film Symposium, 2001.

Puddington, Arch. *Broadcasting Freedom: The Cold War Triumph of Radio Free Europe and Radio Liberty.* Lexington: University Press of Kentucky, 2000.

Rachuk, I. A., ed. *Trudy Vsesoiuznogo nauchno-issledovatel'skogo kinofotoinstituta.* Vol. 60, *Sotsiologicheskie issledovaniia kinematografa.* Moscow: NIKFI, 1971.

Raikin, A. I. *Vospominaniia.* Moscow: Firma "Izd. AST," 1998.

Rajagopolan, Sudha. *Leave Disco Dancer Alone! Indian Cinema and Soviet Movie-Going after Stalin.* New Delhi: Yoda Press, 2008.

Rawnsley, Gary D., ed. *Cold-War Propaganda in the 1950s.* New York: St. Martin's, 1999.

Razzakov, Fedor. *Aktery vsekh pokolenii.* Moscow: EKSMO-Press, 2000.

——. *Dos'e na zvezd: Nashi liubimye fil'my.* Moscow: EKSMO-Press, 2001.

——. *Dos'e na zvezd: 1941–1961.* Moscow: EKSMO-Press, 1998.

——. *Dos'e na zvezd: 1962–1980.* Moscow: EKSMO-Press, 1998.

——. *Nashi liubimye aktrisy.* Moscow: EKSMO-Press, 2000.

——. *Seks-simvoly Rossii. 30–60-e gody.* Moscow: EKSMO-Press, 2000.

——. *Zvezdy televideniia.* Moscow: EKSMO-Press, 2000.

Reid, Susan E., and D. J. Crowley. *Style and Socialism: Modernity and Material Culture in Post-War Eastern Europe.* Oxford: Berg, 2000.

Remington, Thomas F. *The Truth of Authority: Ideology and Communication in the Soviet Union.* Pittsburgh: University of Pittsburgh Press, 1988.

Riazanov, El'dar. *Eti neser'eznye, neser'eznye fil'my.* Moscow: BPSK, 1977.

——. *Ne podvennye itogi.* Moscow: Vagrius, 2000.

Richmond, Yale. *Cultural Exchange and the Cold War: Raising the Iron Curtain.* University Park: Pennsylvania State University Press, 2003.

——. *U.S.-Soviet Cultural Exchanges, 1958–1986: Who Wins?* Boulder, CO: Westview Press, 1987.

Roberts, Graham. *Forward Soviet! History and Non-fiction Film in the USSR.* New York: St. Martin's, 1999.

Rodgers, Rosemarie. "The Soviet Audience: How It Uses the Mass Media." PhD diss., MIT, 1967.

Rodshteina, A. A., ed. *Ekonomika kinematografii.* Moscow: Iskusstvo, 1958.

Rozov, A. Iu., ed. *Shabolovka, 53: Stranitsy istorii televideniia.* Moscow: Iskusstvo, 1988.

Ruzhnikov, V. V. *Lekstii po istorii otechestvennogo radioveshchaniia 1895-2001.* Moscow: GITR, 2002.

Ryback, Timothy W. *Rock around the Bloc: A History of Rock Music in Eastern Europe and the Soviet Union.* New York: Oxford University Press, 1990.

Sappak, Vladimir. *Televidenie i my: Chetyre besedy.* Moscow: Iskusstvo, 1963.

Sarukhanov, V. A. *Byli i skazki televideniia.* Minsk: Nauka i tekhnika, 1990.

Saunders, Frances Stonor. *The Cultural Cold War: The CIA and the World of Arts and Letters.* New York: New Press, 1999.

Sekrinskogo, S. S., ed. *Istoriia strany, istoriia kino.* Moscow: Znak, 2004.

Shane, Scott. *Dismantling Utopia: How Information Ended the Soviet Union.* Chicago: I.R. Dee, 1994.

Sherel', Aleksandr. *Audiokul'tura XX veka.* Moscow: Progress-Traditsiia, 2004.

Sheveleva, G. A., ed. *Pozyvnye trevog i nadezhd: "Maiak," sorok let v efire.* Moscow: Vagrius, 2004.

Shilova, I. *I moe kino: Piatidesiatye, shestidesiatye, semidesiatye.* Moscow: NIIK: Kinovedcheskie zapiski, 1993.

Shklovskii, Viktor Borisovich. *Za 60 let: Raboty o kino.* Moscow: Iskusstvo, 1985.

Shlapentokh, Dmitry, and Vladimir Shlapentokh. *Soviet Cinematography, 1918–1991: Ideological Conflict and Social Reality.* New York: A. de Gruyter, 1993.

Shumiatskii, Boris Zakharovich. *Kinematografiia millionov.* Moscow: Kinofotoizdat, 1936.

Siefert, Masha, ed. *Mass Culture and Perestroika in the Soviet Union.* Oxford: Oxford University Press, 1991.

Slavich, Iu., and E. Lyndina. *Rossiiskie kinozvezdy rasskazivaiut.* Moscow: Panorama, 1998.

Smith, Gerald Stanton. *Songs to Seven Strings: Russian Guitar Poetry and Soviet "Mass Song."* Bloomington: Indiana University Press, 1984.

Solntseva, L. P., and M. V. Iunisov, eds. *Samodeiatel'noe khudozhestvennoe tvorchestvo v SSSR.* St. Petersburg: Gosudarstvennyi institut iskusstvoznaniia, 1999.

Solov'eva, N. V., ed. *Nemnogo o radio i o nas s vami: k 75-letiiu Primorskogo radio.* Vladivostok, 2001.

Sosin, Gene. *Sparks of Liberty: An Insider's Memoir of Radio Liberty.* University Park: Pennsylvania State University Press, 1999.

Starr, S. Frederick. *Red and Hot: The Fate of Jazz in the Soviet Union, 1917–1991.* Updated ed. New York: Oxford University Press, 1983.

Steblov, Evgenii. *Protiv kogo druzhite?* Moscow: Algoritm, 2000.

Stites, Richard, ed. *Culture and Entertainment in Wartime Russia.* Bloomington: Indiana University Press, 1995.

——. *Revolutionary Dreams: Utopian Vision and Experimental Life in the Russian Revolution.* New York: Oxford University Press, 1989.

——. *Russian Popular Culture: Entertainment and Society Since 1900.* Cambridge: Cambridge University Press, 1992.

Strizhenov, Oleg. *Ispoved'.* Moscow: Algoritm, 1999.

Szporluk, Roman, ed. *The Influence of East Europe and the Soviet West on the USSR.* New York: Praeger, 1975.

Tabakov, Oleg. *Moia nastoiashchaia zhizn'.* Moscow: EKSMO-Press, 2000.

Taylor, Richard, and Ian Christie, eds. *The Film Factory: Russian and Soviet Cinema in Documents.* Cambridge, MA: Harvard University Press, 1988.

——, eds. *Inside the Film Factory: New Approaches to Russian and Soviet Cinema.* London: Routledge, 1991.

Taylor, Richard, and D. W. Spring, eds. *Stalinism and Soviet Cinema.* London: Routledge, 1993.

Televidenie—Vchera, segodnia, zavtra. Moscow: Iskusstvo, 1987, 1989.

Thompson, Terry L., and Richard Sheldon, eds. *Soviet Society and Culture: Essays in Honor of Vera S. Dunham.* Boulder, CO: Westview Press, 1988.

Tomoff, Kirill. *Creative Union: The Professional Organization of Soviet Composers, 1939–1953.* Ithaca: Cornell University Press, 2006.

Troianovskii, V., ed. *Kinematograf ottepeli: Kniga pervaia.* Moscow: Materik, 1996.

——, ed. *Kinematograf ottepeli: Kniga vtoraia.* Moscow: Materik, 2002.

Troitsky, A. *Back in the USSR: The True Story of Rock in Russia.* London: Omnibus, 1987.

Tserkover, E., ed. *Vam otvechaet artist (kniga-interv'iu).* Moscow: Molodaia gvardiia, 1969.

Urban, G. R. *Radio Free Europe and the Pursuit of Democracy: My War within the Cold War.* New Haven: Yale University Press, 1997.

Urvalov, V. A. *Ocherki istorii televideniia.* Moscow, 1990.

Vail', Petr, and Aleksandr Genis. *60-e—mir sovetskogo cheloveka.* Moscow: NLO, 1996.

Vasilevskaia, E. V. *Ocherki istorii razvitiia televideniia v zapadnoi Sibiri.* Novosibirsk: Nauka, Sib. otdelenie., 1978.

Vil'chek, V. M. *Pod znakom TV.* Moscow: Iskusstvo, 1987.

Vlasov, M. P. *Sovetskoe kinoiskusstvo 50–60-x godov.* Moscow: VGIK, 1992.

Volkov, I. A., and S. F. Iarmoliuk M. G. Pugacheva, eds. *Pressa v obshchestve (1959–2000): Otsenki zhurnalistov i sotsiologov: Dokumenty.* Moscow: Institut sotsiologii RAN, 2000.

Von Geldern, James, and Richard Stites, eds. *Mass Culture in Soviet Russia: Tales, Poems, Songs, Movies, Plays, and Folklore, 1917–1953*. Bloomington: Indiana University Press, 1995.

Vronskaya, Jeanne. *Young Soviet Film Makers*. London: Allen and Unwin, 1972.

Wettig, Gerard. *Broadcasting and Détente: Eastern Policies and Their Implication for East-West Relations*. London: C. Hurst, 1977.

White, Anne. *De-Stalinization and the House of Culture: Declining State Control over Leisure in the USSR, Poland, and Hungary, 1953–1989*. London: Routledge, 1990.

Wolfe, Thomas. *Governing Soviet Journalism: The Press and the Socialist Person after Stalin*. Bloomington: Indiana University Press, 2005.

Woll, Josephine. *Real Images: Soviet Cinema and the Thaw*. London: I. B. Tauris, 2000.

Youngblood, Denise J. *Movies for the Masses: Popular Cinema and Soviet Society in the 1920s*. Cambridge: Cambridge University Press, 1992.

Yurchak, Alexei. *Everything Was Forever Until It Was No More: The Last Soviet Generation*. Princeton: Princeton University Press, 2005.

Zak, M. E. *Kinoprotsess*. Moscow: Goskino SSSR, 1990.

Zasurskii, Ia. N., ed. *Televizionnaia mozaika*. Moscow: MGU, 1997.

Zhabskii, M. *Kino: Prokat, reklama, metodika, praktika*. Moscow: Soiuzinformkino, 1982.

Zhanry televideniia. Moscow: Gosteleradio NMO, 1967.

Zolotarevskii, Leonid. *Tsitaty iz zhizni*. Moscow: Iskusstvo, 1971.

Zorkaia, Neia Markovna. *Fol'klor, lubok, ekran*. Moscow: Iskusstvo, 1994.

——. *The Illustrated History of Soviet Cinema*. New York: Hippocrene, 1989.

ACKNOWLEDGMENTS

One of the major themes in this book is the power of relationships, personal and institutional, and it is one that speaks directly to the book's own history, too. It is a great pleasure to express my appreciation for all of the support I have enjoyed over the years.

This project got its first footing thanks to funding from Princeton University's Graduate School, Department of History, and Fellowship of Woodrow Wilson Scholars. Additional, much appreciated support came from the International Research and Exchanges Board (IREX) and the Open Society Archives. I am most grateful to Columbia University's Harriman Institute and Harvard University's Academy for International and Area Studies for postdoctoral fellowships. As a faculty member at Queens College of the City of New York, I benefited from a generous PSC-CUNY award for further research. I thank the School of Slavonic and East European Studies of University College London for its financial support as well.

While institutional backing can put a roof over the head of any book project, it is people who make living there worthwhile. And in my case, interactions with other people—mentors, colleagues, friends—have also made the end product inestimably stronger. My first thanks go to my advisers at Princeton, Laura Engelstein and Stephen Kotkin. Anyone with even a passing acquaintance with Soviet history will see my debts to both written all over this book. Laura Engelstein's persistent, uncompromising, and inspired questions helped shape my ideas in every way. I thank her for her generosity of intellect and spirit, and for the gift of her friendship over the years. Stephen Kotkin saw the missing forest in these trees so many times I long ago lost count—and he also goaded me to explore other terrain I would never have contemplated on my own. I am deeply grateful to him for sharing his historical imagination, and for his patience and skill in helping me see my way through thickets again and again.

This project has also benefited immeasurably from the insights of other expert readers over the years. I thank the members of my dissertation committee, Anson Rabinbach and the late Richard Stites, for their thoughtful comments and encouragement, and the members of my writers' group at Princeton without whose brainpower and camaraderie graduate *and* post-graduate life seem unthinkable: Meri Clark, Eduardo Elena, Todd Stevens, Ashli White, and Amanda Wunder. Sergei Kapterev and Anna Fishzon helped me clarify my thinking on fandom with incisive readings in the early days. I am grateful to Susan Morrissey, Alena Ledeneva, Anne Gorsuch, and Stephen Lovell for their shrewd commentary as the project was drawing to a close. In 2008, Harvard's Academy for International and Area Studies sponsored a day-long workshop on a draft of this book. I thank the participants, Thomas Doherty, Terry Martin, Uta Poiger, Susan Reid, Mary Steedly, and Amir Weiner, for their generous engagement with my work—the very model of constructive criticism. I would also like to thank Jorge Dominguez at the Academy for his warm support and mentorship, Jim Clem and Larry Winnie for their help in keeping the wheels of a scholarly life going around, and my fellow scholars for their friendly attacks on my Soviet parochialism. In New York, I am most grateful to Cynthia Hyla Whittaker of Baruch College of the City University of New York for her encouragement and expert advice over the years. I am also indebted to my colleagues at Queens College of the City University of New York and, latterly, the School of Slavonic and East European Studies for their kindness and for intellectual fellowship. John Ackerman and the staff at Cornell University Press were models of flexibility and professionalism in shepherding this project from manuscript to book.

Many of the arguments in this book have been honed in discussions at conferences and seminars over the years. I deeply appreciate the contributions of Ellen Mickiewicz, Mark Von Hagen, and Richard Wortman at the Columbia University Russian history seminar, Amir Weiner and his graduate students at the Stanford University Soviet history seminar, and colleagues at the SSEES Centre for Russian Studies and the Cambridge University Committee for Russian and East European Studies seminar. On a more informal but no less powerful level, my understanding of all things Soviet and Russian (and many other things, too) has been shaped in conversation with a brilliant new cohort of historians. In particular, I thank Miriam Dobson, Victoria Frede, Juliane Fuerst, Steven Harris, Cynthia Hooper, Polly Jones, Kolia Mitrohkin, and Maya Nadkarni for fellow-traveling in the field with wit and wisdom.

One of my greatest pleasures in researching Soviet media culture was spending time with people who once made it. I am forever indebted to Marina Goldovskaya who, having only just met me in Moscow, grabbed the phone in her apartment and set about charming her former Soviet TV colleagues into talking to me. I learned a phenomenal amount from all of my interviewees, but I would like to express particular gratitude to Sergei Muratov in Moscow and Boris Firsov in St. Petersburg for sharing so freely of their time and prodigious knowledge. My thanks, too, to the staff at Gosteleradiofond and the Scientific-Research Institute of Film Art in Moscow and the Open Society Archives in Budapest for their able assistance in my research. Tat'iana Potemkina and her family were wonderful friends and inveterate sceptics of my work—two things for which I will always be grateful. Many years ago, in what turned out to be the last gasp of Soviet power, I spent an unforgettable summer in Leningrad, strolling streets in the endless daylight, mangling Russian around kitchen tables, and thrilling to the realization that all the world was not what I, a very provincial New Yorker, had known or understood it to be. Although I lost touch almost immediately with the people who took me in that summer, I would like to thank them here for helping to pry me open and inspire an enduring fascination with the Soviet world. I am also very grateful to my family, for sending me on that first journey and for humoring and supporting me on all of the subsequent ones. I thank Juna for being Juna. And I thank David Roth-Ey for absolutely everything.

This work incorporates material that appeared in the following publications: "Finding a Home for Television in the USSR, 1950–1970," *Slavic Review* 66, no. 2 (2007): 278–306, and "Playing for Cultural Authority: Soviet TV Professionals and the Game Show, 1950s–1960s," in *Pleasures in Socialism: Leisure and Luxury in the Eastern Bloc,* ed. David Crowley and Susan E. Reid (Evanston, IL: Northwestern University Press, 2010), 147–176.

INDEX

Page numbers followed by letters *f* and *t* refer to figures and tables, respectively.

Brezhnev, Leonid *(continued)*
    on radio broadcasting, 148; on socialist
    culture, 3; stagnation under, 6; and TV
    programming, 201, 279
Britain: film preferences in, 94. *See also* BBC
broadcasting: in post-World War II era, 8;
    and private vs. collective experience, 15;
    in Western Europe, 18. *See also* broad-
    casting, Soviet; radio; television
broadcasting, Soviet: administrative
    overhaul of, 217, 218; goals of, 229, 271;
    importance of, 5; investments in, 217.
    See also radio, Soviet; television, Soviet
Brynner, Yul, 9
byt (everyday, domestic life), television
    and, 198–201, 210, 211

café, television, 123–25
Café of Thirteen Chairs (TV program), 279
Cannes Film Festival, 2, 37, 59, 69, 110,
    110n127
Capote, Truman, 131
Cardinale, Claudia, 115
Carné, Marcel, 115
Carnival Night (film), 84*t*, 98
Caron, Leslie, 57*f*
Case No. 306 (film), 68
CBS (TV network), 192
CC. *See* Central Committee
censorship: of film, foreign, 41, 47; of film,
    Soviet, 30–33, 34–35, 35n35, 50, 52, 56;
    organs of, 5, 144–45, 234; of radio, 146,
    170; of television, 234, 255
Central Committee (CC): and film, 31, 46,
    49; and propaganda, 153; and radio, 147,
    148–49, 159, 161, 163, 169; and television,
    186, 192, 194, 214, 227, 235, 250; writing
    projects of, 161
Central Radio, 150, 158, 159, 162, 169
Central TV, 187, 223n3; programming of,
    122, 123, 184, 197, 228, 261–62; repub-
    lics and, 189; young enthusiasts and,
    239
Chapaev (film), 71, 95, 96, 100, 129, 130
Chesnokov, D. I., 250, 251
children: films for, 25n2, 261; impact of
    foreign films on, 42, 95, 96; impact of
    television on, 204, 206–8; media con-
    sumption by, 14, 82; television program-
    ming for, 157, 158, 212–13, 221, 247, 262,
    274, 275

Chirkov, Boris, 88
choice: and audience segmentation, 72;
    media boom and, 15, 22, 83; moderniza-
    tion and, 62; and movie culture, 74; of
    radio programming, 141; and television
    development, 178, 179; of television pro-
    gramming, 185
Christie, Ian, 33n27, 245
Chukhrai, Grigorii, 37, 58–62, 65, 66, 88
cineastes. *See* film professionals
cinema. *See* film(s)
Club of Film Travel (TV program), 265, 266,
    267; in 1970s, 273, 274, 276
Cold War, cultural, 7, 9, 20; film in, 27,
    65–67, 83, 95–97; music in, 163–64;
    radio in, 135, 153–54, 156–57, 174, 175;
    television in, 178, 209–11
collective experience: film as, 201; media
    boom and move away from, 15, 16, 138,
    156; radio as, 136–37, 136*f*, 138, 156, 159;
    Soviet emphasis on, 4, 134, 209; televi-
    sion as, 208–9, 211, 243, 258
The Color of Pomegranates (film), 88
Confidential (magazine), 117, 120
Conover, Willis, 132
The Cranes Are Flying (film), 65–66, 88,
    110n127; U.S. premiere of, 119*f*
cultural authority/capital: film critics and,
    93; filmmakers and, 54–55, 57, 94n80;
    political elites and, 279; TV enthusiasts
    and, 261, 265–66, 268, 273
cultural exchange: film and, 43, 66, 67–68,
    109; in post-Stalinist era, 9, 29, 36; tele-
    vision and, 231–33, 274
culture: post-World War II transformation
    of, 1–2, 8–9, 17. *See also* culture, Soviet;
    mass culture
culture, Soviet: administration and
    control of, 5; American culture com-
    pared to, 21–22; anxieties about fu-
    ture of, 282; characteristics of, 2–5;
    consumption-side dynamism of, 12–13;
    contradictions of, 1, 4, 8, 16–17, 20,
    27; across decades, 5–6; exceptional-
    ism of, 10, 23, 167; film and, 74, 130;
    foreign infiltration in, 6, 9–10, 16,
    22, 97, 134, 282–83; as formation,
    12, 12n32, 13; functions of, 4, 11, 15,
    16–17, 22, 23, 269, 285; fundamental
    problematic in media age, 285; heroes
    in, 266; ideological commitment to,

Monroe, Marilyn, 45, 116
Mordiukova, Nonna, 32
Morgunov, Evgenii, 73n6
Moscow: film festivals in, 69, 89n61, 99f, 107, 109–10, 109n125; International Youth Festival (1957) in, 164, 238–39, 246, 248; movie theaters in, 76, 77, 79, 80f; Ostankino television tower in, 176, 177f; public TV viewing in, 209
Moscow Does Not Believe in Tears (film), 63, 64, 107, 281–85
Moscow TV. See Central TV
Mosfil'm studio: ETK model and, 60, 61; expansion in post-Stalinist era, 29, 33; most popular films of, 84t–85t; staff at, 64; and television, 231
Motyl', Vladimir, 35, 49n98, 59
movie culture, Soviet, 72–74; film festivals and, 107–10; journalism and, 112–13; paradox of, 127–30; postcards and, 111–12; stardom-fandom dynamic and, 98–106; technological modernity and, 110–11; television and, 121–27
movie theaters, 75–77, 76f, 79, 80f
Mr. Deeds Goes to Town (film), 41
Muratov, Sergei, 200, 239, 243, 265, 267; and KVN show, 254f, 256, 257; and VVV show, 246n83, 249n93, 251n100, 252
music: and film, 80, 90, 127; foreign radio broadcasts and, 132, 133, 134, 143–44; light, preference for, 17, 19; Maiak's approach to, 171–72; in post-Stalinist era, 164–67, 166f; on Soviet radio, 158, 162–63
musical(s), popularity of, 39, 40, 68, 84t–85t
Musical Kiosk (TV program), 265, 271

Nazarenko, Viktor, 185
Nazi Germany, films acquired from, 39–40
Nenashev, Mikhail, 161, 174
newsreels, 42, 80, 80n35, 229
News Relay (TV program), 265–66, 272, 276–77
news reporting: fact vs. commentary in, 170, 173; on radio, 134–36, 152, 158–59, 160, 162, 167–68, 170, 173–74, 229; on television, 178, 220, 227, 248, 262
New Yorker (magazine), 8, 55, 57, 131
New York Times (newspaper), 9, 185, 219, 252n102

Nikulin, Iurii, 73n6
Nixon, Richard, 195, 209, 210
NMO, audience research by, 268–71
Novgorodtsev, Seva, 132

The Oath (film), 41
Ogonek (magazine): film coverage by, 109, 110n127; on TV diktory, 242; on TV viewing, 203, 204f–207f
Operation 'y' and Other Adventures of Shurik (film), 73, 73n6, 74, 84t, 126
Orlov, Viktor, 104
Orlova, Liubov', 100, 100n101, 101, 123
Oscar Awards, 281
Ostankino television center, 176, 177f, 181, 187, 211, 212, 223; cost of, 182; restaurant in, 218
Ostromoukhova, Bella, 259n129
otdykh (relaxation): in Soviet culture, 4, 201, 279; television and, 201–2, 203, 208

Pampanini, Silvana, 113–14
Pant, Val'do, 239
Pasternak, Boris, 222, 272
Pavlenok, Boris, 46, 47
Pavlov, Sergei, 95, 96, 163
Pirates of the Twentieth Century (film), 63, 71, 85t, 281
Pleshakov, Konstantin, 11
Plisetskaiia, Maia, 2, 21
Poland: film publications from, 112n132; foreign radio in, 144; moviegoing in, 78; Soviet films and, 66, 68
political elite: and film, 32, 34–35, 46; and television, 194–95, 211, 212–14, 220–22, 227, 279
Popov, A. S., 137
postcards, cinema, 111–12
postcolonial world: Soviet cinema in, 69–70; Soviet radio broadcasting in, 154
Pozner, Vladimir, 58, 61, 152
Prague Spring (1968), 61, 151, 173, 191–92, 213
Pravda (newspaper), 161; on film, 71, 78; on radio, 140, 155; and radio programming, 173; on television, 208
Presley, Elvis, 8
press, Soviet: film coverage in, 107–9, 108f, 112–13; postwar boom in, 11–12, 14; and radio broadcasting, 173; television

press, Soviet *(continued)*
  coverage in, 179, 195–96, 199–200,
  203–5, 208, 210. *See also specific titles*
Primakov, Evgenii, 152
Prisoner of the Caucasus (film), 84t
Pudovkin, Vsevolod, 33n27
Pugacheva, Alla, 166n128
Putin, Vladimir, 88
Puzin, A., 138, 139, 159, 238, 240
Pyr'ev, Ivan, 33

Queen of the Gypsies (film), 85t, 91

radio: postwar expansion of, 8; television
  compared to, 202
radio, foreign broadcasting, 131–35,
  131n2, 140–46; audience for, 172–73;
  competition with, 160–61, 168–69; vs.
  dissent, 174; explanations for appeal of,
  156–57; jamming of, 131–32, 133, 140–41,
  144–45, 160, 191; popularity of, 143–44,
  162, 168, 174; as solitary activity, 202;
  and television development, 179, 191,
  229
radio, Soviet: administration of, 146–49;
  centralization of, 150; as collective experience, 136–37, 136f, 156;
  criticism of, 159–60; functions of,
  134; growth of, 2, 11, 14; informational
  hierarchy and, 170, 173–74; international broadcasting by, 150, 152–56;
  Maiak and, 167–74; as model for TV
  administration, 187; multilingual
  broadcasting by, 150–52; network of,
  135, 137–39, 150, 156; as private experience, 156, 157f; programming on,
  157–59; shortwave, origins of, 138–39,
  140; shortwave problem in, 144, 148,
  149–50, 154–56, 174–75; and Soviet
  culture, 136, 163, 170, 175; and television, 227–29; uncertain standards in,
  162–63; wartime broadcasting, 136–37;
  wired, 135n13, 136, 137–38; wireless,
  shift to, 138–39
Radio and Television Day, 210, 223
radio clubs, 135
radiofikatsiia ("radiofication"), 135,
  137–39, 150, 156
Radio Free Europe (RFE), 144n51, 147
Radio Liberty (RL), 131, 131n2, 133n7, 145,
  147

Radio Moscow, 150, 152–55; competition
  with foreign radio, 168; foreign correspondents of, 159; multilingual broadcasting by, 151; success of, 22
Rajagopalan, Sudha, 44, 90
Rassadin, S., 93
Razgolov, Kirill, 69
reality, TV enthusiasts and, 223–25,
  236–38, 244
redaktor (editor): film, 30; television,
  214–15
Reid, Susan, 94n80, 104n113, 200n92
relaxation: Soviet culture and, 4, 201, 279;
  television and, 201–2, 203, 208
republics: film industry in, 26, 29, 34, 50,
  86–88; moviegoing in, 81–82, 89–91;
  radio in, 150–52, 153, 158, 161; television in, 181n10, 188–89. *See also specific
  republics*
Riazanov, El'dar, 31–32, 34–35, 98
rock 'n' roll, 22, 164, 165; Soviet, 5, 165–67,
  166f
Rokk, Marika, 39
Roman Holiday (film), 81
Romanov, Aleksei, 35, 63
Romm, Mikhail, 34, 54–55, 240, 242
Rozovskii, Mark, 246n83
rural areas: movie screenings in, 75, 76,
  78, 81; radio broadcasting in, 136f, 139
Russian language: film industry and,
  86–87; radio broadcasting and, 150;
  television broadcasting and, 188
Rybnikov, Nikolai, 32, 98, 106, 112, 120

Salisbury, Harrison, 9, 185
Samoilova, T., 110n127
Sanaev, Vsevolod, 56
Sappak, Vladimir, 199–200, 236–38, 239,
  242, 245
Sartre, Jean-Paul, 37, 38
satellite technology, 187, 191, 210
Schoberova, Olga, 109
Semenov, M., 262
Seventeen Moments of Spring (film), 275
Shabolovka, 226. *See also* Central TV
Shagalova, Liudmila, 120
Sharoeva, E., 234n36
Shelest, Petro, 151
Shepit'ko, L., 61
shestidesiatniki (people of the sixties), 13,
  59, 252, 259. *See also* enthusiasts, TV

Western culture, 6–7; radio broadcasting during, 136–37
Writers' Union, 5, 215

X-ray records, 15

Yermash, Filipp, 30, 34, 58, 60, 62–64, 67n183, 212
Yesenia (film), 43–44, 63, 97, 281
Young Guard (film), 96
youth: depiction in film, 284–85. *See also* children; International Youth Festival; youth audience

youth audience, 73–74, 82–83, 94; and fandom, 103–5; and *KVN* show, 256
Yurchak, Alexei, 20, 141–42

zastoi (stagnation), era of, 6
Zhdanov, Andrei, 7
Zhil'tsova, Svetlana, 241f, 260n134
Zhvanetskii, Mikhail, 254n110
Zolotareva, L., 226
Zolotarevskii, Leonid, 239
Zorkaia, Neia, 91, 92
Zubok, Vladimir, 11